Progress in Tourism, Recreation and Hospitality Management

Volume 4

Edited by
C. P. Cooper and A. Lockwood

Belhaven Press
London

Copublished in the Americas
by Halsted Press an imprint of
John Wiley & Sons Inc., New York

Belhaven Press
(a division of Pinter Publishers)
25 Floral Street, Covent Garden,
London, WC2E 9DS, United Kingdom

First published in 1992

Copublished in the Americas by Halsted Press, an imprint of John Wiley &
Sons, Inc., 605 Third Avenue, New York, NY 10158–0012

British Library Cataloguing in Publication Data
CIP catalogue record for this book is available from the British Library.

ISBN 185293 240 6
ISSN 0952–5424

Library of Congress Cataloging-in-Publication Data
A CIP catalog record for this book is available from the
Library of Congress

ISBN 0–470–21922–X (in the Americas only)

Typeset by Florencetype Ltd, Kewstoke, Avon
Printed and bound in Great Britain by
Biddles Ltd of Guildford and King's Lynn

Contents

List of contributors

Professor Erik Cohen
Department of Sociology and Social Anthropology
The Hebrew University of Jerusalem
Jerusalem 91905
Israel

Erik Cohen is the George S. Wiss Professor of Sociology and Dean, Faculty of Social Science at the Hebrew University of Jerusalem. His principal research interests are in social change, religion, urban life, tourism and tourist arts.

Carlos Manuel Martins da Costa
Department of Management and Industrial Engineering
University of Aveiro
3800 Aveiro
Portugal

Carlos Costa is a faculty member of the Department of Management and Industrial Engineering at the University of Aveiro. His research interests are in the field of planning and development for tourism.

Dr Stephen Curry
Development and Project Planning Centre
University of Bradford
Bradford BD7 1DP
UK

Stephen Curry is Lecturer in the Development and Project Planning Centre, University of Bradford. His research interests are in tourism and developing countries, particularly Jamaica and Tanzania.

Edward Davies
Horwath and Horwath (UK) Ltd
8 Baker Street
London WIM 1DA
UK

Edward Davies is an Associate Director of Horwath and Horwath, UK.

Stephen Dibnah
Proyek Peningkatan Penataan Ruang (P2R)
Kantor Wilayah
Departemen Pekerjaan Umum
Bali
Indonesia

Stephen Dibnah has graduate qualifications in planning from the UK. He is currently doing Volunteer Services Overseas working in Bali with the Indonesian Ministry of Public Works.

Ross K. Dowling
School of Biological and Environmental Sciences
Murdoch University
Perth WA 6150
Australia

Ross Dowling is Research Officer on Tourism and the Environment at Murdoch University. His research interest lies in the field of tourism/ environment relationships and he has acted as consultant and advisor to the New Zealand and Western Australian governments.

David Gilbert
Department of Management Studies for Tourism and Hotel Industries
University of Surrey
Guildford GU2 5XH
UK

David Gilbert is lecturer in marketing and course tutor for the University of Surrey's Diploma/MSc. in Tourism marketing. His research interests relate to aspects of tourism marketing and he is currently examining the factors of consumer behaviour in tourism.

Professor Brian Goodall
Department of Geography
University of Reading
Whiteknights
PO Box 227
Reading RG6 2AB
UK

Brian Goodall is Dean of the Faculty of Urban and Regional Studies, Professor of Geography and Consultant Director of the NERC Unit for Thematic Information Systems. His research interests centre on the structure of the tourism industry, the evolution of resort regions and environmental assessment for tourism.

Dr Yvonne Guerrier
Department of Management Studies for Tourism and Hotel Industries
University of Surrey
Guildford GU2 5XH
UK

Yvonne Guerrier is Senior Lecturer in Organizational Behaviour. Her research interests include managers' careers and management development and work flexibility, especially in the hospitality industry.

Dr Derek Hall
Department of Geography
University of Sunderland
Langham Tower
Ryhope Road
Sunderland SR2 7EE
UK

Derek Hall is Head of Geography and Convenor of the Tourism and Leisure Enterprises Unit at the University of Sunderland. He recently edited *Tourism and Economic Development in Eastern Europe and the Soviet Union*.

Garry Hawkes
Gardner Merchant Ltd
Europe House
Bancroft Road
Reigate RH2 7RA
UK

Garry Hawkes is Managing Director of Gardner Merchant Ltd.

Alan Jefferson
British Tourist Authority
Thames Tower
Blacks Road
Hammersmith
London W6 9EL
UK

Alan Jefferson is International Marketing Director and Deputy Chief Executive at the BTA. He has co-authored *Marketing Tourism—A Practical Guide* and *Developing Tourist Destinations*.

Indira Joshi
Department of Management Studies for Tourism and Hotel Industries
University of Surrey
Guildford GU2 5XH
UK

Indira Joshi is a research student with interests in tourism marketing and quality management. She studies marketing at the University of Strathclyde.

Michael Kipps
Department of Management Studies for Tourism and Hotel Industries
University of Surrey
Guildford GU2 5XH
UK

Michael Kipps teaches in the field of applied science. His research interests are in the application of scientific method to problems in the food service industry.

Professor John Latham
Business Division
Southampton Institute of Higher Education
East Park Terrace
Southampton SO9 4WW
UK

John Latham is Professor of Business Analysis at Southampton Institute. He is a mathematician, with a special interest in research methodology and the analysis of tourism demand.

Andrew Lockwood
Department of Management Studies for Tourism and Hotel Industries
University of Surrey
Guildford GU2 5XH
UK

Andrew Lockwood lectures in operations management aspects of hotels and catering. His research interests include manpower management and work flexibility in hotels and definition and measurement of service quality.

Els Lowyck
Vrije Universiteit Brussel
Faculteit van de Economisce Sociale en Politieke Wetenschappen
Pleinlaan 2
B–1050 Brussels
Belgium

Els Lowyck is a research officer at the Free University of Brussels. She has taken particular interest in the tourist industry from a social development perspective.

Dr Behrooz Morvaridi
Development and Project Planning Centre
University of Bradford
Bradford BD7 1DP
UK

Behrooz Morvaridi is Research Fellow at the Development and Project Planning Centre, University of Bradford. His research interests are in the environment and sustainable development, and in the economic and social effect of processing and dam projects in households, particularly in Eastern Europe.

Sue Newton
Harvester Restaurants
Great West House
Great West Road
Brentford
Middlesex TW8 9DF
UK

Sue Newton is Director of Personnel and Training for Harvester Restaurants

Dr Stephen Page
Centre for Tourism Studies
Department of Geography
Christ Church College
Canterbury CT1 1QU
UK

Stephen J. Page is Senior Lecturer in Tourism Studies at Christ Church College of Higher Education and a member of the Tourism Research Centre, Canterbury Business School, University of Kent. He has published articles on urban tourism and the impact of the Channel Tunnel.

Mrs Elizabeth Pearce
British Standards Institute
Linford Wood
Milton Keynes
MK14 6LE
UK

Elizabeth Pearce is Senior Business Development Officer—food and services—with BSI quality assurance.

Dr Artur da Rosa Pires
Department of Environment and Planning
University of Aveiro
3800 Aveiro
Portugal

Artur da Rosa Pires is Associate Professor in the Department of Environment and Planning at the University of Aveiro. His research interests lie in the field of planning theory and development planning.

Dr Paul Reynolds
Faculty of Business
Northern Territory University
PO Box 40146
Casuarina
Darwin NT
Australia
Paul Reynolds is Associate Professor of Hospitality Management at NTU. His research interests are the ethical considerations of tourism and multinational hotel company strategy.

Cordell W. Riley
Bermuda Department of Tourism
Global House
43 Church Street
Hamilton HM12
Bermuda
Cordell Riley is Statistical and Research Officer for the Bermuda Department of Tourism.

Dr Michael Riley
Department of Management Studies for Tourism and the Hotel Industries
University of Surrey
Guildford GU2 5XH
UK
Michael Riley is Lecturer in Management Studies at the University of Surrey. He specializes in human recource management and is course tutor for the department's Diploma/MSc in International Hotel Management. His research interests lie in labour markets, management development and group behaviour.

Dr Gareth Shaw
Department of Geography
University of Exeter
Amory Building
Rennes Drive
Exeter EX 4 4RJ
UK
Gareth Shaw is a Senior Lecturer in Geography and Joint Director of the Tourism Research Group at the University of Exeter. He has coedited *Tourism and Economic Development: Western European Experiences*, second edition, 1991.

Julie Sheppard
Department of Management Studies for Tourism and the Hotel Industries
University of Surrey
Guildford GU2 5XH
UK

Julie Sheppard is British Gas Research Officer in the Department of Management Studies for Tourism and the Hotel Industries, University of Surrey. She has written widely on food hygiene matters.

Dr Thea Sinclair
Keynes College
Canterbury Business School
at the University of Kent
Tourism Research Centre
Canterbury
Kent CT2 7PD
UK

Thea Sinclair is Director of the Tourism Research Centre and Senior Lecturer in Economics at the University of Kent. She has undertaken a wide range of research on the economics of tourism, including studies for the United Nations Centre of Transnational Corporations and the World Bank, and is an active member of Tourism Concern.

Mrs Silvia Sussmann
Department of Management Studies for Tourism and the Hotel Industries
University of Surrey
Guildford GU2 5XH
UK

Silvia Sussmann is Lecturer in Management Computing. Her current research interests are in intelligent user interfaces and the use of advanced software tools for hospitality research and education.

Carole van der Merwe
Harvester Restaurants
Great West House
Great West Road
Brentford
Middlesex TW8 9DF
UK

Carole van der Merwe is Quality Manager with Harvester Restaurants.

Dr Geoffrey Wall
Faculty of Environmental Studies
University of Waterloo
Waterloo
Ontario N2L 5X4
Canada

Geoffrey Wall is Associate Dean, Graduate Studies and Research, Faculty of Environmental Studies at the University of Waterloo. He has written numerous papers and books on tourism, recreation and parks.

Professor Stephen Wanhill
University of Wales College of Cardiff
65–67 Park Place
Cardiff CF1 3AS
UK

Stephen Wanhill is Professor of Tourism at Cardiff. His main area of research is in tourism planning and development.

Dr Brian Wheeller
Centre for Urban and Regional Studies
University of Birmingham
Edgbaston
Birmingham B15 2TT
UK

Brian Wheeller is Lecturer in Tourism at the University of Birmingham. As Course Director for the Tourism policy and Management MSc., his research interests centre on current attempts at mitigating the negative impacts of tourism.

Dr Alan Williams
Department of Geography
University of Exeter
Amory Building
Rennes Drive
Exeter EX4 4RJ
UK

Alan Williams is a Senior Lecturer in Geography, Joint Director of the Tourism Research Group and Co-Director of the Centre for European Studies at the University of Exeter. He has coedited *Tourism and Economic Development: Western European Experiences*, second edition, 1991.

Editorial preface

Progress in Tourism, Recreation and Hospitality Management was launched in 1989 as a collaborative venture between the University of Surrey and Belhaven Press. It was designed to provide an authoritative, annual and international review of research and major issues of concern in the fields of tourism, recreation and hospitality. **Progress** aimed to provide leadership in research and become an established volume for researchers, students and staff in academic institutions as well as a source book for practitioners. **Progress** thus aimed to fill a gap in the literature; a gap which had arisen owing to the rapid advance of the fields and the difficulties for researchers in consolidating material.

Both the University of Surrey and Belhaven Press decided to review the concept of **Progress** after three annual volumes. Although generally it was felt that **Progress** had met the aims and hopes of its founders, one justifiable area of criticism was a lack of focus. It was decided to reorganize the structure and coverage of **Progress**, and in 1991 a consultation was undertaken of all previous **Progress** authors, the editorial board and the publishers. This exercise was extremely fruitful and has led to the structure of the current volume — groups of chapters centred on two research themes; a new section on tourism statistics and flows; and a series of shorter chapters on critical issues. In addition three editorial advisers have been appointed.

The first of the research themes focuses upon the impact of tourism, and in particular the environmental impact of tourism. As many of the chapters in this volume show, this has become a major concern over recent years and **Progress** has drawn together contributions from the principal researchers and opinion leaders in the subject. The chapters range widely to cover the field. Included in the section are those exploring the history of tourism/environment relationships; the economics of tourism and the environment; emergent techniques for the industry such as environmental auditing; and a number of case examples of environmental problems and strategies for their solution in a variety of contexts around the world. It is clear from the range and quality of the chapters in this section, that much research is under way in this important field; it is also clear that there is an established body of literature and practice in other disciplines which tourism can draw upon in its attempts to ameliorate impacts upon host environments and communities. Yet despite this, it is possible to detect an underlying scepticism, especially towards alternative tourism type solutions. Wheeller's contribution is an overt statement in this regard.

In this volume, Goodall argues that environmental auditing is part of the total quality approach. The second of the research themes expands on this idea of quality and relates it to the tourism and hospitality industry. As the hotel and catering industry begins to wake up to the issue of quality, as shown by the British Hotel and Catering Institutional Management Association's recent interest in the subject, there is a growing need for detailed explanations of the concepts and terminology and examples of good practice from the industry. The section provides just such a combination of academic and industrial contributions. A comprehensive review of the literature on quality management in tourism and hospitality is followed by an example of how some of these concepts have been introduced to a national restaurant chain. In his article on quality in the contract catering industry, Garry Hawkes discusses the relationship between quality and hygiene and the introduction of British Standard 5750 (BS 5750). These two issues are then further expanded through an empirical study of caterers' attitudes to hygiene and quality and a full explanation of the role of BS 5750 in the hotel and catering industry, direct from the British Standards Institution (BSI).

The final two sections of **Progress** focus on tourism statistics and flows, and critical issues in tourism, recreation and hospitality. It is not easy to obtain comprehensive, up-to-date statistical data and independent informed comment on global tourism flows in an easily digestible form, hence the inclusion of a section which aims to do just that. The section on critical issues invites shorter contributions to discuss contemporary themes and stimulate debate. It also aims to provide chapters which centre on a particular geographical region or industrial sector.

In part the restructuring of **Progress** is an attempt to encourage tourism, recreation and hospitality to 'float free' from their disciplinary roots and become a focus of study in their own right. Of course, some would argue that this is already the case with the growing numbers of texts, journals and courses in these fields (see, for example, Sheldon, 1991 for an analysis of recent tourism research publications). Yet recent reviews of the subject areas reiterate fragmentation, lack of a theoretical base and poor development of concepts as the major concern of informed commentators (see, for example, Burton and Jackson, 1989; Graburn and Jafari, 1991). In addition, much work in the fields of concern to this volume are studies which utilize tourism, recreation and hospitality as areas to test and apply research to parent disciplines where the theoretical concepts are well developed. This does little for our own subject areas.

In the first editorial preface to **Progress** these issues were also identified and linked to the immaturity of the subject area (Cooper, 1989). Much of what was written then is still relevant in the early 1990s. To progress the field, Stockdale (1987) has reviewed the methodological issues facing leisure researchers, whilst Burton and Jackson (1989) rightly identify as a priority the need for more holistic, broadly-based and interdisciplinary research. But there are many barriers to this—institutional as well as academic. In part the contribution of **Progress** is to make available a wide range of high quality literature from all disciplines. The drawing together of a body of knowledge, and also exposure to the methods and research traditions of other disciplines (as they impinge on the fields of tourism, recreation and hospitality) should lead to a consistency of terminology, mutual respect and recognition of the validity of research in disciplines other than one's own.

Chris Cooper and Andrew Lockwood
University of Surrey
May 1992

References

Burton, T.L. and Jackson E.L., 1989, 'Leisure research and the social sciences: an exploratory study of active researchers', *Leisure Studies*, 8(2): pp. 263–80.

Cooper, C.P., 1989, Editorial Preface, in C.P. Cooper (ed.), *Progress in Tourism Recreation and Hospitality Management*, Belhaven, London, pp. 1–3.

Graburn, N.H.H. and Jafari, J., 1991, 'Introduction: Tourism—social science', *Annals of Tourism Research*, 18(1): pp. 1–11.

Sheldon, P., 1991, 'An authorship and analysis of tourism research', *Annals of Tourism Research*, 18(3): pp. 473–84.

Stockdale, J.E., 1987, *Methodological Techniques in Leisure Research*, Sports Council, London.

The Impact of Tourism

1 Tourist arts
E. Cohen

Tourist arts as a field of inquiry

Tourist arts, also referred to derisively as *airport art* (Graburn, 1967; Beier, 1968, p. 12; Cornet, 1975, p. 54; Bascom, 1976, p. 308; Mackenzie, 1977; Bassani, 1979) or more seriously as *arts of acculturation* (Gill, 1976, pp. 104–5), *arts by metamorphosis* (Mathieson and Wall, 1982, p. 166), *arts of transformation* (Cole, 1970), or *transitional arts* (Megaw, 1986), are the arts and crafts produced by artisans belonging to touristically *marked* ethnic groups (Graburn, 1984), mostly from the Third and Fourth Worlds (Graburn, 1976c), intended ultimately for sale to members of an *external audience* (Graburn, 1976b, p. 8, Jules-Rosette, 1984, p. 9). The latter could be tourists or other foreigners purchasing the artisans' products directly or indirectly (cf. Aspelin, 1977) on their trip, or members of the general public of developed countries into which such products have been imported.

Tourist arts is a *fuzzy* field (Cohen, 1974, pp. 528–9), with wide margins which overlap with a number of kindred fields, such as *ethnological arts* (Haselberger, 1961, p. 341), or *ethnoart* (Silver, 1979b), *commercial arts*, *souvenirs* (Gordon, 1986), and even *fine art*. *Tourist arts* cannot be empirically sharply distinguished from these other fields, although they can be conceived as an analytically distinct field of inquiry in which social scientists have recently shown a growing interest. Unfortunately, art historians and area specialists are as yet less willing to devote serious attention to this emerging subject.

Though sociologists distinguish between arts and crafts in the modern Western context (Becker, 1978), our subject encompasses both these types of objects; any distinction between *tourist arts* and *tourist crafts* would be wholly artificial, particularly since no distinction between arts and crafts is made in most cultures under consideration (May [1975], p. 125; Sandelowsky 1976, p. 355; Mathieson and Wall, 1982, pp. 165–6).

The study of tourist arts is also not a well-defined or well-established subject. It was dealt with, often as part of a wider study, by a variety of specialists from different social sciences, such as ethnographers, anthropologists, sociologists, geographers, and even development specialists. There are as yet no specialized journals devoted to the subject nor are there good bibliographical sources available. So far, only two collections of articles (Graburn, 1976c; *CSQ*, 1982), a few full-length monographs (e.g. Wagner, 1982; Parezo, 1983; Jules-Rosette, 1984), and a few scores of articles and chapters in books have been devoted to the subject. However, incidental references and longer descriptions can be found in many publications dealing with ethnic tourism in Third World Countries.

The distribution of research among world areas is also not uniform: while there exist many studies on Black Africa, the North American Indians and Latin America, there are only a few studies on Asia, and especially on India and the Middle East. These limitations preclude as thorough a review of the field as one could desire, so the present effort should therefore be seen as merely a preliminary survey.

Types and dynamics of ethnic and tourist arts

A common misconception of ethnic arts is that they are historically stable, *traditional* cultural products, which have been rudely shaken by the acculturative influence of the expanding modern West. In fact, tribal and ethnic arts have been continually changing throughout history under the impact of internal forces and external contacts, although not at the present accelerated rate. Tradition itself is thus in a permanent flux and is frequently *invented* (cf. Hobsbawm and Ranger, 1983). Contact with the modern world has influenced older ethnic traditions and given rise to new ones in a wide variety of ways prior to the expansion of modern tourism. *Tourist arts* should therefore not be seen as an abberation, but as one form of admittedly accelerated cultural change developing from that contact (Bascom, 1976, p. 307).

The rapid and widespread expansion of the production of arts and crafts specifically for the tourist market is a post-World War II phenomenon. However, there were some important historical precedents: thus, Portuguese contacts with West Africa in the sixteenth century led to the emergence of a particular syncretic type of craft products, known as Afro-Portuguese ivory (Fagg, 1939; Cornet, 1975, p. 54; Bascom, 1976, p. 309; Vogel, 1989). The Chinese, from the seventeenth century onward started a distinct line of porcelain production, destined expressly for the West, made for Western uses and decorated with Western motifs, known as *Chinese export porcelain* (Scheurleer, 1974). During the nineteenth century native skills were utilized throughout the world for the manufacture of new kinds of products adapted to the needs and tastes of traders, settlers and colonial officials. Some completely new crafts, such as the Haida argillite carvings (Kaufmann, 1976), indeed emerged during early contact periods as a response to the penetration of Western influences in remote areas. Many of these items in time became cultural markers of the artisans' ethnic group, although they were in fact from the outset produced for foreigners, and have not been part of any indigenous *tradition*.

With the penetration of modern industrial goods into Third World countries, many well-established local crafts declined significally or even disappeared (Beier, 1968, pp. 3–10; Bascom, 1976, pp. 305–6; Biebuyck, 1976; Kent, 1976, p. 91; O'Hear, 1986). Others underwent far-reaching changes as a result of contact with Western materials, technologies and ideas long before the arrival of modern tourism (cf. Hawthorn, 1961, p. 69;

Graburn, 1976c, *passim*; Wilpert, 1982, p. 16). In fact, much of the *traditional* ethnic art which is presently affected by tourist demand has already been much changed during pre-tourist times, and should more properly be referred to as *neo-traditional* to distinguish it from earlier, indigeneous forms (cf. Graburn, 1984, p. 397).

Pre-contact *traditional* and many of the older *neo-traditional* arts are presently traded primarily in the collectors' rather than the tourists' market (May [1975], pp. 127–8). Such arts can serve, however, as a point of departure or *baseline* (Kent, 1976, p. 98; Parezo, 1983, XIX) for the formulation of a typology, and a developmental or evolutionary scheme, for tourist arts.

The early critics of modern mass tourism tended merely to contrast what for them was *true* tribal and ethnic culture with tourist kitsch (e.g. Giesz, 1975), or with the *phoney folk-culture* (Forster, 1964, p. 226) created by tourism. Art historians, particularly of African art, tended to dismiss tourist arts as valueless or inferior, and to exclude them from their studies (cf. Crowley, 1970, p. 43; Silver, 1979a, p. 191).

The approach of the early researchers to commercialized ethnic arts as *arts of acculturation* or *transitional arts*, while avoiding a derisive terminology, still viewed them as ephemeral phenomena on an often implicit unilinear and unidirectional continuum, ranging from tradition to modernity, and progressing irreversibly on a single route from allegedly anonymous and stylistically uniform traditional ethnic crafts to ethnically unmarked individualistically distinctive artistic creations.

Some authors made several further distinctions along that continuum. Thus May ([1975], p. 125) proposes a not wholly value-neutral scale of categories of Papua New Guinean arts, ranging from *pure* traditional art through contact-influenced traditional art (our *neo-traditional*) and pseudo-traditional art (which 'at its worst' includes *airport art*) to syncretic art forms combining traditional art with individual creativity, and eventually to wholly introduced art forms which are the work of individual creative artists.

As research progressed, however, it became clear that such simplistic unilinear typologies are untenable, since commercialized ethnic arts may change along several distinct lines. Moreover, such developments are occasionally looplike: new art products, developed initially for an external public tend to be reintegrated into the (current) *tradition* of the group, becoming a marker of its (external) identity. Some are even used or collected by members of the group; Graburn (1976b, p. 8; 1984, p. 396), working with a two-dimensional model based on the variables of *intended audience* (internal or external) and the aesthetic source of the art (internal to the group, synthetic or external), distinguished six principal types of ethnic and tourist arts (Table 1.1; see also Graburn, 1976b, pp. 4–9). Graburn (1984, p. 399) consequently situated these six types on an evolutionary model of the process of change in ethnic arts, based on the additional variables of culture change (from tradition to modernity) and relative importance of the type of art to the ethnic group itself (Figure 1.1).

Cohen, proceeding along Graburn's lines, distinguished four variables

Table 1.1   *Categories of ethnic and tourist arts*

	Destination of the art forms	
Sources of art forms	Local/ethnic society	Visiting/tourist society
Local/ethnic society	*Functional traditional* e.g., religious figures, Dogon Granary doors, ritual masks	*Commercial traditional* Upper Sepik shields, Asmat *bisj* poles, Karen textiles
Novel or synthetic	*Reintegrated* Cuna *molas*, older *kachina* figures Andean clothing	*Souvenir novelty* Seri, Makonde carvings, Mexican *amate* paintings, Inuit sculptures
National/international genres	*Popular arts* Zaïre painting, older Navajo jewellery, Ghanaian *asato* arts	*Assimilated fine arts* Namatjira watercolours, Sante Fe Indian painting, Eskimo prints

Source: Graburn, 1984, p. 396.

for the classification of ethnic arts, namely, perpetuation v. innovation in artistic production, the orthogeneity v. heterogeneity of the process of artistic change, the internal v. external nature of the audience for the arts, and the extent to which the initiative for artistic production was spontaneous, i.e., originated in the ethnic group itself, or derived from outside agents (Cohen, 1983). A typology of types of change in ethnic music in Israel was developed on the basis of these variables (Shiloah and Cohen, 1983). Since it is analytical and general in nature, this typology is equally applicable to ethnic arts (Table 1.2).

Such typologies do not, of course, demarcate a closed domain. It is particularly important to point out two contrary lines of development beyond the limits of ethnic or *tourist arts*, emerging from the two types situated at the lower end of Graburn's typology in Figure 1.1. On the one hand, popular souvenirs, as they become standardized, tend to be industrially produced by people often unrelated to their original producers (e.g. Maori *tikis* or North-West Indian totem poles made of plastic) (Deitch, 1977, p. 184); though touristic, they are thus neither *ethnic* nor *art* any more, even if they have preserved their character as (external) ethnic markers. On the other hand, some assimilated ethnic fine artists tend eventually to lose the ethnic label as they integrate into a national art world, and their art thereby ceases to be an ethnic marker (cf. Graburn, forthcoming).

Theoretical approaches to tourist arts

Since tourist arts are a new field of inquiry, there exist as yet only few explicit and comprehensive theoretical statements formulating basic ques-

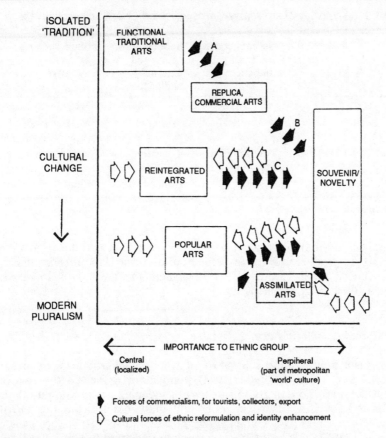

Figure 1.1   *Processes of change in tourist arts*

Source: Graburn, 1984, p. 399.

tions, hypotheses or programmes for empirical research. Nevertheless, one can discern in the literature four major approaches to tourist arts, differing in their wider ideological and paradigmatic perspective as well as in the theoretical orientation of their respective protagonists.

The politico-economic approach

Protagonists of this approach typically depart from a neo-Marxist or dependency theory (e.g. Wagner, 1982, pp. 131ff.) and deal with the impact of the incorporation of local artisans into the wider national and international market upon the forms of their production and upon their socio-economic position. Special emphasis is paid to the manner of their subordination and exploitation by middlemen and marketing agencies, reflected in

Table 1.2   *A typology of stylistic dynamics in Jewish Oriental music in Israel*

	Spontaneous: internal audience	Spontaneous: sponsored external audience	Spontaneous: external audience
Perpetuation— Orthogenetic	(1) Traditional	(2) Conserved	(3) Museumized
Innovation— Ortho/Heterogenetic	(4) Neotraditional	(5) Transitional	(6) Pseudoethnic
Innovation— Heterogenetic	(7) Popular	(8) Ethnic fine	(9) Fine

Source: Shiloah and Cohen, 1983, p. 238.

such indices as the share of the final price accruing to the producer, and the return to the producer for the investment of his or her labour (Hirschfield, 1977; Lauer, 1978; Littlefield, 1979; Eshelman, 1981; Novelo, 1981; Barnard, 1984, p. 2; Stephen, 1987).

The culture-critical approach

Protagonists of this approach, most of whose background is in art or cultural history (e.g. Boorstin, 1964), tend more to bewail the loss of authenticity and the denigration or loss of meaning of traditional ethnic arts through tourism, than to examine and analyse empirically the tourist products themselves (e.g. Hanna, 1972; Turner and Ash, 1975, pp. 140–3; Mackenzie, 1977; *CSQ*, 1982), or formulate constructive theoretical approaches to their study.

   Though the criticism expressed in this approach is in many respects well placed and of practical significance, it is often too global, superficial and prejudiced to be of much avail for a deeper understanding of tourist arts. Moreover, the critics tend to disregard the fact that *traditional* arts were threatened by the penetration of modernity all over the world and have often disappeared in the past, and that tourism helped to salvage or revive some of them (Cohen, 1989a, pp. 162–4). However, whatever the flaws of the approach, its representatives were among the first to draw attention to the emergent tourist art phenomena and helped thereby to set the research agenda for more value-neutral and insightful social science approaches to the study of the meaning of tourist arts.

The socio-cultural approach

This is the dominant approach in the recent literature and informs most of the empirical case studies of tourist arts, particularly those of anthropologists. The basic assumption of this approach is that tourist arts have to be dealt with in an unprejudiced and value-free manner within the general framework of the study of social and cultural change. Although there are, obviously, wide variations within this approach, its common distinctive feature is the readiness to deal with tourist arts as a subject of research in its own right, and not only as an index of politico-economic dependency or of cultural degeneration. Emphases on specific problems vary from descriptions of the processes of commercialization and the consequent changes in the arts themselves (e.g. Graburn, 1976c, McKean, 1976; Johnson, 1978; Boynton, 1986; de Kadt, 1979, pp. 68–76; Parezo, 1983), to a concern with the role tourist arts play for the ethnic groups' changing identity in the wider world (Graburn, 1984; Nason, 1984). Most authors who adopted this approach emphasize the adaptation of the tourist arts to the market (see especially Graburn, 1976c, *passim*). However, some seek to discover unexpected and often unconscious new meanings in the tourist products (e.g. Silver, 1979a; Cohen, 1990; Conquergood, forthcoming). This last endeavour links the present approach to the following one.

The semiotic approach

The protagonists of this approach seek to disclose the message encoded in tourist arts, using the techniques of semiological analysis (Szombati-Fabian and Fabian, 1976; Jules-Rosette, 1984). Some of them proceed on the assumption of a homology between language and art (Ben-Amos, 1977; Graburn, 1984, pp. 402–9). While this approach is applied by few researchers so far, it is one of the most promising avenues for the future study of tourist arts.

The production of tourist arts

The emergence of tourist arts is closely related to the recent growing interest in the industrialized world in ethnic craft products and the opening up of hitherto remote and inaccessible areas to modern means of communication, although not necessarily to tourist visits (cf. Aspelin, 1977). Within this general context, no systematic reasons can be adduced to why their production started in one location rather than another in the ethnic area (cf. Parezo, 1983, pp. 136–42). However, it appears that at least in the initial developmental stage (ibid., p. 151) of production of a tourist art, the artisans will tend to be *culture brokers* or *marginal men* (Smith, 1977), people who are well versed in their ethnic culture, and had at least some acquaintance with and experience in the wider society (Parezo, 1983, p. 161). Such people, in turn, may serve as teachers or advisers to less widely experienced artisans entering the tourist market.

Entrance to the tourist market involves a reorientation of production from an often poor internal to a generally well-to-do (Novelo, 1981, p. 206; cf. Littlefield, 1979, pp. 481–2) external (touristic) audience, i.e., an audience which is not conversant with the culture of the producers and their religious and aesthetic norms. Such a reorientation sometimes progresses gradually, the artisans at first selling the same product to both audiences. Soon, however, a differentiation between types of products takes place for aesthetic, religious (Parezo, 1983) or economic reasons, the same artisans sometimes producing simultaneously for both markets (e.g. Ben Amos, 1976, pp. 326–7; Salvador, 1976, p. 180; Eshelman, 1981, p. 246; Lambrecht, 1981, pp. 65–6; Boynton, 1986). Typically, however, the tourist market tends eventually to take over completely (e.g. Kooijman, 1977, p. 159; Johnson, 1978, pp. 58–9; Richter, 1978, pp. 325–6). During the reorientation of production, far-reaching changes tend to take place in the products intended for the tourist market. In some instances, indeed, new kinds of art emerged in response to tourist demands, such as Kamba or Eskimo sculptures (Elkin, 1958, p. 314ff; Graburn 1976a), or the bark paintings of the Australian aborigines (Williams, 1976); these have only a tenuous connection with the *traditional* arts of the group. In other cases, declining or forgotten arts have been revived through the emergence of a tourist market (Bascom, 1976, p. 319; Boyer, 1976).

Artisans may have diverse reasons to turn to commercialized production of their arts (Parezo, 1983, pp. 144–5), including the preservation of their cultural heritage (Williams, 1976, pp. 280–1; Parezo, 1983, pp. 148–9). However, the principal motive is invariably economic—whether to supplement a meagre agricultural or other source of principal income, or to turn art production into the principal source itself (Graburn, 1976a, p. 46; Kent, 1976, p. 95; Low, 1976, p. 224; Stromberg, 1976, p. 149; Parezo, 1983, pp. 144ff). Hence, their readiness to commercialize their ethnic arts increases with economic hardship, particularly under radically changing circumstances, such as worsening agricultural conditions (Parezo, 1983, pp. 6–9), foreign occupation (Nason, 1984, p. 436), and forced migration or flight caused by persecution or war (Cohen, 1982, 1989b; Conquergood forthcoming). Such hardships help to overcome cultural barriers or religious taboos against commercial production (Parezo, 1983, pp. 75–99). Such production in turn opens for members of the group a new channel of communication—the transmission of messages to the surrounding environment or even the wider world (Parezo, 1983, pp. 149–50; Jules-Rosette, 1984; Cohen, 1990; Conquergood, forthcoming). The latter endows the newly emergent tourist art with a vitality and expressiveness, especially during its formative period. Aesthetic or cultural or even political motives for the production of tourist arts thus tends to accompany the dominant economic one. These cannot be reduced to the latter and have to be studied and analysed independently (Jules-Rosette, 1984, pp. 15–19), as indeed they are in the study of art in general.

Traditionally, ethnic arts were produced on a small scale, either as part of widely practiced leisure activities of members of households, or as specialized occupations (such as smiths or silversmiths).

The transition to tourist arts does not in the majority of cases radically change the previous small-scale forms of production (Cook, 1982, p. 19).

However, in some instances, large-scale workshops (e.g., Elkan, 1958, p. 319; Jules-Rosette, 1984, p. 105; Smithies, 1988) and even production-line factories for standardized products (Bascom, 1976, pp. 312–3) have emerged. Even here, however, the craft-like nature of production has been generally preserved. There are two reasons for this continuity: the hand-made character of the products is their principal trade mark (e.g., Littrell, 1990, p. 239), hence their production remains labour-intensive despite some changes in technology; while the limited resources of most local producers and the difficulties they encounter in securing loans limit the expansion of enterprises and the introduction of capital-intensive techniques of production. Tourist arts enterprises are therefore typically based on low investments in raw materials, implements, or machinery (e.g., Eshelman, 1981, p. 251; Parezo, 1983, p. 148; Leon, 1983, p. 49), and they are labour rather than capital-intensive. Thus the units of production are small. Tourist arts are produced predominantly by individual artisans working alone, or with the help of members of their family, a few apprentices (Silver, 1981) or employees (e.g., Littlefield, 1979, pp. 475–6). They are basically *cottage industries* (Williams, 1976, p. 281; Boynton, 1976 pp. 462–3; Johnson, 1978, pp. 57–8): work is mostly done within the household, often during periods of leisure (e.g. Deitch, 1977, p. 181; Eshelman, 1981, p. 248; Wilpert, 1982, p. 35; Stephen, 1987, pp. 46–7; Smithies, 1988, p. 53), or in separate workshops attached to the habitation.

Despite this continuity in the basic mode of production, commercialization of ethnic arts nevertheless introduces some significant changes in the nature and organization of production. The mere expansion in the quantity of products—in comparison with the period before commercialization—leads to the increase in the intensity of production (e.g., Forster, 1964, p. 221) and to some specialization between the more skilled artisans and their helpers (e.g., Wilpert, 1982, pp. 21–2). In some cases people belonging to social categories which were traditionally excluded from the production of a certain art or craft move into it—especially men into women's work or women into that of men (Wilpert, 1982, pp. 29–30; Parezo, 1983, pp. 81–2).

The turn to production for an external audience intensifies the changes in the structure of production, which have often been initiated already in earlier times. Particularly, there is a tendency to substitute industrial for natural raw materials (cf. Graburn, 1976c, *passim*), such as industrial for homespun thread, machine-made for home-woven cloth, industrial paints for natural colours, or even plastic for rattan or bamboo. Many raw materials are bought, rather than prepared by the artisans themselves (e.g. Ben Amos, 1976, p. 323). Hence, the range of activities of the artisans is narrowed down in comparison with earlier periods, when their work embraced, typically, the complete production process.

Most commercialized art products remain in some sense *handmade*, as preferred by the tourists. However, substantial technological innovations in production methods (Jules-Rosette, 1984, pp. 181–9) have taken place. Only in few instances have *traditional* production methods been *frozen* (*ibid.*, p. 183). In most cases modern tools have been substituted for older ones (e.g., Wilpert, 1982, p. 21). Even machinery has been introduced in some places. This ranges from the widespread use of sewing-machines (e.g., Salvador, 1976, pp. 177–8) in the making of clothing and other textile products, to the introduction of electric drills and similar tools for working in wood, stone or metals (e.g., Jules-Rosette, 1979/80, p. 118; 1984, p. 65; Barck and Kihlberg, 1981).

Traditional craft producers were typically independent, selling their products, if at all, at their workshops or in the local market. Such arrangements still continue in some areas of small-scale production of tourist arts (e.g. Littlefield, 1979, pp. 475–6; Connelly-Kirch, 1982; Wagner, 1982). However, in general the producer of tourist arts is cut off from the market, which contributes in some instances to changes in the organization of production. The simplest new organizational form is a variety of the *putting-out* system (Littlefield, 1979, pp. 476–7; Silver, 1981, pp. 47–8; Cook, 1982, p. 19; Jules-Rosette, 1984, pp. 147–8; Stephen, 1987, p. 46), in which an entrepreneur distributes orders and materials to individual artisans and pays for their work on a piece-rate basis. Though the artisans continue to work at home, they become de facto employees of the entrepreneur.

Another new organizational form is producer associations (Levinsohn, 1980, p. 57) and co-operatives (Beier, 1968, p. 12; Salvador, 1976, p. 181; Swain, 1977, pp. 77–8; Barnard, 1984, p. 7; Jules Rosette, 1984, pp. 113–27; Crowley, 1985a, pp. 69–70; Leon, 1987, pp. 50–1). In many cases, these were not spontaneously established by the producers, but rather emerged under the tutelage of governments, advisers or non-profit marketing agencies (e.g., Graburn, 1976a, p. 48; Silver, 1981, p. 46; Donnelly, 1986). However, being an unaccustomed form of organization, co-operatives often suffered from management problems and internal strains and conflicts (e.g., Swain, 1977, p. 77; Silver, 1981, p. 46; Jules-Rosette, 1984, p. 119; Donnelly, 1986; Stephen, 1987, pp. 47–8). Moreover, the more successful artisans, who have little to gain from co-operation, tend to leave them and deal as individuals in the market (Jules-Rosette, 1984, p. 146).

The commercialization and marketing of tourist arts

Tourist arts are, almost by definition, commercialized arts. *Commercialization* of artistic products, however, has often a negative connotation and is hence perceived as having a detrimental impact on ethnic art (cf. Jules-Rosette, 1984, p. 11). However, the cultural significance and the social consequences of commercialization in fact vary widely according to the context in which it occurs and the manner in which it is brought about. These are completely different when a still viable craft is suddenly commercialized through outside initiative, from when a moribund craft is revived spontaneously by local people (e.g. Zerner, 1982; Parezo, 1983).

Accordingly, different types of commercialization of ethnic crafts should be distinguished (Cohen, 1989a) (Table 1.3). These types could probably be further elaborated by specific comparative studies of the processes of commercialization.

Table 1.3 *Processes of types of commercialization of ethnic arts*

Culture	Source of initiative	
	Spontaneous	Sponsored
Vital	(A) Complementary commercialization	(C) Encroaching commercialization
Declining	(B) Substitutive commercialization	(D) Rehabilitative commercialization

Source: Cohen, 1989, p. 162.

Ethnic and tourist art markets are frequently described in the literature. The most extensive surveys were conducted by Crowley (1970; 1980; 1981; 1983; 1985a; 1985b), who described most of the important markets around the world. A systematic typology of marketing channels for tourist arts has, however, not yet been developed (although see Crowley, 1970, pp. 43–4; Graburn, 1984, p. 398).

A basic distinction in tourism studies is that between direct and indirect tourism (Aspelin, 1977). The former comprises direct contact between tourists and representatives of an ethnic culture, whereas the latter entails the mediation of such contact through intermediaries. This dichotomy is a useful starting-point for developing a typology of the marketing of tourist arts. However, it has to be further refined by turning it into a continuous variable, namely, that of the relative distance between the original producer and the ultimate consumer of tourist art products. This can be defined as the number of intermediate steps separating them. Four points on this variable represent the principal empirical types of marketing of tourist arts.

(1) *Direct purchase.* The tourist or other foreigner visits the artisan's locale and purchases direct from him. The purchase may take place in the producer's household, his workshop or shop, in restaurants, in the market, the street or the hotel lobby (e.g., Elkan, 1958, p. 314; Abramson, 1976, p. 257; Ryerson, 1976, p. 135; Richter, 1978, p. 335; Silver, 1981, p. 46; Connelly-Kirch, 1982; Wagner, 1982). A variation of this type, at a slightly greater distance, is purchase by the tourists from one of the members of the artisan's family. This is common in situations where one of the spouses produces the wares and the other sells them.

This type is found principally in underdeveloped commercialization, where no organized, wider marketing system has yet emerged (cf. Hirschfield, 1977, pp. 115–16). It has the advantage of creating direct contact between producer and consumer and of remunerating the producer with the full price of his wares (Ryerson, 1976, p. 135), even if the price is often low and the quantity sold limited.

All the other types require intermediaries of various kinds. The greater the number of intermediaries, the smaller the producer's share in the final price of his product (Knab, 1981, p. 238; Ribeiro, 1981). However, the expansion of the market increases demand and hence the volume of production, thus creating more work for individual producers, or for more individuals. This is a crucial factor since tourism arts are a buyer's market: the producers can almost always increase production if demand grows. Since the producers in indirect tourism are cut off from the customers and hence face an anomymous audience (Jules-Rosette, 1984, p. 23), they depend almost completely on the feedback from the market they receive from the intermediaries about the kinds of products demanded, their style, size, ornamentation, etc. (*ibid.*, p. 194; Silver, 1981, p. 47; Cohen, 1983; Parezo, 1983, pp. 170ff). The greater the distance between producer and consumer, the more important this feedback becomes. Three types of indirect purchase in the realm of tourist arts ordered by the relative distance between producer and ultimate purchaser can be distinguished:

(2) *Purchase from local markets and stores in producers' countries.* The tourist visits the *region* in which the tourist art originates, although he does not reach the often remote ethnic village or outlying urban neighbourhoods in which it is produced. Hence, he makes his purchases in markets or stores which carry local art and craft products (e.g. Crowley, 1970, p. 44; Silver, 1979a, p. 194; Parezo, 1983, pp. 173ff). These may arrive there either directly from the artisan or through a local intermediary. The latter is sometimes one of the producers, who purchases or collects the work of his or her co-producers for a fee or commission and brings them to the market (e.g., Eshelman, 1981, p. 249), and sometimes an outsider, frequently a trader, from one of the middlemen minorities (Bonacich, 1973), who developed personal trading relations with the artisans' ethnic group.

(3) *Purchase from centrally located tourist shops and galleries in the producer's country.* The tourist visits a principal *centre* of the producer's country and here purchases the latter's products, often in shops and galleries carrying a wide variety of products from different regions of the country, or even from surrounding countries (cf. Crowley, 1981, p. 67; Jules-Rosette, 1984, p. 260). The products typically reach these shops and galleries through dealers or wholesalers, who in turn depend for their supplies on regional intermediaries.

(4) *Purchases from galleries, craft shops and department stores in the consumer's country.* The consumer in this type is not strictly speaking a *tourist* since he does not leave his place of residence to purchase the artisan's wares. Rather, these wares are imported into his country and put on sale there, typically in galleries, specialty craftshops or department stores (Ichaporia, 1982). Here, the ethnic products are brought to the

consumer, rather than vice versa as in tourism. The consumer is thus in a position relative to the art he purchases, paralleling that of the museum visitor relative to the ethnic objects he views. The chain of intermediaries here is the longest and typically leads from the original producers, through local intermediaries and wholesalers, to exporters, and from there to importers, and finally retail outlets in the purchaser's country. Thus there is an almost total cultural disjunction between the original producer and the ultimate purchaser. The producer is ignorant of his product's destination and the purchaser has only a vague idea, if any, of the provenance of the products he buys (Hawthorn, 1961, p. 69; Jules-Rosette, 1984, p. 28).

Direct sale to tourists and other visitors frequently starts spontaneously (Eshelman, 1981, p. 246), with the first visitors—often collectors (May [1975], pp. 127–8), or ethnographers—purchasing objects in local use, or ordering copies of such objects. The sale to tourists in such situations is an extension of the sale to these earlier visitors.

While the development of indirect sales may also happen spontaneously, it is frequently sponsored by individual outsiders, such as traders, shopkeepers, or missionaries (Williams, 1976, p. 272; Ribeiro, 1981; Wilpert, 1982, p. 23). At a later stage, however, it is often taken over by external institutional agencies which direct production, product development and market expansion (Aspelin, 1977, pp. 150–1; Cohen, 1989b). These agencies vary widely in nature, interests and policies. Four kinds of such agencies can be distinguished.

(1) *Museums.* Some modern museums actively encourage production of arts and crafts by contemporary artisans (Hawthorn, 1961, p. 69; Parezo, 1983, p. 28; Ganslmayr, 1988). Nevertheless, their principal interest is often in the preservation of *traditional* styles and objects. Hence they usually ask for copies of *traditional* objects, often to be sold in their own outlets, the museum shops (Crowley, 1970, p. 44).

(2) *Non-governmental organizations (NGOs).* These non-profit-making bodies, whose central offices are usually in one of the developed countries, while their agencies in Third World countries are managed by expatriates, seek to combine, to varying degrees, an interest in the preservation of ethnic aesthetic traditions with an interest in furthering the income of needy marginal or dislocated ethnic groups (Ichaporia, 1982, p. 13; Cohen, 1983; Leon, 1987, pp. 51–2; Bonnier, 1988).

(3) *Governmental agencies.* Governments of many Third World countries established special agencies dealing with the promotion and marketing of ethnic and tourist arts, whether as their principal function (e.g., Crowley, 1970, p. 44; Knab, 1981, pp. 237–8) or as part of their alleged role of helping and protecting tribal and other minorities (such as SPI/FUNAI in Brazil (Aspelin, 1977, p. 151) or BANCOFO and FONART in Mexico (Ryerson, 1976, p. 136; Stromberg, 1976, p. 160; Stephen, 1987, pp. 47–8). While nominally concerned with the development of minorities and the preservation of their aesthetic traditions, such agencies have primarily a

commercial concern, directed not so much to the benefit of the producers as to the earning by the government of foreign currency through the sale to tourists and the export of ethnic arts and crafts.

(4) *Commercial establishments*. These establishments, whose common primary interest is explicitly commercial, nevertheless initiated a wide range of business policies, dependent upon their relative emphasis on expensive, high quality products, as against cheap souvenir-type mass-produced articles. Galleries (Crowley, 1970, p. 43) with at least a nominal concern for aesthetic standards promote primarily high quality products and their policies come close to those of the museums, although they may be less restrictive and more innovative. Large trading companies such as the Hudson Bay Company, active in the trade of Inuit art, (Graburn, 1970, 1976a, pp. 45ff) or the Fred Harvey Company, active among the South-West Indians in the United States (Deitch, 1977, pp. 176–8; Parezo, 1983, pp. 27–8), have directly promoted the production of tourist arts and purchased the products in large quantities.

In the last few decades the bulk of the trade in tourist arts passed into the hands of wholesalers, exporters and importers (e.g., Elkan, 1958, p. 320; Low, 1976, p. 222; Stromberg, 1976, p, 156; Ichaporia, 1982; Jules-Rosette, 1984 *passim*), who deal in them both within their countries of origin and especially abroad. These enterprises are the main factor encouraging, through their trading policies, the standardization and simplification of tourist arts, and thereby bring about the decline in their variety and aesthetic appeal. However, these enterprises also demand good workmanship and reject shoddy work; they are therefore a major factor in the preservation of quality of production.

The marketing of tourist arts tends in recent times to become increasingly integrated into wider touristic facilities and attractions, some of which, such as *art fairs* (Nason, 1984, p. 441) and native handicrafts market (Crowley, 1985, p. 72), are of a temporary character, while others, such as *craft villages* (Crowley, 1981, p. 71), and native cultural centres are permanent establishments. Many of these establishments feature cultural performances and exhibitions, as well as demonstrations of native arts and crafts production (e.g., Low, 1976, p. 217), and include art and souvenir shops in which local as well as other ethnic art products can be purchased by the visitors.

The consumers of tourist art

Of the various components in the process of commercialization of tourist arts, we have the least systematic or detailed information on the ultimate destination of these arts: the consumers.

Several authors described the encounters between local sellers and foreign buyers of tourist art in markets (e.g., Connelly-Kirch, 1982, pp. 394–5), or in shops (Loeb, 1977). The fullest theoretical explication of the producer–consumer relationship was proposed by Jules-Rosette (1984, pp. 12), who interprets it as a double, symbolic and economic, exchange. However, none of these authors attempted to distinguish between different kinds of consumers of tourist arts, whether in terms of the historical development of their audience, or the different styles of travel and preferences of contemporary tourists.

It is possible to reconstruct a composite historical profile of the changing character of the external audience for ethnic arts. Tourists were usually not the first outsiders who purchased or ordered ethnic craft products in remote areas of the world. These were generally earlier visitors of various kinds: travellers, adventurers and sailors looking for *curios* (Haselberger, 1961, p. 342; Kaufmann, 1976, p. 58), explorers, ethnographers and anthropologists making collections for their research or for museums, private collectors (May [1975], p. 128) and traders (Sandelowski, 1976, pp. 360–2). The early contacts were sporadic and the purchases casual. As ethnic groups were opened up to outsiders—often in the wake of foreign conquest or penetration by national governments—more permanent relations with traders or amateur patrons of ethnic arts have sometimes been established (e.g., Brody, 1971; 1976; Ben Amos, 1976, pp. 332–3; Neich, 1982, p. 33). These relations were at the outset often of a personal nature, mixing commercial and ethnographic interests. The general trend of change in the external audience of ethnic arts can thus be conceived as a gradual decline of such personal relations between individual traders or patrons and a narrow circle of artisans (Maduro, 1976, pp. 239–41), and the growing exposure of the ethnic producers to an expanding, heterogeneous and increasingly impersonal consumer audience. Members of this audience are frequently only vaguely, if at all, aware of the ethnic identity and cultural background of the producers of the arts they are buying, and are certainly ignorant of their symbolic meaning (cf. Hawthorn, 1961, p. 69; Sandelowsky, 1976, p. 362). However, they may attribute new and different meanings to the object they are purchasing. Owing to this circumstance, a discrepancy often emerges between the meaning of the same art objects for their producer and their consumer (Jules-Rosette, 1984, p. 18). Thus art objects which had a religious or magic meaning for the producers and their group, are now appreciated primarily for their aesthetic or ethnological qualities. This discrepancy appears to be a principal factor in the gradual adaptation of the art products to the perceived tastes and preferences of the external public. However, since the tourist arts do not usually become a purely commercial venture, completely adapted to consumer demand, but continue to express meanings and to contain overt or hidden messages on part of the producers (Silver, 1979a; Jules-Rosette, 1984), the discrepancy persists to some extent even in the mature stages of commercialization. The differential perceptions of tourist art products by producers and consumers therefore constitute a most fruitful, though little explored area of research (Jules-Rosette, 1984, pp. 15–19).

Some authors (e.g. May [1975], pp. 127–8) attempted to list the different kinds of purchasers of ethnic and tourist arts. However, until recently no attempt was made to propose a typology based on variables significant in a broader sociology of tourism.

Two partly overlapping variables of theoretical import appear to be relevant to such a typology: the mix of strangeness and familiarity desired by the tourists on their trip (Cohen, 1972) and the degree of their concern with authenticity (MacCannell, 1973; Cohen, 1979; 1988a). The first of these could be used to create a typology of customers by the extent to which they prefer to purchase *extraordinary* (Gordon, 1986), strange or novel, exotic, as against more customary or familiar-looking objects. Such a typology would parellel Cohen's (1972, pp. 167–8) typology of tourist roles. Tourists seeking ethnically marked (stereo-)typical objects would fall in the middle of such a typology. It should be noted, however, that tourists often desire novelty (or *typicality*) of some aspect of the product, e.g. motifs or designs, whereas they prefer familiarity in others, such as colours, colour combinations, forms and functions. Any typology based on the strangeness–familiarity variable will therefore have to take into account all the aspects of the products purchased by the tourists.

Moreover, customers for tourist arts are not a culturally homogeneous group. They differ in their culturally determined tastes, not only in what they consider extraordinary or strange, but also in what they consider *customary*. Thus, European, North American and Japanese tourists in Thailand manifest quite different cultural preferences for colours and colour combinations in hill tribe textiles, for example (my observation; cf. also Wilpert, 1982, p. 34); these preferences, in turn, lead to a differentiation in the appearance of tourist art products destined for different markets.

Consumers could also be classified by the depth of their concern for authenticity. Such a classification would run roughly parallel to the left to right diagonal in Graburn's diagram of tourist arts (Figure 1.1), with consumers most concerned with authenticity looking for traditional arts or, in their absence, for replicas, and those least concerned with authenticity, purchasing mass-produced popular arts or souvenirs. Authenticity, however, is not a quality of the object itself, but is attributed to it by the tourists (Cohen, 1988a); hence, whether an object is seen as authentic or not depends upon the criteria of authenticity employed by them. These vary considerably in accordance with the tourists' depth of concern with authenticity. For those less concerned, the information that an object is decorated with *traditional* ethnic or tribal designs, or that it is *handmade* is thus usually a sufficient marker of authenticity (Cohen, 1988a, p. 378; Littrell, 1990, p. 237).

A recent study shows that in addition to authenticity and strangeness, other factors, such as the shopping experience and personal meanings play a major role in the consumers' appreciation of the symbolic significance of touristic textiles in their possession (Littrell, 1990). Littrell's study is the first to propose an analytical typology of consumers of tourist arts, which incorporates these various sources of significance. However, the typology relates only to objects purchased for keeping and use. Nevertheless, many tourists do not purchase products, especially souvenirs, merely for themselves; they purchase gifts to be distributed to kin, friends, and colleagues. These have to fit the circumstances of their relationships (cf. Graburn,

1983, pp. 44–5). Hence, many tourists purchase a *basket* of different products, often ranging from a few more expensive items purchased primarily for themselves, and a larger number of smaller and cheaper ones, for distribution at home. Mass tourism therefore generates a disproportionately growing demand for small souvenirs and other trinkets.

The principal audience of tourists arts, particularly in the early stages of their development, is usually composed of foreigners. Domestic tourists and other members of the local majority population initially tend to show only little if any interest in the arts of the ethnic minorities of their country; they usually become customers of locally produced tourist arts only at a later stage (e.g. Eshelman, 1981, p. 251). However, domestic tourists and other nationals at that stage may become an important component in the total demand for tourist arts (Jules-Rosette, 1984, p. 210). Thus Wilpert (1982, p. 34) claims that even in little Western Samoa, about 50 per cent of the customers are Samoans (who buy the objects as presents to take abroad).

The consequences of the commercialization of ethnic arts for tourism

Ethnic arts were historically in a process of permanent, though often slow, change. The intensified contact between many isolated groups and the outer world speeded up change, sometimes transforming and often destroying local cultures, including arts and crafts (e.g., Graburn, 1976b, pp. 12–13). Tourism, both direct and indirect, is part and parcel of a wide range of external impacts upon ethnic arts, and though it has specific consequences of its own, these have to be considered within this wider context of externally induced changes. Moreover, the broader significance of the consequences can be gauged only against this wider context. Therefore, extreme alternatives in an ethnic art form, which were introduced by an NGO to achieve maximum participation in the production of tourist arts by refugees who are devoid of other sources of income, has quite a different significance than the same alternatives would have were they the consequence of the initiative of an external entrepreneur, who sought to utilize the craftmanship of an isolated population with a vital culture merely to produce cheap objects for the mass market (Cohen, 1989b).

Within the scope of this review, however, we shall be able to outline only the principal concrete kinds of consequences. We shall not attempt to estimate their significance within all the changing contexts in which they have occurred.

The production of most kinds of tourist arts follows a similar pattern. Immediately following the commercialization and the opening up of the tourist market, there is often an upsurge of creativity in response to the challenge of new opportunities (Graburn, 1976c; Cohen, 1983) and the decline of traditional normative or religious constraints. Soon, however, routinization and standardization set in, often accompanied by the decline in the quality of the products (Hawthorn, 1961, p. 69; Universitas Udayana and Francillon, 1975, p. 733; Stromberg, 1976; Graburn, 1984, p. 406). This is especially so when a mass market for cheap souvenirs develops. Once a product becomes popular in the market, outsiders to the ethnic group which has originated the product often penetrate the market, copying designs and producing ever simpler, lower quality products (Eshelman, 1981, p. 256; Jules-Rosette, 1984, p. 27). As a consequence the market declines. Government agencies and NGOs then sometimes intervene in an attempt to preserve the craft through quality control (e.g. Leon, 1987, p. 52), occupational instruction as part of the curriculum in schools (Johnson 1978, p. 60), training courses (de Kadt, 1979, pp. 71–3; Leon, 1987, p. 51; Bonnier, 1988), or even special ethnic art schools and academies (Universitas Udayana and Francillon, 1975, p. 747; Okotai *et al.*, 1976, p. 6; Neich, 1982, p. 34), established to safeguard the long-term survival of traditional skills and styles.

While the general trend in the production of tourist arts is towards the standardized production of easily recognizable *ethnic* products, competition between the producers serves as an incentive for some individual differentiation and innovation (Graburn, 1976c, *passim*, Okotai *et al.*, 1976; Jules-Rosette, 1979/80, p. 117) in order to gain an advantage in the market (Stromberg, 1976, p. 158). Although much of tourist art is anonymous, this tendency leads to the emergence of signed works (Jules-Rosette, 1984, p. 149), and sometimes of *ethnic* artists known by name, some of the latter acquiring a considerable personal reputation (Graburn, 1976b, p. 22; Knab, 1981, pp. 239–40; Parezo, 1983, pp. 169–72, Jules-Rosette, 1984, pp. 142–53), and even occasionally penetrating the general art market (Graburn, forthcoming).

It is impossible to survey here all the various changes which occur in the tourist art products in the course of their commercialization. However, this process is characterized by contrary trends in several major aspects of tourist arts, and a review of these trends summarizes well the divergent changes in tourist arts.

Traditionalism v. innovation in motifs and designs

Motifs and designs are perhaps the principal aspect from which the style of ethnic arts is generally determined, hence it is a major indicator for the classification of these arts in the theories of evolution outlined above. Since motifs and designs are also the most important ethnic *markers*, there is, at least in the early stages of commercialization, a tendency to reproduce the mostly *neo-traditional* motifs and designs which were current at its baseline (e.g., Silver, 1979a, p. 198). Two contrasting trends of change from the baseline are discernible. The *traditionalist* trend consists of a return to earlier, sometimes even archaic (Brody, 1976, pp. 75–6) or prehistoric motifs and designs. These are in many instances reintroduced to the group by outsiders, or copied from museum catalogues or archaeological publications (e.g., Boyer, 1976, pp. 195–6). The *innovative* trend ranges from the adaptation of extant styles, motifs and designs to suit the tastes of an external public, or to make them more attractive to it (Johnson, 1978, p. 59; Knab, 1981, p. 241; Cohen, 1983; Boynton, 1986, p. 460), through the development of new *synthetic* (Abramson, 1976, p. 259), or *syncretic* (Jules-Rosette, 1979/80, p. 128) styles, to the introduction of completely novel *heterogenetic* ones (Shiloah and Cohen, 1983, pp. 237–8), such as pictorial representations in cultures which earlier possessed only ornamental designs (Kent, 1976, p. 95; Megaw, 1982; Jules-Rosette, 1984, pp. 142ff.; Cohen, 1990). Although the artisans may sometimes invent the new motifs and designs spontaneously, they probably more often borrow them from the modern popular culture (e.g., Parezo, 1983, pp. 94–9) or receive them from outside agents (e.g. Boyer, 1976, pp. 195–6; Sandelowsky, 1976, p. 363).

Naturalism v. abstraction motifs

Motifs or ethnic arts are usually stylized to some degree, even though there are huge differences between cultures in the extent of stylization. In tourist art two contrary trends can be observed. On the one hand, a turn towards naturalism (Bascom, 1976, pp. 313–4), result in the destylization of products (Graburn, 1976a, p. 52). Although the symbolic significance of traditional motifs may thereby be impoverished, the product becomes more accessible to an external audience, since the motifs are more readily recognizable (cf. Silver, 1979a, p. 204). On the other hand, there is a contrary trend of progressive abstraction (Kent, 1976, p. 97), or *stylization* of more naturalistic motifs (Beier, 1968, pp. 11–12; Stromberg, 1976, p. 152), often in a manner which makes them resemble modern Western arts styles. Thus some African tourist arts are made to look Picassoesque (Jules-Rosette, 1979/80, p. 120) — an ironic development considering the fact that Picasso was inspired by African art in developing the cubist style (Rubin, 1984).

Standardization v. individualization of products

Artisans traditionally made similar though not identical objects. While art products of a tribal or ethnic group were readily recognizable, they were not identical or standarized like industrial wares. Commercialization engenders two contrary trends of change. One is standardization: the progressively more standardized mass production of tourist art objects (Maduro, 1976, p. 241; Stromberg, 1976, p. 156; Cohen, 1983, p. 16). This trend is typical in small, cheaper products intended as souvenirs and in craft production for the export market. Preparation of catalogues by marketing agencies (Kent, 1976, pp. 96–7) seems to reinforce that trend.

The opposite trend is that of progressive individualization (e.g., Graburn, 1976b, pp. 21–3; Stromberg, 1976, p. 160): artisans, becoming aware of the value of individuality in Western art, seek to endow their

work with a personal imprint and to become artists known by name
(Graburn, 1976b, p. 22; Brody, 1976, p. 76; Sandelowsky, 1976, pp. 363–
4; Williams, 1976, p. 279; Knab, 1981, p. 241). Some artisans sign their
work to express or emphasize their individuality and increase thereby the
value of their products (Kent, 1976, p. 97). However, the signing of tourist
art products may sometimes in itself be a gimmick to make standarized
products appear differentiated.

Simplication v. elaboration of motifs and designs

Motifs and designs of tourist arts tend, on the one hand, to become
gradually simplified and ever grosser in comparison with the baseline
ethnic arts. Especially in mass-produced tourist arts, fine details, which
may have been of considerable significance for the group, are eliminated,
since the meaning is lost for an outside audience (cf. Lathrap, 1976,
pp. 202–5; McKean, 1977, p. 103; Jules-Rosette, 1984, p. 219; Leon, 1987,
p. 49). Complex motifs are parried down to a few recognizable marks. On
the other hand, an opposite tendency toward conspicuous elaboration of
motifs and designs on tourist arts is occurring. Freed from ritual or other
restrictions, having access to new materials and colours, and in a competitive market, artisans seek to enhance the attractiveness of their wares by
increasing the complexity of motifs and designs, adding ornamentation and
otherwise elaborating them, and thereby embellishing the products (cf.
Cornet, 1975, p. 55; Lathrap, 1976, pp. 199–202; Levinsohn, 1980, p. 57,
Boynton, 1986, p. 464).

Restraint v. exaggeration

Given the stylistic qualities of ethnic arts at the baseline, two contrasting
trends can be observed. On the one hand, there is a tendency to restrain
the buoyancy of much of ethnic art in order to adapt it to the more subdued
tastes of a Western art public (e.g. Stromberg, 1976, p. 158). On the other
hand, the demand of part of the external audience for *exoticism* and even
grotesqueness (Crowley, 1970, pp. 47–8; Bascom, 1976, p. 314; Graburn,
1976b, p. 18), in the *primitive* products, induces artisans to introduce
exaggerations into their work (Cornet, 1975, p. 55), which are typically
completely unrelated to their culture. Indeed, according to Silver (1979a,
pp. 200–2), grotesque and sensationalist works are such a blatant inversion
of native culture that they dialectically serve to reinforce the adherence to
the proper aesthetic canon of the group.

Gigantism v. miniaturization

In comparison with the customary size of ethnic art object at the baseline,
two contrasting trends can be distinguished. On the one hand, tourist art

products are occasionally made increasingly bigger, sometimes reaching
gigantic proportions (Abramson, 1976, p. 258; Bascom, 1976, p. 314;
Graburn, 1976b, p. 18; Salvador, 1976, p. 18). More often they are
reduced in size to facilitate production, reduce the price of the products
and make it easier for tourists to carry them in their luggage (Maduro,
1976, p. 241), or to use them in their homes (e.g., Brody, 1976, p. 76; Gill,
1976, pp. 108–9, Lathrap, 1976; Sandelowski, 1976, p. 362; Stromberg,
1976, p. 158; Johnson, 1978, p. 59; Leon, 1987, p. 49).

Introduction of novel materials v. return to native materials

During their development prior to becoming tourist arts, many ethnic
artisans have substituted new industrial materials and colours for those of
older, native origin. This trend was intensified with the production for the
tourist market for different reasons: exhaustion of native resources, convenience in production, and preservation and maintenance of the products
or the development of new types of products (Beier, 1968, p. 10; Graburn,
1976b, p. 28; Maduro, 1976, p. 242; Stromberg, 1976, p. 156; Knab, 1981,
p. 234; Lambrecht, 1981, p. 63). However, as a reaction to this trend by
the more sophisticated and **purist** segment of the buying public, a contrary
purposeful return to native materials has taken place in some instances,
e.g., in the return from artificial to natural materials in basketry (Lambrecht, 1981, p. 65–6), or in the substitution of traditional handspun and
handwoven materials, dyed in natural colours, for industrial cloth used in
the production of touristic textile products among the Karen of northern
Thailand (my observation).

Product for show v. use

Ethnic craft products were functionally integrated in the whole lifestyle of
the people who used them: they were *functional arts*. Early explorers and
collectors collected them mainly to be displayed, out of context, in exhibitions and museums. Contemporary tourist arts reflect both these practices in a novel form: while modern tourists do not usually collect *authentic*
objects representing a given culture, they often seek objects to be put on
show as decorations for their homes (de Kadt, 1977, p. 72). Much of the
tourist art is produced in response to this demand and its form changed to
serve that purpose: e.g., embroideries on costumes are framed like paintings (Salvador, 1976, p. 181), and sand paintings and amate paintings are
made into pictures (Stromberg, 1976, p. 156; Parezo, 1983). Contrariwise,
in search of new outlets and markets, new products are developed for
specific uses. Such products may be quite different from those customary in
the producer's own culture (e.g., Salvador, 1976, p. 181; Johnson, 1978,
p. 60; Jules-Rosette, 1979–80, p. 117). Thus, ironically, bookmarkers and
tablecloths are produced by South-East Asian tribal people, who have
neither books nor tables. In some instances, semi-finished ethnic products,

such as embroidered pieces of cloth, are employed by non-ethnics for the production of modern Western products, such as ethnically ornamental fashionable garments (Cohen, 1988b).

These contrasting pairs of consequences of the commercialization of ethnic arts for the tourist market appear in many different configurations under the influence of a wide variety of factors such as the culture of the group, the kind of art under consideration, the type and size of the market, and the nature of the mediating and marketing agencies. Although there is insufficient information on the relative effect of each of these factors, it appears that the major influence on the direction of change in tourist arts is exercised by the mediating and marketing agencies. The policies of these agencies on quality v. quantity of production, preservation of ethnic *traditions* v. adaptation to market demands, and stress on artistic freedom v. intervention in the artisan's work largely determine the different outcomes of commercialization.

Conclusion

Tourist arts are an ill-defined target field, studied by researchers from various disciplines and with widely differing ideological and theoretical perspectives, in a bewildering variety of locations around the world. Hence, a reviewer attempting to piece together an integrated picture of the state-of-the-art in the field faces serious difficulties. The strategy adopted here has been a rather down-to-earth approach, centring on concrete arguments and findings regarding the processes which engender and determine the production, marketing and consumption of tourist arts and their consequences for the art itself. It remains to indicate briefly some wider issues which have not been given sufficient attention in the body of this review.

As some of the in-depth anthropological studies of artisans and their communities have shown, the commercialized production of tourist arts, once it becomes a principal occupation of a large number of members of the community, may have wide-ranging social consequences in economic development and the differentiation, stratification and structure of social relations between local groups, etc. (Johnson, 1978; Richter, 1978; Sander, 1981; Knab, 1981; Connelly-Kirch, 1982, pp. 399–400; Stephen, 1987). These wider repercussions should be made into a major focus of study, as the perspective of researchers of tourist arts becomes gradually widened from a concentration on the immediate production and exchange of tourist arts to a concern with the broader effects of these processes. Hence we need more holistic studies of ethnic communities in which the production of tourist arts has become the principal economic activity.

Like tourism in general, tourist arts are also an important factor in the formation of a new *external* identity of ethnic groups in the Fourth World (Graburn, 1976b, pp. 26–7; 1984, p. 408; Low, 1976, pp. 224–5; Deitch, 1977, p. 181; Parezo, 1983, p. 150). Groups such as the Eskimos or the Kamba (Elkin, 1958, p. 314; Jules-Rosette, 1984, pp. 106ff) have become known and are attributed a distinctive identity through their tourist arts, even though this *art* may be a recent invention and be little related to the groups' *traditional* culture. Moreover, in some instances the ethnic arts of a particular Fourth World group may be utilized as distinguishing symbols not only of the group but also of the wider society in which it is located (Graburn, 1976b, p. 29; 1984, pp. 413–4).

A major concern of many students of tourist arts is the extent to which commercialization changes, impairs or destroys *traditional* cultures. It is clear from our presentation that there is no general answer to this question. There is little doubt that commercialization is a factor of change. However, when evaluating its overall significance, one has to take into account three important considerations. First, no culture is completely static; tourism and the production of ethnic arts for the tourist market are just another kind of influence which make for change, even though its intensity and rapidity may be exceptional. Second, tourism is only one factor of change in ethnic arts and crafts emanating from the modern world, and often, moreover, a late-comer. This is particularly true in societies such as those of the United States, Latin America and parts of Asia, in which Western influences on the native populations have been strong long before the coming of modern tourism. Finally, in any evaluation of the impact of commercialization, the alternative has to be taken into account—and in many cases that alternative is not the preservation of pristine ethnic arts, but their complete disappearance as they succumb to modern industrial mass consumer goods (de Kadt, 1979, p. 69).

Moreover, the direct effects of commercialization are not unequivocal. There is no doubt that it often led to a decline in standards and the production of aesthetically fairly worthless, banal objects, known as *airport art*. However, sometimes the impetus of the new market has helped the preservation, conservation or even revival of moribund ethnic arts (Brody, 1976; Wilpert, 1982, p. 23). Elsewhere, the production of the arts has indirectly helped to preserve an ethnic culture (McKean, 1976; Connelly-Kirch, 1982, p. 400). Finally, and perhaps most important, at least in some cases new aesthetically significant genres and even new art forms have appeared during the development of tourist arts, while in other cases, these arts have been found to convey important symbolic messages to their novel audience.

A final issue is the complicated problem of authenticity in tourist arts. Although this is just one specific manifestation of the wider problem of authenticity in tourism, and the even wider one of the meaning and significance of the concept of *authenticity* in the modern world (see Trilling, 1972), it is important and deserves detailed consideration. This is especially so, since the question of authenticity is frequently raised in publications on tourist arts (e.g. Barnard, 1984), and since much of the discussion surrounding this question is muddled owing to conceptual and theoretical difficulties.

We should note, first, that *authenticity* and such related concepts as *originality*, *copy*, *reproduction* and even *fakery* are not qualities of an object, but socially constructed attributions by the members of a culture.

Hence, whether a piece of ethnic art is considered to be *authentic* or *inauthentic*, a *copy*, or even a *fake*, will depend very much on the criteria of judgement which happen to be employed by the observer or potential customer. In cross-cultural evaluations there is the additional complication that the producers and consumers belong to different cultures, and therefore may have widely differing criteria of judgement. Moreover, in some cases the cultural group of the producers may not possess such concepts as *authenticity*, *originality* or *fakery*.

Second, in this late modern or post-modern age there is considerable and growing confusion surrounding these concepts even in the Western world, as such composites as *original reproduction* and *authentic reconstructions* testify. Indeed, it is increasingly obvious that the older puristic concepts of *authenticity* and *originality* (Cohen, 1988a, pp. 374–5) are becoming increasingly irrelevant in a culturally as well as technologically rapidly changing world (cf. Beier, 1968, p. 12). As ethnic groups adopt new artistic genres, seek to express in their work new messages directed at an external audience and acquire new technical skills, restrictive conceptions of authenticity are of little practical use, even though they express a nostalgic yearning for an allegedly pristine, uncontaminated cultural world, which seems to have disappeared forever.

Third, there is the phenomenon of *emergent authenticity* (Cohen, 1988a, pp. 379–80). Newly produced objects, even some *airport art*, which are presently considered blatantly unauthentic may acquire in due time a patina of authenticity (Cornet, 1975, p. 54), just as similar products of the past have acquired in recent times.

Fourth, the claim of *authenticity* or *originality* for a product is often made by the sellers, rather than the producers of tourist art. These intermediaries are frequently *keying* (Goffman, 1974, pp. 45ff), misrepresenting (e.g. Maduro, 1976, p. 241) or even faking the provenance of the object, the background of its producers or the techniques of production (e.g., Bascom, 1976, p. 314; Loeb, 1977). The intermediaries, rather than the producers *stage authenticity* (MacCannell, 1973), often mislead unsuspecting and ignorant tourists into buying an object which in fact is not what it is represented to be.

Finally, some ethnic groups, aware of the appreciation of their *traditional* culture and the value of *antiquities*, have embarked upon the production of replicas, often by copying old pieces from museums or art books (Eshelman, 1981, p. 247; Bernard, 1982; Wilpert, 1982, p. 23), and other objects which are presently not in use in their culture. In so far as these are exact copies they become *authentic reproductions*. However, in some instances, such objects are consciously aged by various techniques (Crowley, 1970, p. 48; Bascom, 1976, p. 316; Eyo, 1976, p. 54), to produce *instant antiques* (Sutliff, 1981), which are then sometimes sold as the real thing by unscrupulous dealers. Such cases exemplify an at least tacit collusion between producers and intermediaries. It is ironic that this type of fakery, when practised on a large scale, gives rise to what for some authors is a new genre of tourist arts—the *counterfeit industry* (Schaedler, 1979, pp. 149–51).

The concrete areas of study reviewed in the body of this chapter certainly necessitate more examination, especially in comparative and longitudinal studies, which will approach their subject emically, i.e. through the eyes of the producers' culture and within the wider economic, social and political context, (cf. Cohen, 1979, pp. 30–2). However, the issues briefly referrred to in this concluding section appear to me to be intellectually and theoretically the most challenging ones, and therefore deserve particular attention in the future.

References

Abramson, J.A., 1976, 'Style change in an upper Sepik contact situation', in N.N.H. *Graburn* (ed.), 1976, *Ethnic and Tourist Arts*, University of California Press, Berkeley, 249–65.

Aspelin, P.L., 1977, 'The anthropological analysis of tourism: indirect tourism and political economy in the case of the Mamainde of Mato Grosso, Brazil', *Annals of Tourism Research*, 4(3): pp. 135–60.

Barck, A. and K. Kihlberg, 1981, *Sameslojd*, LTs forlag, Stockholm.

Barnard, B., 1984, 'But is it authentic: the tourist arts of Southeast Asia', *Universities Field Staff International Reports*, Asia, No. 14.

Bascom, W., 1976, 'Changing African art', in N.N.H. *Graburn* (ed.), 1976, *Ethnic and Tourist Arts*, University of California Press, Berkeley, 303–19.

Bassani, E., 1979 '19th century airport art', *African Arts*, 12(2): pp. 34–5.

Becker, H.S., 1978, 'Arts and crafts', *American J. of Sociology*, 83: pp. 862–89.

Beier, U., 1968, *Contemporary art in Africa*, Pall Mall Press, London.

Ben-Amos, P., 1976, '"A la recherche du temps perdu"': On being an ebony-carver in Benin', in N.N.H. *Graburn* (ed.), 1976, *Ethnic and Tourist Arts*, University of California Press, Berkeley, 320–33.

Ben-Amos, P., 1977, 'Pidgin languages and tourist arts', *Studies in the Anthropology of Visual Communication*, 4(2): pp. 128–39.

Bernard, P., 1982, 'Repliques d'objets archaïques en Mélanésie', *Res*, No. 3: pp. 108–13.

Biebuyck, D.P., 1976, 'The decline of Lega sculptural art', in N.N.H. *Graburn* (ed.), 1976, *Ethnic and Tourist Arts*, University of California Press, Berkeley, 335–49.

Bonacich, E., 1973, 'A theory of middlemen minorities', *American J. of Sociology*, 38(5): pp. 583–94.

Bonnier, J., 1988, 'Afroart, a new idea', in *Craft Reports from all around the World*, World Crafts Council, Copenhagen, pp. 36–9.

Boorstin, D.J., 1964, *The Image: A Guide to Pseudo-events in America*, Harper and Row, New York.

Boyer, R. McD., 1976, 'Gourd decoration in Highland Peru', in N.N.H. *Graburn* (ed.), 1976, *Ethnic and Tourist Arts*, University of California Press, Berkeley, 183–96.

Boynton, L.L., 1986, 'The effect of tourism on Amish quilting design', *Annals of Tourism Research*, 13(3): pp. 451–65.

Brody, J.J., 1971, *Indian painters and white patrons*, University of New Mexico Press, Albuquerque.

Brody, J.J., 1976, 'The creative consumer: survival, revival, and invention in Southwest Indian Arts', in N.N.H. *Graburn* (ed.), 1976, *Ethnic and Tourist Arts*, University of California Press, Berkeley, 70–84.

Cohen, E., 1972, 'Toward a sociology of international tourism', *Social Research*, 39(1): pp. 164–82.
Cohen, E., 1974, 'Who is a tourist? A conceptual clarification', *Sociological Review*, 22(4): pp. 527–55.
Cohen, E., 1979, 'Rethinking the sociology of tourism', *Annals of Tourism Research*, 6(1): pp. 18–35.
Cohen, E., 1982, 'Refugee art in Thailand', in *Cultural Survival Quarterly*, 6(4): pp. 40–2.
Cohen, E., 1983, 'The dynamics of commercialized art: Meo and Yao of northern Thailand', *J. of the National Research Council of Thailand*, 15(1), part II: pp. 1–34.
Cohen, E., 1988a, 'Authenticity and commoditization in tourism', *Annals of Tourism Research*, 15(3): pp. 371–86.
Cohen, E., 1988b, 'From tribal costume to pop fashion: the "boutiquisation" of the textiles of the hill tribes of northern Thailand', *Studies in Popular Culture*, 11(2): pp. 49–59.
Cohen, E., 1989a, 'The commercialization of ethnic crafts', *Journal of Design History*, 2(3): pp. 161–8.
Cohen, E., 1989b, 'International politics and the transformation of folk crafts—the Hmong (Meo) of Thailand and Laos', *J. of the Siam Society*, 77(1): pp. 68–82.
Cohen, E., 1990, 'Hmong (Meo) commercialized refugee art: from ornament to picture', in D. Even, E. Cohen, B. Danet (eds), *Art as a Means of Communication in Pre-literate Societies*, The Israel Museum, Jerusalem.
Cole, H. 1970, *African Arts of Transformation*, The Art Galleries of the University of California, Santa Barbara, Calif.
Connellly-Kirch, D., '1982, Economic and social correlates of handicraft selling in Tonga', *Annals of Tourism Research*, 9(3): pp. 383–402.
Conquergood, D., forthcoming, 'Fabricating culture: the textile art of Hmong refugee women', in J. Speer and E. Fine (eds), *Performance, Culture and Identity*, Indiana University Press, Bloomington.
Cook, S., 1982, Craft production in Oaxaca, Mexico, *CSQ*, pp. 18–20.
Cornet, J., 1975, 'African art and authenticity', *African Arts*, 9(1): pp. 52–5.
Crowley, D.J., 1970, 'The contemporary traditional art market in Africa', *African Arts*, 4(1): pp. 43–9.
Crowley, D.J., 1980, 'The art market in Easter Island, Tahiti, and Samoa', *African Arts*, 13(2): pp. 66–70.
Crowley, D.J., 1981, 'African crafts as communication', *African Arts*, 14(2): pp. 66–71.
Crowley, D.J., 1983, 'The traditional art market in Southeast Asia', *African Arts*, 16(4): pp. 65–70.
Crowley, D.J., 1985a, 'The art market in Southern Oceania', *African Arts*, 18(2): 68–74.
Crowley, D.J., 1985b, 'The circumpolar art market', *African Arts*, 19(1): pp. 70–4.
CSQ, 1982 'Ethnic arts: works in progress?', *Cultural Survival Quarterly*, 6(5): pp. 1–42 (Special Issue).
de Kadt, E., 1979, *Tourism: Passport to Development?*, Oxford University Press, New York.
Deitch, L., 1977, 'The impact of tourism upon the arts and crafts of the Indians of the Southern United States', in V.L. *Smith* (ed.), 1977, *Hosts and Guests*, University of Pennsylvania Press, Philadelphia, 173–84.
Donnelly, N.D., 1986, 'Factors contributing to a split within a clientelistic needlework cooperative engaged in refugee resettlement', in G.L. Hendricks, B.T.

Downing and A.S. Deinhard (eds), *The Hmong in Transition*, Center for
Migration Studies of New York Inc., New York, and The Southeast Asia
Refugee Studies of the University of Minnesota, 159–73.

Elkan, W., 1958, 'The East African trade in woodcarvings', *Africa*, 28(4): pp. 314–
23.

Eshelman, C.G., 1981, 'Arte y comercio Nahua: el amate pintado de Guerrero',
America Indigena, 41(2): pp. 245–63.

Eyo, E., 1976, 'Tourism and control', *African Arts*, 9(3): pp. 53–4.

Fagg, W., 1939, *Afro-Portuguese Ivories*, Batchworth, London.

Forster, J., 1964, 'The sociological consequences of tourism', *International J. of
Comparative Sociology*, 5(2): pp. 217–27.

Ganslmayr, 1988, 'What can museums do?', in *Craft Reports from all around the
World*, World Crafts Council, Copenhagen, 106–10.

Giesz, L., 1975, 'Kitsch-man as tourist', in G. Dorffles (ed.), *Kitsch: The World of
Bad Taste*, Bell Publishing, New York, 156–74.

Gill, R.R., 1976, 'Ceramic arts and acculturation at Laguna', in N.N.H. *Graburn*
(ed.), *Ethnic and Tourist Arts*, University of California Press, Berkeley, 102–13.

Goffman, E., 1974, *Frame Analysis*, Harper, New York.

Gordon, B., 1986, 'The souvenir, messenger of the extraordinary', *J. of Popular
Culture*, 20(3): pp. 135–46.

Graburn, N.H.H., 1967, 'The Eskimos and airport art', *Trans-Action*, 4(10):
pp. 28–33.

Graburn, N.H.H., 1970, 'The marketing of Canadian Eskimo art', paper, Annual
Meetings of the Northeastern Anthrop. Assoc.

Graburn, N.H.H., 1976a, 'Eskimo art: the Eastern Canadian Arctic', in *Graburn*
(ed.), *Ethnic and Tourist Arts*, University of California Press, Berkeley, 39–55.

Graburn, N.H.H., 1976b, 'Introduction: arts of the Fourth World', in *Graburn*
(ed.), *Ethnic and Tourist Arts*, University of California Press, Berkeley, 1–32.

Graburn, N.H.H. (ed.), 1976c, *Ethnic and Tourist Arts*, University of California
Press, Berkeley.

Graburn, N., 1983, 'To pray, pay and play: the cultural structure of Japanese
domestic tourism', *Les Cahiers du tourisme*, Series B, No. 26.

Graburn, N.H.H., 1984, 'The evolution of tourist arts', *Annals of Tourism
Research*, 11(3): pp. 393–419.

Graburn, N.H.H. forthcoming, 'Ethnic arts and the Fourth World: the view from
Canada'.

Hanna, W.A., 1972, 'Bali in the seventies; part I: cultural tourism', *AUFSR,
Southeast Asia Series*, 20(2): pp. 1–7.

Hasselberger, H., 1961, 'Methods of studying ethnological arts', *Current
Anthropology*, 2(4): pp. 341–84.

Hawthorn, H.B., 1961, 'The artist in tribal society: the Northwest coast', in M.W.
Smith (ed.), *The Artist in Tribal Society*, Routledge and Kegan Paul, London,
59–70.

Hirschfield, L.A., 1977, 'Art in Cunaland: ideology and cultural adaptation', *Man*,
12: pp. 104–23.

Hobsbawm, E. and T. Ranger (eds), 1983, *The Invention of Tradition*, Cambridge
University Press, New York.

Ichaporia, N., 1982, 'Imports and exportomania', in *CSQ*, pp. 12–14.

Johnson, R.B., 1978, 'The role of tourism in Tongan culture', in V.L. Smith (ed.),
Tourism and Behavior, Studies in Third World Societies, No. 5, 55–68.

Jules-Rosette, B., 1979/80, 'Technological innovation in popular African art: A
case study of some contemporary art forms in transition', *J. of Popular Culture*,

13: pp. 116–30.

Jules-Rosette, B., 1984, *The Messages of Tourist Art: An African Semiotic System in Comparative Perspective*, Plenum, London.

Kaufmann, C.N., 1976. 'Functional aspects of Haida argillite carvings', in N.N.H. Graburn (ed.), 1976, *Ethnic and Tourist Art*, University of California Press, Berkeley, 56–69.

Kent, K.P., 1976, 'Pueblo and Navajo weaving traditions and the Western world', in N.N.H. Graburn (ed.), 1976, *Ethnic and Tourist Art*, University of California Press, Berkeley, 85–101.

Knab, T., Artesania y urbanización: el caso de los Huicholes, *America Indigena*, 41(2): pp. 231–43.

Kooijman, S., 1977, *Tapa on Moce Island, Fiji*, Brill, Leiden.

Lambrecht, D., 1981, 'New basketry in Kenya', *African Arts*, 15(1): pp. 63–6.

Lathrap, D.W., 1976, 'Shipibo tourist art', in N.N.H. Graburn (ed.), 1976, *Ethnic and Tourist Art*, University of California Press, Berkeley, 197–207.

Lauer, M., 1978 'Artesania y capitalismo en el Perú', *Analisis* (Lima), No. 5: pp. 26–48.

Leon, L., 1983, 'Artisan development project', *Cultural Survival Quarterly*, 11(1): pp. 49–52.

Levinsohn, R., 1980, 'Rural Kwazulu basketry', *African Arts*, 14(1): pp. 52–7.

Littlefield, A., 1979, 'The expansion of capitalist relations of production in Mexican crafts', *J. of Peasant Studies*, 6(4): pp. 471–88.

Littrell, M.H., 1990, 'Symbolic significance of textile crafts for tourists', *Annals of Tourism Research*, 17(2): pp. 228–45.

Loeb, L.D., 1977, 'Creating antiques for fun and profit: encounter between Iranian Jewish merchants and touring coreligionists', in V.L. Smith, (ed.), *Hosts and Guests*, University of Pennsylvania Press, Philadelphia, 185–92.

Low, S.M., 1976, 'Contemporary Ainu wood and stone carvings', in N.N.H. Graburn, (ed.), *Ethnic and Tourist Art*, University of California Press, Berkeley, 211–25.

MacCannell, D., 1973, 'Staged authenticity: arrangements of social space in tourist settings', *Am. J. of Sociology*, 79(3): pp. 589–603.

McKean, Ph.F., 1976, 'Tourism, culture change, and culture conservation in Bali', in D.J. Banks (ed.), *Changing Identities in Modern Southeast Asia*, Mouton, The Hague, 237–47.

McKean, Ph.F., 1977, 'Towards a theoretical analysis of tourism: economic dualism and cultural involution in Bali', in V.L. Smith (ed.), *Hosts and Guests*, University of Pennsylvania Press, Philadelphia, 93–107.

MacKenzie, M., 1977, 'The deviant art of tourism: airport art, in B.H. Farrell (ed.), *The Social and Economic Impact of Tourism on Pacific Communities*, Center for South Pacific Studies, University of California, Santa Cruz, Calif. 83–4.

Maduro, R., 1976, 'The Brahmin painters of Nathwara', Rajasthan', in N.N.H. Graburn (ed.), *Ethnic and Tourist Arts*, University of California Press, Berkeley, 227–44.

Mathieson, A. and G. Wall, 1982, *Tourism: Economic, Physical and Social Impacts*, Longman, London.

May, R.J. [1975], 'Tourism and the artifact industry in Papua New Guinea', in B.R. Finney and K.A. Watson (eds), *A New Kind of Sugar: Tourism in the Pacific*, East–West Center, Honolulu, 125–33.

Megaw, J.V.S., 1982, 'Western Desert acrylic painting—artifact or art', *Art History*, 5(2): pp. 205–18.

Megaw, V., 1986, 'Something but for whom? Ethics and transitional art', *Cultural Survival Quarterly*, 10(3): pp. 64–9.

Nason, J.D., 1984, 'Tourism, handicrafts, and ethnic identity in Micronesia', *Annals of Tourism Research*, 11(3): pp. 421–49.

Neich, R., 1982, 'The Maori woodcarvers of Rotura and the Museums of New Zealand', *CSQ*, pp. 32–5.

Novelo, V., 1981, 'Para el estudio de las artesanias mexicanas', *America Indigena*, 41(2): pp. 195–210.

Okotai, T., Henderson, P. and I. Fogelberg, 1976, 'The cultural impact of tourism: art forms—revival or degradation', University of South Pacific Extension Service PEACESET Conference, Impact of Tourism Development in the Pacific, (Suva, Fiji) 3 May 1976.

O'Hear, A., 1986, 'Pottery making in Ilorin: a study of the decorated water cooler', *Africa*, 56: pp. 175–92.

Parezo, N.J., 1983, *Navajo Sandpainting, from Religious Act to Commercial Art*, University of Arizona Press, Tucson.

Ribeiro, B.G., 1981, 'O artesanato cesteiro como objeto de comercio entre os indios do alto Rio Negro, Amazonas', *America Indigena*, 41(2): pp. 289–309.

Richter, D., 1978, 'The tourist art market as a factor in social change', *Annals of Tourism Research*, 5(3): pp. 323–38.

Rubin, W., 1984, 'Picasso', in *W. Rubin* (ed.), *Primitivism in 20th century art*, The Museum of Modern Art, New York, Vol. I, pp. 241–342.

Ryerson, S.H., 1976, 'Seri ironwood carving: an economic view', in N.N.H. *Graburn* (ed.), *Ethnic and Tourist Arts*, University of California Press, Berkeley, 119–36.

Salvador, M.L., 1976, 'The clothing arts of the Cuna of San Blas, Panama', in N.N.H. *Graburn*, (ed.), *Ethnic and Tourist Arts*, University of California Press, Berkeley, 165–82.

Sandelowsky, B.H., 1976, 'Functional and tourist art along the Okavango River', in N.N.H. *Graburn*, (ed.), *Ethnic and Tourist Arts*, University of California Press, Berkeley, 350–65.

Sander, H.J., 1981, 'Beziehungen zwischen Tourismus, landlichen Kunsthandwerk und Agrarstruktur in einigen Dorfern Zentralmexikos', *Erdkunde*, 35(3): pp. 201–9.

Schaedler, K.-F., 1979, 'African arts and crafts in a world of changing values', in E. de Kadt, *Tourism: Passport to Development?*, Oxford University Press, New York, 146–56.

Scheurleer, D.F.L., 1974, *Chinese Export Porcelain*, London.

Shiloah, A. and Cohen, E., 1983, 'The dynamics of change in Jewish Oriental ethnic music in Israel', *Ethnomusicology*, 27(2): pp. 227–52.

Silver, H.R., 1979a, 'Beauty and the "I" of the beholder: identity, aesthetics and social change among the Ashanti', *J. of Anthropological Research*, 35(2): pp. 191–207.

Silver, H.R., 1979b, 'Ethnoart', *Annual Review of Anthropology*, 8: pp. 267–307.

Silver, H.R., 1981, 'Carving up the profits: apprenticeship and structural flexibility in a contemporary African crafts market', *American Ethnologist*, 8(1): pp. 41–52.

Smith, V.L. (ed.), 1977, *Hosts and Guests*, University of Pennsylvania Press, Philadelphia.

Smith, V.L., 1977, 'Eskimo tourism: micro-models and marginal men', in V.L. *Smith* (ed.), *Hosts and Guests*, University of Pennsylvania Press, Philadelphia, 51–70.

Smithies, M., 1988, 'Tourism, carving and change in Bali', *Living in Thailand*, 17(6): pp. 44–6, 53.

Stephen, L., 1987, 'Zapote weavers of Oaxaca: development and community control', in *Cultural Survival Quarterly*, 11(1): pp. 46–8.

Stromberg, G., 1976, 'The amate bark-paper painting of Xalitla', in N.N.H. *Graburn*, (ed.), *Ethnic and Tourist Arts*, University of California Press, Berkeley, 149–62.

Sutliff, J.P., 1981, 'Old and new—instant antiques', *Sawadd*, March–April: pp. 21–5.

Swain, M.B., 1977, 'Cuna women and ethnic tourism: a way to persist and an avenue to change', in V.L. *Smith* (ed.), *Hosts and Guests*, University of Pennsylvania Press, Philadelphia, 71–82.

Szombati-Fabian, I. and Fabian, J., 1976, 'Art, history and society: popular painting in Shaba, Zaïre', *Studies in the Anthropology of Visual Communication*, 3(1): pp. 1–21.

Trilling, L., 1972, *Sincerity and Authenticity*, Oxford University Press, London.

Turner, L. and Ash, J., 1975, *The Golden Hordes*, Constable, London.

Universitas Udayana and G. Francillion, 1975, 'Tourism in Bali—its economic and socio-cultural impact: three points of view', *International Social Science J.*, 27: pp. 721–47.

Vogel, S., 1989, 'Africa and the Renaissance: art in ivory', *African Arts*, 22(2): pp. 84–9.

Wagner, V., 1982, *Catching the Tourist: Women Handicraft Traders in the Gambia*, University of Stockholm, Department of Social Anthropology, Stockholm Studies in Social Anthropology, Stockholm.

Williams, N. 1976, 'Australian aboriginal art at Yirrkala: introduction and development of marketing', in N.N.H. *Graburn* (ed.), 1976, *Ethnic and Tourist Arts*, University of California Press, Berkeley, 266–84.

Wilpert, C.B., 1982, 'Traditionell und touristisch: Kunsthandwerkliche Holzarbeiten in Samoa', *Mitteilungen aus dem Museum für Volkerkunde Hamburg*, 12: pp. 15–36.

Zerner, Ch., 1982, 'Tourism and the arts in Southern Sulawesi', in *CSQ*, pp. 21–3.

2 Tourism and environmental integration: the journey from idealism to realism

R.K. Dowling

Introduction

The environment–tourism relationship has incorporated four phases over the last four decades. In the 1950s it was viewed as being one of coexistence (Zierer, 1952). However, with the advent of mass tourism in the 1960s, increasing pressure was put on natural areas for tourism developments. Together with the growing environmental awareness and concern of the early 1970s the relationship was perceived to be in conflict (Akoglu, 1971). During the next decade this view was endorsed by many others (e.g. Cohen, 1978; OECD, 1980; Mathieson and Wall, 1982). However, at the same time a new suggestion was emerging that the relationship could be beneficial to both the environment and tourism (e.g. Budowski, 1976; Pigram, 1980; Romeril, 1985).

Over recent years the relationship has increasingly been viewed as one with considerable potential for either conflict or symbiosis. Pursuing the latter view it has been suggested that environmental conflicts caused by natural area tourism developments may be reduced and that environmentally compatible tourism developments may be achieved through an integrated approach fostering sustainable development (Farrell and McLellan, 1987; Farrell and Runyan 1991). Such an approach will be attained only through environmentally appropriate tourism planning (Inskeep, 1991a and b).

Early stirrings: the 1950s to the early 1970s

Forty years ago the prevailing view was that tourism had few impacts on the natural environment. 'A notable characteristic of the tourist industry and recreation industry is that it does not or should not lead to the destruction of natural resources' (Zierer, 1952; p. 463). However, tourism's professional body, the International Union of Official Travel Organizations (IUOTO; predecessor of the World Tourism Organisation, WTO), did recognize the possibility of adverse impacts. In 1954 it introduced into its General Assembly a section on the protection of the tourist heritage which dealt with the protection of tourism 'capital' or resources from potentially adverse physical and social effects.

The advent of mass tourism which characterized the 1960s spawned a plethora of research on the evaluation of tourism. The IUOTO demonstrated through various surveys that natural tourism resources were the primary factor that attracted tourists, even in countries with an outstanding cultural heritage. This led to the first studies on what was termed the *ecological impact* of tourism and it convinced the IUOTO of the need for an integrated approach to tourism development.

In Tahiti the association between the environment and tourism development was examined in the light of tourist-induced environmental degradation (Beed, 1961). Concern was expressed that the tourist invasion could induce ecological imbalance within the island's ecosystem if it was not carefully managed. Another study outlined the impact on fragile sites by visitors destroying vegetation, collecting souvenir rock specimens, and causing trail erosion (Darling and Eichhorn, 1967). On the other hand studies of tourism developments in America (Waters, 1966) and Africa (Makame, 1968) purported that they were beneficial to the environment. Later in the decade the IUCN began its first study of tourism and conservation when it met for its Tenth Technical Meeting on **Ecology, Tourism and Recreation** (IUCN, 1967).

As international tourism developed, concomitant with it emerged high expectations of its potential role in economic growth and overall development for many countries. However, environmental concerns that were beginning to emerge at this time gained greater credence. An early example was in the Caribbean where a strong rationale for conservation of nature and historical sites was fostered as an integral part of tourism (Carlozzi and Carlozzi, 1968). They argued that integrated environment–tourism development would provide a major opportunity for achieving a measure of economic self-sufficiency in the Lesser Antilles.

During the 1960s increasing public environmental awareness paralleled the advent of mass tourism. Therefore, it was inevitable that the two would interact and in many cases conflict. Early stirrings of widespread global environmental awareness and concern had been made by Carson in her book **Silent Spring** (1962) and by Hardin in his classic **The Tragedy of the Commons** (1969). These were quickly followed by major statements of global environmental problems in **Ecoscience: Population, Resources and Environment** (Erhlich *et al.*, 1970) and **The Environmental Revolution** (Nicholson, 1970).

This awareness which had already embraced the tourism industry was endorsed in a **Tourist Review** article 'Tourism and the problem of environment' (Akoglu, 1971). In the same year the IUOTO adopted an environmental tourist policy. Central to it was the recommendation that at the national level countries should establish an inventory of natural tourist resources. Implicit in the policy directive was the concept of classifying or zoning, whereby areas with a particularly sensitive or fragile environment would be developed only on a small scale, if at all. Another key feature of the tourist environmental policy was the establishment of guidelines for the development of new tourist resorts. The IUOTO suggested that environmental considerations be incorporated in the commissioning of the design of any new tourist development so that buildings blended in with their surroundings and any adverse environmental impacts were minimized.

These policies were shared at the United Nations **Conference on the Human Environment** at Stockholm in 1972. During this meeting an important concept was formulated which would have far reaching implications for the future. This was the birth of the *ecodevelopment strategy* which suggested that economic development should take place only if it was linked to environmental protection. A corollary to this strategy was the notion that any resulting environment–tourism development should be entirely compatible with local values and culture. These views were also endorsed by a World Bank study which concluded that planning should be integrated to avoid disparities in the standards of amenities for the visitor and local population (Seth, 1985).

The debate widens: the 1970s

Over the next few years the diverging themes of the environment–tourism relationship began to gain momentum with cases being argued both for and against tourism. Some indicated that tourism provided the incentive for conservation through the establishment of national parks (e.g. in East Africa; Myers, 1972), heritage values (Basque, Spain; Greenwood, 1972) and natural and cultural resources (Agarwal and Nangia, 1974; Dower, 1974). Others argued that tourism created unacceptable costs owing to pollution (Young, 1973; Goldsmith, 1974) and impacts on fauna (Crittendon, 1975; Mountfort, 1975) or flora (Liddle, 1975; McCabe, 1979). However, it was two tourism professionals who provided the strongest support for acknowledgement of the link between tourism and the natural environment. Haulot, the Commissioner General of Tourism in Belgium, and Krippendorf, the Director of the Swiss Tourism Association, both espoused tourism–environment integration (Haulot, 1974; Krippendorf, 1975). Their books were the first on the theme of tourism and the environment and after the consideration of a wide range of tourism's effects on the environment they concluded that the two must be kept in balance.

The year 1976 was a landmark in the environment–tourism debate with a major paper by Dr Gerardo Budowski, the Director General of the IUCN, exploring the relationship between those promoting tourism and those advocating the conservation of nature (Budowski, 1976). He suggested that the relationship is particularly important when tourism is partly or totally based on values derived from nature and its resources, and added that the relationship could be one of conflict, coexistence or symbiosis. He said that they are in conflict when tourism induces detrimental effects on the environment and are in coexistence particularly when there is little contact and each remains in isolation. He postulated that the two are in symbiosis when each derives benefits from the other, that is, natural attributes are conserved whilst tourism development is attained and suggested that this approach fosters environment–tourism integration.

Budowski indicated that the environment–tourism relationship at that time was more often one of conflict than coexistence. He challenged both conservationists and tourism developers to change their attitudes and work towards integration, which he suggested would in turn lead to a symbiotic relationship. Budowski proposed that if this approach were followed then conservation and tourism would benefit mutually. He said, 'tourism helps by lending support to those conservation programmes which will develop educational, scientific and recreational resources with the objective that they in turn will attract more and different kinds of tourists' (Budowski, 1976, p. 29).

The symbiotic approach was soon to be fostered in the Mediterranean where tourism was having a devastating effect on the natural, human-made and socio-cultural environments, especially in the coastal areas (Tangi, 1977). To protect and preserve the region's environmental quality the United Nations Environment Programme (UNEP) sponsored **Mediterranean Action Plan**, and **Regional Seas Programme** devised a number of tourism development strategies to overcome the adverse impacts of mass tourism. The approaches were described as alternative development strategies and included spatial, temporal and educational aspects.

In the latter part of the decade an attempt was made to assess systematically the environmental impacts of tourism (Cohen, 1978). The environment was described as the *physical environment* with both natural and cultural components and impacts classified as either positive or negative. The factors of the environmental impacts of tourists were described as depending upon the intensity of tourist site-use, the resilience of the ecosystem, the time perspective of the developers and the transformational character of touristic developments. An evolutionary phase was proposed for natural areas in which the original tourist destinations become environmentally degraded through intensive use. Finally, Cohen stated that the environment–tourism relationship could be viewed in two ways, either as protecting the environment **for** tourism, or **from** tourism. He concluded that the latter approach was particularly important, especially in developing countries.

During the same year the American Conservation Foundation put together a compilation of case studies of tourism in natural areas in eight different developed countries (Bosselman, 1978). It outlined many of the problems associated with tourism impacts on natural areas, and concluded that tourism can be most beneficial if it makes the tourist more aware of the special qualities of places. While both Cohen and Bosselman were pointing out the potential environmental risks posed by tourism, the alliance of tourism and the environment was being proposed by Gunn (1978). Although he endorsed Budoswki's view that the environment–tourism relationship had evolved from coexistence through conflict to symbiosis, he went further in suggesting their synergistic possibilities. To explore these, Gunn advocated the need for an international alliance of tourism, recreation and conservation.

The 1970s were a decade which can be best summarized as one in which the potential conflicts of tourism and the natural environment were realized. Parallel with this was an associated increase of interest in the relationship between the social and cultural environment and tourism. Research was centred on the tourist, the host and the tourist–host relationship (Turner and Ash, 1975; Smith, 1977; de Kadt, 1979). Also, it ushered in an awareness that tourism development with its predominantly economic slant had to be tempered with the realization that it brought with it associated social impacts which could be either negative (Thomason *et al.*, 1979) or positive (Cohen, 1979).

The debate deepens: the early 1980s

The beginning of the new decade ushered in a wave of interest in tourism and conservation issues and 1980 was a landmark year for the environment–tourism relationship. In March the United Nations Environment Programme (UNEP) and the WTO formally signed an agreement on tourism and the environment. In September at the World Tourism Conference in the Philippines, the **Manila Declaration on World Tourism** was generated. Also that year the Organization for Economic Co-operation and Development (OECD) published the results of a three-year investigation by a **Group of Experts on Environment and Tourism** (1980). The publication summarized the situation at the time, as being one in which the environment and tourism were in conflict owing to the adverse environmental impacts caused by tourism. Its prediction for the future was that 'tourism is involving more and more people and is becoming a virtual mass phenomenon whose uncontrolled expansion can be seriously damaging for the environment' (OECD, 1980, p. 41).

While these environmental initiatives were being made by tourism (WTO) and development (OECD), the world's major environmental organizations, the IUCN, UNEP and the World Wildlife Fund (WWF; later to be known as the World Wide Fund for Nature), joined forces to present a global conservation plan: **The World Conservation Strategy** (IUCN, 1980). The strategy argued that development can only be sustained by conserving the living resources on which it depends as well as by the integration of development and conservation. Living-resource conservation was defined as being specifically concerned with plants, animals and micro-organisms, and with those non-living elements of the environment on which they depend. It was advanced that living resources have an important property which distinguishes them from non-living resources: that they are renewable if conserved and are degradable if not. The same argument was applied to water, soil and air resources. This policy took the earlier concept of *ecodevelopment* linking environment and development, and added the notion of the *integration* of the two in order for the earth to be able to continue supporting humankind in the future. This was to shape the future direction of conservation for the remainder of the decade and gained increasing importance when, during the same year, the Brandt

Commission Report on **North–South** relations stated that development must include the care of the environment (Brandt Commission, 1980).

In 1982 UNEP and the WTO issued a joint declaration formalizing interagency co-operation for the purpose of 'protection, enhancement and improvement of man's environment for the harmonious development of tourism'. They added, 'similarly, rational management of tourism may contribute to a large extent to protecting and developing the physical environment and the cultural heritage as well as improving the quality of man's life' (UNEP and WTO, 1982). At the same time a major survey and summary of the environmental impacts of tourism reached a different conclusion (Mathieson and Wall, 1982). Taking up Budowski's (1976) theme of coexistence, conflict or symbiosis they explored the latter two views in detail, and concluded that more often than not the relationship was in conflict for 'there is little evidence to indicate the widespread existence of a symbiotic relationship between tourism and the environment' (p. 101).

However, attempts were being made in different parts of the world to achieve tourism–environment compatibility. In Nepal the Sagamartha (Mt Everest) National Park was established largely to ameliorate the adverse environmental impacts of back-packing tourists. One of its main objectives was to promote tourist and visitor use suitable to the environment and conditions of the park to the extent compatible with the other objectives (including conservation of nature, water, soil, religious and historic values) in a manner which would provide economic benefit to the local population and to Nepal (Jefferies, 1982). In Australia the Great Barrier Reef Marine Park, which had been established in 1975, underwent classification in 1981 into five zones in order to separate areas for environmental protection and tourism use (Kelleher and Kenchington, 1982). In East Africa attempts were also being made to harmonize conservation and development. While tourism development was fostered consideration was being given to the protection of coastal and marine areas visited by foreigners to ensure that essential ecological processes were left undisturbed (Kundaeli, 1983).

By now the environment–tourism debate was being widened to include the socio-cultural aspects which had been the focus of separate research in the 1970s. A social theory base for tourism was advanced by Travis (1982) and a community-based environmental approach advocated by Murphy (1983). It was argued that tourism is essentially resource-based and by ignoring social (as well as ecological) implications the industry was in danger of undermining its very existence. It was suggested that benefits would accrue for the industry and the destination community from the development of a mutually symbiotic relationship.

From idealism to realism: the late 1980s

By the mid-1980s the environment–tourism relationship was beginning to be more clearly understood. A review was made of the major issues and literature of the time by Dunkel (1984) and the positive aspects advanced

(OAS, 1984). The importance of the environment to any aspect of development had been asserted through the **World Conservation Strategy** and close co operation between the environment and tourism had been advocated (UNEP/WTO, 1983) and initiated (Mlinaric 1985). In addition, environmental impacts ascribed to tourism had been described (OECD, 1980; Mathieson and Wall, 1982; Pearce, 1985), and the need for social and cultural components to be included in planning aspects had been advanced (Travis, 1982; Murphy, 1985; 1988).

Co-operation between conservation and tourism was advocated at a European Heritage Landscapes Conference held in 1985 by Adrian Phillips, the Director of the Countryside Commission of the United Kingdom. He stressed their interrelationship pointed to the need for their future co-operation and argued that there are three reasons why conservation should seek the support of tourism. These are that tourism provides conservation with an economic justification, it is a means of building support for conservation, and it can bring resources to conservation (Phillips, 1985).

A special edition of the **International Journal of Environmental Studies** (25 (4) 1985) concentrated on the topic, and the relationship was described as moving closer together, with 'Budowski's ideal [being] much more a reality now than it was in 1976' (Romeril, 1985; p. 217). The view that tourism can be a major agent for landscape conservation was also endorsed by Lusigi, 1981; Murphy, 1986a; and Leslie, 1986. At the same time the integration of the relationship was also being advanced for its benefits to both business (Murphy, 1986b) and regional development (Pearce, 1985). Other aspects of the relationship were also being examined, notably the biological impacts of the environment and tourists on each other (Edington and Edington, 1986) as well as the environmental carrying capacity of tourism (**UNEP Industry and Environment** (9 (1) 1986)).

By the end of the year it was clear that the idealism of the environment–tourism relationship as advocated through symbiosis was being tempered by the realism that in actual fact the underlying conflicts were ever present. This was demonstrated during a symposium held in March 1986 in Canada by the Alberta Chapter of the Canadian Society of Environmental Biologists. The symposium theme of 'Tourism and Environment: Conflict or Harmony?' was debated by leading Canadian researchers and academics. For example, 'The expanding importance from a global perspective of the tourism interface with wildlife and natural environments' was presented by J. Butler, and others were given by R. Butler, P. Murphy and J. Ritchie. However, whereas the Vice-President of the Tourism Industry Association of Alberta presented a paper on 'Tourism and the environment: a natural partnership' (Mackie, 1986), the Director of the Environmental Council of Alberta countered with his one entitled 'The — tourists are ruining the parks' (Landals, 1986).

Towards integration: the 1990s

By the middle of the last decade the environment–tourism relationship had embraced aspects of the three states of coexistence, conflict and symbiosis. Today it can be argued that all three relationships exist simultaneously depending on location and issue (Hall, 1991). Although the relationship in symbiosis has been sought after as the *ideal* in reality, it has been largely one of conflict (Smith and Jenner, 1989). Therefore a new orientation for the relationship has been advanced, in which both the environment and tourism are viewed as making a unified whole (Dowling, 1990). This is the state of integration where the possibilities of coexistence, conflict and symbiosis are recognized and environmentally appropriate tourism opportunities are advanced. Such activities and developments are fostered if they are environmentally compatible, minimize adverse impacts and maximize benefits. This is the essence of sustainable development which was advocated in a major global statement by the World Commission on Environment and Development (WCED, 1987). Entitled **Our Common Future** and generally referred to as **The Brundtland Report**, it examined the world's critical environmental and development problems and concluded that only through the sustainable use of environmental resources will long-term economic growth be achieved (Brundtland, 1987). Hence the term *sustainable development*, which had previously been coined, was now brought into wide use and the concept began to shape the nature of the future environment–tourism relationship.

This approach was proposed in a special issue of the **Annals of Tourism Research** (14 (1) 1987) which centred on *Tourism and the Physical Environment*. It suggested that the environment and tourism must be integrated in order to maintain environmental integrity and successful tourism development (Farrell and McLellan, 1987). They also advanced the notion that 'a symbiosis between tourism and the physical environment is the second strand of a dual braid of concern, the first being the contextual integration of both physical and social systems' (p. 13). Their argument is that

the true physical environment is not the ecosystem, the central core of ecology. This is an environment (better still an analogue model) perceived by those occupying a subset of the scientific paradigm, and their viewpoint is not exactly the same as the abiotic vision of landscape perceived by the earth scientist or the more balanced landscape or region, the core of the geographer's study. (p. 12)

Their reasoned approach for a more holistic view is advanced with the need for integration of community concern and involvement in tourism development as contended by Travis (1982) and Murphy (1983, 1985). This integrative approach is one in which the 'resource assets are so intimately intertwined with tourism that anything erosive to them is detrimental to tourism. Conversely, support of environmental causes, by and large, is support of tourism' (Gunn, 1987; p. 245).

Similar concerns were also expressed by Romeril (1989a, b). Whereas

just four years before he had championed Budowski's environment–
tourism symbiotic relationship (Romeril, 1985), he now concluded that
'the goal is to maintain a profitable and viable tourism industry without
detriment to the environment, an objective which must surely become the
norm in the 1990's' (Romeril, 1989a; p. 208). In addition he stated that 'the
symbiotic ideal of Budowski and Romeril will remain a distant goal while
such detrimental change is still seen' (1989b; p. 111). Romeril suggests the
increase of *alternative* or *green* tourism as a possible future way towards
environment–tourism integration. This is also proposed by CART, the
Centre for Advancement of Responsive Travel (Millman, 1989). However,
alternative tourism is often used as a synonym for *appropriate* tourism,
although questions are now being raised of whether or not this is so
(Cohen, 1989; Butler, 1990; Farrell and Runyan, 1991).

Conclusions

Today the integration of tourism and the environment is being carried out
at different levels in a number of places for a variety of reasons. They range
in size from small-scale (e.g. Yankari Game Reserve, Nigeria; Olokesusi,
1990) to large-scale (Lake Baringo, Kenya; Burnett and Rowntree, 1990),
and include conservation (Brake, 1988), cultural (Gale and Jacobs, 1987),
heritage (Millar, 1989), social (Brockelman and Dearden, 1989) and
spatial benefits (Jansen-Verbeke and Ashworth, 1990). On a global scale
this integrative approach is being fostered by principles of both conservation (McNeely and Thorsell, 1989; McNeely, 1990) and development
(GLOBE '90, 1990).

To conclude, the nature of the environment–tourism relationship at
present can be best summarized as one which is in equipoise. The view that
tourism and the environment are a symbiotic or even synergistic panacea
must be tempered by the fact that the relationship is still one of conflict in
many parts of the world. Therefore it is through their integration that
conflicts can be minimized and symbiotic possibilities advanced. This view
has been advocated by the IUOTO in the 1960s, Haulot and Krippendorf
in the 1970s, Romeril in the 1980s and is the basis of the current sustainable
development thrust. Whilst in the past, natural area tourism development
to enhance economic growth has been described as being either in coexistence, conflict or having symbiotic possibilities, the emergent view is that
continued tourism development will be sustained only by the recognition of
the interdependencies that exist among environmental and economic issues
and policies. This is the concept of *sustainable development* which is
recognized by both those who describe the conflicts (Smith and Jenner,
1989) as well as those who advocate a symbiotic approach (Romeril, 1989 a
and b). It has been advanced that

an aware and completely changed industry can sustain tourism. In terms of modern
thinking and ecodevelopment, if tourism is sustained significant steps have then

been taken toward maintaining environmental integrity. A healthy environmental integrity means the possibility of successful tourism, which, when managed properly, becomes a resource in its own right. (Farrell and McLellan, 1987; p. 13)

References

Agarwal, R.K. and Nangia, S., 1974, *Economic and employment potential of archaeological monuments in India*, Asia Publishing House, New Delhi.

Akoglu, T., 1971, 'Tourism and the problem of environment', *Tourist Review*, 26: pp. 18–20.

Beck, B. and Bryan, F., 1971, 'This other Eden: a study of tourism in Britain', *The Economist*, 240: pp. 66–83.

Beed, T.W., 1961, 'Tahiti's recent tourist development', *Geography*, 46: p. 368.

Blake, G.H. and Lawless, R.I., 1972, 'Algeria's tourist industry', *Geography*, 57(2): pp. 148–51.

Bosselman, F.P., 1978, *In the Wake of the Tourist: Managing Special Places in Eight Countries*, The Conservation Foundation, Washington DC.

Brake, L.A., 1988, 'Tourism as a tool for conserving arid lands', *Australian Parks and Recreation*, 24(3): pp. 37–40.

Brandt Commission, 1980, *North–South: A Programme for Survival*, Pan Books, London.

Brockelman, W.Y. and Dearden, P., 1990, 'The role of nature trekking in conservation: a case study of Thailand', *Environmental Conservation*, 17(2): pp. 141–8.

Brundtland, G.H., 1987, 'Our common future—call for action', *Environmental Conservation*, 14(4): pp. 291–4.

Budowski, G., 1976, 'Tourism and environmental conservation: conflict, coexistence or symbiosis?', *Environmental Conservation*, 3(1): pp. 27–31.

Burnett, G.W. and Rowntree, K.M., 1990, 'Agriculture, research and tourism in the landscape of Lake Baringo, Kenya', *Landscape and Urban Planning*, 19: pp. 159–72.

Butler, R.W., 1990, 'Alternative tourism: pious hope of trojan horse?', *Journal of Travel Research*, 28(3): pp. 40–5.

Carlozzi, C.A. and Carlozzi, A.A., 1968, *Conservation and Caribbean Regional Progress*, The Antioch Press.

Carson, R., 1962, *Silent Spring*, Fawcett, Greenwich, Connecticut.

Clare, P., 1971, *The Struggle for the Great Barrier Reef*, Collins, London.

Cohen, E., 1978, 'The impact of tourism on the physical environment', *Annals of Tourism Research*, 5(2): pp. 215–37.

Cohen, E., 1979, 'A phenomenology of tourist experiences', *Sociology*, 13: pp. 179–202.

Cohen, E., 1989, 'Alternative tourism—a critique', in T.V. Singh, L. Thenus and F.M. Go (eds), *Towards Appropriate Tourism: The Case of Developing Countries*, Peter Lang, Frankfurt am Main, Germany, pp. 127–42.

Crittendon, A., 1975, 'Tourism's terrible toll', *International Wildlife*, 5(3): pp. 4–12.

Darling, F.F. and Eichhorn, N.D., 1967, 'The ecological implications of tourism in national parks', in *Ecological Impact of Recreation and Tourism upon Temperate Environments*, IUCN Proceedings and Papers, New Series No. 7, Morges, Switzerland, pp. 98–101.

de Kadt, E. (ed.), 1979, *Tourism: Passport to Development*, Oxford University Press, Oxford.
Dower, M., 1974, 'Tourism and conservation: working together', *The Architects' Journal*, 18(159): pp. 939–63.
Dowling, R.K., 1990, 'Integrating tourism and conservation', in S.R. Verma, S. Singh and S. Kumar (eds), *Environmental Protection—A Movement*, Nature Conservators, New Delhi, pp. 5–25.
Dunkel, D.R., 1984, 'Tourism and the environment: a review of the literature and issues', *Environmental Sociology*, 37: pp. 5–18.
Edington, J.M. and Edington, M.A., 1986, *Ecology, Recreation and Tourism*, Cambridge University Press, Cambridge.
Ehrlich, P.A., Ehrlich, A.H. and Holdren, J.P., 1970, *Ecoscience: Population Resources and Environment*, W.H. Freeman, San Francisco.
Farrell, B.H. and McLellan, R.W., 1987, 'Tourism and physical environment research', *Annals of Tourism Research*, 14(1): pp. 1–16.
Farrell, B.H. and Runyan D., 1991, 'Ecology and tourism', *Annals of Tourism Research*, 18(1): pp. 41–56.
Gale, F and Jacobs, J.M., 1987, *Tourists and the National Estate*, AGPS, Canberra.
GLOBE '90, 1990, 'Global Opportunities for Business and the Environment: Conference and Trade Fair—Tourism Stream', Vancouver, Canada, 19–23 March.
Goldsmith, E., 1974, 'Pollution by tourism', *The Ecologist*, 48(1): pp. 47–8.
Greenwood, D., 1972, 'Tourism as an agent of change: a Spanish Basque case study', *Ethnology*, 11: pp. 80–91.
Gunn, C.A., 1978, 'Needed: an international alliance for tourism–recreation–conservation', *Travel Research Journal* 2: pp. 3–9.
Gunn, C.A., 1987, 'Environmental designs and land use', in J.R.B. Ritchie and C.R. Goeldner (eds), *Travel, Tourism and Hospitality Research: A Handbook for Managers and Researchers* Wiley, New York, pp. 229–47.
Hall, C.M., 1991, *Introduction to Tourism in Australia: Impacts, Planning and Development*, Longman Cheshire, Melbourne.
Hardin, G., 1968, 'The tragedy of the commons', *Science*, 162: pp. 1243–8.
Haulot, A., 1974, *Tourisme et environnement: la recherche d'un equilibre*, Marabout Monde Moderne, Verviers, Belgium.
Inskeep, E., 1991a, *Tourism Planning: An Integrated and Sustainable Development Approach*, Van Nostrand Reinhold, New York.
Inskeep, E., 1991b, 'Planning for sustainable tourism development'. Paper presented at the *World Tourism Organisation Seminar on Sustainable Tourism Development*, Naimey, Niger, 9–12 December.
IUCN, 1967, *Ecology, Tourism and Recreation*, proceedings of the Tenth Technical Meeting, IUCN Morges, Switzerland.
IUCN, 1980, *World Conservation Strategy*, IUCN, Gland, Switzerland.
Jansen-Verbeke, M.C. and Ashworth, G., 1990, 'Environmental integration of recreation and tourism', *Annals of Tourism Research*, 17(4): pp. 618–22.
Jefferies, B.E., 1982, 'Sagamartha National Park: the impact of tourism in the Himalayas', *Ambio*, 11(5): pp. 274–82.
Kelleher, G.G. and Kenchington, R.A., 1982, 'Australia's Great Barrier Reef Marine Park: making development compatible with conservation', *Ambio*, 11(5): pp. 262–7.
Krippendorf, J., 1975, *Die Landschaftsfresser*, Hallwag Verlag, Berne, Switzerland.
Kundaeli, J.N., 1983, 'Making conservation and development compatible', *Ambio*,

12(6): pp. 326–31.

Landals, A.G., 1986, 'The —— tourists are ruining the parks', in *Tourism and the Environment: Conflict or Harmony?* Proceedings of a Symposium sponsored by the Canadian Society of Environmental Biologists, Alberta Chapter, Calgary, Canada, 18–19 March 1986. CSEB, Alberta, pp. 89–99.

Leslie, D., 1986, 'Tourism and conservation in national parks', *Tourism Management*, 7(1): pp. 52–6.

Liddle, M.J., 1975, 'A selective review of the ecological effects of human trampling on natural ecosystem', *Biological Conservation*, 7: pp. 17–36.

Lusigi, W.J., 1981, 'New approaches to wildlife conservation in Kenya', *Ambio*, 10(2–3): pp. 87–92.

Mackie, I.B., 1986, 'Tourism and the environment: a natural partnership', in *Tourism and the Environment: Conflict or Harmony?*, Proceedings of a Symposium sponsored by the Canadian Society of Environmental Biologists, Alberta Chapter, Calgary, Canada, 18–19 March 1986, CSEB, Alberta, pp. 17–22.

Makame, H., 1968, 'Tourism', *African Development*, 2(3): pp. 3–5.

Mathieson, A. and Wall, G., 1982, *Tourism: Economic, Physical and Social Impacts*, Longman, Harlow.

McCabe, J., 1979, 'The Iwasaki proposal—some background on a conservation resource', *Habitat Australia*, 7(1): pp. 16–17.

McNeely, J.A., 1990, 'How conservation strategies contribute to sustainable development', *Environmental Conservation*, 17(1): pp. 9–13.

McNeely, J.A. and Thorsell, J.W., 1989, 'Jungles, mountains and islands: how tourism can help conserve the natural heritage', *World Leisure and Recreation* 31(4): pp. 29–39.

Millar, S., 1989, 'Heritage management for heritage tourism', *Tourism Management*, 10(1): pp. 9–14.

Millman, R., 1989, 'Pleasure seeking v. the "greening" of world tourism', *Tourism Management*, 10(4): pp. 275–8.

Mlinaric, I.B., 1985, 'Tourism and the environment: a case for Mediterranean Cooperation', *International Journal of Environmental Studies*, 25(4): pp. 239–45.

Mountfort, G., 1974, 'The need for partnership: tourism and conservation', *Development Forum*, April: pp. 6–7.

Murphy, P.E., 1983, 'Tourism as a community industry: an ecological model of tourism development', *Tourism Management*, 4(3): pp. 180–93.

Murphy, P.E., 1985, *Tourism A Community Approach*, Methuen, New York.

Murphy, P.E., 1986a, 'Tourism as an agent for landscape conservation: an assessment', *The Science of the Total Environment*, 55: pp. 387–95.

Murphy, P.E., 1986b, 'Conservation and tourism: a business partnership', in I.B. Mackie, 1986, *Tourism and the Environment: Conflict or harmony?* Proceedings of a Symposium sponsored by the Canadian Society of Environmental Biologists, Alberta Chapter, Calgary, Canada, 18–19 March 1986, CSEB, Alberta, pp. 117–27.

Murphy P.E., 1988, 'Community driven tourism planning', *Tourism Management*, 9(2): pp. 96–104.

Myers, N., 1972, 'National parks in savannah Africa', *Science*, 178: pp. 1255–63.

Myers, N., 1973a, 'The people crunch comes to Africa', *Natural History*, 82: pp. 10–15.

Myers, N., 1973b, 'Impending crisis for Tanzanian wildlife', *National Parks and Conservation Magazine*, 47(8): pp. 18–23.

Nicholson, M., 1970, *The Environmental Revolution*, Hodder and Stoughton,

London.

OAS, 1984, 'Reference guidelines for enhancing the positive socio-cultural and environmental impacts of tourism', Volume 5, *Enhancing the Positive Impact of Tourism on the Built and Natural Environment*, Organization of American States, Washington DC.

OECD, 1980, *The Impact of Tourism on the Environment*, Organization for Economic Co-operation and Development, Paris.

Olokesusi, F., 1990, 'Assessment of the Yankari Game Reserve, Nigeria: problems and prospects', *Tourism Management*, 11(2): pp. 153–63.

Ovington, J.D., Groves, K.W., Stevens, P.R. and Tanton, M.T., 1973, *A Study of the Impact of Tourism at Ayers Rock—Mt Olga National Park*, Environmental Consultant Group, Department of Forestry, Australian National University, AGPS, Canberra.

Pearce, D.G., 1985, 'Tourism and environmental research: a review', *International Journal of Environmental Studies*, 25(4): pp. 247–55.

Phillips, A., 1985, 'Opening address', in *Tourism, Recreation and Conservation in National Parks and Equivalent Reserves*, A European Heritage Landscapes Conference, Peak National Park Centre, Peak Park Joint Planning Board, Derbyshire, England, pp. 9–14.

Pigram, J.J., 1980, 'Environmental implications of tourism development', *Annals of Tourism Research*, 7(4): pp. 554–83.

Romeril, M., 1985, 'Tourism and the environment—towards a symbiotic relationship (introductory paper)', *International Journal of Environmental Studies*, 25(4): pp. 215–18.

Romeril, M., 1989a, 'Tourism and the environment—accord or discord?', *Tourism Management*, 10(3): pp. 204–8.

Romeril, M., 1989b, 'Tourism—the environmental dimension', in C.P. Cooper (ed.), *Progress in Tourism, Recreation and Hospitality Management*, Belhaven, London, pp. 103–13.

Seth, P.N., 1985, *Successful Tourism Management*, Sterling Publishers, New Delhi.

Smith, C. and Jenner, P., 1989, 'Tourism and the environment', *EIU Travel and Tourism Analyst*, 5: pp. 68–86.

Smith, V.L. (ed.), 1977, *Hosts and Guests: The Anthropology of Tourism*, University of Philadelphia Press, Pennsylvania.

Spiegel, 1972, 'In zehn Jahren sind das hier Slums', *Der Spiegel*, 3 July, 26(28): pp. 56–64.

Tangi, M., 1977, 'Tourism and the environment', *Ambio*, 6(6): pp. 336–41.

Thomason, P., Crompton, J.L. and Van Kamp, B., 1979, 'A study of the attitudes of impacted groups within a host community toward prolonged staying tourist visitors', *Journal of Travel Research* 18(3): pp. 2–7.

Travis, A.S., 1982, 'Managing the environment and cultural impacts of tourism and leisure development', *Tourism Management*, 3(4): pp. 256–62.

Turner, L. and Ash, J., 1975, *The Golden Hordes: International Tourism and the Pleasure Periphery*, Constable, London.

UNEP and WTO, 1982, *Joint Declaration Between the United Nations Environmental Programme and the World Tourism Organisation*, WTO, Madrid.

UNEP and WTO, 1983, *Workshop on the Environmental Aspects of Tourism*, WTO, Madrid.

Waters, S.R., 1966, 'The American tourist', *Annals of the American Academy of Political and Social Sciences*, 368: pp. 109–18.

WCED, 1987, 'Our common future', *Report of the World Commission on Environment and Development* (The Brundtland Commission), Oxford

University Press, Oxford.

Young, G., 1973, *Tourism: Blessing or Blight?* Penguin, Harmondsworth, England.

Zierer, C.M., 1952, 'Tourism and recreation in the west', *Geographical Review*, 42: pp. 462–81.

3 Tourism, development and the environment: the eternal triangle
G. Shaw and A. Williams

Tourism–environment relationships

The relationship between tourism, its associated developments and the environment are both complex and dynamic, not least because they are set within broader economic, societal and political changes. Evidence of such complexities is partly provided by Budowski (1976) who argued that the links between the tourism industry and the environment lobby exist in three quite different forms. The first of these is where each group is in isolation, with both camps promoting their respective views although having little or no contact with each other. This position usually gives way rapidly to either a second form of relationship, whereby the tourism industry and environmentalists are in open conflict, or a third form where both parties are mutually supportive. The evidence, such as it is, suggests that open conflict is the most common form of relationship (Mathieson and Wall, 1982). Alternative perspectives have attempted to demonstrate that tourism, far from conflicting with environmental conservation, can be credited with enhancing concern and appreciation for the environment (Gunn, 1978). However, Budowski's view provides a useful starting-point, despite the fact that it ignores the broader setting of tourism–development relationships.

The nature of tourism–environment relationships are obviously contingent on the particularities of the area under consideration. Thus, much of the literature on tourism impact has emphasized negative aspects, constructed around a tourism industry entering and despoiling some undeveloped, *natural* area. Whilst this view may reflect the experiences of many countries and regions, it is clearly a simplistic perspective. Tourism development takes place in a diverse range of environments. As Figure 3.1 suggests, in some situations the environment is so damaged by past industrial processes that tourism development is expected to upgrade environmental quality. This is certainly true in many inner-city areas, where tourism projects are being used to promote urban regeneration (Law, 1991). Similarly, although in a number of older seaside resorts the past development of tourism may have created problem environments, hope for future enhancements still very much depends on attracting tourism investment (ETB, 1991). This latter example also serves to underline the

dynamic nature of tourism–environment relationships and the short-term
character of tourism investment. The tourism industry has a notoriously
short product cycle. While new markets and products are constantly being
sought, in doing so, investment levels and infrastructure in older resorts
are neglected and decline. Such shifts in development, and their consequent problems, lie at the heart of resort-cycle models, which can be used
to provide another insight into tourism–environment relationships (Butler,
1980).

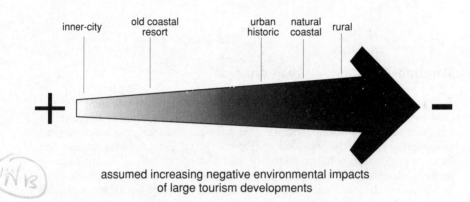

inner-city   old coastal   urban   natural   rural
              resort   historic coastal

assumed increasing negative environmental impacts
of large tourism developments

Figure 3.1 *Standard views of tourism–environmental impacts*

A further level of complication in these relationships is added by the
changing societal notions of tourism. The most obvious example of societal
change is the rise of *green tourism*, which has been promoted as much by
the green movement itself as by any original political initiatives, with
Krippendorf's (1984) so-called *critical consumer tourists* leading the
demand for environmentally-sound holidays. This process represents one
form of change in societal attitudes towards tourism and development,
though its roots are set within the wider group of ecological values of the
green consumer (Elkington and Mailes, 1992). These changes in holiday
tastes and demand, by at least one important set of tourists, are causing the
tourism industry to reassess its image, leading to some tour and travel
companies offering *ecological holidays*. For example, **Natural Habitat**, a
US-based operator, and **Nature Track**, specialize in holidays observing
wildlife on high quality natural history adventures (*The Times*, 1992).
Without entering the debate on the real ecological value of such tours,
these examples do show the demand-led form of this type of tourism which
has caused, in some cases, a dramatic shift in the relationship between
tourism and the environment. Some, like Urry (1990), argue that this shift
is related to postmodernism and the reaction to mass tourism as a form of
mass consumption, with the service class being very much in the vanguard
of such movements.

A final factor complicating tourism–environment relations is that of political pressures applied through public policy at all levels of government. Of course in many instances societal and political views converge, making them difficult to disentangle, and it is by no means clear whether political parties lead or follow public opinion in this field. Nevertheless, we can recognize a broadly changing pattern of government and public interest in the impact of tourism development on the environment. It can be noted, however, that policies, even within the same country or region, are not consistent, neither are they often clearly directed. Various elements of government, whether parties, bureaucracy, or competing sectors (departments), can have strongly divergent interests, being subject to different external pressures. This, for example, is the case with the countryside in the United Kingdom, which is a policy battleground between the Ministries of Agriculture and the Environment. Tourism, of course, cuts across both these sectional interests as well as touching on other government departments such as Transport and Industry.

Within such a context, the aim of this chapter is to explore the nature of tourism–environment relationships through an examination of public policy and societal attitudes. Specific attention will be given to the policies of economic development and environmental constraint, as illustrated by a case study from South-West England. This will be used to analyse what are often construed to be the seemingly intractable problems of promoting tourism development whilst safeguarding the environment. Before considering such issues, it will be useful to review the broader levels of public policy application at both international and national levels, since these strongly impinge on local policy-making attitudes. Having established the policy framework and objectives, the remainder of the chapter proceeds to examine the changing perceptions of the tourists themselves. The contradictions in their perceptions of the tourism–development relationship serve only to reinforce further the *eternal triangle* of tourism, development and the environment. Tourists are a force for both development and conservation.

Tourism and the environment: reawakening political interests

Despite widespread concern over tourism's impact on a range of Third World environments, few truly international policy statements have been forthcoming. UNESCO (1976) has centred on cultural environmental impacts, although its scheme of recognizing World Heritage sites is aimed at wider elements of conservation. In a more general way the OECD (1980) have produced a review of tourism's impact on the natural, man-made and cultural environments, although, for obvious reasons, this is not couched in policy-making terms. In contrast to these more general statements, recent activity by the European Commission and the Council of Ministers has stimulated an increasing number of policies and statements on tourism and the environment. One of the earliest of these to achieve prominence was the European Coastal Charter, formally approved by the

European Parliament in 1982 and ratified by the Council of Ministers in 1986. Whilst not specifically aimed at tourism, its objectives—to ensure that coastal development is in a manner which balances economic and environmental criteria—obviously touches on many schemes for coastal resorts or holiday centres (ECTARC, 1989, pp. 17–18).

A wider-ranging set of European-based policies are heralded by the Commission's **Charter for Cultural Tourism**, with its emphasis on developing a responsible tourism policy. This not only has implications for the development of cultural tourism, but is also being viewed as a means to relieve the environmental pressures caused by mass tourism in many coastal regions (ECTARC, 1989). Although insufficient information is available, as yet, to judge whether such claims are over-optimistic, the more important point is that tourism is becoming an increasingly political issue at a European level. Indeed, earlier EC directives, namely 85/337/EEC, already call on member states to undertake environmental impact assessments for certain large-scale projects, including tourism developments that affect the natural and man- made environments.

The detailed basis of the **Charter for Cultural Tourism** is to move away from the short-term gains of tourism towards 'the realisation of longer-term economic, cultural and physical environmental benefits, avoiding the danger of exploitation ultimately damaging the environment' (ECTARC, 1989, p. 92). Such goals cut across much of the established relationships between tourism and the environment. Through a series of broad recommendations (Table 3.1), they aim to provide a programme of sustainable tourism. These suggestions cover a range of restrictive policies (especially those directed at the physical environment) through to those aimed at encouraging local participation in establishing and promoting tourism development. As we shall see in South-West England, such ideas have fed through into regional and local tourism planning, and many places are for the first time trying to co-ordinate tourism and environmental policies in a range of ways rather than just through negative planning.

Within the United Kingdom, interest in such issues has developed along a number of different lines. One of the most traditional routes has been the development of new strategies toward rural tourism, with the ETB (1988) and Countryside Commission (1988) both producing reports which stress that tourism in the countryside should support the objectives of conservation. A more radical departure has been the establishment, in 1990, of a government task force charged with finding solutions to the impact of tourism on the environment. In announcing its formation, the Secretary of State for the Environment restated the nub of these conflicts, when he stressed that 'we must ensure that its [tourism] development is not at the expense of the environment and heritage' (*The Times*, August 1990). The terms of reference of this government task force were twofold: first, to examine the size and nature of environmental problems caused by large numbers of visitors at particular sites; and second, to draw up guidelines on how tourism activities can be harmonized with the need to conserve and preserve the environment (ETB, 1991, pp. 4–5). The whole project was based on a series of case studies including historic towns, heritage sites,

Table 3.1 *Recommendations to the EC, concerning tourism and the physical environment*

(1) Tourism projects should be supported only when adequate means of monitoring airborne, water, noise and waste pollution are established.

(2) Cultural tourism developments should whenever possible use traditional transport and make use of pedestrianization schemes.

(3) Preference should be given to tourism projects that do not require extensive new infrastructure.

(4) Regional and local authorities should be responsible for the approval of new tourism developments as well as the conservation of existing structures.

(5) Legislation should be introduced at the EC level restricting trade in plants, animals and fossils.

(6) Codes of conduct should be provided for visitors using sensitive areas.

Source: ECTARC, 1989, p. 94.

seaside resorts and rural environments. In this context, therefore, the task force attempted to tackle the full spectrum of tourism–environment relationships as outlined in Figure 3.1, centring on problems of overcrowding, traffic congestion, wear and tear on the physical fabric, inappropriate developments, and conflicts with the host community. Of course, such issues are nothing new, since most regional and local tourist authorities have been grappling with these problems certainly since the 1960s.

Table 3.2 *The management of tourism–environmental problems*

A. *Key issues*
1. Better management information:
     Visitor surveys
     Site survey (determine carrying capacity)
     Regular monitoring

2. Effective co-ordination:
     Need for partnership approach, stresses importance of tourism
     development action programmes, town centre management schemes

3. Adequate resourcing:
     Stresses role of both private and public sectors in funding

B. *Practical management approaches*
1. Assessment of capacity
2. Transport management
3. Marketing and information
4. Conservation and adaptation
5. Design and control of development
6. Involvement of local community

Source: ETB, *Tourism and the Environment*, 1991.

The significance of the report lies more in the fact that it has brought tourism–environment relationships back on to a national political agenda. Furthermore, it remains to be seen whether the solutions suggested by the report (see Table 3.2) can act as a template for tourist organizations, local authorities and conservationists to resolve their differences. Much of the material from the report is, as previously stated, drawn from case studies, thus implying that the solutions can work in certain environments. However, the question must be asked of whether these selected case studies are exhaustive in their coverage? The thrust of this chapter is that in regions such as Devon and Cornwall the relationships between tourism, planning and the environment are extremely complex. This complexity derives not only from the scale and variety of tourism activities but equally from the changing and often contradictory local authority perspectives on tourism. These have ranged from a complete *laissez-faire* attitude to open hostility, as well as encompassing a period of strong encouragement to gain economic benefits from tourism.

Cornwall and Devon: policy ambivalence

In the early history of tourism in Cornwall and Devon, tourism–environment relationships largely accorded with the first stage of Budowski's (1976) model: an isolated situation. Exmouth and Teignmouth had started to develop as local watering-places for Exeter's merchants by the mid-eighteenth century. Thereafter the pace of development quickened, and Sidmouth, Dawlish and Torquay emerged as small resorts. The prime attractions at this time were the scenery, the mild climate and the growing fashion of sea-bathing. South Devon was especially popular, not least because of the belief in the health-giving properties of its coastal environment. Cornwall's remoteness meant that it was relatively untouched by tourism at this stage, although Penzance was given a boost by medical praise of the virtues of its 'Mediterranean' climate (discussed further in Shaw and Williams, 1991). Tourism did, of course, also influence the environment at this stage, but tourist numbers were so small that the effects were mostly insignificant.

From the mid-nineteenth century onwards, the coming of the railways changed the parameters for tourism development (Simmons, 1982). New hotels were opened at the coastal termini of the railway network, and in Cornwall resorts such as Newquay and St Ives were seen to revive and grow at a rapid rate. However, the real impact of the railways came in the early twentieth century. Successful marketing by the Great Western Railway of the 'Cornish Riviera' led to a sharp rise in tourist numbers. Again the environmental qualities of the area—this time compared to the Italian Riviera—were a major attraction for the tourists. Nevertheless, by the end of the nineteenth century Torquay was ceasing to be a fashionable watering-place and was emerging as an important coastal tourist resort. Tourism, however, remained highly polarized on a small number of resorts and the growing impact on the environment was still uncontroversial. In

Torquay, for example, the 1902 Corporation Bill allowed a one penny rate to be levied for advertising the resort. Although this was opposed for reasons of financial prudence, there was little opposition on environmental grounds. Cornwall and Devon remained in the first stage of Budowski's model.

From the 1920s and 1930s the pace of tourism growth quickened, although it was still largely within highly constrained resort areas. However, the major impact of tourism was to come later, during the 1950s. The growth of mass tourism brought with it the demand for cheaper holiday accommodation. This was met by chalets, caravan and camping sites as well as by more traditional serviced accommodation. In Cornwall, for example, there was a 310 per cent increase in the number of chalets between 1954 and 1964 (Heck, 1966). At the same time the growing shift to personal transport meant that tourism became more spatially diffuse. The result was growing pressure on the environment, particularly on the coastal zones, parts of the National Parks and other rated 'beauty spots'. Congested roads also became a notorious feature of the summer season, and a seemingly endless series of improvements were undertaken to increase road-carrying capacities. The South-West was entering the second phase of Budowski's model as the tourism industry and environmentalists came into more open conflict.

The pressures on coastal areas were particularly intense in Cornwall and this led the County Council to declare 'saturation' areas from 1959 onwards. Devon had similarly designated areas 'Approaching Capacity for Holiday Development', in which further camping and caravanning were discouraged. The distribution of both sets of zones is shown in Figure 3.2. These declarations were followed by the designation of a plethora of areas of environmental constraints such as Areas of Outstanding Natural Beauty (AONBs) and Coastal Preservation Areas during the 1960s. As a result, only 15 per cent of the coastline of Cornwall was not affected by some form of control. The growing conservationist lobby was increased by large numbers of middle-class immigrants. Having been drawn to the region by its attractive environment, they were determined to conserve this in the face of pressures from tourism and other forms of economic development.

From the late 1970s onwards, however, there was a shift in public policy perspectives on tourism. The economic crisis of the late 1970s and 1980s led to a search for new means of creating jobs. This eventually came to the notice of national government, whose policies for tourism became far more supportive. This percolated through to the local level with, for example, Devon being offered £1 million of grants by the English Tourist Board in 1983 to develop new attractions. At the same time, the stagnation of tourist numbers after 1980 (and decline in some resorts) led to renewed interest in promoting tourism. As a result, the County Council strategies in both Cornwall and Devon have given more support to encouraging tourism as a key element in economic development. However, antipathy to tourism remains, for it is seen to undermine the traditional character of settlements (especially in Cornwall), to add to congestion on the roads, and to threaten rural landscapes (for example, see Deacon et al., 1985). There are hopes

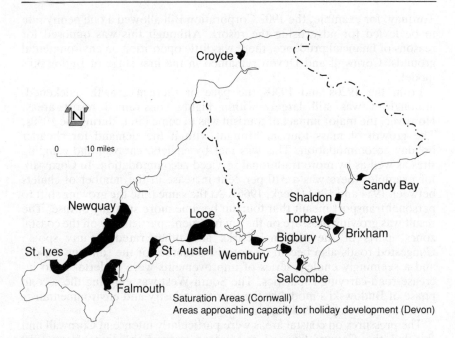

Figure 3.2   *Areas of tourism restriction in Devon and Cornwall*

Sources: Cornwall CC Holiday Industry 1966; Devon CC Development Plan 1961.

that the advent of critical green tourists may move tourism–environment
relationships into the third phase of Budoswki's model, where the tourist
industry and environmentalists become mutually supportive. The next
section of this chapter considers the prospects for this in the light of
research on tourist behaviour and visitor attitudes.

Cornwall's tourists: consumers of the environment and conservationists?

In most analyses of the conflict between tourist developers and environmentalist movements, it was traditionally assumed that tourists were
unthinking mechanisms for the environmental devastation brought about
by the tourism industry. This is clearly a gross over-simplification as, for
example, Krippendorf's (1987) work on the critical tourist suggests.
However, even the polarization between the mass tourist and the critical
tourist is an over-simplification. Not only is there a continuum in attitudes
and interests, but individuals are also likely to hold a mixture of—often
contradictory—attitudes. This may be demonstrated by detailed research
on tourists in Cornwall. The wider background to this research programme

is discussed elsewhere (Shaw and Williams, 1991). Here, we refer to just one part of this survey of tourists undertaken in 1990 (William *et al.*, 1991). This was a questionnaire survey of 4,855 tourists in the county, which examined visitor behaviour, their attitudes to Cornwall as well as their expectations of a holiday experience.

Table 3.3   *Tourists in Cornwall, 1990: general perceptions and activities*

(a)   *Perceptions of Cornwall*

% of visitors who 'agree' or 'agree strongly' with the following statements:

Rank		%
1	Beautiful scenery	97.2
3	Good beaches	84.3
8	Good car parking	52.9
9	Roads not congested	46.1

(b)   *Most important holiday activities*

% of visitors considering activity to be 'very' or 'fairly important':

Rank		%
2	Sightseeing by car/coach	77.6
3	Going to the beach	77.2
5	Strolling in the countryside	65.1

(c)   *Suggested improvements to Cornwall*

% of visitors suggesting:

Rank		%
1	Protect natural beauty	31.7
2	Improve cleanliness	11.3
3	Improve roads	15.4
4	Improve parking	8.1

Source: Cornwall Visitor Survey, 1990.

The 1990 visitor survey confirms that visitors to Cornwall continue, as was the case in the nineteenth century, to be attracted by its environmental features. For example, beautiful scenery and good beaches are two of the three aspects of the county which receive the strongest endorsement with more than 90 per cent of all visitors agreeing or strongly agreeing with these descriptions. At the other extreme, we can note that less than 41 per cent of visitors were able to agree with the views that roads were not congested and that there was 'lots to do if the weather is bad'. However, when it came to holiday activities more people ranked sightseeing by coach or car, rather than strolling in the countryside as being an important part of their holiday activities (Table 3.3). There is, then, a classic contradiction between a high value placed on the environment and an equally high value being placed on personal mobility by car which causes many of the problems of congestion and possible environmental degradation. This is further

underlined by the improvements that visitors suggested would improve
Cornwall as a tourism destination. The highest-ranked priority was protection of the natural beauty, yet the third ranked suggestion was 'improve the
roads'. Tourists to Cornwall therefore represent a double-edged weapon in
the conflict between development and the environment. At one level they
are a strong force for conservation. Thus, it is the 'natural' beauty of the
County and its clean beaches which bring most tourists to the County. Yet
their individual consumption interests also led them to suggest road improvement schemes which may damage the environment directly and may
go on to attract increased numbers of tourists into the area. Therefore,
tourists as well as local communities, remain deeply ambivalent in their
perception of the tourism–environment relationships. It is within this set of
contradictions that policy-makers have to operate.

Conclusions

In the introduction to this chapter it was argued that the relationship
between tourism, its associated development and the environment are both
complex and dynamic. This chapter has investigated some of these basic
relationships, illustrating the arguments by reference to a case study of
Cornwall. Figure 3.3 presents a schematic summary of the major changes
over time in these relationships. The four main phases can be summarized
as follows:

1. **First phase**, pre-twentieth Century–1940s, is characterized by limited
   tourist numbers, a policy vacuum, and little or no major effects on the
   environment. As tourist numbers increase in the inter-war period and
   the industry develops, no planning policy exists.
2. In the **second phase**, 1950s–70s, mass tourism develops, and there is an
   isolation of entrepreneurs from the local community. Positive and
   negative attitudes towards and effects on the environment are common
   as are policies of containment as negative planning increases. There is,
   however, only limited public authority promotion.
3. During the **third phase**, 1980s, mass tourism continues. However, more
   positive policies to encourage tourism can be identified strongly mixed
   with remnants of more restrictive policies. Some tourism entrepreneurs
   are partly incorporated in policy-making (via increased consultation,
   Tourist Development Action Programmes and Tourist Boards). The
   impact of tourism and attitudes of tourists all tend to become more
   positive, as the economic benefits of tourism are increasingly stressed.
4. The **fourth phase**: future unspecified. A growing number of critical
   consumer tourists, with more supportive public policy, have a positive
   impact on the environment. Additionally, there is a parallel reinteg-
   ration of tourism entrepreneurs into the community, as ideas about
   sustainable tourism and community-level tourism become accepted
   practice.

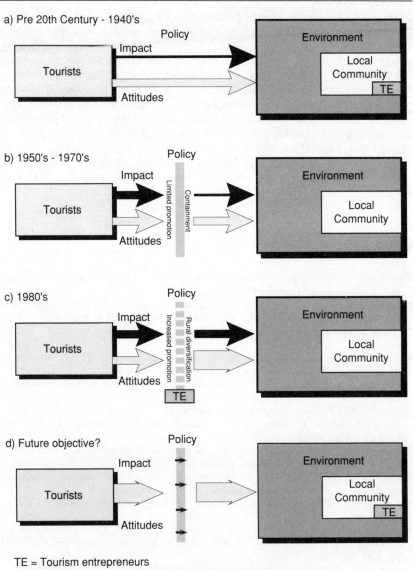

a) Pre 20th Century - 1940's

b) 1950's - 1970's

c) 1980's

d) Future objective?

TE = Tourism entrepreneurs
⇨ Positive effects and attitudes   → Negative effects and attitudes

Figure 3.3   *Tourism and the environment in Cornwall*

All of these relationships are more complex than can be presented in this simple diagrammatic form. However, the policy *box* is perhaps the most complex. There are international, national and local policies for tourism, and these can be acting in contradictory directions. This is further compounded by different political and sectional interests at each level. This is particularly evident in parts of South-West England where there is little consensus on the future direction of tourism, even within the industry itself. Certainly, there are signs that policy-making bodies are moving toward the ideas of community-level tourism (Devon County Council, 1991). Equally, however, many of the major points of the tourist industry can be sustained in its present form only by mass tourism. If tourism policies can be rooted in a community-wide consensus (Budowski's third phase), then it is likely that there will be a convergence of tourism–environment relationships towards the utopian fourth stage of Figure 3.3. Should this happen on any large scale then the region's tourist industry would have to change quite dramatically. Such changes would involve important restructuring and inevitably lead to major shifts in the tourism economy.

References

Budowski, G., 1976, 'Tourism and conservation: conflict, coexistence or symbiosis', *Environmental Conservation*, 3: pp. 27–31.

Butler, R.W., 1980, 'The concept of a tourist area cycle of evolution: implications for management of resources', *Canadian Geographer*, 24(1): pp. 5–12.

Deacon, B., George, A. and Perry, R., 1988, *Cornwall at the Crossroads*, Truran, Redruth.

Devon County Council, 1991, *Devon Action for Tourism and the Environment: A Consultative Document*, Devon County Council, Exeter.

Elkington, J. and Mailes, J., 1992, *Holidays that don't Cost the Earth*, Gollancz, London.

ECTARC, 1989, *Contribution to the Drafting of a Charter for Cultural Tourism (Tourism and The Environment)*, European Centre for Traditional and Regional Cultures, Llangollen.

English Tourist Board (ETB), 1991, *Tourism and the Environment: Maintaining the Balance*, English Tourist Board, London.

Gunn, C.A., 1978, 'Needed: an international alliance for tourism, recreation, conservation', *Travel Research Journal*, 2: pp. 3–9.

Heck, H.W.J., 1966, *Survey of the Holiday Industry*, Cornwall County Council, Truro.

Katz, C. and Kirby, A., 1991, 'In the nature of things: the environment and everyday life', *Transactions of the Institute of British Geographers*, 16(3): pp. 259–71.

Krippendorf, J., 1984, *Die Ferienmenschen. Für ein neves Verständnis von Freizeit & Reisen*, Orell Füssli, Zurich.

Krippendorf, J., 1987, *The Holiday Makers*, Heinemann, London.

Law, C.M., 1991, 'Tourism as a focus for urban regeneration', in *The Role of Tourism in the Urban and Regional Economy*, Regional Studies Association, London.

Mathieson, A. and Wall, G., 1982, *Tourism: Economic, Physical and Social Impacts*, Longman, London.

OECD, 1980, *General Report: The Impact of Tourism on the Environment*, Paris, OECD.

Shaw, G. and Williams, A.M., 1991, 'From bathing hut to theme park: tourism development in South West England', *Journal of Regional and Local Studies*, 11(1–2): pp. 16–32.

Simmons, J., 1982, 'The railway in Cornwall, 1835–1914', *Journal of the Royal Institution of Cornwall*, 37: pp. 11–30.

The Times, 'Task Force ordered to assess tourism impact', 2 August 1990 and 12 January 1992.

UNESCO, 1976, 'The effects of tourism on socio-cultural values', *Annals of Tourism Research*, 4: pp. 74–105.

Urry, J., 1990, *The Tourist Gaze: Leisure and Travel in Contemporary Societies*, Sage Publications, London.

Williams, A. and Shaw, G., 1990, *To Return or not to Return*, Tourism Research Group, University of Exeter, Exeter.

Williams, A., Greenwood, J. and Shaw G., 1991, *Cornwall Tourist Visitor Survey 1990*, Tourism Research Group, University of Exeter, Exeter.

4 Environmental auditing for tourism

B. Goodall

Tourism and environment

Environment is a core feature of the tourism product. Tourists are there-fore 'consumers of environment', travelling to the producer's location, the tourist destination, in order to consume the product. Thus tourism is dependent upon the attractive power of a destination's environment, that is, its primary resources of climate, scenery, wildlife, cultural and historic heritage. Often much of that environment takes the form of open-access resources, which are not owned by anyone and for which no market exists, so making avoidance of overuse more difficult. Environmental degradation may well follow and the despoiled destination loses its attraction.

The rapid global growth of tourism has led to a devastating impact on the environment. Growth creates problems, especially where fragile and re-mote environments are visited. To enable tourists to experience a destina-tion's primary resources, secondary resources, such as accommodation, transport facilities and service infrastructure have to be provided, resulting in the major physical restructuring of the destination by the extension of its built environment (Cater and Goodall, 1992). Such mass market and other environmentally destructive forms of tourism continue to dominate the industry world-wide. There exists a circular and cumulative relationship between tourism development, the environment and socio-economic development in the destination area: most tourism development places additional pressures on the environmental resources upon which it is based, compromising the future prospects of the host population. Even in staging major events, such as the Olympic Games, which boost the local economy and increase employment as well as attracting more tourists, the massive preparation, over ten years at Albertville for the 1992 Winter Olympics, wreaks havoc with the environment (Keating, 1991). This exploitative approach of much tourism development neglects the industry's resource dependency.

Even allowing for the fact that tourism is a competitive, high-risk industry, given its dependence upon the environment it is only to be expected that it should be concerned to conserve heritage, both natural and cultural, and to maintain and enhance the quality of the environment. As quality of life and quality of service become increasingly important to consumers, so tourism firms and organizations in both public and private sectors will seek to act in environmentally responsible ways. Indeed, in the latest market research, evidence of consumers' concern for the environment and human relations is strong and thought to be sufficiently deep-rooted to influence purchasing behaviour and product development throughout the 1990s (Gordon, 1991). Thus there is both a push factor away from environmentally destructive tourism and a pull factor towards green or sustainable tourism which makes sensitive use of natural environments and cultural heritage attractions.

Sustainable tourism requires that the demands of increasing numbers of tourists are satisfied in a manner which continues to attract them whilst meeting the needs of the host population with improved standards of living, yet safeguarding the destination environment and cultural heritage. Although this view of sustainable tourism is generally accepted, how it can be implemented, given the loose and fragmented structure of the tourism industry, including the public sector, is another matter. Ideally, the principle of sustainability should be central to the tourism policies of both tourism-generating and tourism-receiving countries. However, what does it entail in practice for tourism firms and organizations? What constitutes good environmental practice by the tourism industry and how can tourism firms and organizations monitor their activities in this context?

Tourism's environmental objectives (and responsibilities)

Society demands products which are supplied (for tourists this means holidays and other travel products), and accepts, albeit sometimes involuntarily, that there are environmental risks in so doing. However, tourist destinations, the tourism industry and the tourists themselves appear to share a common interest in ensuring that the environment, their primary resource, is sustained. In essence the constant natural assets rule (Pearce, 1991) applies, whereby the overall stock of environmental assets available to future generations (of tourists and non-tourists) must not be reduced. Thus the overall objective of the tourism industry, including private firms and public sector organizations, must be to conduct business in an environmentally acceptable manner compatible with the character of destinations, on a scale which their host environments and cultures can absorb and welcome.

Is the tourism industry ready to accept its responsibility for the environment? Indeed, not only should this question be asked on a destination scale but also globally, because tourism in its use of transport services, contributes to global environmental change (pollution). The diversity and fragmentation of the industry is important in considering its response: in particular, recognition of the very different roles performed by commercial firms (whether tour operators, travel agents, transport carriers, attraction or accommodation operators, etc.) and the public sector (whether national, regional or local governments or agencies such as national tourist offices or local tourist information centres). The former will be supplying a total tourism product or some component of the product to make profits. The latter do not, usually, have a tourism product *per se* to sell, although they may participate in promotional activities and supply infrastructure and public services. Their role, however, may be crucial on the destination scale where tourism development and expansion proposals emanating from many, small, independent firms can have a substantial environmental impact in the aggregate. Regulatory and planning roles of public sector organizations therefore have a particular role to play in safeguarding primary resources on the destination scale.

A distinction needs to be made between existing tourism activity and proposed tourism development. The latter, as a condition of proceeding, can be made to conform more readily to current *best* standards of environmentally acceptable practice. Full advantage can be taken of the latest technical advances for example, in energy-efficient buildings, vehicles and other equipment. Large-scale development proposals can be made the subject of, as in the European Community, an environmental impact assessment (EIA)—a balanced appraisal of the **potential** total effects of the proposed development on the natural and human environments. Only where the result of the EIA clearly demonstrates that the development will be environmentally responsible and sustain the destination's primary tourism resources should planning permission to proceed normally be granted. Planning authorities in destination areas are therefore in an influential position to ensure new tourism development maintains and enhances environmental quality (although it has to be admitted that destination planners and politicians have to balance environmental and other priorities).

Existing tourism activities and facilities, however, would at best have been developed to past standards (if any such existed) at a time when environmental considerations may not have been a factor in the development decision. Many established tourism businesses may be operating in an environmentally inefficient, even polluting, manner. Continuing profitability, unexpired economic lives of indivisible factors of production (buildings, equipment, etc.), habit and inertia make it difficult to change the nature of existing tourism activities. Indeed, the capital cost of any change for environmental reasons and/or loss of revenue can be a deterrent. Nevertheless opportunities for (environmental) improvement do occur when equipment needs replacing, buildings refurbishing and supply contracts renewing. Ongoing tourism activities therefore need to be subjected to an **environmental audit** which is a management tool providing a systematic, regular and objective evaluation of the environmental performance of the organization, its plant, buildings, processes and products. In essence, environmental audit and EIA have the same goals and are complementary tools in the struggle to achieve sustainable tourism.

Increasingly there is evidence that the tourism industry at large is seeking to act in environmentally responsible ways. The lead often comes at a national government level. In the United Kingdom, for example, the **Tourism and Environment Task Force**, established by the Secretary of State for Employment in 1990, was charged

to draw up guidance on how the tourism industry and other agencies might ensure that their present activities and policies as well as future tourism developments are in harmony with the need to conserve and preserve the environment, and to serve the well being of the host populations. (Tourism and Environment Task Force, 1991, p. 2)

Elsewhere in Europe, Portugal's national tourism plan seeks to conserve the national and cultural heritage (Lewis and Williams, 1991), Switzerland is trying to develop tourism facilities in harmony with the environment, observing ecological constraints (Gilg, 1991), and France has regulated development in mountainous and coastal areas (Tuppen, 1991). Tourism policy in Cyprus now places greater emphasis on preservation and improvement of environment (Witt, 1991). Kenya's objectives in developing tourism include the reduction of undesirable social and economic consequences and the conservation, protection and improvement of environment and wildlife (Dieke, 1991). The Philippines' national tourism plan aims for that level of tourism development which will ensure protection of the natural environment and preserve the country's ecological balance (Choy, 1991).

To implement such policy and planning goals tourism development needs to be subject to EIA and existing tourism activity to environmental audit. Since the general principles of EIA application to tourism have been outlined elsewhere (see Green and Hunter, 1990), the emphasis here is on environmental auditing as a management tool for monitoring the environmental performance of existing tourism activity. Tourism activity and development in both the public and private sectors are equally amenable to environmental audit and environmental impact assessment.

There are certain implications which follow from the adoption of an environmentally responsible code of behaviour by tourism firms and organizations. At the development proposal stage particular attention has to be paid to choice of location and site selection in relation to environmental capacity concepts and to the design and integration of any buildings and infrastructure. During the construction phase efforts have to be made to minimize environmental disturbance and to ensure restoration where any environmental damage has occured. Once operational it requires adherence to appropriate on-site landscape and ecological management practices and the choice of working processes and routines which respect principles of natural resource conservation e.g. entailing energy efficiency, waste management (recovery and recycling), and source reduction of inputs. This is where environmental auditing comes into its own for the individual tourism firm or organization: although such firms and organizations have to comply with various health, safety and environmental legislation, environmental auditing goes much further.

Principles of environmental auditing

It must be emphasized that environmental auditing is a means to an end: audits can be undertaken for any firm or organization—including those which exploit the environment! However, such audits are likely to be undertaken voluntarily as part of normal business practice only by firms committed to an environmentally responsible policy. These firms will, therefore, have already formulated an environmental policy as an integral part of their overall business strategy, designed to give total quality management. The place of environmental auditing within the firm's operating structure is highlighted in Figure 4.1.

What objectives are likely to be contained in the environmental policy of firms committed to *green* or *environmental* corporatism? Their policy statements should indicate, for both current and future activities:

1. compliance with the spirit as well as the letter of environmental legislation and participation in the development of reasonable and workable environmental regulations;
2. avoidance of negative environmental impacts of their proposed developments and reduction of any negative impacts of current activities (e.g., emission of pollutants);
3. promotion of increased efficiency in the use of resources, including waste minimization, and the substitution of environmentally benign inputs and equipment wherever feasible;
4. development of products which are environmentally friendly; and
5. fostering amongst staff, and maybe also customers and the communities in which they function, an understanding of environmental issues.

Wherever possible, specific goals or targets should be established. On adoption of a green policy, environmental auditing of the firm's activities would identify the firm's relevant operational problems. Subsequently it needs to be undertaken regularly to monitor progress and to ensure adequate feedback to management. Esso, for example, review environmental performance monthly at director level (Essoview, 1991). It should be stressed that where a firm or organization adopts such a comprehensive environmental policy, then benefits will accrue to the *global* environment as well as the *local* one. Benefits of auditing are also enjoyed by the firms themselves, including identification of potential cost savings; availability of a full up-to-date environmental database for future planning, use in training programmes and in response to emergencies, as well as liaison with public authorities; facilitation of insurance cover for environmental damage liability; and promotion of the firm's environmental image.

All aspects of a firm's operations may be reviewed under environmental audit. Inputs, in varying forms and amounts are required by all firms and organizations, and where a firm *thinks green* the use of environmentally benign materials, substances and equipment will be encouraged. This means that inputs are selected which are environmentally beneficial because they reduce demand on natural resources, e.g., recycled paper, or which do not contain environmentally-damaging ingredients, e.g., phosphate-free detergents and cleaners, CFC-free aerosols, whilst environmentally unfriendly inputs, such as asbestos, pesticides, toxic and corrosive materials are phased out. In the production of a good or the rendering of a

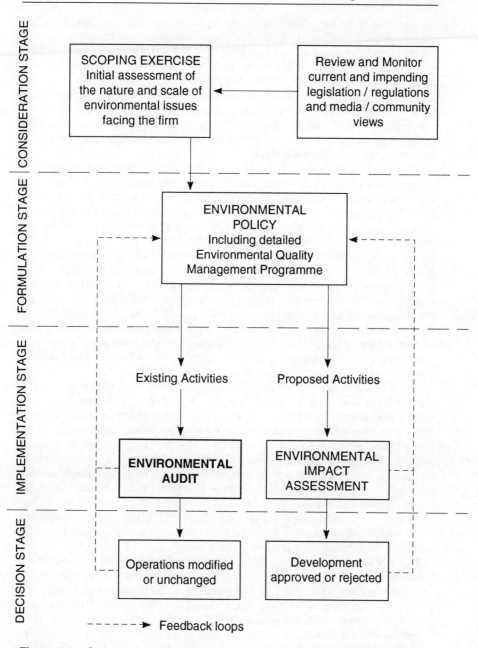

Figure 4.1 *Corporate environmentalism—the place of environmental auditing*

service, the resource efficiency of the processes, particularly their energy efficiency (including that of buildings and vehicles), will be evaluated. In addition the production and disposal of wastes from production will be examined with a view to source reduction, recovery and reuse within the firm, and recycling off-site where disposal is necessary. Where any wastes are potential pollutants, particular attention will be given to controlling, progressively reducing and ultimately eliminating such emissions. Similarly the firm's product can be designed to meet higher environmental standards, e.g. motor vehicles which run on unleaded petrol, or to be *green*, e.g., walking or cycling holidays.

What is feasible? Acting in an environmentally responsible way has consequences for a firm's costs and revenues, the incidence of which may vary over time. For example, improving the energy efficiency of an existing hotel by installing wall and roof insulation and double-glazed replacement windows will incur an immediate capital outlay in anticipation of lower, future fuel costs. There may also be changes to revenues: positive if the higher comfort standard attracts more visitors; negative if average occupancy declines because of any associated price increase. Elimination of all pollution or environmentally damaging action is therefore neither technologically nor economically feasible. Even where technologically feasible, the adoption of environmentally friendly practices and materials will reflect the trade-off between costs and benefits of such action, particularly for private sector firms. Thus, in the situation of an optimum use of the environment, the marginal pollution abatement costs are equal to the marginal environmental damage costs.

The principles evolved under industrial pollution control can be used to demonstrate the minimum that can be expected of tourism firms and organizations volunteering to act in an environmentally responsible way and the considerations which should exercise public authorities when formulating environmental regulations which impinge upon tourism activity. The fundamental basis of the British approach to anti-pollution legislation for a century and a half has been the **best practicable means** (BPM) which took account of the cost of pollution abatement and its effect on the viability of the industry. This led to presumptive emission limits, set and updated by HM Inspectorate of Pollution (HMIP) after consultation with industry. Compliance with the set limit value was normally taken as evidence that the BPM were being used.

This approach has recently been refined in the proposals for **integrated pollution control** (Royal Commission on Environmental Pollution, 1976) incorporated into the 1990 UK Environmental Protection Act. Integrated pollution control was to have been based on the concept of the **best practicable environmental option** (BPEO), i.e., that option which provided the most benefit or the least damage to the environment as a whole, at acceptable cost, in the long term as well as the short term. A BPEO pollution control strategy for a particular industry could be so expensive as to be uneconomic e.g., a technique which reduced emissions by 95 per cent although it was four times as expensive as an alternative which reduced emissions by only 90 per cent, could be judged as acceptable if the emissions were particularly hazardous. In fact the 1990 UK Environmental Protection Act has incorporated the EC Directive on combating industrial pollution which is based on the **best available technique not entailing excessive cost** (BATNEEC). This is a concept not far removed from the BPM. Under the BATNEEC, the HMIP again impose conditions specifying emission levels from plants which can be up-graded in line with technological developments from time to time. The BAT will normally apply, although the presumption can be modified where it can be shown that the costs of applying the BAT would be excessive compared with the environmental protection achieved. Even so there may be a further *let-out*, albeit temporary, via derogation, entailing the modification of legislation (specifically for application of EC directives), e.g., relaxing of emission standards, compliance dates, etc.

Even allowing for acceptance of the *polluter-pays principle* (whether interpreted as the polluter paying for the cost of prevention or the cost of the environmental damage), tourism firms and organizations may be expected, as part of their environmental policy, to behave according to the BPM/BATNEEC principles. It therefore has to be admitted that whilst such behaviour will mitigate the environmentally damaging consequences of tourism, it will not necessarily eliminate them. For example, if tourism is expanding at a particular destination, even though existing firms comply with emission standards and similar (or more stringent) standards are imposed on new firms, incremental growth of the tourism industry could still lead to the capacity of the destination environment to absorb potential pollutants, such as sewage effluent, being exceeded. Environmental deterioration may ensue unless emission standards for existing firms and new entrants are tightened further.

Environmental auditing will allow a tourism firm to evaluate the environmental consequences of its current range and level of activities, to determine the extent to which its current operations measure up to the BPM principles, and therefore to project an environmentally responsible image. In practice environmental audits may vary in their comprehensiveness and Table 4.1 summarizes, and illustrates in a tourism context, the different types that may be used. Audits of compliance, for example, have a narrow emphasis, whereas an issues audit would reveal a tourism firm's acute concern for the wider global environment. The audit *trail* in any firm may include some or all of these types, the most comprehensive range being used by transnational companies critically aware of the importance of their corporate environmental image world-wide.

Applying environmental auditing to tourism

Theoretically environmental auditing can be applied to the activities of any tourism firm or organization at any spatial scale from site, through neighbourhood, to regional, national and global. The World Travel and Tourism Council (WTTC) (1991) recommends that the tourism industry make a proactive commitment to environmentally responsible growth, acknowl-

Table 4.1 *Different types of environmental audit that can be undertaken by tourism firms*

Audit	
Activity	An overview of an activity or process which crosses business boundaries in a company, e.g., staff travel by employees of a hotel chain.
Associate	Auditing of firms which act as agents, subcontractors or suppliers of inputs, e.g., tour operators using only hotels which have adequate wastewater and sewage treatment or disposal facilities and which are in keeping with the character of a destination.
Compliance	Relatively simple, regular checks to ensure the firm complies with any current environmental regulations affecting its operations, e.g., airline checking on noise levels of its aircraft at take-off.
Corporate	Typically an audit of an entire company, especially a transnational one, to ensure that agreed environmental policy is understood and followed throughout the firm.
Issues	Concentration upon a key issue, e.g., ozone depletion, and evaluation of company operations in relation to that issue, e.g., hotel chain checks aerosols used are CFC-free, uses only alternatives to CFC-blown plastic foams for insulation and retrieves any CFCs used in air-conditioning plant for controlled disposal.
Product	Ensuring that existing products and proposed product developments meet the firm's environmental policy criteria, e.g., tour operator designs holiday based on walking once destination reached, using locally owned vernacular accommodation and services.
Site	Audit directed at spot checks of buildings, plant and processes known to have actual or potential problems, e.g., hotel checking energy efficiency of its heating and lighting systems, airport authority checking aircraft noise levels near to landing and take-off flight paths.

edging as part of this the requirement of annual environmental audits for all on-going tourism activities. Environmental auditing may be undertaken by individual tourism firms for their products, e.g., package holidays; for essential activities, e.g., transport; for buildings, especially hotels; for linked firms, e.g., suppliers of foodstuffs and furniture to hotels; as well as to the broader issues/corporate dimension, e.g., acid rain. Although there is little or no evidence to date that tourism firms are undertaking formal environmental audits, many have drafted or are formulating environmental policies and it is likely that product and activity/site (operational) audits will become commonplace.

Consider tourism products. A product audit will reveal how environmentally responsible the firm's present product range is and suggest how products can be adapted to make them environmentally more friendly. For example, tour operators offering hire cars as part of a package holiday can ensure that they operate on lead-free petrol (as in the Sun Blessed Holidays); those operating coach tours can arrange that routes in historic towns are selected so as not to damage the foundations of medieval buildings (e.g., Moswin Tours). Tour operators can also select accommodation that is owned and managed locally: this helps sustain the local economy, the more so where hotels in particular use mainly local produce (the latter having a further environmental benefit if fewer transport inputs are used). Indeed, a tour operator, e.g., Pure Crete, may encourage the restoration of derelict, traditionally built properties for use as tourist accommodation. A product audit may therefore lead to a change in both the width and depth of the firm's product range, with new or revamped products formulated to be environmentally friendly such as the introduction of wildlife conservation holidays, e.g., Beach Villas, Wildlife Travel, and conservation working holidays, or restricting the numbers participating in particular wildlife and natural history tours (e.g., Zoe Holidays).

Formulating an environmentally friendly tourism product may be only half the battle since there is the matter of how that product is *consumed* by the holiday-makers, some of whom are less environmentally aware than others. It may therefore be argued that tour operators have a duty of care towards destination environments and their host populations, which requires tour operators to help educate holiday-makers about the customs, culture and environmental issues of those destinations. Thus, tour operators like Saga Holidays, Allegro Holidays, Eurocamp and CV Travel include briefing packs and/or advice on a destination's cultural and ecological background amongst the information they distribute to their tourists. Such *consumer education* in the form of tour operator-issued code of conduct for behaviour at a destination will become increasingly common.

Tourism firms can also *go green* operationally by seeking to minimize their use of resource inputs (i.e., source reduction), by substituting environmentally benign inputs, by controlling waste discharges and encouraging recovery and reuse, and by giving staff *environmental* training. This operational context applies to all activities of tourism firms, including those which take place in tourist origin areas or entail transport between tourist origins and destination. Source reduction of inputs presents the tourism industry with considerable difficulty where the transport component of the product is concerned. Whilst some saving may be possible by substituting public for private transport and increasing load factors, all fossil fuels contribute to global warming. Hence any increase in the long-haul tour market adds to that problem, however well-maintained the aircraft engines. Certain tourism firms have reduced or are seeking to reduce energy consumption in their buildings. For example, Disney World have reviewed all building specifications at both their California and Florida sites from the viewpoint of electrical energy (and water) conservation (Woolf, 1991). On a much smaller scale, the Hotel Ucliva, Waltensberg,

Switzerland installed a heating system which uses locally grown wood, managed on sustainable forestry principles and burnt in a pollution-free, high temperature furnace (Lane, 1990).

Substitution of environmentally benign for environmentally harmful inputs is also taking place, although the availability of such inputs depends on the environmental policies adopted by firms in other industries. However, large tourism firms, e.g., Disney World, use the power of their massive purchasing budget to make suppliers provide environmentally friendly products. Toiletries and cleaning materials which are CFC and phosphate-free are insisted upon by some firms, e.g. Consort Hotels. Organic produce is appearing on certain hotel and restaurant menus. Many firms run their motor vehicles on unleaded petrol, e.g. British Airways, Consort Hotels. Indeed, the latter provide staff living within 5 miles of their York hotel with bicycles, as well as having two courtesy bicycles for guests' use (Evans, 1990). Stationery and other paper products used by hotels (e.g., Consort), tour operators (e.g., Saga Holidays) and airlines (e.g., British Airways), is made increasingly from recycled paper. These examples illustrate the possibilities: activity and site audits would confirm whether and the extent to which tourism firms operate in an environmentally responsible manner.

An integral part of a tourism firm's corporate environmental policy will be a positive attitude towards minimizing waste and encouraging recycling. Much waste from tourism firms, especially from hotels and other tourist accommodation, is similar in composition to domestic household rubbish and is normally disposed of by burial at landfill sites. Even where the waste is biodegradable this is not a totally satisfactory solution to waste disposal, since landfill sites are in increasingly short supply, there is some danger of pollution from leachate, and even vegetable waste is hard to break down in a landfill site when surrounded by plastic and lacking oxygen. If biodegradable rubbish does eventually decompose it still releases methane (which contributes to global warming). However, waste minimization and pollution reduction is a step in the right direction: British Airways, for example, is reviewing its operations, seeking to reduce aircraft noise, CFC emissions from its engineering processes, and toxic paint wastes, as well as its catering operations, where increasing use is being made of reusable crockery.

Recyclability is preferable to biodegradability. Efforts should therefore be made to recycle as many materials as possible, e.g., aluminium and 'tin' (steel) cans, paper and cardboard, glass, plastic, other scrap metals, cooking oils and lubricants, etc. Even energy can be *recycled* in a sense, e.g., heat energy from refrigeration units can be used to heat water and buildings. Recycling has the advantage that it may also reduce primary resource consumption, e.g., if a car hire firm installs a car wash which cleans and recycles its water (rather than discharging dirty water into mains drainage) it will use only 9 litres of fresh water per wash (instead of the usual 210 litres where there is no recycling). In particular recycling can save on energy use (although these benefits are only indirect to the tourism industry), e.g., the energy consumed in making one new aluminium can would make twenty recycled ones. Hotels and other tourist buildings could fit low-energy compact fluorescent bulbs which not only use far less energy but last up to eight times longer than standard light bulbs (although they do cost more initially). Such reductions in energy consumption will assist in stemming global warming.

However recycling opportunities may be differentially available to tourism firms, a reflection of their size. Small firms, such as independent hotels and guest-houses would need to sort, store and either arrange collection or delivery of recyclable materials, whereas large firms, such as transnationals, may have *in-house* opportunities, based on scale economies, to benefit from recycling. For example, Disney World in Florida has its own sewage works linked to an organic composting factory which converts sewage sludge into organic fertilizer for use on the flower-beds and trees of the Magic Kingdom and also recycles irrigation water to reduce demand on water supply. Consideration is currently being given to the building of a large reverse osmosis plant which would enable recycled water to be used in swimming-pools (Woolf, 1991). Again, activity and site audits would indicate how *green* the tourism firm was operationally and target processes and activities for improvement.

Whilst all tourism firms can undertake the range of internal environmental audits, the tour operators are in a position to influence the environmental friendliness of the total tourism product by carrying out associate audits of firms acting as their agents or subcontractors in supplying the components of their package holidays. There is evidence to suggest that some tour operators, especially smaller specialist ones, select tourist accommodation on the basis that it is locally owned and managed, is of vernacular design and construction, etc. (e.g., Saga Holidays, Pure Crete, Arctic Experience, Sunvil Travel and VFB Holidays), even if they do not go so far as to undertake associate audits. Perhaps, in Europe at least, EC Directive 990/314/EEC on Package Travel, Package Holidays and Package Tours (to be implemented from 31 December 1992), which clearly imposes certain responsibilities on tour operators (and/or travel agents) regarding their products, will encourage European tour operators to consider such audits.

Corporate audits are hardly appropriate for the many small firms which form a large part of the fragmented tourism industry. It would therefore be sufficient if such small independent firms carried out activity, product and site audits as part of their regular management function. However, for large firms, especially transnationals, with numerous *local bases*, e.g. multiple travel agencies, hotel chains and mass tour operators, the role of the corporate audit assumes importance in ensuring knowledge of the company's environmental policy and comparability of implementation in each of the company's operative bases or establishments. In practice this may focus on internal communications and on the training and motivation of all company staff. The latter is perhaps the one area where some firms are showing an awareness of their wider environmental responsibilities, although the fact that tour operators, such as Allegro Holidays and Eurocamp, provide a range of environmental training for their staff (including destination representatives and agents) cannot be represented as even an embryo corporate audit.

Issues audits are likely to adopt a rather different format, not least because they do not need to be undertaken as part of a regular environmental monitoring schedule, being required only when a particular (new) environmental issue is recognized. In all other respects, if a firm has adopted regular environmental monitoring, employing the other forms of audit, then issues audits could well be redundant. Within the tourism industry many firms, especially tour operators, are demonstrating an awareness of wider environmental issues such as wildlife conservation and global warming: for example, Moswin Tours provide their tourists who visit the Black Forest in Germany with an opportunity to learn about acid rain. Tour operators also participate in a practical way at the destination scale, e.g. CV Travel has been advising communities in certain destinations about rubbish disposal; Sunvil Travel assisted, with staff time and other aid in kind, in the creation of Cyprus's first national park on the Akemas peninsula; and Turkish Delight have provided financial support to the conservation foundation attempting to *save* the Dalyan Delta (important for loggerhead turtles) from development. Similarly, other tour operators offer general (financial) help to wildlife conservation, e.g., Arctic Experience support both the Wildlife Trust and the Whale and Dolphin Conservation Society, although they may link such support to the numbers of tourists purchasing their package holidays. Thus Cox & Kings will buy one acre of Belize rainforest for conservation for every traveller on their wildlife programme, or offer a week's sponsorship for a researcher from the Whale and Dolphin Conservation Society for each tourist on one of their whale-watching holidays.

Conclusions

Environmental auditing offers management a procedural framework within which judgements can be made on how environmentally responsible a tourism firm's or organization's current operations and products are. It is a means to an end. Implementation of environmental audit is therefore dependent upon a clear commitment by tourism firms and organizations to total quality management, of which environmental policy is an integral part.

At first sight it appears obvious that the long-term common interest of the tourism industry is the adoption of policies which conserve tourism's primary resource base, the environment, since this must underpin the sustainability of tourism at any destination. However, environmental auditing itself requires a commitment of resources and the question must be asked whether the benefits and costs of taking action consequent upon the results of an environmental audit are clear-cut.

Although environmental auditing may identify why and where tourism products, activities and processes are damaging the environment, remedial action may be another matter. If a compliance audit shows a firm is failing to meet legal requirements, immediate action can be expected (otherwise the firm risks prosecution and fines). However, where activity, associate, product and site audits indicate environmentally damaging consequences, a positive response can clearly be expected where a firm's profitability will benefit, which may be true where a hotel reduces its energy consumption. Action may be less likely, though, where the benefits are largely enjoyed by third parties or the general public, such as the reduction of pollution from motor vehicle emissions. In these cases, if remedial action entails greater costs the individual firm could be at a disadvantage *vis-à-vis* competitors (who take no action) unless it is able to offset these higher costs by even greater revenue. Can more tourists be attracted if the firm markets its products as *greener* than those of its competitors? Herein lies the uncertainty! If consumers' current search for quality embraces an increasing environmental awareness, the tourism industry would face demand-led pressure to adopt environmental auditing more widely. Until that happens, although some tourism firms will take advantage of the niche market for *green holidays*, generally the competitive nature of the industry will slow the widespread adoption of environmental auditing.

References

Cater, E. and Goodall, B., 1992, 'Must tourism destroy its resource base?', in A.M. Mannion and S.R. Bowlby (eds), *Environmental Issues in the 1990s*, London, Wiley, 97–114.

Choy, D.J.L., 1991, 'National tourism planning in the Philippines', *Tourism Management*, 12(3): pp. 245–52.

Dieke, P.U.C., 1991, 'Policies for tourism development in Kenya', *Annals of Tourism Research*, 18(2): pp. 269–94.

Essoview, 1991, 'Green routine', *Essoview*, 3, September: 2–3.

Evans, M., 1990, 'Green tourism—a hotelier's view', *Insights*, September: D9–11, English Tourist Board.

Gilg, A.W., 1991, 'Switzerland: structural change with stability', in A.M. Williams and G. Shaw (eds), *Tourism and Economic Development: Western European Experiences*, London, Belhaven, 130–52.

Gordon, C., 1991, 'Sustainable leisure', *Ecos*, 12(1): pp. 7–11.

Green, D.H. and Hunter, C., 1990, 'Assessing the environmental impact of tourism', *Proceedings of the Tourism Research into the 1990s Conference*, University College, Durham Castle, 10–12 December, 338–53.

Keating, M., 1991, 'Bad sports', *Geographical Magazine*, 63(12): pp. 26–9.

Lane, B., 1990, 'Green accommodation', in: B. Bramwell (ed.), *Shades of Green: Working Towards Green Tourism in the Countryside, Conference Proceedings*, Cheltenham, Countryside Commission; English Tourist Board, Rural Development Commission, 81–3.

Lewis, J. and Williams, A.M., 1991, 'Portugal: market segmentation and regional specialisation', in A.M. Williams and G. Shaw (eds), *Tourism and Economic Development: Western European Experiences*, London, Belhaven, 107–29.

NSCA, 1991, *Pollution Handbook*, Brighton, National Society for Clean Air and Environmental Protection.

Pearce, D., 1991, 'Towards the sustainable economy: environment and economics'. *Royal Bank of Scotland Review*, 172, December: pp. 3–15.

Royal Commission on Environmental Pollution, 1976, *Air Pollution Control: An Integrated Approach*, Fifth Report, London, HMSO.

Tourism and Environment Task Force, 1991, *Tourism and the Environment: Maintaining the Balance*, London, English Tourist Board and Employment Department.

Tuppen, J., 1991, 'France: the changing character of a key industry', in A.M. Williams and G. Shaw (eds), *Tourism and Economic Development: Western European Experiences*, London, Belhaven, 191–206.

Witt, S.F., 1991, 'Tourism in Cyprus—balancing the benefits and costs', *Tourism Management*, 12(1): pp. 37–46.

Woolf, J., 1991, 'The greening of Mickey Mouse', *Observer*, 10 February: p. 57.

WTTC, 1991, *WTTC Policy—Environmental Principles*, Brussels, World Travel and Tourism Council (mimeographed).

5 Tourism, economic development and the environment: problems and policies
M. Thea Sinclair

Foreign currency receipts from tourism can constitute a catalyst to economic development in countries which have limited possibilities of exporting manufactured goods. Developing countries appear to have a comparative advantage in tourism owing to their environmental resources, including coastal and scenic attractions, wildlife and climatic features. However, developing countries experience the problems of over-utilization of some of their resources, and under-utilization of others. Deterioration in the quality of the environment resulting from over-utilization, *ceteris paribus*, implies a worsening of the tourism product supplied, in a context in which tourists are generally demanding higher quality tourism. Environmental degradation can cause some tourism demand to switch to alternative, more environmentally attractive areas, with a consequent decline in total and/or per capita foreign currency earnings in the original destination. Under-utilization of resources implies a loss of scarce foreign currency earnings which could contribute to the country's development.

The economics literature on tourism and development has paid little attention to estimating the effects of environmental change on tourism receipts. Much of the literature has instead been concerned with quantifying the foreign currency earnings which developing countries receive from international tourism (for example, Baretje, 1988; English, 1986; Lee, 1987) and the income and employment generated by tourism (for example, Archer, 1977; 1989; Fletcher and Archer, 1991; Pye and Lin, 1983; Varley, 1978). Although the complex nature of the tourism product has deterred researchers from estimating supply functions for tourism (Sinclair and Stabler, 1991), demand has been more widely studied (Archer, 1976; Sheldon, 1990; Syriopoulos, 1990; and Witt and Martin, 1989, provide useful reviews).

There is considerable scope for further research on the pricing of environmental resources. In the context of natural resources, Stabler (1991) has discussed the issue of market failure with respect to wildlife as a tourism product. Market failure frequently results from the environmental component of tourism products being a public good, from which no potential consumer can be excluded and which is not priced. For example, many nature reserves have been freely accessible to tourists, although the population of the destination country has often had to finance, via taxation payments, the infrastructure providing the tourists' means of access. Where environmental resources have been valued, their prices have often failed to reflect the social costs of provision. Thus, when fees for entry to reserves have been charged, they have often failed to cover the provision costs which the destination country has incurred as the result of tourism. The effect of zero or under-priced environmental resources has often been to stimulate a level of demand which has damaged the quality of the resources.

The problem of over-utilization results from the past lack of recognition of the true value of environmental resources. Although a variety of studies and reviews of the effects of tourism on the environment have been carried out, by both public organizations and individual researchers (for example, Boo, 1990; Farrell and Runyan, 1991; Pearce, 1985; Romeril, 1989), little research has been undertaken on the evaluation of environmental resources which are consumed by tourists. Most of the applied economic research on environmental evaluation has been undertaken in the area of leisure and recreation (for example, Bishop and Heberlein, 1979; Brookshire et al., 1983; Desvousges et al., 1983). The methodologies which have been used include cost-benefit analysis (Adger and Whitby, 1990; Campen, 1986), the hedonic pricing technique (Brookshire et al., 1982), the contingent valuation method (Bishop and Heberlein, 1986; Cummings et al., 1986; Garrod and Willis, 1991) and the travel cost model (Bishop and Heberlein, 1980; Willis and Benson, 1988). The last two methodologies have been applied to safari tourism by Brown, Jr and Henry (1989). The Delphi technique is a judgemental method which has been used to assess the environmental effects of tourism (Green et al., 1990).

The application of the preceding methodologies has demonstrated the often considerable value of environmental resources. The positive value of environmental resources consumed by tourists has been acknowledged in policies for alternative tourism, in vogue at the beginning of the 1990s and described as sustainable tourism development. For example, green tourism or nature tourism is increasingly promoted, ostensibly as a sustainable, environment-friendly form of tourism, although its commercialization may result in the contrary effects, as Long (1991) points out. Sustainable development entails maintaining the quality of the environment, and can be distinguished from economic growth, which is concerned with increases in national income. Sustainable development requires the maintenance of a constant value or a constant stock of resources, and is necessary if decreases in the quality of tourism products are to be avoided. A constant value of resources could be achieved by a reduced quantity of more highly priced resources. Hence Pearce et al., (1989) argue that a more appropriate definition of sustainability is that of constant natural capital, entailing the maintenance of a constant stock of environmental resources. De Kadt (cited in Nash and Butler, 1990) has pointed to the need to make conventional tourism more sustainable, as well as to develop alternative forms of tourism.

Although sustainable tourism development can be attained by regulation and the setting of standards, it can often be achieved more efficiently via the price mechanism (Wanhill, 1980). Fees or taxes on the use of environmental resources can be imposed such that the price takes account not only of the marginal private cost of the use of the resources, but also the marginal external cost of any damage incurred by their use, and of the marginal. user-cost which results from the depletion of the resources. The incidence of the tax on suppliers and tourists varies from case to case, depending upon the sensitivities of supply and demand to a change in price. Some cross-subsidization can occur, if local residents are charged preferential rates relative to foreign tourists, as has recently been the case for national wildlife parks and reserves in Kenya (Sinclair, forthcoming). A third means of achieving sustainable development is by the imposition of quantity restrictions, which prevent the utilization of resources beyond their carrying capacity. An example of quantity constraints is the limitations on the numbers of tourists who are allowed to visit the Galapagos (Marsh, 1987), although since official quotas may be exceeded (Agardy, 1990), effective implementation is important.

Alternative measures are appropriate in different contexts as Favoro (1983) argued during a discussion of tourism and fishing in Uruguay, and may include a combination of restrictions on tourist numbers and taxation to alter prices. Price controls may be combined with restrictions on numbers where the aim is to prevent excessive price rises. The number and type of regulatory measures varies greatly between different countries, since the imposition of regulations may depend upon pressure group activity (Favoro, 1983), and regulations may not be enforced (George, 1987).

At the microeconomic level, a number of projects now include the explicit aim of conserving the local environment (Arndell, 1990). Financial support from governments and international organizations (Lee, 1991; Davis and Simmons, 1982) has been important in stimulating the development of rural areas which are not part of popular tourist circuits, thereby decreasing the under-utilization of environmental resources. Such planned investment has the additional advantage of channelling income and employment from tourism to poorer members of the population. However, the goal of sustainable tourism development requires not only an appropriate economic pricing and/or quota policy, but also the support and on-site participation of local residents, as Long (1991) argues.

Although policies can be implemented in an attempt to tackle the problems of over- or under-utilization of environmental resources by tourists, their effectiveness may be limited if control of tourism development lies mainly with firms in industrialized countries. Britton (1982), for example, contended that the metropolitan companies retain the major share of control over the form and extent of tourism development in the Third World. Firms from industrialized countries not only supply much of the transport which tourists use (Cleverdon, 1979), but also affect the environment within destination countries, through ownership and contracts with local enterprises (Bote and Sinclair, 1991; UNCTC, 1982). For example, hotel management companies are commonly contracted to

design, construct and operate large hotels, thereby changing the environment of the destination.

The governments of developing countries sometimes introduce measures
designed to support local enterprises, although limited knowledge of and
influence over the terms of contracts made between domestic and foreign
enterprises decreases the effectiveness of the measures (Sinclair *et al.*,
1992). Detailed knowledge of environmental resources in the destination
country can form the basis for the supply of specialist holidays by local tour
operators, who can tap demand from particular segments of the market
with a strategy of *niche marketing* (Goodall *et al.*, 1989). Local tour
operators may thus compete successfully alongside foreign tour operators
who aim at mass market sales. The small-scale agro-tourist co-operatives,
supported by the socialist government and run by women in rural areas in
Greece, are an example of a means of conserving the local environment, as
well as providing the women with an income, increased control and
independence (Castelberg-Koulma, 1991). However, even if foreign control is constrained, local élites frequently obtain control over the use of
resources (Richter, 1989), and may subordinate the objective of sustainable tourism development to one of maximizing short-term profitability.
Under these circumstances, there is likely to be a case for increased
management of environmental resources by governments or international
organizations.

Plans requiring greater management of tourism development have been
formulated for a number of areas. The tourism development plan for south
Sulawesi, for example, recommended increased local participation and
management, along with the spatial deconcentration of tourism development (Suwelo, 1991). Coastal resources in Hawaii have been managed by
planning and zoning, and proposals for greater local participation in environmental impact studies, the determination of carrying capacities and
environmental monitoring studies have been put forward (Tarnas, 1991).
Some internationally-funded projects have also recognized the contribution of management to sustainable tourism. For example, the Pacific
Regional Tourism Development Programme, financed by the European
Community, formulated environmental guidelines for tourism development including criteria for environmental impact assessments, environmental monitoring and tourist behaviour management (Arndell, 1990).

In the greater management of tourism development, the role which
economists can play is to provide guidelines on the levels of prices,
taxation, subsidies or restrictions on tourist numbers, by which means the
twin objectives of tourism development and environmental sustainability
can be attained. Thus, the literature on the economics of sustainable
tourism development is of practical relevance and is likely to be reflected
in applied studies and projects in an increasing number of tourist
destinations.

Acknowledgements

I should like to thank Mike Stabler for his constructive comments on an earlier draft of this chapter.

References

Adger, N. and Whitby, M., 1990, *Appraisal and the Public Good: Environmental Assessment and Cost-Benefit Analysis*, Working Paper 7, Countryside Change Unit, Department of Agricultural Economics and Food Marketing, University of Newcastle upon Tyne.

Agardy, T., 1990, 'Integrating tourism in multiple use planning', paper presented at the Congress on Marine Tourism, 23–29 May, Honolulu, Hawaii.

Archer, B.H., 1976, *Demand Forecasting in Tourism*, Occasional Papers in Economics, No. 9, University of Wales Press, Bangor.

Archer, B.H., 1977, *Tourism Multipliers: The State of the Art*, Occasional Papers in Economics, No. 11, University of Wales Press, Bangor.

Archer, B.H., 1989, 'Tourism and island economics: impact analyses', in C.P. Cooper (ed.), *Progress in Tourism, Recreation and Hospitality Management*, Volume One, Belhaven, London, pp. 125–34.

Arndell, R., 1990, 'Tourism as a development concept in the South Pacific', *The Courier*, No. 122: pp. 83–6.

Baretje, R., 1988, 'Tourisme international du tiers monde: l'enjeu des devises', *Teoros* 7(3): pp. 10–14.

Bishop, R.C. and Heberlein, T.A., 1979, 'Measuring values of extra-market goods: are indirect measures biased?', *American Journal of Agricultural Economics*, 61(5), pp. 926–30.

Bishop, R.C. and Heberlein, T.A., 1980, *Stimulated Markets, Hypothetical Markets and Travel Cost Analysis: Alternative Methods of Estimating Outdoor Recreation Demand*, Department of Agricultural Economics Staff Paper No. 187, University of Wisconsin.

Bishop, R.C. and Heberlein, T.A., 1986, 'Does contingent valuation work?', in R. Cummings, D.S. Brookshire and W.D. Schulze (eds), *Valuing Environmental Goods: An Assessment of the Contingent Valuation Method*, Rowman and Allanfield, Totowa, New Jersey.

Boo, E., 1990, *Ecotourism: The Potential and Pitfalls*, World Wildlife Fund, Washington DC.

Bote Gómez, V. and Sinclair, M.T., 1991, 'Integration in the tourism industry: a case study approach', in M.T. Sinclair and M.J. Stabler (eds), *The Tourism Industry: An International Analysis*, CAB International, Wallingford, pp. 67–90.

Britton, S.G., 1982, 'The political economy of tourism in the third world', *Annals of Tourism Research*, 9(3): pp. 331–58.

Brookshire, D.S., Eubanks, L.S. and Randall, A., 1983, 'Estimating option prices and existence values for wildlife resources', *Land Economics*, 59(1): pp. 1–15.

Brookshire, D.S., Schulze, W.D., Thayer, M.A. and d'Arge, R.C., 1982, 'Valuing public goods: a comparison of survey and hedonic approaches', *American Economic Review*, 72(1): 165–77.

Brown, Jr and Henry, W., 1989, *The Economic Value of Elephants*, London Environmental Economics Centre Paper 89–12, University College London.

Campen, J.T., 1986, *Benefit/Cost and Beyond*, Ballinger, New York.

Castelberg-Koulma, M., 1991, 'Greek women and tourism: women's co-operatives as an alternative form of organization', in N. Redclift and M.T. Sinclair (eds), *Working Women: International Perspectives on Labour and Gender Ideology*, Routledge, London and New York, pp. 197–212.

Cleverdon, R., 1979, *The Economic and Social Impact of International Tourism on Developing Countries*, Economist Intelligence Unit, London.

Cummings, R., Brookshire, D.S. and Schulze, W.D., (eds), 1986, *Valuing Environmental Goods: An Assessment of the Contingent Valuation Method*, Rowman and Allanfield, Totowa, New Jersey.

Davis, H.D. and Simmons, J.A., 1982, 'World Bank experience with tourism projects', *Tourism Management*, 3(4): pp. 212–17.

Desvousges, W.S., Smith, V.K. and McGivney, M.P., 1983, *Comparison of Alternative Approaches for Estimating Recreation and Related Benefits of Water Quality Improvements*, US Environmental Protection Agency, EPA-230-05-83-001, Washington DC.

English, E.P., 1986, *The Great Escape? An Examination of North–South Tourism*, North–South Institute, Ottawa.

Farrell, B.H. and Runyan, D., 1991 'Ecology and tourism', *Annals of Tourism Research*, 18(1): pp. 26–40.

Favoro, E., 1983, 'Dos enfoques para el análisis de externalidades: examen de la interacción pesca vs. turismo en La Paloma', in M. Arana *et al.*, *Medio ambiente y turismo*, Consejo Lationoamericano de Ciencias Sociales, Buenos Aires, pp. 107–18.

Fletcher, J.E. and Archer, B.H., 1991, 'The development and application of multiplier analysis', in C.P. Cooper (ed.), *Progress in Tourism Recreation and Hospitality Management*, Volume Three, Belhaven, London, pp. 28–47.

Garrod, G. and Willis, K.G., 1991, *Some Empirical Estimates of Forest Amenity Value*, Working Paper 13, Countryside Change Unit, Department of Agricultural Economics and Food Marketing, University of Newcastle upon Tyne.

George, V., 1987, 'Tourism on Jamaica's north coast', in S. Britton and W.C. Clarke (eds), *Ambiguous Alternative Tourism in Small Developing Countries*, University of the South Pacific, Suva, Fiji, pp. 61–77.

Goodall, B., Radburn, M., Stabler, M., 1989, *Market Opportunity Sets for Tourism*, Geographical Papers No. 100, Tourism Series 1, University of Reading.

Green, H., Hunter, C. and Moore, B., 1990, 'Assessing the environmental impact of tourism development. Use of the Delphi technique', *Tourism Management*, 11(2): pp. 111–20.

Lee, G., 1987, 'Tourism as a factor in development cooperation', *Tourism Management*, 8(1): pp. 2–19.

Lee, G., 1991, 'Lomé IV and the tourism sector', *Tourism Management*, 12(2): pp. 149–51.

Long, V., 1991, 'Nature tourism: environmental stress or environmental salvation?', paper presented at The World Leisure and Recreation Association International Congress, 16–19 July, Sydney (Department of Geography, University of Waterloo, Canada).

Marsh, J.S., 1987, 'National parks and tourism in small developing countries', *Ambiguous Alternative, Tourism in Small Developing Countries*, University of the South Pacific, Suva, Fiji, pp. 25–45.

Nash, D. and Butler, R., 1990, 'Towards sustainable tourism', *Tourism Management*, 11(3): pp. 263–4.

Pearce, D., Markandya, A., Barbier, E.B., 1989, *Blueprint for a Green Economy*,

Earthscan Publications, London.

Pearce, D.G., 1985, 'Tourism and environmental research: a review', *International Journal of Environmental Studies*, 25(4): pp. 247–55.

Pye, E.A., and Lin, Tzong-biau (eds), 1983, *Tourism in Asia: The Economic Impact*, Singapore University Press, Singapore.

Richter, L.K., 1989, *The Politics of Tourism in Asia*, University of Hawaii Press, Honolulu.

Romeril, M., 1989, 'Tourism—the environmental dimension', in C.P. Cooper (ed.), *Progress in Tourism, Recreation and Hospitality Management*, Volume One, Belhaven, London, pp. 103–13.

Sheldon, P.J., 1990, 'A review of tourism expenditure research', in C.P. Cooper (ed.), *Progress in Tourism, Recreation and Hospitality Management*, Volume Two, Belhaven, London, pp. 28–49.

Sinclair, M.T., forthcoming, 'Tour operators and policies in Kenya', *Annals of Tourism Research*.

Sinclair, M.T., Alizadeh, P., Atieno Adero Onunga, E., 1992, 'The structure of international tourism and tourism development in Kenya', in D. Harrison (ed.), *Tourism and the Less Developed Countries*, Belhaven, London.

Sinclair, M.T. and Stabler, M.J., 1991, 'New perspectives on the tourism industry', in M.T. Sinclair and M.J. Stabler (eds), *The Tourism Industry: An International Analysis*, CAB International, Wallingford, pp. 1–14.

Stabler, M.J., 1991, 'Where will the birds go? The threats of recreation and tourism development to estuarial wildlife: an economic critique', paper presented at the Third Global Congress of Heritage Interpretation International 3–8 November, Honolulu, Hawaii.

Suwelo, I. Sutanto, 1991, 'Preservation of the megalithic culture, nature and tourism development in Toraja, south Sulawesi, Indonesia, through deconcentration of tourist service centres and integrated zoning system', paper presented at the Third Global Congress of Heritage Interpretation International 3–8 November, Honolulu, Hawaii.

Syriopoulos, T., 1990, 'Modelling tourism demand for Mediterranean destinations', PhD thesis, University of Kent at Canterbury.

Tarnas, D., 1991, 'Coastal resources management in Kona, Hawaii—towards sustainable tourism development', paper presented at the Third Global Congress of Heritage Interpretation International, 3–8 November, Honolulu, Hawaii.

United Nations Centre on Transnational Corporations, 1982, *Transnational Corporations in International Tourism*, Report for the UNCTC by J.H. Dunning and M. McQueen, United Nations, New York.

Varley, R.C.G., 1978, *Tourism in Fiji: Some Economic and Social Problems*, Occasional Papers in Economics, No. 12, University of Wales Press, Bangor.

Wanhill, S.R.C., 1980, Charging for congestion at tourist attractions, *International Journal of Tourism Management*, 1(3): pp. 168–74.

Willis, K.G., and Benson, J.F., 1988, A comparison of user benefits and costs of nature conservation at three nature reserves, *Regional Studies*, 22(5): pp. 417–28.

Witt, S.F. and Martin, C.A., 1989, 'Demand forecasting in tourism and recreation', in C.P. Cooper (ed.), *Progress in Tourism, Recreation and Hospitality Management*, Volume One, Belhaven, London, 4–32.

6 Perspectives on the environmental impact of the Channel Tunnel on tourism in the 1990s

S.J. Page

Introduction

During the last decade there has been increasing sophistication among the needs and aspirations of tourists reflected in the development of a *new tourism* (Poon, 1989), which has seen greater emphasis on the consumer requirements of tourists particularly their search for more authentic holiday experiences and individual tourism products (Krippendorf, 1986). One consequence of this *new tourism* phenomenon is a greater concern for the natural and built environment in which tourism activities are undertaken (South-East Economic Development Strategy 1989a), and its impact in different localities. This greater awareness of environmental issues[1] related to tourism (Smith and Jenner, 1989) has been reflected in the rapid expansion and diversity of research on this theme which has considered *green tourism* (Wood and House, 1991), *alternative tourism* (Travis, 1988), *sustainable tourism* (Pigram, 1980; Smith and Eadington, 1992; Turner, 1988), and *ecological tourism* (Place, 1991; Boo, 1990; Chaplin, 1990), all of which have implicitly or explicitly emphasized the need for a more holistic assessment of how tourism affects the environment (Cohen, 1978; Farrell and Runyan, 1991).

Recent reviews of research on the environmental dimension in tourism have identified the scope and nature of this growing body of knowledge as well as the existing weaknesses in the structure and form of such studies (Pearce, 1985; Farrell and Runyan, 1987). The recognition of the symbiotic relationship between conservation and tourism (Budowski, 1976; Romeril, 1985) has led to the requirement for a greater integration of interdisciplinary and multidisciplinary approaches to research on tourism and the environment to achieve sustainable tourism development (Pigram, 1990; McMillan-Scott, 1990). This has concentrated on the need to overcome tourism's tendency to destroy sometimes the very resources upon which it depends (Holder, 1988), thereby maintaining a 'profitable and viable tourism industry without detriment to the environment, an objective which must surely become the norm in the 1990s' (Romeril, 1989a, p. 208). This very objective was the focus of the recent **Tourism and the Environment**

Report (Department of Employment, 1991), aimed at encouraging the UK tourism industry to accept that the environment is its very lifeblood and that it must consider the long-term consequences of tourism activity and development. Although Romeril (1989b, p. 107) has argued that this *mutual dependence* of tourism and the environment requires appropriate strategies and methodologies to understand the complex interrelationships between the interaction of tourism and the environment, no universal environmental methodology appears to have been adopted by researchers in their assessment of tourism's impact on the environment.

An examination of the Channel Tunnel and proposed £3.5 billion International High Speed Rail Link (IRL) from London to the Tunnel are examples of major infrastructure projects which illustrate how analytical techniques such as environmental impact assessment (EIA) can be used to assess the environmental consequences of such large-scale tourism projects. The Channel Tunnel, is therefore both a major tourism project and an essential tourism infrastructure project which removes one of the 'missing links' in Europe's transport network (Holliday, Marcou and Vickerman, 1991: p. 166) and a potential constraint on cross border tourist flows between the United Kingdom and mainland Europe. Thus, the Channel Tunnel is also likely to have a potential generative effect on tourist flows as it facilitates a greater ease of travel between the United Kingdom and continental Europe, which may increase the environmental impact on tourism. EIA provides a methodological framework for systematically analysing how tourism may affect the environment. It may also facilitate a more holistic view of the relationships between tourism and the environment, thereby establishing a set of techniques which can be applied to research on the environmental impact of major tourism projects in other localities. Furthermore, this review of the Channel Tunnel's potential environmental effect on tourism is timely in view of the statutory requirement for an EIA in all European Community (EC) countries for tourism projects that are likely to have a *significant impact* on the environment (Department of the Environment, 1989).[2] To understand the Channel Tunnel case, the different environmental techniques and methodologies used to assess the impact of major tourism infrastructure projects are considered. This provides a context in which to assess the significance of the recent EC directive on EIA and recent research on the environmental aspects of the Channel Tunnel project from a tourism perspective.

The Channel Tunnel: assessing the environmental impact of a major tourism infrastructure project

The Channel Tunnel is currently the largest project in Europe for the transport of tourists, and is expected to cost in excess of £8 billion at 1990 prices. According to SERPLAN (1989), the Channel Tunnel could generate an additional 450,000 tourists for the South-East of England in 1993 and the British Tourist Authority has suggested that the Tunnel could add 0.5 per cent to the annual growth rate for international tourist arrivals in

London. Whilst not wishing to reiterate the issues discussed in the chapter on the Channel Tunnel by Jefferson (1992), it is evident that the Tunnel project will create a new tourist gateway between the United Kingdom and mainland Europe, thereby facilitating more choice in the available modes of cross-Channel travel for tourists after 1993. Tourist use of the Tunnel will be broadly related to time-saving and convenience compared with existing forms of sea and air travel (Figure 6.1), although psychological factors, such as an aversion to travelling in a tunnel underneath the English Channel (Manning-Shaw, 1991) and customer preference for sea travel, may play an important role in tourist patronage of available modes of crossing the Channel after 1993. The extent to which the opening of the Channel Tunnel will directly and indirectly affect physical and man-made tourism environments in the 1990s has largely been overlooked in recent research on the Channel Tunnel. There has been a tendency to concentrate on three areas of research in tourism. First, there has been a strong emphasis on the regional and local impact of the Tunnel on tourism in different areas (Touche Ross, 1988; Charlton and Essex, 1989; Vickerman, 1987; Vickerman and Flowerdew, 1990; Channel Tunnel Joint Consultative Committee, 1986; 1987; 1989; 1990). Second, a range of studies have examined the economic aspects of the Tunnel (Kay *et al.*, 1989; Button, 1990; SERPLAN, 1989). Lastly, there are those studies which have emphasized the transport dimension of the Tunnel and the likely effects on travel habits and infrastructure requirements for tourism in the United Kingdom (Manning-Shaw, 1991; Gibb, 1986; 1988; 1989; Whitelegg, 1988; Page and Sinclair, forthcoming) and mainland Europe (Vasseur, 1988; Barre, 1988; Therain, 1989).[3]

The environmental dimension has not received the same attention, with the exception of the controversy over the routing of the high speed rail link through Kent (Kent County Council, 1986; 1988; Channel Tunnel Joint Consultative Committee, 1989; Environmental Resources Limited, 1988; 1989) and Belgium (Sevrin, 1988). In the United Kingdom the environmental lobby (Environmental Resources Limited, 1985; Council for the Protection of Rural England, 1985) has been particularly concerned with the physical impact (Mitchell, 1986; Department of Transport, 1988; Sullivan, 1989), although the majority of such studies have centred on a specific impact or issue rather than a broader framework in which to assess the Tunnel's effect on different tourism environments in the 1990s. In France, however, there has been a more favourable response to the Tunnel and high speed rail link as the landscape of the Nord-Pas-de-Calais is perceived to be of a poorer environmental quality than Kent and the regional economy has experienced problems from deindustrialization. Consequently, the Tunnel has been viewed as a mechanism to stimulate economic growth in northern France (Mauroy, 1988) while the 'ecological lobby is weak and poorly organised in an area whose people have little romantic attachment to the countryside and see environmental protection as something of a luxury' (Grayson, 1990, p. 71). The environmental dimension can, however, form a useful starting-point for an evaluation of the Tunnel's impact on tourism after 1993.

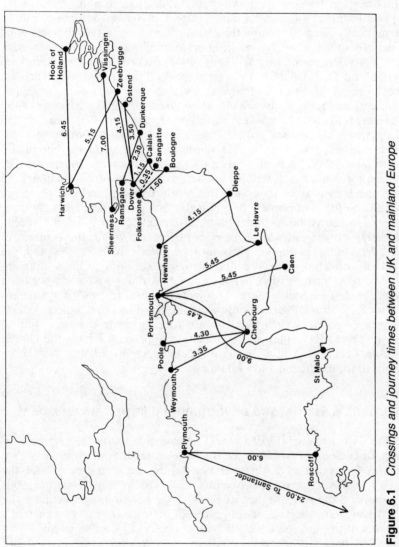

Figure 6.1 *Crossings and journey times between UK and mainland Europe*

Note: Times shown in hours and minutes

Analysing the environmental impact of the Channel Tunnel: a methodological framework

To understand the environmental impact of the Channel Tunnel requires a methodological framework in which the scale, nature and extent of the project's influence on existing and future tourism environments can be systematically assessed. Within the existing literature on the environmental impact of tourism, a number of different methodological approaches exist, which were documented by Williams (1987) according to their analytical function and the techniques they employ. As Table 6.1 shows, there are three levels at which environmental research on tourism can be undertaken, corresponding to the *identification*, *prediction* and *evaluation* of the environment likely to be affected by the planning and design, construction and operation of tourism projects that may give rise to both direct and indirect impacts. Williams (1987) summarizes five main methodologies used to assess the effects of tourism on the environment. These cover *ad hoc teams of specialists* describing impacts within their professional field of study, the *map overlay approach* frequently used in land use planning, *checklists* of different impacts of physical development related to tourism, networks to assess the secondary and tertiary effects of tourism projects, and lastly, more *sophisticated matrices* of impacts within the confines of EIA.[4] EIA as a methodological tool considers the activities and the potentially affected environmental elements resulting from a tourism-related project such as the Channel Tunnel. Although EIA has not been specifically designed with tourism projects in mind, it does offer a potentially useful methodological tool to examine the direct and indirect effects of a project on the existing and future tourism environment within an integrated research framework. Guidelines required for EIA in the United Kingdom (Table 6.2) fulfil the criteria outlined by Williams (1987) for identification, prediction and evaluation.[5]

The Channel Tunnel and environmental impact assessment

The EC Directive (85/337/EEC) on EIA coincided with the UK government's **Invitation to Promoters for the Development, Financing, Construction and Operation of a Channel Fixed Link between France and the United Kingdom** (Department of Transport, 1985, p. 80). Wathern (1990) has examined the recalcitrance of certain member states, particularly the United Kingdom, towards adopting the directive since the government's commitment to push the Channel Tunnel project to fruition as quickly as possible in 1985. By using the parliamentary device of the Hybrid Bill (Anderson, 1987; Holliday and Vickerman, 1990; Holliday *et al.*, 1991), no public planning inquiry was needed, which avoided any obligatory participation in an EIA to comply with the impending EC Directive since 'the Directive does not apply to projects . . . which are authorised by a private or Hybrid Bill' (Department of the Environment, 1989, p. 23), although 'the promoter of such a Bill should provide an environmental statement

Table 6.1   *Functional classification of environmental assessment approaches in tourism*

Function	Methodological thrust
1. Identification	Description of the existing environmental system Determination of the components of the tourism project Definition of the environment modified by the tourism project (including all components of the project)
2. Prediction	Identification of environmental modifications that may be significant Forecasting the quantity and/or spatial dimensions of change in environment identified Estimation of the probability that the impact (environmental change) will occur (time period)
3. Evaluation	Determination of the incidence of costs and benefits to user groups and populations affected by the project Specification and comparison of the trade-offs (costs or effects being balanced) between various alternatives

Source: Williams, 1987, p. 387.

which can be considered by the select or standing committees . . . on the Bill' (Department of the Environment, 1989, p. 23). The latter situation applied to the four shortlisted promoters of the Fixed Link project (Channel Tunnel Group, Channel Expressway, Eurobridge and Euroroute), who were required to comply with the EC Directive in 1985. This meant that rather than preparing a simple environmental statement, a detailed EIA was required from each promoter, minimizing the cost to the government by requiring the private sector to fund a detailed environmental analysis. As a result, the EIAs of the Fixed Link project are a landmark in EIA in the United Kingdom,[6] the first to comply with the EC Directive 85/337.

The four shortlisted promoters' EIA reports submitted in 1985 were subsequently appraised by Land Use Consultants (1985) who reviewed the content, coverage, accuracy and presentation of the reports in relation to their ability to meet the requirements of the draft EC Directive 85/337. Their summary appraisals of each promoter's EIA report are outlined in Table 6.3. Evaluating EIAs is a complex process (Ross, 1987; Elkin and Smith, 1988) in view of the problems of understanding and forecasting the secondary effects and consequential development such projects may generate. For example, the Channel Tunnel Group's EIA (Channel Tunnel Group, 1985) underestimated the potential impact of a Fixed Link on tourism, arguing that the Tunnel in itself would not directly stimulate a growth in the demand for cross-channel travel. Yet this overlooks the new tourism markets which will be made more accessible to the United Kingdom and Europe by the Tunnel and improvements to the high speed European rail network and road. Thus, while the Channel Tunnel Group EIA dealt with the physical impacts of the construction of the Tunnel, it

Table 6.2 *Information and content of environmental statement[1] in the UK as set out in Schedule 3 to the Town and Country Planning (Assessment of Environmental Effects) Regulations, 1988*

1. An environmental statement comprises a document or series of documents providing for the purpose of assessing the likely impact upon the environment of the development proposed to be carried out, the information specified in paragraph 2 (referred to in this Schedule as 'the specified information').

2. The specified information is:
   (a) a description of the development proposed, comprising information about the site and the design and size or scale of the development;
   (b) the data necessary to identify and assess the main effects which that development is likely to have on the environment;
   (c) a description of the likely significant effects, direct and indirect, on the environment of the development, explained by reference to its possible impact on:
   human beings;
   flora;
   fauna;
   soil;
   water;
   air;
   climate;
   the landscape;
   the interaction between any of the foregoing;
   material assets;
   the cultural heritage;
   (d) where significant adverse effects are identified with respect to any of the foregoing, a description of the measures envisaged in order to avoid, reduce or remedy those effects; and
   (e) a summary in non-technical language of the information specified above.

3. An environmental statement may include, by way of explanation or amplification of any specified information, further information on any of the following matters:
   (a) the physical characteristics of the proposed development, and the land use requirements during the construction and operational phases
   (b) the main characteristics of the production processes proposed, including the nature and quantity of the materials to be used;
   (c) the estimated type and quantity of expected residues and emissions (including pollutants of water, air or soil, noise vibration, light, heat and radiation) resulting from the proposed development when in operation
   (d) (in outline) the main alternatives (if any) studied by the applicant, appellant or authority and an indication of the main reasons for choosing the development proposed, taking into account the environmental effects;
   (e) the likely significant direct and indirect effects on the environment of the development proposed which may result from:
   (i) the use of natural resources;
   (ii) the emission of pollutants, the creation of nuisances, and the elimination of waste;

Table 6.2—continued

(f) the forecasting methods used to assess any effects on the environment about which information is given under subparagraph (e); and

(g) any difficulties, such as technical deficiencies or lack of know-how, encountered in compiling any specified information.

In paragraph (e), 'effects' includes secondary, cumulative, short, medium and long-term, permanent, temporary, positive and negative effects.

4. Where further information is included in an environmental statement pursuant to paragraph 3, a non-technical summary of that information shall also be provided.

Note: 1. In this context, an Environmental Statement is a 'document setting out the developer's own assessment of his project's likely environmental effects' (Department of the Environment, 1989, p. 2), and a checklist of the detailed matters to be considered as part of the Environmental Impact Assessment can be found in the Department of the Environment's (1989), pp. 37–42) *Environmental Assessment: A Guide to the Procedures*.

Source: Department of the Environment, 1989, pp. 35–6.

---

failed to make a detailed assessment of the consequences of a growth in visitor arrivals induced by the Fixed Link. Criticisms of the Channel Tunnel Group's EIA have also pointed to the voluminous and unintelligible nature of the study (Lee and Wood, 1988).[7] Despite the failure to consider the potential environmental impacts of a sustained growth in visitor arrivals and departures once the Tunnel opened, it is possible to identify how tourist use of the Tunnel will affect the environment.

First, there is the immediate environmental impact of constructing the Tunnel and its effect on existing tourism resources. Second, there are potential environmental pressures which will result from tourists travelling by car to the Tunnel terminals at Cheriton and Frethun. Third, there are direct environmental costs of the new high speed train service following the construction and operation of a proposed new IRL between London and Kent and the TGV network in North-West Europe. Although these potential costs have not been quantified in the United Kingdom,[8] they can be assessed from an EIA of the Belgian high speed rail link. Fourth, there may be environmental costs and benefits generated by additional tourist use of alternative forms of infrastructure serving the Tunnel if the planned provision of additional capacity cannot meet tourist demand. These environmental costs will result from tourists who are forced to travel by road owing to the lack of train services to meet the demand and the lack of an interchange facility at the proposed International Passenger Terminal at Ashford. Lastly, there is the indirect impact of increased car-borne visitors, which is difficult to predict owing to the degree of flexibility in visiting destination compared with rail-borne visitors, whose initial impact will be determined by the location of interchange and terminal facilities in Kent and London.

Table 6.3   *Land Use Consultants' summary appraisals of the Channel Fixed Link EIA*

Channel Expressway (1985)	The EIA accords in outline with the government's requirements, although some important areas of potential impact are only covered in a cursory manner. The method of approach tends to place excessive emphasis on the scope for amelioration and mitigation of certain key impacts, notably on landscape and ecology, and, as a result, the statements fail to reflect the full extent of unavoidable impacts.
Channel Tunnel (1985)	In general, the EIA is thorough, methodical and supported by good technical detail. It meets the government's requirements in almost all respects. Site descriptions and project baselines are clear and well evaluated. They lead into logical impact analysis and positive proposals for mitigation.
Eurobridge (1985)	The EIA does not conform, in almost all respects, to what we judge to be an acceptable standard of presentation and its contents are inadequate. The statements do, however, point to some of the long-term environmental issues which need to be considered for any Channel Fixed Link.
Euroroute (1985)	Euroroute has produced an EIA which accords with the government's requirements and is generally of high standard. The report is laid out in a clear and logical sequence and is well designed. Baseline environmental conditions are carefully described and efforts have been made to quantify the magnitude and significance of potential impacts. However, the origin of some of the statements is difficult to identify (i.e. whether they are value judgements of the EIA team or are based on detailed research).

Source: Land Use Consultants, 1986.

The environmental impact of constructing the Tunnel on existing tourism resources

The construction of the Tunnel is extremely well documented in recent research and so are the conservation issues associated with the project which have aroused the concerns of amenity bodies such as the Council for the Protection of Rural England and the Nature Conservancy Council. Ardill (1987) examined the conservation lobby's concern for the impact on the landscape, and the 'land irretrievably lost or damaged due to the construction of the Channel Tunnel (see Plates 1 and 2), the terminals, associated infrastructure and the high speed link' (South-East Economic Development Strategy, 1989b, p. 99). The effects of consequential development on the South-East from selective land releases for tourism or

Plate 6.1   *Aerial view of the site where Eurotunnel's UK terminal is under construction, March 1991 (Courtesy of Channel Tunnel Group Ltd)*

motorway service areas at interchanges are also of concern since many of the preferred development sites will create pressure on the green belt and protected areas. Anderson (1987) commented on the visual amenity of the Kent landscape affected by the Tunnel and indirectly examined some of the tourism resources that consequential development may affect and which is likely to be detrimental to the image of Kent as the *Garden of England*. Although Anderson (1987) was interested in the existing planning restrictions on development in Kent, the Kent Impact Study (Channel Tunnel Joint Consultative Committee, 1986) declared that it was the local authorities and planning bodies like Kent County Council who were responsible for the environmental aspects of consequential development of the Channel Tunnel (Ardhill, 1987). The Channel Tunnel Joint Consultative Committee (1986) argued that there would be only a limited environmental impact, based on the fact that although there had been a threefold growth in the demand for cross-Channel travel since 1970, this had not generated any consequential development nor led to any dramatic change in the county's economic geography. However, the absence of a completed M20 and recent developments in Kent's economic geography reveal that distribution companies have moved towards arterial routes like the M2 for fast access to the ports and London. Ardhill concluded that the physical impact of 'the Channel Tunnel is a project of immense magnitude and

Plate 6.2   *Aerial view of Eurotunnel's French terminal site, with the town of Calais beyond, May 1991 (Courtesy of Channel Tunnel Group Ltd)*

complexity: a complexity of schemes, many of which themselves constitute by an ordinary scale a major development with profound and widespread implications' (Ardhill, 1987, p. 206), indicative of the need to look beyond the immediate environmental consequences to consider the extent to which tourism will have a long-term effect on the environment.

Tourist use of the Tunnel and the potential effects on the environment

According to Land Use Consultants (1986, p. 49) the Tunnel could affect tourism as

a potential source of employment and induced development, both of which can be regarded as positive benefits. However, unless adequately managed and controlled, tourism and recreation can create their own pressures on the physical and social environment . . . [and is] likely to increase the attraction of East Kent for foreign tourists, particularly for areas within easy reach of the terminal which can provide opportunities to relax after a potentially stressful journey.

This general assessment requires some clarification of the scale of the potential impact of tourism in relation to the number of tourists using the Tunnel once it is open. According to SETEC (1989), the traffic forecasting consultants to Eurotunnel, in 1993 they expect 15.8 million road passengers to travel through the Tunnel via the shuttle service and 13.6 million by rail, although more recent forecasts indicate somewhat reduced passenger numbers. This will virtually double the capacity for cross-Channel crossings after 1993 and the potential environmental impacts largely depend on the extent to which demand grows to fill this increased capacity and the degree of market capture by Eurotunnel of existing ferry and air traffic. The environmental consequences of tourist use of the Tunnel have been examined by Kent County Council (1990) in relation to the proposed development of a new dedicated transport corridor through Kent to London (assuming that the eventual route of the IRL is synonymous with a large part of the M20). This raises the question of how tourist use of the Tunnel can be accommodated within the existing environment and the cumulative effects of additional tourists travelling through Kent after 1993.

Table 6.4 *Environmental impact assessment of road/rail options between London and the Channel Tunnel*

OPTION 1: ADDITIONAL LANES ON M20/M25 (one lane in each direction)

Assessment

Existing motorway alignment allow for additional lanes to be constructed.
No construction costs assessed.
An additional motorway lane is assumed to have a capacity of 1,200 cars per hour
  at safe distances of 50 mph (which approximates to 6 trains per hour in one
  direction on a new rail link with a load factor of 3.85 people/car and full
  occupancy of a high speed train of 770 people).

OPTION 2: A DOUBLE-TRACK, HIGH SPEED RAILWAY, ROUTED ALONG EXISTING MOTORWAY CORRIDORS

Assessment

The rail link would approximate to one additional motorway lane in each
  direction.
Proximity to the existing motorways would minimize the environmental impacts
  compared with routing the line through a new area.
Visual, noise and vibration impacts would aggregate to produce a greater net
  impact on the existing population living near to the new 'motorway–railway'
  corridor.
The high speed railway would avoid/minimize additional noise, land take, visual
  intrusion and impacts on other areas.

OPTION 3: A TOTALLY NEW ALIGNMENT FOR A HIGH SPEED, DOUBLE-TRACK RAILWAY

Assessment

Owing to commercial and engineering attractions, the route would be planned,
  where possible, to avoid major population centres, areas of natural beauty.
The new railway would probably use the motorway corridors for part of its
  length, although it would require separate alignment in other areas, resulting in
  environmental impacts.

Source: Steer Davies and Gleave, 1989.

According to Steer Davies and Gleave (1989), to assess the environmental costs and benefits of the Tunnel and related infrastructure for tourist and non-tourist use requires an 'adoption of social costs benefit appraisal rather than the existing financial criteria associated with investment decisions associated with the project' (Steer Davies and Gleave, 1989, p. iii). Their report **The Right Tracks to Europe: The Regional and Environmental Impact of the Channel Tunnel** produced an EIA of three rail/road options for tourist and non-tourist travel between London and the Tunnel (see Table 6.4). Despite the delay in a decision on the final route for a IRL, their assessment considered a range of environmental consequences of additional infrastructure to meet traffic needs to and from the Tunnel, concluding that a new rail link built within an existing motorway corridor would have the least environmental impact. SERPLAN (1990) argued that there was a need to 'minimise the effect of Tunnel traffic on the [South-East] region's roads . . . [which] would represent a real environmental gain' and that a new rail link should have 'the highest standards of environmental protection . . . using government finance in the same way as for a major new road' (SERPLAN, 1990, p. 31).[9] Kent County Council (1990, p. 31) also acknowledged that 'environmental design and protection should always be key factors in the planning, development and importantly, in the management of transport corridors'.

Direct environmental costs of tourist use of Tunnel-related transport infrastructure

The actual impact of major road and rail infrastructure to serve Tunnel traffic has been assessed within Belgium as part of the EIA for the proposed high speed TGV link from Lille to Brussels,[10] due for completion after 1993. This provides an insight into the real environmental costs of both road and rail travel by tourists and non-tourists. The purpose of the EIA by the European Centre of Regional Development of the Walloon Region (CEDRE, 1990) was to assess the *micro-ecological effects* — the environment in which the infrastructure is to be established. The *micro-ecological effects* are of interest here because CEDRE considered the abiotic impact (e.g. changes in geology, hydrology, noise and vibration), the biological impact (e.g. on flora, fauna and the interactions between the two) and the human impact (e.g. the effect on agriculture, residential areas, traffic, transport and the human elements of the landscape). Their assessment of pollution (see Table 6.5) reveals the potential impact tourist travel may have on the environment through which they travel — in this case a dedicated transport corridor. Tourist travel by rail and road produce pollutants, though on balance, rail is considered to be the more *environmentally friendly option*, more energy-efficient and less intrusive. However, it still has a significant impact as Table 6.5 implies since it will generate much noise pollution. For this reason, CEDRE (1990) listed £40 million of environmental protection measures which would be required in Belgium when constructing the high speed link. A similar, if not more costly, set of

Table 6.5 *A comparison of pollution from the TGV and motor traffic using the motorway in Belgium*[1]

Pollutant	TVG Gram/km travelled	CAR Gram/km travelled
Sulphur dioxide[2]	0.124	0.090
Nitrous oxide[3]	0.071	1.460
Aerosol	0.044	0.049
Carbon monoxide[4]	0.005	1.109
Hydrocarbon[5]	0.002	0.179
Carbon dioxide[6]	228.907	135.000
Safety:		
Number of persons killed per billion km travelled	0.8 (train) 0 (French TGV)	20.0 (roads) 6.7 (motorway)

Notes: 1. The accuracy of the pollution measurements listed in the table will depend on the meteorological conditions and prevailing winds as to whether pollutants concentrate at particular locations or disperse over a wider area.
2. Sulphur dioxide may impair health and it contributes to acid rain as sulphuric acid.
3. Nitrous oxide is a major component in photochemical smog, and nitric acid contributes to acid rain. The major emission source is motor vehicles and power stations.
4. Although carbon monoxide does not directly cause health-related problems, it can induce complications among people suffering from cardiac-related diseases. Concentrations of carbon monoxide in confined areas is harmful as it can reduce the oxygen-carrying capacity of the blood.
5. Partially burnt hydrocarbons are carcinogenic (cancer-forming) agents and they also contribute to photochemical smog.
6. Carbon dioxide contributes to the 'greenhouse effect'.

Source: CEDRE, 1990.

measures may well be required in Kent once the IRL route is decided to minimize the environmental damage and potential pollution from tourist and non-tourist use of transport corridors.

The environmental costs and benefits of tourist use of the international passenger terminals

Visitors travelling by rail or road will also generate an environmental impact on their tourist destination(s). In London it will largely be caused by the international passenger terminal at Waterloo and the second terminal to be built at King's Cross by the year 2003. In Kent many of the direct environmental impacts will occur at the Tunnel terminal and at the Ashford international passenger terminal, which is likely to be the focus for rail and car travellers from the South-East wishing to board the Channel Tunnel rail services. The scale of the environmental impact is evident at Waterloo which expects to be able to accommodate between 9.4

and 11.1 million passenger trips per annum after 1993. The environmental impact at Waterloo and Ashford, once it is constructed, will result from increased pressure on public and private transport networks, which in London seem unlikely to be able to accommodate such a growth in demand at peak times (Touche Ross, 1988; Page and Sinclair, forthcoming).This will inevitably lead to a reduction in the quality of tourism experience for visitors and a deterioration in the immediate environment for local residents with increased pressure on car parking, accommodation and tourist service. The environmental impact of increased tourist traffic in Ashford town centre and the proposed construction of the £100 million Ashford international passenger terminal (IPT) may transform the town into a rail gateway to Europe (British Rail/YRM, 1990). Consultants for British Rail identified a problem of potential congestion in and around Ashford town centre caused by traffic generated by the IPT, which is likely to intensify between 1990 and the year 2008 in view of a predicted 45 per cent growth in rail travel from Ashford to London and European destinations (A. Gibb, 1990). Although 20 per cent and 80 per cent of the demand is likely to occur within Ashford and the wider South-East area respectively, a large proportion of tourists will arrive at the station by car. The provision of car parking and congestion may concentrate the environmental problems, especially pollution, in a small area of the town.

The indirect environmental impact of increased numbers of car tourists on tourist destinations

An associated problem relates to additional car visitors who may stop in Ashford *en route* to the Tunnel for leisure shopping and accommodation, adding to the potential congestion. Although Ashford is unlikely to suffer what Romeril (1989b, p. 105) called *saturation tourism*, which results from factors such as a seasonally induced peak in flows of tourists, other small historic towns in Kent such as Canterbury, Tunbridge Wells and the county town of Maidstone already experience some environmental changes in the peak season owing to increased numbers of visitors. The volume of tourists in towns such as Canterbury, which receives over 2.25 million visitors at the Cathedral alone, testifies to the pressure on such areas without the advent of the Channel Tunnel. Although the South-East Economic Development Strategy (1989b) pointed to the potential problems of unplanned and unmanaged tourism in a number of historic towns in the South-East, it is evident that planned visitor management strategies will not be able to overcome all of the problems, particularly once the Tunnel is open. The tourism-carrying capacity in Kentish towns like Canterbury is already nearing saturation point in the peak season, although the Tunnel **may** only have a marginal impact on visitor arrivals in view of its location in East Kent, requiring a detour from the main M20–M25 access route to and from the Tunnel. However, the Tunnel will certainly generate the potential for more tourist visits to the County of Kent after 1993: assessing where, when and the duration of these visits among domestic and overseas tourists likely to use the Fixed Link remains a difficult process since the Tunnel has not opened and there are few examples of similar projects upon which to base an estimate. Whatever locations the potential tourists visit, the existing environmental pressures and long-term sustainability of tourism at certain destinations in the South-East and London are likely to be greatly reduced if the seasonality and distribution of visitors is not extended further.

Conclusion

Environmental issues have developed a prominent role in tourism research over the last decade and the complexity of assessing the direct and indirect impacts on different localities has led to the application of research methodologies such as EIA to understand the symbiotic relationship of tourism and the environment. Although the Channel Tunnel has not yet opened, assessing the impact additional tourists will pose for the environment is an important exercise for both the private and public sectors in preparing strategies to accommodate potential changes in the patterns and processes likely to affect tourism after 1993. Large-scale tourism-related projects such as the Channel Tunnel and IRL have raised environmental awareness of the potential impact of development resulting from increases in tourism, raising short and long-term issues on the sustainability of tourism at destinations likely to be directly affected by the operation of the Tunnel. In the short term, the success of visitor management strategies in the Kentish towns and Central London will influence the ability of destinations to absorb and service the needs of additional tourists, even though the tourism environments will be under greater pressure. In the long term, the Channel Tunnel's impact on the environment raises issues of government policy and the need for an interventionist approach through additional investment in infrastructure which is in the national interest to ensure the long-term sustainability and success of tourism throughout Britain. As the BTA (1988, p. 5) argued, 'constructing a new [high speed railway] track through Kent would be expensive, cause environmental problems [but] . . . the whole nation will benefit if major cities are linked with the European high speed rail network'. The contrast in state participation in infrastructure provision for the Channel Tunnel in France and Britain may reveal inadequacies in the long-term consideration of the environmental impact of consequential Tunnel-related tourism development in Britain. Although the emphasis on the private sector construction and operation of the Tunnel may have required a detailed EIA, this was narrowly defined and unable to assess the impact on tourism. Furthermore, investment constraints in public agencies like British Rail who are charged with meeting the infrastructure needs of the Tunnel (e.g. the building of the £3.5 billion IRL) will almost inevitably lead to a greater environmental cost in pollution and the social impact of tourism congestion from increased road travel and at rail interchanges in London and Ashford. These issues should have been examined more systematically in the initial EIAs prepared in 1985 for the Channel Tunnel Group and subsequently updated with references to the restricted environmental reports prepared for British Rail in 1988 and 1989 (Environmental Resources Limited, 1988; 1989). There is a fundamental weakness in the short-term monitoring by the Kent Impact Study Team of the Channel Tunnel's impact on tourism. Moreover, inadequate co-ordination of public and private sector research on the indirect impact of the Tunnel on tourism environments has meant that the environmental impacts have been largely on the transport corridors connected with the Fixed Link. Whilst it is not possible to forecast precisely where the major tourism impacts will occur after 1993, the tourism industry does need to consider and plan for the Tunnel's opening: it must ensure that short-term economic gains are not emphasized to the detriment of the environment. This may guarantee the long-term viability of tourism throughout the United Kingdom, particularly in the South-East which is likely to experience many of the environmental costs of developing the Channel Tunnel. The extent to which South-East England will receive the benefits of a growth in tourism resulting from the Tunnel after 1993 will largely be conditioned by the provision of appropriate tourist infrastructure.

Notes

1. According to Romeril (1989b, p. 104), research on the environmental impacts of tourism 'are generally categorized under three main headings; physical, biological and socio-economic (which includes cultural) . . . [and] it is inevitable that impacts in one category do not occur in isolation but inter-relate and overlap with one another'.
2. The formulation of the EC Directive (85/337/EEC) on EIA and its subsequent adoption by the United Kingdom in July 1988 has been documented by Tomlinson (1986), Lee and Wood (1988) and Kivell (1989).
3. Other related lesser-known studies are documented in Grayson's (1990) recent bibliographical survey of the rapidly expanding literature of the Channel Tunnel.
4. EIA can be defined as a technique for assessing the likely effects of a new development prior to a project receiving planning permission and it has been described as

   the assessment of the environmental effects likely to arise from a major project (or other type of action) significantly affecting the environment. EIA is intended to form an integral part of the process formulating, evaluating and reaching a decision upon a proposed action . . . which may then be modified or even abandoned to mitigate the forecast environmental impacts. (Lee and Wood 1988b)

   while the Department of the Environment (1989, p. 3) considered it to comprise:

   a technique and process by which information about the environmental effects of a project is collected, both by the developer and from other sources, and taken into account by the planning authority in forming their judgement on whether the development should go ahead . . . the emphasis [is] on systematic analysis, using the best practicable techniques and best available sources of information, and on the presentation of information in a form which provides a focus for public scrutiny of the project and enables the importance of the predicted effects, and the scope for magnifying or mitigating them.

5. The development and application of EIA as a method of environmental analysis has been extensively documented in the United States where it is used in the environmental review (Goodenough, 1983). More recently, the application and use of EIA has been examined in the United Kingdom (Wathern, 1990; Clarke and Hetherington, 1988) as a direct result of the adoption of EC Directive (85/337/EEC).
6. The French EIAs on the Channel Tunnel were prepared as part of the public inquiry on the project, although as Anderson (1987) has shown, EIAs have been obligatory in France since 1976 for large projects.
7. Some eighteen specialist studies on the environmental effects of the Tunnel were produced and subsequently audited by Environmental Resources Limited (1985) and the interrelationships between these specialist studies were presented in the summary volume as an overview of the environmental impact. Once construction of the Tunnel commenced, a further twenty specialist studies were undertaken in 1986–7, referred to as the baseline studies. All of these reports can be consulted at the Eurotunnel Exhibition Centre Library, St Martin's Plain, Cheriton, near Folkestone, Kent.
8. Although British Rail commissioned Environmental Resources Limited in 1988 and 1989 to undertake a number of EIAs of the construction of a high speed rail link between the Channel Tunnel and London, these have remained confidential owing to the highly sensitive nature of the contents. The Secretary of State for Transport also announced in Parliament (1 July 1991) that once the preferred route of the high speed rail link from London to the Channel Tunnel was announced, it would be subject to a full EIA, thereby leading to a further set of EIA studies which will also have to be audited.
9. Under Section 42 of the Channel Tunnel Act the government is prevented from investing public money in a new rail link, although it is not restricted in providing funding for environmental safeguards and protection.
10. In Belgium, this was the first major infrastructure project to be preceded by an EIA.

References

Anderson M.A., 1987, 'Planning and environmental considerations: position paper and discussion', in C.H. Church (ed.), *Approaching the Channel Tunnel*, University Association for Contemporary European Studies, Kings College, London, pp. 34–55.

Ardhill, J., 1987, 'The environmental impact', in B. Jones (ed.), *The Tunnel: The Channel Tunnel and Beyond*, Ellis Horwood, Chichester, pp. 177–212.

Barre, A., 1988, 'Le Tunnel sous la Manche: une nouvelle donne pur l'aménagement régional', *Hommes et Terres du Nord*, 1–2: pp. 6–12.

Boo, E., 1990, *Ecotourism: The Potentials and Pitfalls*, World Wildlife Fund, Washington DC.

British Railways Board/YRM, 1990, *Ashford International Passenger Station and British Railways Development Sites: Environmental Statement*, YRM Architects and Planners, London.

Brown, P.D. and Goss, A., 1987, *The Channel Tunnel and the London Region*, Council for the Protection of Rural England.

Buchanan, C.R.S., 1988, 'The impact of the Channel Tunnel', *Tourism Management*, 9(4): pp. 330–1.
Budowski, G., 1976, 'Tourism and environmental conservation: conflict, coexistence or symbiosis', *Environmental Conservation*, 3(1): pp. 27–31.
Button, K., 1990, 'The Channel Tunnel—the economic implications for the South East of England', *Geographical Journal*, 156(2): pp. 187–99.
CEDRE, 1990, *Transports à grande vitesse: développement régional et aménagement du territoire, rapport de synthèse*, Centre Européen du Développement Régional, Strasburg.
Chaplin, M., 1990, 'The silent jungle: ecotourism among the King Indians of Panama', *Cultural Survival Quarterly*, 14(i): pp. 42–5.
Charlton, C. and Essex, S., 1989, *The Impact of the Far South West with particular Reference to Devon and Cornwall: Tourism*, Poly Enterprises Ltd, Plymouth.
Clarke, M. and Hetherington, J., 1989, *The Role of Environmental Impact Assessment in the Planning Process*, Mansell, London.
Cohen, E., 1978, 'The impact of tourism on the physical environment', *Annals of Tourism Research*, 5: pp. 215–37.
Council for the Protection of Rural England, 1985, *The Channel Fixed Link: What Price for the Countryside? Evidence Submitted to Select Committee on Transport*, Council for the Protection of Rural England, London.
Department of Employment, 1991, *Tourism and the Environment: Maintaining the Balance*, HMSO, London.
Department of the Environment, 1989, *Environmental Assessment: A Guide to the Procedures*, HMSO, London.
Department of Transport, 1988, *Transport and the Environment*, HMSO, London.
Elkin, T.J. and Smith, P.G.R., 1988, 'What is a good environmental impact statement? Reviewing screening reports from Canada's National Parks', *Journal of Environmental Management*, 26: pp. 71–89.
Environmental Resources Ltd, 1985, *Environmental Effects in the UK: Environmental Assessors' Report*, Channel Tunnel Group, London.
Environmental Resources Ltd, 1988, *Channel Tunnel Phase 3 Study: Stage 3 Final Report*, British Railways Board, London.
Environmental Resources Ltd, 1989, *Second Channel Tunnel Terminal: Environmental and Planning Considerations*, Channel Tunnel Rail Link Project, London.
Farrell, B.H. and Runyan, R.W., 1987, 'Tourism and physical environment research', *Annals of Tourism Research*, 14: pp. 1–16.
Farrell, B.H. and Runyan, R.W., 1991, 'Ecology and tourism', *Annals of Tourism Research*, 18: pp. 26–40.
Gibb, A., 1990, *Ashford International Passenger Station: Traffic Impact Study, Volume 1*, Alexander Gibb, London.
Gibb, R., 1986, 'The impact of the Channel Tunnel rail link on South East England', *Geographical Journal*, 139(2): pp. 255–77.
Gibb, R., 1988, 'Geographic implications of the Channel Tunnel', *Geography Review*, 2(2): pp. 2–13.
Gibb, R., 1989, *The Impact of the Channel Tunnel on the Far South West*, Poly Enterprises Ltd, Plymouth.
Goodenough, R., 1983, 'Recent developments in California's environmental review process—an evaluation of the use of environmental impact reports', *International Journal of Environmental Studies*, 20: pp. 181–90.
Grayson, L., 1990, (ed.), *Channel Tunnel—Le Tunnel sous la Manche*, The British Library, London.

Holder, J.S., 1988, 'Pattern and impact of tourism on the environment of the Caribbean', *Tourism Management*, 9(2): pp. 119–27.

Holliday, I., Marcou, G. and Vickerman, R., 1991, *The Channel Tunnel: Public Policy, Regional Development and European Integration*, Belhaven, London.

Holliday, I. and Vickerman, R., 1990, 'The Channel Tunnel and regional development: policy responses in Britain and France', *Regional Studies*, 24: pp. 455–66.

House of Commons Select Committee on the Channel Tunnel Bill, 1986, *Minutes of Evidence*, HMSO, London.

Jefferson, A., 1992, '1993 Cross-Channel opportunities', in C.P. Cooper (ed.), Volume Four, *Progress in Tourism Recreation and Hospitality Management*, Belhaven, London.

Kay, J., Manning, A. and Szymanski, S., 1989, 'Economic benefits of the Channel Tunnel', *Economic Policy*, April: pp. 212–34.

Kent County Council, 1988, *Kent County Council and the Channel Tunnel*, Kent County Council, Maidstone.

Kent County Council, 1986, *The Channel Tunnel and the Future of Kent*, Kent County Council, Maidstone.

Kent County Council, 1990, *The Transport Challenge: A New Approach for Kent*, Kent County Council, Maidstone.

Kivell, P., 1989, 'Protecting the Euro-environment', *Geography*, 74(1): pp. 47–52.

Krippendorf, J., 1986, 'Tourism in the system of industrial society', *Annals of Tourism Research*, 13: pp. 393–414.

Land Use Consultants, 1985, *The Channel Fixed Link: Environmental Appraisal of Alternative Proposals. A Report Prepared for the Department of Transport*, HMSO, London.

Lee, N. and Wood, C., 1978, 'Environmental impact assessment of projects in EEC countries', *Journal of Environmental Management*, 6: pp. 57–71.

Lee, N. and Wood, C., 1980, 'Environmental impact assessment in the EEC', *Environmental Impact Assessment Review*, 1(3): pp. 287–300.

Lee, N. and Wood, C., 1988, 'The European Directive on environmental impact assessment: implementation at last?', *The Environmentalist*, 9(3): pp. 177–86.

McMillan-Scott, E., 1990, 'The growth of tourism: can the environment cope?', in M. Quest (ed.), *The Horwath Book of Tourism*, Macmillan, London, 240–9.

Manning-Shaw, J., 1991, 'The Channel Tunnel', *Tourism Management*, 12(1): pp. 5–8.

Mitchell, I., 1986, 'The missing link', *Landscape Design*, 159(2) pp. 4–5.

Mauroy, P., 1988, 'Tunnel sous la Manche, TGV nord-européen, une opportunité pour le développement d'une métropole régionale à l'éhelle européenne', *Hommes et Terres du Nord*, 1–2: pp. 30–1.

Page, S. and Sinclair, M.T., forthcoming: 'The Channel Tunnel: an opportunity for London's tourism industry?', *Tourism Recreation Research*.

Pearce, D., 1985, 'Tourism and environmental research: a review', *International Journal of Environmental Studies*, 25(4): pp. 247–55.

Pigram, J.J., 1980, 'Environmental implications of tourism development', *Annals of Tourism Research*, 7: pp. 554–83.

Pigram, J.J., 1990, 'Sustainable tourism—policy considerations', *Journal of Tourism Studies*, 1(2): pp. 2–9.

Place, S.E., 1991, 'Nature tourism and rural development in Tortuguero', *Annals of Tourism Research*, 18: pp. 186–201.

Poon, A., 1989, 'Competitive strategies for a "new tourism"', in C. Cooper (ed.), *Progress in Tourism, Recreation and Hospitality Management*, Volume One, Belhaven, London, 90–102.

Romeril, M., 1985, 'Tourism and the environment—towards a symbiotic relationship', *International Journal of Environmental Studies*, 25: pp. 215–8.

Romeril, M., 1989a, 'Tourism and the environment—accord or discord?', *Tourism Management*, 10(3): pp. 204–8.

Romeril, M., 1989b 'Tourism—the environmental dimension', in C. Cooper (ed.), *Progress in Tourism, Recreation and Hospitality Management*, Volume One, Belhaven Press, London, 103–13.

Ross, W.A., 1987, 'Evaluating environmental impact statements', *Journal of Environmental Management*, 25: pp. 137–47.

SERPLAN, 1989, *The Channel Tunnel: Impact on the South East Region*, SERPLAN, London.

SERPLAN, 1990, *The Channel Tunnel Monitor*, SERPLAN, London.

SETEC/Wilbur Smith Associates, 1989, *Review of Market Trends and Forecasts*, Eurotunnel, Paris.

Sevrin, R., 1988, 'Le TGV à travers le Hainaut Occidental', *Hommes et Terres du Nord*, 1–2: pp. 70–3.

Smith, C. and Jenner, P., 1989, 'Tourism and the environment', *Travel and Tourism Analyst*, 5: pp. 68–86.

Smith, V. and Eadington, W. (eds), forthcoming, 'Tourism Alternatives: Perspectives on the Future of Tourism.

South-East Economic Development Strategy, 1989a, *The Last Resort: Tourism, Tourist Employment and Post Tourism in the South East*, SEEDS, London.

South-East Economic Development Strategy, 1989b, *The French Connection: The Impact of the Channel Tunnel on the South East*, SEEDS, London.

Steer Davies and Gleave Ltd, 1989, *The Right Tracks to Europe: The Regional and Environmental Impact of the Channel Tunnel*, Transport 2000, London.

Sullivan, M.A., 1989, *How Green is your Railway? High Speed Railway Construction and the Environment: Lessons from Europe*, Council for Protection of Rural England, London.

Therain, P., 1989, 'Tunnel sous la Manche et tourisme: l'Euro-région sort du Tunnel', *Espaces*, 96: pp. 20–2.

Tomlinson, P., 1986, 'Environmental assessment in the UK: the EC Directive', *Town Planning Review*, 57(4): pp. 458–86.

Touche Ross, 1988, *London Tourism Impact Study*, Touche Ross, London.

Travis, A., 1988, 'Alternative tourism', *Naturopa*, 59: pp. 25–7.

Turner, T. (ed.), 1988, *Sustainable Environmental Management*, Westview Press, Boulder.

Vasseur, J., 1988, 'Tunnel TGV nord-européen: une opportunité pour la localisation d'enterprises nouvelles et le développement régional de la Picardie', *Hommes et Terres du Nord*, 1–2: pp. 89–91.

Vickerman, R., 1987, 'The Channel Tunnel: consequences for regional growth and development', *Regional Studies*, 21: pp. 187–97.

Vickerman, R. and Flowerdew, A., 1990, *The Channel Tunnel: Economic and Regional Impact*, Economist Intelligence Unit, London.

Whitelegg, J., 1988, *Transport Policy in the EEC*, Routledge, London.

Wathern, P., 1990, *Environmental Impact Assessment: Theory and Practice*, Unwin Hyman, London.

Williams, P.W., 1987, 'Evaluating environmental impact on physical carrying capacity in tourism', in J.R.B. Ritchie *et al.* (eds), *Travel, Tourism and Hospitality Research*, Wiley, New York, 385–97.

Wood, K. and House, S., 1991, *The Good Tourist: A Worldwide Guide for the Green Traveller*, Mandarin, London.

7 Tourism development along beaches and waterfronts: the Portuguese situation

A. da Rosa Pires and C.M.M. Costa

Tourism development in Portugal

Tourism plays an important and highly strategic role in the Portuguese economy. In fact, tourism accounts for about 20 per cent of foreign exchange earnings and contributes significantly to the equilibrium of the balance of payments. It is worth stressing that the Portuguese trade balance is traditionally in deficit and that both tourism earnings and emigrants' remittances make an important and decisive contribution to restoring the equilibrium of the balance of payments. Furthermore, tourism is estimated to be responsible for about 4 per cent of total employment in Portugal and just over 6 per cent of the gross domestic product (for a comparative overview of the relevance of tourism in southern European countries see Yannopoulos, 1988).

In Portugal the importance of tourism has grown gradually though steadily during the last three decades and particularly since the late 1970s (Tables 7.1 and 7.2). The exception is the period between 1973 and 1976 in which the combined effects of the first oil crisis and the 1974 revolutionary coup in Portugal produced a drastic reduction in tourist flows (Table 7.1). In fact, despite some early attention to the tourism phenomenon (the Tourism Directorate was created in the Ministry of Development as early as 1911), it acquired economic significance only in the 1960s. Until then, tourism was basically confined to the national market, relying on spas scattered throughout the country and on a few selected, affluent tourist resorts on the west coast. After World War II, however, tourism flows and particularly international tourism flows started to increase, showing a fivefold rise from 76,000 in 1950 to 352,000 in 1960. It was in the 1960s, however, that tourism growth really *took-off*: by 1967 the number of international arrivals was already just below 2.5 million (Cavaco, 1970; Ribeiro, 1990).

This sudden and large increase in tourism flows was associated with major changes in both the dominant forms and nature of tourism as well as in the main tourist destinations. Indeed, following the world-wide trend towards mass tourism, it was the sea, sand and sun factor (i.e., sunlust-type tourism) which became hegemonic and shifted the location of the main tourist destination areas to the southern coast (the Algarve). There, low

Table 7.1 *International arrivals in Portugal*

Year	Number of arrivals (millions)
1970	3.44
1971	3.87
1972	3.92
1973	4.08
1974	2.62
1975	1.97
1976	2.18
1977	2.97
1978	3.39
1979	5.29
1980	6.98
1981	7.28
1982	7.30
1983	8.88
1984	9.81
1985	11.69
1986	13.06
1987	16.17
1988	16.08

Table 7.2 *International tourism arrivals in Portugal*

Year	Number of arrivals (millions)
1979	2.26
1980	2.71
1981	3.02
1982	3.16
1983	3.71
1984	4.12
1985	4.99
1986	5.41
1987	6.10
1988	6.62

costs, a beautiful and (then) unspoilt landscape, the calm and warm waters and a Mediterranean climate, to which a regional airport was added in the mid-1960s, combined to make the Algarve a very attractive tourist destination. With the exception of the coast around Lisbon, the traditional west coast resorts gradually lost much of their importance. This was particularly true around Cascais and Estoril.

In the early 1990s, the Algarve region alone accounts for about 40 per cent of all Portuguese bedspaces in the hotel sector (i.e., hotels, motels, *pousadas*, *estalagens* and boarding-houses). Perhaps more significantly, the Algarve claims 49 per cent of all international tourist bednights in the hotel sector. If one adds to this analysis the Lisbon coastal region, then 10 per cent of the national territory (coast of Lisbon plus Algarve) accounts for 60 per cent of all the bedspaces in the hotel sector and 70 per cent of international tourist bednights (Figure 7.1). This geographically unbalanced pattern of tourism growth is just one consequence of its spontaneous nature. In fact, a striking feature of tourism development throughout the last decades is the absence of a meaningful policy framework, at both the national and at the regional levels.

Only in the mid-1980s was a first tentative effort made to establish a global policy framework for tourism development. That was done through the preparation of the National Tourism Plan 1986–9. This document contained a wide-ranging analysis of the tourism phenomenon, aiming to assess its articulation with, and role within, the wider process of regional development. In the plan different forms of tourism were considered, as well as their social, economic and environmental implications. Furthermore, their different geographical settings and policy requirements were to a varying extent also taken into account, and a targeted policy framework did emerge from such proposals. Nevertheless, the implementation of the plan was fraught with difficulties and many policy measures and recommendations can hardly be said to have become effective. More importantly, the expected review of the Plan, which was due in 1991 has not yet been completed.

The Portuguese tourism administrative structure

In Portugal, tourism is represented at government level by a **Secretary of State** under the **Minister of Trade and Tourism**. However, in the recent past (until 1987) the **Secretary of State for Tourism** (STT) was directly answerable to the Prime Minister, on account of the interaction of tourism matters with many other departments. The institutional association between tourism and trade, which still remains a controversial issue, can partly be explained by the structure of the Department of Trade which supports and promotes, to a large extent, the tourism marketing and promotional activities abroad.

The STT has under its direct dependence several departments, the most important of which is the **Directorate General for Tourism** (DGT). The DGT has the responsibility of supervising and co-ordinating almost all fields of tourist activity and is supported by a large administrative structure (see Costa, 1991; for a further development of this issue). In parallel, there are other departments concerned with more specific areas, namely training (**National Institute for Tourism Training**), promotion (**Institute of Tourism**

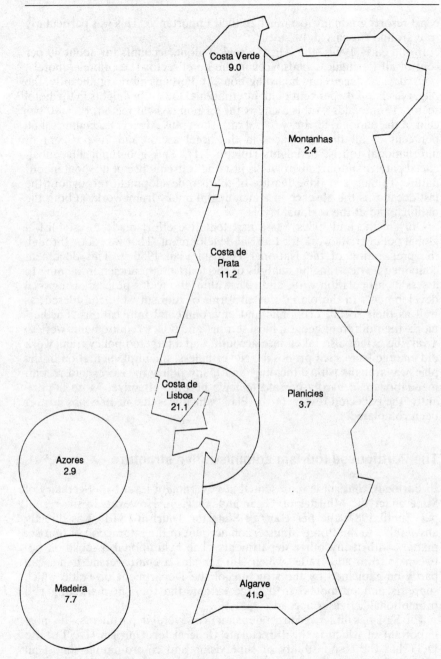

Figure 7.1 *Bednights spent in all means of accommodation (by tourism promotional regions, 1988)*

Source: Directorate General For Tourism, Lisbon, 1991

Promotion), financing (**Fund of Tourism**), gambling (**General Inspectorate of Gambling**), and the management and planning of public interests in the tourism field, such as the *pousadas* (**National Enterprise of Tourism**).

At the regional level, the main administrative agents are the **Regional Tourist Boards** (RTBs). The RTBs are based upon the voluntary association of municipalities, and their structure includes an executive as well as a regional commission. In the latter, the majority of the seats belong to the municipalities who created the RTB, and the other seats are taken by public and private agents who are seen to have an important role in regional tourism development. It is this regional commission who elects the executive commission. The RTBs are economic and administratively autonomous and constitute a quite widespread phenomenon in Portugal, consisting of more than 200 of the 304 Portuguese municipalities. There are in fact nineteen RTBs which cover about 80 per cent of the Portuguese territory. Their main sources of finance are a given proportion of the receipts of the (regional) tourism VAT and gambling activity. Although the relevant legislation allows for a wide scope of intervention, the lack of financial and technical resources leads the RTBs to intervene mainly in the promotion and support of regional tourist attractions and activities. The planning and development functions remain largely untouched.

At the local level there is a third type of voluntary tourism organization, the **Junta de Turismo**, which tends to exist only in municipalities, or in a very small group of municipalities, where the tourism phenomenon is not only very important but is also rooted in a very specific issue (e.g., local gastronomy, local history/culture). The first **Juntas of Tourism** were established more than half a century ago, and indeed the current survival of some of them must also be explained by the weight of tradition. Lack of resources is again of crucial importance to understand their main role: to provide information locally and carry out promotion. The more recent legislation concerning the regional and local levels of tourism organization (Law Decree 287/91) favours the integration of the Juntas into the RTBs.

One of the most striking issues of tourism administrative structures in Portugal is the lack of management and planning functions at regional and local levels. Furthermore, this absence is compounded by the lack of a coherent and guiding policy framework at national level, as mentioned before. Thus, the longstanding passive attitude towards the highly unbalanced geographical pattern of tourism growth should not come as a surprise. The problem, however, is that this standpoint has resulted on the one hand, in the underuse of natural (tourism) resources in many regions, which means that the national tourism potential has not been fully realized. On the other hand, it has also produced a very high dependence upon a specific type of tourism (sunlust travel) and, almost inevitably severe congestion in certain tourist destinations. As is well known, these circumstances can easily result in the destruction of the very conditions which sustained the original impetus of tourism growth. In other words, the lack of both a coherent development strategy at national level and of a decentralized and institutionalized policy on tourism development can have important repercussions not only at national but also at the local/regional level. This is particularly true in areas subjected to very high growth pressures, such as the Algarve, an example which will be examined in greater detail below.

Coastal tourism development: the Algarve

The development of the Algarve as a tourist resort started in the early 1960s. Then, a few high quality hotels were built during the opening up of the country to foreign investment and interests by a hitherto strictly nationalist Portuguese corporatist regime. The high quality standards of these early initiatives were to become the international hallmark of the Algarve. It was at this time that the regional School for Hotel Studies was created, a fact whose importance was reinforced by the government's requirement to the applicants for investment funds to employ a minimum number of persons trained in the school. Also in the 1960s, the regional airport (in Faro) started to operate, giving a new impetus to tourism development.

In the 1970s the basic characteristics of growth were maintained and consolidated through the emergence of a new form of quality tourism: the *tourist villages*. Although this concept was initially developed in Sardinia, according to Horácio Cavaco (1990), the chairman of the Regional Tourist Board, 'the Algarve was the first region to adapt it fully to tourism development'. Between 1974 and 1977 there was a marked reduction in tourist flows, for reasons already referred to above; however, the Algarve eventually recovered from that situation.

The 1980s are seen by many as the period of the breakdown of the high quality model of tourism development in the Algarve. Some even argue, as Cavaco (1990) does, that one should speak of *building industry* expansion rather than *tourism* expansion. According to Cavaco, bedspaces mushroomed in the Algarve from 78,000 in 1980 to an estimated quarter of a million ten years later, although, as Pinto (1991) points out, only about a third of them are officially registered. This property boom took place in the almost total absence of, or lack of commitment to, a guiding policy framework. Silva and Silva (1990) argue that the almost total dependence on foreign tourism operators selling 'transport and accommodation' packages, whose competitiveness was often based on low prices, not only contributed significantly to this property boom but also had a detrimental impact on the nature and quality standards of tourism development. Environmental quality and urban design were clearly sacrificed to the ever-rising demand for (non-serviced) accommodation. Not surprisingly, Silva and Silva (1990) notice that by the end of the decade, the regional employment profile does reveal a clear deficit of skilled labour.

It can be said, then, that the rapid and intensive development of the Algarve in the 1980s took place in an unplanned and disorderly way. In these circumstances, much of this development damaged, and in some instances definitively disrupted, the image of high quality tourism which underpinned that very development. In fact, there has never been an effective policy framework covering:

1. the forms of tourism that were desired;
2. the specific requirements of such forms;
3. the kind of policies that should be pursued to satisfy those requirements;
4. the way in which other development proposals should be dealt with in order not to endanger such requirements; and
5. the administrative and institutional apparatus which should support the implementation and enforcement of the necessary policy measures.

Some of the most obvious and visible consequences of this situation will be only briefly examined here.

Two of the first victims of the spontaneous and uncontrolled growth are the the urban form and the urban structure. It is interesting to note that four out of the sixteen municipalities which constitute the Algarve region concentrate 80 per cent of the tourist bednights of the Algarve. Indeed, building densities in particular places reach unacceptable levels. Furthermore, the issues of urban and environmental design are ostensibly forgotten in many areas. The wall effect at the seafront without any provision of open space, the emergence of high-rise hotels without any concern for the surrounding area and the provision of basic infrastructures are two examples of the disregard for basic amenities. The ways in which the *new* and the *old* urban fabric were integrated and the articulation between new developments and existing infrastructure also leaves much to be desired: the task of managing and producing urban change in a rapidly changing environment without well-thought and clearly-framed policy objectives and guidelines can hardly achieve satisfactory results.

A further and no less important consequence of the anarchic growth of the 1980s is the lack of concern for landscape planning and the disrespect for the natural resources and conditions. In fact, many of the new developments are not only aesthetically unpleasant but also damage the environment to an extent that can endanger the very security of buildings and people. Of course, one can also find in the Algarve the opposite situation. In some areas, the issues of urban design and structure were duly considered, housing density and building standards were well thought out and the provision of infrastructure, open space and supporting services were taken into account. Curiously, most of these good examples correspond either to some of the early (comprehensive) development projects or to a late reaction to the concrete jungle into which some places in the Algarve were turned mainly during the last decade.

Indeed, local and regional authorities as well as many other social and economic agents are increasingly aware of the need to establish and shape in a different way the tourism product on offer in the Algarve. The aim is to go beyond the sun, sand and sea formula and to diversify tourism attractions. This can be achieved not only through a better living environment but also by offering activities ranging from learning a sport or a typical craft to visiting walking in the surrounding hills of the inland (and yet unspoilt) areas of the Algarve. The promotion of local specificity is also a growing concern. To this end, the local cultural and historical heritage is being rediscovered, reassessed and revitalized. The promotion of local gastronomy is a good example of this. However, undoubtedly more important is the decision to create an open-air museum dedicated to the Discoveries period, which is going to be located near Sagres, where the Nautical School of the legendary Prince Henry is said to have existed.

This product diversification, which includes the cultural component as we have seen, will necessarily require an upgrading of skills. It is no coincidence that the regional and new University of Algarve, like some others in Portugal for that matter, is already promoting higher education studies on tourism. The overall attitude towards tourism is certainly changing in Portugal. Meanwhile, however, many local authorities are now learning to cope with, and possibly others have not yet realized, the social, environmental and economic costs of a mono-product model of tourism growth. The high capital investment in the expansion of infrastructures and the heavy current spending on the maintenance of those infrastructures and the associated support services still constitute for many a hidden cost of tourism development.

Conclusion

The history of the Algarve as an international tourism resort shows that although central government provided initially some support a high quality model of tourism, it was unable or unwilling to maintain it when the Algarve experienced a period of spontaneous and intensive growth. The passive attitude taken by the government in the face of a huge and uncontrolled growth in tourism is certainly not unrelated to the strategic role of tourism in the Portuguese economy as a provider of much needed foreign exchange earnings. This constitutes a good illustration of the different and sometimes conflicting interests inherent in tourism development. It is increasingly recognized, however, that a full appreciation of these interests must not be devoid of time-scale considerations.

The unplanned and disorderly way in which tourism growth took place not only exacerbates the negative impacts of tourism and reduces competitiveness, so endangering growth prospects, but also places a very heavy burden on local authorities. On the one hand, they are blamed for not having fulfilled their role of safeguarding public amenities in both the natural and the built environment. On the other hand, they are faced with the need to engage in very high levels of capital and current spending for the creation and maintenance of public infrastructures and related support services—which remain in fact underutilized for most of the year. One of the key mechanisms by which Local Authorities are affected by the pressures and consequences of tourism growth is the physical planning system (Portas, 1989). It is the granting or the refusal of planning permissions which ultimately influences the quality of the living environment, although it is obvious that it also depends on the (aggregate) quality of the individual development proposals. Furthermore, the existence of a well-structured planning framework and clearly defined planning guidelines does favour the emergence of conforming development proposals. Nevertheless, without a clearly defined tourism policy, it is very unlikely that local authorities can endorse and practise adequate and effective planning.

However, few would disagree that a coherent tourism policy cannot be defined exclusively at local authority level. It is also true that local authorities cannot be excluded from policy formation. Indeed, the effectiveness of a tourism policy requires a broader and inter-sectoral policy attitude and local authorities are strategically positioned to assume such an attitude. As the Algarve experience clearly illustrates, development proposals *a priori* classified as *tourism* proposals are only a small part of the more complex but decisive process of urban change. There is also an interdependence between the local and the regional and/or the central levels of the state. This relationship must be recognized and developed, both administratively and institutionally.

In addition to the situation portrayed above is the argument that planning powers do not rely exclusively on local authorities. In the littoral areas, maritime authorities also have a role to play in the change of land use. The conclusion, then, is that as well as the *vertical* links suggested above, an effective tourism policy requires the establishment of *horizontal* links. These links should also bring together state and private agencies. It was mentioned before how the strategies of tourism operators based upon short-term objectives led to negative impacts which endanger the sustainability of development prospects. To exploit an area and then move somewhere else when resources in that particular area are exhausted, although having some logic from a strictly business perspective, is totally unacceptable from a community as well as from a long-term economic point of view. Indeed, although tourism development is highly dependent upon private enterprise, the use of public amenities inevitably induces the state to perform an intervening role. The enhancement of a sensitive private tourism sector (through, for instance, organization building and the upgrading of tourism management skills) becomes of key importance in the establishment of a fruitful partnership between the state and private enterprise. These considerations, if taken together with the realization of the fragmented nature of the tourism industry, lead to a different and complementary type of argument, that of the need to create a *tourism culture*.

By *tourism culture* one means a socio-political and economic environment in which the tourism phenomenon, with its several and diversified dimensions, is known and understood in greater depth and by a larger number of people than has been so hitherto. To that end, and as Vitorino also argues, one should start by establishing tourism as a scientific and research priority at the higher education level. This would certainly constitute, *inter alia*, a political recognition by the state of the need to raise and widen the awareness of the determinants, requirements and impacts of tourism growth. Indeed, such an educational priority and co-ordinated effort to enlarge and upgrade skills for tourism management is fully justified given (1) the diversity and plurality of the agents who directly or indirectly participate in or influence tourism; (2) the cross-sectoral nature of tourism industry; and, last but not the least, (3) the scale and range of the impacts of tourism development. In this sense, the emergence of a *tourism culture*, meaning a wider awareness of the nature of the tourism phenomenon and an enhanced ability to deal with its dynamics and consequences, should be raised as a central concern in any comprehensive attempt to create, develop and implement an effective tourism policy.

References

Cavaco, H., 1990, 'O Algarve Precisava de uma Crise a Sério . . .' (The Algarve was in need of a real crisis . . .), *Turismohotel*, *116*, pp. 54–64.

Costa, C.M.M., 1991, 'Planning for Tourism in Portugal: a Comparison Between the Tourist Organization in Portugal and England', unpublished MSc thesis, University of Surrey, Guilford.

Pinto, F. M. (1991) *Turismo Algarvio e Estratégia de Crescimento* (Tourism in Algarve and a Development Strategy), Comissão de Coordenação Regional do Algarve, Faro.

Portas, N., 1989, 'O Desenho Urbano em Situações de Costa' (Urban Design in Coastal Resorts), paper presented at a Conference on O Ordenamento do Território e o Turismo, organized by the Sociedade Portuguesa de Urbanistas, 26–8 October, Lagos.

Ribeiro, P.H.R.M., 1990, O Desenvolvimento de Actividades de Recreio e Turismo (The Development of Leisure and Tourism Activities), mimeo, Department of Environment and Planning, University of Aveiro, Aveiro.

Silva, J.B. and Silva, J.V., 1990, 'Algarve: Crescimento Turístico e Estruturação de um Espaço Regional (Algarve: Tourism Development and the Structuring of a Regional Environment), Paper presented at the 30th European Congress of the Regional Science Association, 28–31 August, Istambul.

Yannopoulos, G.N. 1988, 'Tourism, Economic Convergence and the European South', *Estudos de Economia*, *8*, 197–216.

8 Impacts of tourism on indigenous communities — the Australian case

P.C. Reynolds

Introduction

Over the post-war period, tourism in Australia has grown to become an important economic, social and cultural activity. Growth in inbound tourism in recent years has been rapid, and foreign exchange earnings from tourism now exceed those from wool or coal. It is estimated that tourism contributed 5.1 per cent ($A23.4 billion) to Australia's GDP in 1989–90, of which 72 per cent was attributed to domestic tourism.

The effect of the growth of foreign interest is potentially significant from a cultural impact perspective. It is important for tourism that Australia's cultural authenticity be preserved, rather than for it to be manipulated or swamped by external influences. At the same time it should not be trivialized by being turned into a tourism commodity, but should be seen as a genuine national asset.

Participation in tourism has been identified as a potential major source of economic growth for Aboriginal and Torres Strait Islander communities. However, these opportunities may have negative impacts on the quality of life in these communities and therefore require careful management. There are five principal areas of participation in tourism for Aboriginal people: employment, investment, the arts and crafts industry, cultural tours and joint ventures. None of the five is without its problems for Aboriginal participants. For example the impact of tourism on the natural environment is often linked to concerns about Aboriginal heritage protection for sites of religious, historical and archaeological significance (Sullivan, 1984; Gale and Jacobs, 1987). If tourism is going to continue to grow, it must be managed in an ecologically and culturally sustainable way to protect the very heritage that the traveller has come to see. This chapter therefore concentrates on the impacts of tourism upon Aboriginals in remote areas, rather than urban dwellers.

The social and cultural impacts of tourism

It is hard for a people who are trying to come to terms with the twentieth century to realise that what the twentieth century wants from them is their primitiveness.

(Manager of the Tjapukai Aboriginal Dance group in *The First Australians*, ABC television 28 November 1991)

The Australian tourism industry makes considerable use of Aboriginal culture in advertising and promoting the country as a tourist destination. Ironically, Aboriginal people have had minimal employment in the industry themselves.

The Australian tourism industry relies on Aboriginal culture which, in reality, is not as accessible as promotional activity indicates. Furthermore, it seems that while the industry clearly profits from its promotion of Aboriginal culture, it generally does not seem to acknowledge any such transaction (Birgin, 1991; Kesteven, 1987). Many Aboriginal people have negative associations with tourism. These associations originate in past and present experiences. In the 1970s Aboriginal participation was generally of a *passive* nature and was largely exploitive. Secondly, non-Aboriginal people were interpreting Aboriginal culture to tourists, often offending Aboriginal people in the process (Altman, 1988, 1989b; Bosselman, 1978).

Impacts of tourism on Aboriginal communities

Some studies of Aboriginal tourism highlight specific impacts of tourism on Aboriginal communities. Ecological perspectives recognize the potential for tourism to diminish the quality of life in Aboriginal communities. Assessments often concentrate on environmental impacts that negatively affect traditional economic activities, such as hunting and gathering, and how such negative effects might, in turn, affect the cultural fabric of Aboriginal community life. Dillon (1987) argues that if Aboriginality is viewed as a tradeable commodity, this might provide grounds for financial compensation when cultural impacts impinge on Aboriginal identity and lifestyle.

Traditional Aboriginal society does not have any equivalent to tourism, and this has to be recognized as a major obstacle to participation in the industry. Aboriginal people tend to be reluctant to *appear* in public. Tourism can threaten the nature of traditional culture to the detriment of Aborigines themselves. This is especially possible if the Aborigines concerned are not empowered in decision-making over what and how tourism occur.

The impact of Western culture poses many problems for the Aborigines. Although issues such as education, health and housing are important to Aborigines and non-Aborigines alike, the approach in addressing these issues must be different, for there are remarkably different specific issues which cause concern (Miller *et al.*, 1985). In practice it is important to recognize that all domains of Aboriginal life and the diverse impacts of tourism are neither discrete nor easily separated from each other, even for analytical purposes. Furthermore, research indicates that impacts vary from case to case (Altman 1989b; Birgin 1991).

Aboriginal participation in tourism

The Royal Commission into Aboriginal Deaths in Custody: National Report (Commonwealth of Australia, 1991) identifies Aboriginal participation in tourism as a potentially major source of economic growth for aboriginal communities. The report acknowledges that these opportunities are likely to have negative impacts on the quality of life in these communities and would therefore require careful management. The Royal Commission reviews the literature and identifies five principal areas of participation for Aboriginal people:

Employment.   Employment opportunities exist in the tourism industry for Aboriginal people, in both service provision to tourists and in national parks.

Investment.   Aboriginal communities could invest in enterprises which service the tourist industry. A notable example of such investment is the Gagudju Association which holds sole equity in the Four Seasons Cooinda Hotel and Four Seasons Crocodile Motel, both in Kakadu National Park in the Northern Territory. Purchase of the property was financed from mining royalties paid as 'areas affected' moneys with respect to the Ranger Uranium Mine at Jabiru (Altman, 1988).

The arts and crafts industry.   In some Aboriginal communities indirect participation in tourism is a preferred option. This is possible via the arts and crafts industry. A successful enterprise such as the community-owned Maruku Arts and Crafts in Uluru National Parks in the Northern Territory is an exemplary model for this form of enterprise (Altman, 1989a). However, in general, Aboriginal participation in the arts and crafts industry has had varying commercial success. A primary concern for the artists and their promoters is whether to produce material for the fine art market or the tourist market (Altman, 1989a; Finlayson, 1990). Funding bodies interpret the issue as a choice between culture or commerce and debate whether it is feasible or desirable to merge the two. The review of the Aboriginal Art and Craft Industry (Altman, 1989a) discussed extensively various points in connection with this issue (see also Altman and Taylor, 1990).

Cultural tours   The development of cultural tourism has worked successfully in communities where the enterprise centres on an individual or family group and is maintained as a small-scale operation. Ipolera Tours, based at a small outstation group in central Australia, illustrates how a small-scale, family-based commercial venture can work successfully. However, it is crucial to this success that the venture is a family rather than a community enterprise. In north Queensland the Mossman Gorge Aboriginal Community offers guided walking tours through the Gorge National Park. The tours are staffed only by those members of the community who wish to participate and who feel comfortable in their interaction with tourists. This keeps the enterprise informal and small-scale.

Joint ventures. Joint ventures in cultural tourism offer opportunities for Aboriginal people to participate jointly with non-Aboriginals in the provision of goods and services to the tourism industry. This option has received little attention from government funding bodies and has met with some resistance from Aboriginal groups who are sensitive to issues of aboriginal control. This concern over equity and control is greater in enterprises which are privately funded than in those where governments finance projects with public money.

None of the above five areas outlined by the Royal Commission is without problems for Aboriginal participants. Employment in some occupations in tourism-related industries requires literacy and communication skills and may require the adoption of cultural styles which can be foreign and daunting. Factors like these limit the employment opportunities for Aboriginal employees and inevitably confine their participation in the service industries to unskilled or semi-skilled work. Few Aboriginal employees in the hospitality sector of the tourism industry hold managerial positions. Participation in hospitality and other tourism-related services also demands direct and intensive social interaction with tourists which many Aboriginal people are unwilling or unable to undertake. In national parks, like Kakadu (Kesteven, 1987) and Uluru (Altman, 1987), most Aboriginal people have avoided employment opportunities in tourism for reasons of this kind and have shown definite preference for indirect economic participation in the industry, as is possible with manufacturing arts and crafts for retail sales (Altman, 1989a). However, some more gregarious individuals have been willing to undertake both training and employment, especially for park ranger positions.

Other forms of Aboriginal participation in cultural tourism, such as bush food tours or camping trips, also require intense social interaction with tourists. Again, its interpersonal aspects can be both uncomfortable and confronting experiences for many Aboriginal people (and probably for many tourists). However, in some communities this problem is overcome by self-selection, where Aboriginal volunteers, with the right sort of personality, staff such *intercultural* enterprises. Alternatively, enterprises may draw on a pool of staff who are available and happy to work on casual terms more appropriate to their personal requirements.

In situations where Aboriginal cultural enterprises cater to specific consumer markets within the tourism industry, it is possible for service provision to be more flexible. Such flexibility can be an advantage. However, all aboriginal enterprises need to be familiar with the structure and demands of the tourism industry in order to market their product successfully. In North Queensland, residents of the Mossman Gorge community retain their individual style of presentation and low-key interaction with tourists, while their non-Aboriginal partners, Australian Pacific Tours, market the bush tours as an option in a range of day trips by bus through the district.

Conclusions

The tourism industry is vital to Australia's future. In 1989–90 it contributed 5.1 per cent of the GDP (BTR, 1991). Many advertisements for Australia as a destination feature Aboriginal heritage and culture as a part of the holiday package. Tourists are frequently disappointed at the lack of actual contact with this aspect provided in their holiday (Birgin, 1991; BTR, 1990). The tourism industry has recognized this fact, and has set up various reviews and working parties to examine this possibly lucrative aspect. There are several reasons why the past projects have failed. These range from a simple lack of training and education, both in supply and in take-up of opportunities, to a real desire of several Aboriginal groups not to become involved in tourism, and many incidents of unscrupulous behaviour by operators (Birgin, 1991; Altman, 1989b; NTTC, 1989).

In dealing with the impacts on indigenous groups, it is interesting to compare studies of the indigenous American communities (Indians) with experiences in Australia. The former have taken part in tourism for many years, although the same sources of tension between the tourists and the hosts persist (Laxson, 1990). The problems and lack of solutions are now being repeated in Australia, especially in ceremonial activities (where the dances are perceived by the tourist as show and put on for their benefit rather than a part of a living tradition), and in the general area of social stress. Tourists either ignore residents or try to interact with them in an inappropriate way, such as personal space being violated with contact and touching, and (mostly accidental) desecration of traditional sites and artefacts.

Several solutions and strategies have been suggested to cope with *authentic* culture without destroying or trivializing the genuine and understanding the gap between the visitor and the visited. Many of these solutions rely on the growth of *responsible* tourism and the education of the tourist. This may well be naïve and misplaced (Wheeler, 1991; May, 1991). For many the two words *responsible* and *tourism* are conflicting and incompatible.

If tourism is to play a constructive part in the maintenance of the natural and cultural environment of the developing world, it needs to consider the values which developers, host communities and tourists alike place on their environment. Tourism should not be a zero-sum game, where only one party wins. Variable-sum models are in the best long-term interests of all. This may mean convincing the international travel industry and governments to think in new and innovative ways. The tourism industry must be made more socially responsible to ensure that the social or environmental conditions in which the host community lives do not deteriorate as a result of touristic development.

Tourism has been a force for preservation of both natural beauty and man-made wonders. It has provided new markets for crafts and traditions which were threatened by extinction. At some point, however, the long-term costs to the host community must be examined and a non-exploitive relationship between host and guest be determined. If responsible cultural tourism is going to have an important place in the future of Australia, then care must be taken now to protect the heritage, and notice be made of impacts of tourism on other indigenous communities, for one of conventional tourism's saddest impacts in the developing world is the schism between leisured tourists and the impoverished host culture.

References

Altman, J.C., 1987, *The Economic Impact of Tourism on the Mutitjulu Community, Uluru (Ayres Rock-Mount Olga) National Park*, Working Paper No. 7, Department of Political and Social Change, Research School of Pacific Studies, Australian National University, Canberra.

Altman, J.C., 1988, *Aborigines, Tourism and Development: The Northern Territory Experience*, ANU, North Australian Research Unit, Monograph, Darwin.

Altman, J.C. (Chairman), 1989a, *The Aboriginal Arts and Crafts Industry Report of the Review Committee*, Australian Government Publishing Service, Canberra.

Altman, J.C., 1989b, 'Tourism dilemmas for Aboriginal Australians', *Annals of Tourism Research*, 16: pp. 456–76.

Altman. J.C., 1990, 'Selling Aboriginal art' in J.C. Altman and L. Taylor (eds), *Marketing Aboriginal Art in the 1990s*, papers presented to a workshop in Canberra, 12–13 June 1990, Institute Report Series, Aboriginal Studies Press, Canberra.

Altman, J.C. and Taylor, L. (eds), 1990, *Marketing Aboriginal Art in the 1990s*, papers presented to a workshop in Canberra, 12–13 June 1990, Institute Report Series, Aboriginal Studies Press, Canberra.

Birgin, R., 1991, *Aboriginal People and Tourism in the Northern Territory*, NTTITC.

Bosselman, F.P., 1978, 'Dreamtime at Ayres Rock', in F.P. Bosselman, *In the Wake of the Tourist*, The Conservation Commission, Washington, DC.

Brayley, R., Var T. and Sheldon, P., 1990, 'Perceived influence of tourism on social issues', *Annals of Tourism Research*, 17(2): pp. 285–8.

BTR (Bureau of Tourism Research), 1991, *Australian Tourism Data Card*, BTR, Canberra

Bull, A., 1990, 'Australian tourism: effects of foreign investment', *Tourism Management*, 11(4): pp. 325–31.

Cohen, E. (ed.), 1979, 'Sociology of tourism', *Annals of Tourism Research*, Special Edition, 6(1&2): 18–35.

Commonwealth of Australia, 1991, *Royal Commission into Aboriginal Deaths in Custody*, Canberra.

DASSETT, 1991, *Cultural Tourism in Australia*, a study commissioned by DASSETT and prepared by consultants Peter Brokenshaw and Hans Guldberg.

Dillon, M.C., 1987, *Aborigines and Tourism in North Australia: Some Suggested Research Approaches*, East Kimberly Working Paper No 14, Centre for Resource and Environmental Studies, Australian National University, Canberra.

Finlayson, J., 1990, 'Tourist art versus fine art', in J.C. Altman and L. Taylor (eds), *Marketing Aboriginal Art in the 1990s*, papers presented to a workshop in Canberra, 12–13 June 1990, Institute Report Series, Aboriginal Studies Press, Canberra.

Gale, F. and Jacobs, J. (eds), 1987, *Tourists and the National Estate: Procedures to*

Protect Australia's National Heritage, Australian Government Publishing Service, Canberra.

Jafari, J., Pizam, A. and Przeclawski, K., 1990, 'A sociocultural study of tourism as a factor of change', *Annals of Tourism Research*, 17(3): pp. 469–72.

Kesteven, S., 1987, *Aborigines in the Tourist Industry*, East Kimberly Working Paper No. 14, impact assessment project AIAS and Anthropology Department UWA and Academy of the Social Sciences in Australia.

Laxson, J.D., 1991, 'How 'we' see 'them': tourism and native Americans', *Annals of Tourism Research*, 18(3): pp. 365–91.

May, V., 1991, 'Tourism, environment and development', *Tourism Management*, 12(2): pp. 112–18.

Miller, M., Bin-Sallik, M., Coombs, H.C., Hall, F. and Morrison, T. (Review Committee), 1985, *Aboriginal Employment and Training Programmes* (known as the Miller Report), Australian Government Publishing Service, Canberra.

Nash, D. and Smith V.L., 1991, 'Anthropology and tourism', *Annals of Tourism Research*, 18(1): pp. 12–25.

NTTC (Northern Territory Tourist Commission), 1989, *Towards Year 2000*, Vol. 1, final report, NTTC/Peat Marwick, Sydney.

Perdue, R.R, Long, P.T. and Allen, L., 1990, 'Resident support for tourism development', *Annals of Tourism Research*, 17(3): pp. 586–99.

Pizam, A., 1978, 'Tourism's impacts: the social costs to the destination community as perceived by its residents', *Journal of Travel Research*, 6(3): pp. 8–13.

Richter, L.K., 1987, 'The search for appropriate tourism: focus on the Third World', *Tourism Recreation Research*, 12(2).

Richter, L.K., 1989 *The Politics of Tourism in Asia*, University of Hawaii Press, Hawaii.

Sullivan, H. (ed.), 1984, *Visitors to Aboriginal Sites: Access, Control and Management*, Proceedings of the 1983 Kakadu workshop, Australian National Parks and Wildlife Service, Canberra.

Wheeler, B., 1991, 'Tourism's troubled times', *Tourism Management*, 12(2): pp. 91–6.

9 The changing status of tourism in Bali, Indonesia

G. Wall and S. Dibnah

Introduction

The purpose of this chapter is to examine the recent and very rapid rate of growth in tourism in Bali, Indonesia in order to identify some of the problems arising from the development of tourism, and to discuss recent initiatives which are being taken to plan for and manage tourism there.

Bali is a small island in the Indonesian archipelago. In an area of 5,600 square kilometres resides a permanent population of 2.8 million people at a density of approximately 500 per square kilometre. To these must be added nearly 1 million international and domestic tourists annually. Thus, although Bali is not a poor area of Indonesia, population density is high and there are considerable pressures on natural resources (Figure 9.1).

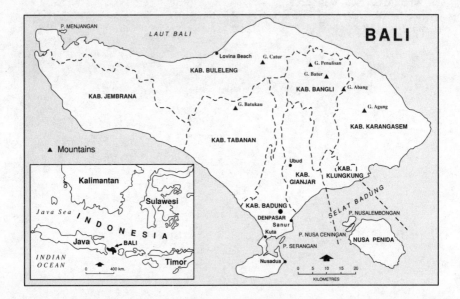

Figure 9.1 Bali

Bali is a Hindu island in a Muslim sea—almost all residents of Bali are Hindu in a country which is predominantly Muslim. The manifestations of Balinese Hinduism are evident in the landscape, in the numerous family and village temples, traditional architecture, and in the many colourful religious ceremonies which are distinctive to Bali and set it apart from the rest of the world.

The tourism context

Tourism has grown rapidly in recent years in Bali and is expected to continue to expand in the foreseeable future. It has become an extremely important sector of the Balinese economy in its own right, constituting approximately one-fifth of gross provincial product if related craft industries are included, and it also overlaps with and has implications for most other economic sectors. For example, the agricultural landscape, the production of handicrafts and the rich cultural traditions encourage visitors out of the major resorts into rural areas. Dance and musical performances and ceremonies, including cremations, have become tourist attractions. Thus, the landscape and the very way of life of the Balinese people constitute a major part of the resource base which draws visitors. While the government of Indonesia has viewed tourism as a positive economic force with the potential to generate foreign exchange and raise standards of living in Bali, the cultural traditions of Bali have resulted in the development of *cultural tourism* in which the contact between visitors and the Balinese people and their way of life, particularly in its more colourful expressions, constitute a major part of the tourist experience. It follows that while it is essential that the activities of tourists and participants in the tourist industries be understood thoroughly, by itself this is insufficient. Attention must also be directed at understanding the many forms of interactions which exist between tourists and residents, and between the tourist industry and other economic sectors.

Present status of tourism in Bali

The growth of tourism is a recent phenomenon in the long history of Bali. Before 1945 the number of tourists was small and the rapid growth of tourism did not take place until the 1960s. In 1964 the whole of Indonesia had 35,915 visitors; in 1965 there were only 29,367; and in 1966 the number declined further to 19,311, of whom only 2,150 went to Bali. Many of these visitors were travelling on business rather than for pleasure. The first guidebooks did not appear until the early 1970s.

In 1966 the Bali Beach Hotel opened on Sanur Beach with 300 rooms. Since that time it has been joined in Sanur by the Bali Hyatt and numerous smaller establishments. The international airport was enlarged, permitting the use of larger planes, and in 1968, 5,000 people flew to Bali. The rate of growth was very rapid: in 1969 there were 10,000 arrivals; 23,000 by 1970;

133,000 in 1978; and 158,000 in 1981. The preceding figures refer only to international arrivals and the number of domestic visitors must be added to have a complete picture of the volume of tourists. Mabbett (1985) has suggested that in 1982 domestic visitors occupied more than a third of the rooms rented out in the better hotels. Of the foreign visitors, the largest group (65,000) in 1982 were Australians, against 32,000 from Europe, 30,000 from Japan and 16,000 from North America.

From 1968 to 1975 the number of tourist accommodations in Bali increased by 300 per cent. In April 1975 there were 116 hotels with a total of 3,072 rooms. Of these, 109 were small hotels with less than 50 rooms. However, with the expansion there was a gradual shift of ownership out of the hands of the Balinese. In 1982 the Bali office of Indonesia's Directorate General of Tourism classified 24 hotels as being worthy of star grading and they were all located in either Sanur, Kuta or Denpasar. Nearly 2,000 of their 2,763 rooms were in Sanur. To these must be added the recent developments in Nusa Dua, which will be discussed below, as well as further expansions in Kuta, Sanur and other resorts such as Ubud and Candi Dasa. The same organization listed 157 restaurants with places for 10,000 people, although 132 of these, with places for 8,500 people, were in Badung regency. Thus the tourists and tourism infrastructure are highly concentrated in one regency in the south of the island.

Hotel employment is the major direct source of income from tourism for the Balinese. In 1974 total employment was estimated at 5,438, of which 4,076 were Balinese, and each twin-bedded room averaged 1.5 employees. Women accounted for approximately 17 per cent of all hotel workers. However, hotel employment has affected many more persons than this since employee turnover averaged 21 months. There has been migration to Badung District from elsewhere in Bali as well as from Java: before Bali Hyatt opened in 1974 there were 7,000 applicants for 400 jobs and many of these were from districts other than Badung. Most of the lower-level jobs were filled by Balinese; the supervisory, managerial and administrative jobs were generally held by non-Balinese.

According to Mabbett (1985), the Bali Hotel in Denpasar is where tourism in Bali really began. It was here that most of the small number of visitors stayed in the 1930s, and it was here that the first commercial dance performances were presented. The hotel was built by a Dutch shipping company, although since 1956 it has been under Indonesian control as part of the country-wide Natour group, and it has been modernized extensively.

Tourists began arriving in Kuta in small numbers in the late 1960s. At that time Kuta had only one hotel, the Kuta Beach, which was founded in 1955 as a successor to one of the same name which opened in 1935 and then closed in 1942 with the arrival of the Japanese. Perhaps the first lodging-house, or *losman*, Komala Indah opened in 1970, since when it has been joined by scores of others, the majority of which are in Balinese hands. In 1973 Pertamina Cottages opened for business near the airport, and the Legion Beach Hotel followed in 1975. The Bali Oberoi came later, and by 1985 there were eight hotels in Kuta with star ratings in the official Indonesian hotel guide, at least six more which appeared to be in a similar class. Altogether there are more than 200 establishments in Kuta providing accommodation for tourists, with more than 2,000 rooms.

Future numbers

The number of foreign arrivals in Bali has been projected to increase by 15 per cent per annum during the Fifth Five-Year Plan (Repelita V) to reach 700,000 by 1993. This would constitute a doubling of tourist arrivals within a five-year period. To this must be added a 5 per cent annual increase in domestic tourists who will likely number 500,000 in 1993. Thus, total tourist arrivals was projected to be 1.2 million in 1993. Such an increase in numbers will place strains on the infrastructure and environment, and will require improvements in various supporting facilities, including better airport and transportation services as well as additional hotel rooms. For example, it was suggested that it will be necessary to increase the number of hotel rooms to 34,000 by 1993 from the 1988 figure of approximately 11,000. However, no plan appears to be in place which indicates how this is to be done. In fact, there has been a hotel building-boom in Bali and the number of rooms projected in Repelita V as being necessary by 1993 had already been achieved by 1991.

At the same time, the market for tourism in Bali has softened as a result of the world recession, which has been particularly severe in Australia, which has now been replaced by Japan as the leading source of visitors. At the same time, the Gulf War discouraged air travel throughout the world and came at a time when prospective visitors to Bali might have been expected to be booking their vacations. The result is that there is an over-supply of tourist accommodation in the early 1990s.

The Bali Tourism Study

The most important document in the early history of tourism in Bali is the **Bali Tourism Study** which was undertaken by SCETO, a consortium of French consultants. The study was sponsored by the United Nations Development Programme and the International Bank for Reconstruction and Development. The report, in six volumes, was released in 1971 and is the template which, until recently, has guided the development of tourism in Bali. The structure of the report is as follows:

1. Main report
2. The master plan
3. Technical data: roads; 3B technical plan: roads
4. Technical data: infrastructure
5. Economics
6. Master plan implementation

The Bali Tourism Study is a plan for the development of tourism in Bali. It is concerned with tourism throughout the island. Although it is an impressive document on tourism it is not a comprehensive plan for there is only a limited attempt to link tourism with other sectors of the economy. The Bali Tourism Study has served its purpose well and many, perhaps most, of its recommendations have been implemented. However, more than fifteen years have elapsed since the completion of the study, which was designed to set guidelines for development in 1985. The majority of the data on which the study is based was collected in the late 1960s and much has changed in tourism in Bali since that time. Thus, there is a need to take stock anew of the status of tourism in Bali and to suggest new strategies to accommodate the growing number of tourists.

The Nusa Dua Development Plan

As recommended in the Bali Tourism Study, a major tourism development was initiated in Nusa Dua, a fairly dry area near the southern tip of the island. Pacific Consultants K.K. of Tokyo were contracted to prepare a development plan for the area and following upon the completion of an interim report in 1972, the final (draft) report was submitted in eight volumes in 1973. The contents of the report are as follows:

1. General
2. Ecology
3. Landscape and architecture
4. Road
5. Water supply, sanitary sewage and storm drainage system
6. Electrical system and telecommunications
7. Waste disposal system
8. District cooling system

The Nusa Development Plan provides a detailed assessment of the physical resource base of Nusa Dua as well as guidelines for the development of the area. Nusa Dua has been and is being developed under the direction of the Bali Tourism Development Corporation which draws up site contracts and has considerable independence, acting in a very similar fashion to a Crown Corporation in Canada. Prior to the development of tourism, Nusa Dua was predominantly coconut plantation with some coastal fishing. However, the agricultural resource is poor. The area is now the location of a growing number of luxury hotels and a conference centre situated in a tourist enclave. Nusa Dua was expected to offer about 2,700 hotel rooms by 1990, which was as many as the combined accommodation of Sanur and Kuta. While the development is extremely impressive, there has been no official attempt to date to evaluate the economic, environmental and social consequences of the Nusa Dua resort. It would be appropriate to assess the strengths and weaknesses of the Nusa Dua development in order to learn from the experience, prior to the initiation of additional resort developments in Bali and elsewhere in Indonesia.

Excursion roads

A series of reports on excursion roads were completed in 1978 and 1979. The excursion roads were designed to facilitate the movement of tourists from the three major accommodation nodes in the south to various attractions in the interior of the island. The intention was to spread the positive economic impacts of tourism without encouraging adverse socio-cultural impacts which might result from large numbers of visitors staying overnight in the interior. The excursion routes are mapped in great detail and the maps may provide a bench-mark against which some types of change may be measured.

Academic literature

There is a small but growing academic literature on tourism in Bali. Most of that which exists post-dates the reports which have been mentioned above and draws heavily upon them, particularly the SCETO report.

In 1975 Francillon published a paper based primarily upon three reports prepared by staff at Udayana University in Denpasar as follows: Report on the influence of Mass Tourism on the way of Life in Balinese Society; Report of the Development of Tourism in Bali; The Impact of Tourism on Socio-Economic Development in Bali (Universitas Udayana and Francillon 1975; Francillon 1979). (Others also appear to reference these reports but it is not always clear if it is these or other reports because of the small differences in the translation of titles.) Francillon discusses the characteristics of tourists, their seasonal distribution and spending-patterns, Balinese handicrafts, employment structure, land tenure and culture. He concludes by suggesting that so-called cultural tourists may have more negative impacts than mass tourism because the former are likely to have more penetrations, 'encroachments and interactions'. Somewhat similarly, French anthropologist Picard (1983), in a number of publications, has stressed the possible negative impacts of tourism in Balinese culture.

However, American anthropologist McKean (1973; 1977) has displayed a more sanguine attitude towards the impacts of tourism. He points out that the interests of tourists have stimulated the spread and revitalization of some elements of traditional culture. He draws attention to the paradox that while tourists are an agent of change, they also have a strong interest in the traditional customs and crafts of Bali. He suggests that both conservatism and economic necessity encourage the Balinese to maintain their skills as carvers, musicians and dancers, and that provided appropriate safeguards are taken, the impacts of tourism on Balinese culture could be benign.

Noronha (1979) provides an excellent overview of many aspects of tourism in Bali. However, his data are derived primarily from the Udayana University reports, and although he does make some interesting observations on the SCETO report and the Nusa Dua report, his observations predate the construction of the latter.

Rodenburg (1980), in an important paper, examines the effects of scale in the tourism industry on economic development in Bali. Tourism enterprises are divided into three categories. Large-scale tourism corresponds to hotels of international standard; small industrial tourism refers to economy class hotels; and craft tourism consists of homestays (*losman*), independent restaurants and souvenir shops. Rodenburg concludes that smaller-scale enterprises offer a greater opportunity for profit and control to local people than do those on a larger scale. Jenkins (1982), in a paper which undertakes a critical review of Rodenburg's analysis, argues that although large-scale developments are likely to be inevitable because of external economies of scale and market structures in international tourism the consequences of such developments can be foreseen and mitigated by pre-project planning. However, the nature of such planning and the method of implementation are not discussed. The analysis in these papers is primarily economic and there is only a limited examination of environmental and socio-economic consequences of different scales of development. Rodenburg admits that the question of scale-dependent social and cultural effects of development have not been addressed. Furthermore, the analyses were conducted prior to the development of the Nusa Dua project, using planned budgets. It is known that the Husa Dua project was not completed on schedule and it is questionable whether likely impacts were foreseen accurately. The spatial implications of these developments merit further consideration, as do the characteristics and behaviour of tourists of different cultures who patronize various types of development, for these factors are also likely to influence the nature of impacts. Thus, although the studies of Rodenburg and Jenkins are provocative and address important questions, their findings must be regarded as tentative given their timing in relation to the Nusa Dua project. Furthermore, some types of impact, particularly environmental and social, have yet to be investigated adequately.

The present status of tourism in Bali

It has been argued above that the recent growth of tourism in Bali has led to an imbalance between the number of tourists and the supporting infrastructure. Development is concentrated in the south of the island, leading to pressures upon the quantity and quality of water supplies, difficulties of waste disposal, problems of coastal erosion, traffic congestion, regional imbalance in economic opportunities, and concern over the continued viability of Balinese culture. Although these challenges cannot be addressed in detail in this chapter they are no less real for that. As has been explained above, the existing tourism plan has run its course so that these and other problems as well as recent tourism developments, have occurred in the absence of a current tourism plan.

However, the challenges of tourism are being met with a number of responses. Four major initiatives have been taken which may have far-reaching implications for tourism in Bali and for the lives of its people:

1. the development of a **Spatial Arrangement Plan** for Bali;
2. the creation of a **National Tourism Strategy**;
3. **United Nations Development Programme** initiatives to produce a new tourism plan and an associated management strategy for Bali; and
4. the formulation of a **Sustainable Development Strategy** for Bali.

Space does not permit the detailed examination of each of these initiatives although each will be discussed briefly.

The spatial arrangement plan

Faced with growing regional imbalances resulting from the marked concentration of tourism in Badung regency in the south of the island, in 1988 the Governor of Bali in Decision Letter Number 15 designated fifteen centres for future tourism development. Shortly thereafter a sixteenth centre was added to the list. To some extent this can be seen as a recognition of what was already happening, for many developments were taking place in a seemingly haphazard fashion. Nevertheless, it constituted the reversal of a policy which had previously favoured concentrated development in the south to a new policy dispersion of tourism. Although the sixteen areas identified for development include the existing major coastal resorts, new areas for tourism development are also added, in both coastal and inland areas, throughout the island. It remains to be seen if the Spatial Arrangement Plan will be enforced and if it will be modified as a result of the other initiatives which are described below. However, the Spatial Arrangement Plan could lead to a substantial spread of tourism to previously undeveloped parts of the island.

The National Tourism Strategy

The National Tourism Strategy has yet to be released. However, it is likely that it will reflect a desire to promote international tourism more widely in Indonesia. Reflecting Indonesia's tropical island physiography and its cultural diversity, *Beach Plus* may provide a unifying marketing concept. The established market importance of Bali may encourage it to be viewed, from a national perspective, as a *hub* to facilitate *spoke* developments in other regions, with priority for tourism development being given to eastern Indonesia. From a national perspective, tourism may be viewed as **the** leading economic sector in Bali and as a catalyst for stimulating development elsewhere. In contrast, the Balinese may wish to stress more balanced development sectorally, with three leading sectors: agriculture, tourism and small industry. National and provincial priorities could result in conflicting policies, national strategy encouraging shorter stays in Bali to redistribute tourists to locations elsewhere in Indonesia, whereas Bali

province may wish to encourage longer stays to occupy excess accommodation capacity.

United Nations Development Programme initiatives

The United Nations Development Programme is currently supporting two
related initiatives: a project concerning the **Management of Tourism in
Bali** and the development of a **Comprehensive Tourism Development
Plan**. Very briefly, in recognition of the lack of adequate systems for
physical, socio-economic and financial management, and planning and
control of tourism development, the following problems are being
addressed:

1. an inadequate plan framework for the island;
2. lack of co-ordination and optimal use of resources;
3. lack of response to indigenous organizations;
4. the inadequate provincial and local tax base;
5. inadequate information systems and an unreliable data base; and
6. inadequate skilled and trained professional staff.

This work should be completed by the end of 1992.

The Bali Sustainable Development Project (BSDP)

The BSDP is a collaborative venture between the University of Waterloo,
Canada, and Gadjah Mada University in Yogyakarta, Java, with the
assistance of Udayana University, Bali, Indonesia. The project is funded
by the Canadian International Development Agency. Although not a
tourism project specifically, because tourism is a major agent of change in
Bali it has received considerable attention.

The BSDP has had to develop a definition of sustainable development
appropriate to Bali (BSDP, 1991). It is worth noting that the World
Commission on Environment and Development does not mention tourism
in its report **Our Common Future**, which is perhaps the key source
document among devotees of sustainable development, and it is a moot
point whether, and in what form, tourism might be a sustainable activity.
The BSDP definition of sustainable development is in line with those of the
World Commission on Environment and Development and its predecessor, the World Conservation Strategy, although it differs from them in
the additional emphasis given to culture in the BSDP definition. This
reflects the great significance of culture to the Balinese and the policy of
cultural tourism which acknowledges culture as being a primary tourist
attraction. Thus, a concept of sustainable development had to be formulated which encompasses the continuity of culture as well as that of natural
resources and production.

An important strategic element of the BSDP is the ongoing linkage of
the programme and its components to the needs of policy-makers in Bali,

in particular Bali's central planning agency BAPPEDA. Following more than three years of research, workshops and exchanges, a preliminary sustainable development strategy was tabled in June 1991. A refined version of this strategy will be presented in Bali in June 1992 in time to provide input into Repelita VI, the next five-year plan.

Conclusions

The initial phase of mass tourism in Bali took place according to a plan. Although the plan was not always followed in detail, it did largely determine the present spatial distribution of tourism in Bali. Although international tourism has grown and is projected to grow rapidly in Bali, the existing plan is obsolete. In the absence of an enforceable plan, gaps have appeared between elements of supply and demand, leading to economic, environmental and, possibly cultural imbalances. A number of initiatives are being taken to address the problems but it is at present unclear if their recommendations will be compatible or if the political will exists to enforce them. However, in recent years the pace of change has been so rapid that strong direction is required to ensure that in the words of local dictums, 'cultural tourism' and 'tourism for Bali' do not become 'Bali for tourism' and 'tourist culture'.

Acknowledgements

This chapter has benefited from collaboration with colleagues at Gadjah Mada University, Udayana University and the University of Waterloo, through participation in the Bali Sustainable Development Project which is funded by the Canadian International Development Agency.

References

Francillon, G., 1979, *Bali: Tourism, Culture, Environment*, Udayana University and UNESCO.
Jenkins, C.L., 1982, 'The effects of scale in tourism projects in developing countries', *Annals of Tourism Research*, 9(2): pp. 229–49.
McKean, P.F., 1973, 'Cultural involution: tourists, Balinese, and the process of modernization in an anthropological perspective', unpublished PhD thesis, Brown University, Providence, RI.
McKean, P.F., 1977, 'Towards a theoretical analysis of tourism: economic dualism and cultural involution in Bali', in V. Smith (ed.), *Hosts and Guests: The Anthropology of Tourism*, University of Pennsylvania Press, Philadelphia, 93–108.
Mabbett, H., 1985, *The Balinese*, January Books, Wellington, NZ.
Noronha, R., 1979, 'Paradise reviewed: tourism in Bali', in E. de Kadt (ed.), *Tourism — Passport to Development?*, Oxford University Press, Oxford 177–204.

Picard, M., 1983, *Community Participation in Tourist Activity on the Island of Bali: Environment, Ideologies and Practices*, UNESCO/URESTI-CNRS, Paris.

Rodenburg, E., 1980, 'The effects of scale on economic development: tourism in Bali', *Annals of Tourism Research*, 7(2): pp. 177–96.

Universitas Udayana and Francillon, G., 1975, 'Tourism in Bali—its economic and socio-cultural impact: three points of view', *International Social Science Journal*, 27: pp. 721–57.

10 Sustainable tourism: illustrations from Kenya, Nepal and Jamaica

S. Curry and B. Morvaridi

Introduction

The question of sustainability is most commonly discussed in the light of agricultural or industrial development. However, the main themes of most definitions of sustainable development—concern for the environment and provision of an economic resource base for future generations, dealing with the question of poverty and the preservation of culture (Morvaridi, forthcoming)—can be identified as directly relevant to tourism. This chapter will begin by setting tourism and sustainability in a theoretical context. Case studies will then be examined and the chapter will conclude with some policy recommendations on sustainable tourism development.

Tourism and sustainability

Tourism includes several forms of directly and indirectly productive activities. To be sustainable, it requires the establishment of an industry which includes consideration of the long-term effects of economic activity in relation to resources and, therefore, concern for the twin needs of this and future generations. Sustainability depends on the persistence or desirability of a system's productivity under known or possible conditions (Conway et al., 1990), and on consumption not exceeding resources, thereby to secure a steady resource base. The twin emphasis of sustainable development on the *needs* of existing and future generations puts economic activity, in this case tourism, into a new perspective (WCED 1987; Pearce, Barbier and Markandya, 1990).

A key problem for sustainable development is the trade-off between present and future needs (Pearce and Barbier, 1990). Assessment of the extent of such a trade-off in tourism includes consideration of whether tourism developers have taken account of any long-term effects on the environment or the socio-economic welfare of local people. The establishment of new game parks in South Africa and Kenya, for example, can entail relocating peoples against their best interests or wishes. It is important that planners are concerned with not only developing popular tourist centres for immediate use and revenue, but also the human and physical environments they will affect.

The physical environment is important to tourism, and often provides the main attraction for visitors. There has been a considerable interest in the effects of tourism on the physical environment (OECD, 1980; Roberts, 1983). This has concentrated on specific forms of tourism where the environment is thought to be particularly susceptible to greater numbers of tourists, such as parks, coastal strips, alpine zones, and islands and reefs (Farrell and McLellan, 1987). The context and conclusion of such studies has been the need to maintain the physical environment for long-term purposes, and therefore to restrain economic uses such as tourism. Emphasis is placed on maintaining the quality of the environment and of the tourists' experience. In more detail, the possible consequences of tourism on the environment have been listed as water and noise pollution, loss of landscape, destruction of flora and fauna, degradation of historic sites, and congestion, amongst others (Vigus, 1990).

One aspect of the environmental effects of tourism is the conflict that can arise over the use of resources, most obviously between those operating in the tourism sector—hoteliers, restaurateurs, shopkeepers, tour operators —and the rest of the local population who may not benefit as owners or as workers from the influx of tourists. This has given rise to a more recent emphasis on sustainable tourist development: 'The relationship of tourists, communities, managers, developers, and policy makers to each other, and especially to their environment, is the substance of ecological tourism and, certainly, sustainable development' (Farrell and Runyan 1991, 27). This approach also sees sustainability as linked to acceptability: '[The view that] formulas and prescriptions suited to other places, but not tried or accepted locally, should be rejected. The concept of sustainability is totally sub-scribed to it' (Farrell and McLellan, 1987, p. 8).

Whilst still related especially to the physical environment, sustainable tourism development has redirected attention on different actors and groups affected by tourism, and is thus distinct from a simple concentration on conservation. However, sustainability in tourism continues to have an economic interpretation, without which other concerns will evaporate. This economic sustainability centres on quality; in addition, it reinterprets acceptability in terms of the distribution of the benefits and costs of tourism.

De Kadt (1990) identifies scale and distribution as two components of sustainable development which can also be applied to tourism. Even if the carrying capacity of tourism locations can be improved, it will always have a maximum. Alternatively, tourism can be more dispersed, less capital-intensive, and scaled down to provide more room for small and family enterprises. These changes, desirable in themselves, would also have the effect of ensuring a wider distribution of net benefits, possibly between generations as well as at any one time. Nevertheless, the growing poverty of most people in developing countries means that 'for LDCs, then, the issue of sustainability is primarily one of how to maintain the productivity of resources' (de Kadt, 1990, p. 11).

A main objective of sustainable development is to reduce the poverty of the world's poor by providing lasting and secure livelihoods, which entails minimizing resource depletion, cultural disruption and social instability. Sustainable tourism, therefore, places emphasis on the host population's economy, society and culture. Encouragement of sustainable tourism would mean considering not only the needs of tourists but also the needs of local people. Few industries have such widespread linkages as tourism.

Sustainable development requires the assessment of hazards which may threaten the successful continuation of economic activity. Tourism markets are rather short-lived. The population of tourists changes in income, age and other characteristics. Tastes also change as a result. On the other hand, some tourism assets like hotels and tourist roads have long physical lives, assuming normal maintenance. Sustaining tourism entails periodic reinvestment in tourism plant. In part this is because of changing technology. More importantly, it is to maintain the quality of the plant, which in itself is a key attraction. This problem of reinvestment is most acute in areas of mass tourism where a country is more reliant on the sector and where there has been a larger indirect investment in support of tourism.

Tourism is subject to a form of product life cycle. Sustaining tourism from the viewpoint of tour operators can mean relocation to new areas. Sustaining tourism from the viewpoint of particular destinations must include reinvestment. The implications of periodic reinvestment in tourism plant and related services are easier to work out than the effects of tourism on the physical environment, and are equally important to sustaining tourism quality.

Periodic reinvestment is also required in indirectly productive activities to maintain the standard of supply. Some of these can be financed from revenues derived from tourism itself; some of them cannot and must rely on general revenues. To a considerable extent, indirectly productive facilities will be common to tourists and non-tourists, so an acceptable distribution of the costs must be found. This is more important where tourism is only one of several activities in an area—the crowding effects of tourism are more visible than those of other activities.

The distributional effects of infrastructure provision can be particularly acute in small economies where an extended runway can mean no hospital or fewer schools. These impacts have to be added to those from directly productive activities. It has been argued that the outflow of foreign exchange as profits, management and other fees can exceed its outflow for purchasing operating and capital items Bryden, 1973). Domestically, incomes generated through tourism may extend little beyond the sector itself and those participating in it. Where tourism develops, there is often an opportunity cost in other economic activities, which can be particularly important where agriculture declines rather than grows. Overall, the experience may resemble that of Tanzania, where 'A financial surplus was mobilized from other sectors and re-directed toward tourism through government institutions, a process sustained for two decades' (Curry, 1988, p. 240). Sustainable development of tourism must take distributional effects into account in circumstances where they cannot be measured precisely nor seen immediately.

Overall, the most important contribution of the various approaches to sustainable development is the recognition of a fundamental *cumulative causation* with regard to poverty, environmental degradation and underdevelopment (Chambers, 1987, Morvaridi, forthcoming).

To illustrate these issues, three brief case studies are presented from different places and at different times. In each, a proposed tourism-related investment can be seen to raise questions of tourism quality and at the same time income distribution.

Quality and distribution: the cases of Kenya, Nepal and Jamaica

Kenya in the mid-1970s

From an early date, its wildlife attractions have been important to Kenyan tourism. Already in the mid-1970s, concern was expressed by tour operators and investors over the management of wildlife areas. Increasing tourist numbers and investment had led to congestion in some areas, combined with a threat of increased poaching. A large-scale project was devised for World Bank funding oriented to the development of wildlife areas. This project had several components including a reorganization of wildlife planning and management.

A main conclusion from several ecological and tourism studies was that game parks and reserves were not self-contained ecological units. Most herbivores dispersed on a seasonal basis to surrounding areas that could be several times as large as the parks themselves. These dispersions were being met by an increase in land entitlement and use in the surrounding areas. Not only did the dispersals affect agriculture and forestry, but the restriction of dispersals also led to overgrazing in the park and reserve areas. A conflict between tourism, conservation and agriculture threatened the quality of the parks and the growth of the tourist industry.

New ways of managing the wildlife areas was the main component of the project. Out of the many wildlife areas in Kenya three in particular were identified for investment and improvement, because they were major attractions for tourists and because the viability of park game populations was dependent on continued wildlife access to dispersal areas.

The proposed solution was managed dispersals implemented through game barriers. Where elephant or rhino were important, barriers would take the form of moats; otherwise they would take the form of fences. Game barriers were thought to be more reliable than the *ad hoc* alternatives of thunder flashes and gun-firing which in any case did not control dispersals and therefore would not properly protect alternative land uses. The project was to provide funding for the construction of game barriers. The maintenance of the barriers would fall to different authorities in different areas, although central subsidy might be justified if the incremental income from tourists in game areas yielded a tax base that could be redistributed within Kenya.

Several land uses and users would be affected by a game barrier policy.

In some areas, it would be smallholder agriculture developing livestock production; in other areas it would be large-scale farming developing grain production; in other areas it would be Masai settlement schemes. In each circumstance, maintaining game dispersals would mean a loss of economic activity. This raised a serious problem of distribution. The ultimate benefits of the game protection were seen as a growth in tourist numbers and expenditure; the loss of income and opportunity in dispersal areas was one of the major costs.

A policy was proposed to address these distributional issues and make the changes in wildlife management acceptable. If game barriers were to allow dispersals through land with alternative uses, the land-users would need an income from the migrating game itself, or from some other source to make up for what they lost. A policy was devised to allow land-users to earn income from the game. This could come from hunting or culling, under licence, or it could come from expansion into game-based tourism through establishing lodges and camps.

These opportunities would be greater in some areas than others. In any case, they might not fully compensate for lost production from alternative uses. The government would also adopt a policy, for specified land-users in specific dispersal areas, of guaranteeing a 'Minimum Return from Wildlife'. What was not earned through wildlife-related activities would be made up by a direct concession fee, a cash payment that would ensure a minimum revenue from land reallocated through the game barrier investments.

These proposals were made in the light of the direct distributional consequences of a specific game conservation measure. Additional features of the overall project would deal with quality improvement in park areas themselves, of which game dispersals were a necessary condition. However, the funding arrangements required that before game park investments were approved, the government should have reached agreements including direct concession fee payments for land-users in surrounding areas. It was no use apparently improving the quality of the tourism experience without ensuring its sustainability.

The game barrier and compensation schemes brought distributional issues directly into the realm of project financing. It posed a broader issue of government revenue sources from tourism and their control. The government had the means to raise further revenues from tourism to meet the additional project costs, through park entry fees or hotel taxes. Alternatively, it could rely on an increased growth of tourism under existing tax and revenue arrangements. In either case, the government would be acting as the main agent in ensuring the conditions for a long-term expansion of wildlife-related tourism.

Nepal in the early 1980s

The main income and foreign exchange-generating tourism in Nepal is city tourism. Trekking and climbing generate incomes in other regions at much less cost, although at much lower levels of expenditure by tourists. Climbing generates demands for supplies (as well as rubbish) in a concentrated area around the base camps. Trekking generates demands along some well-established routes.

A principal need for these forms of tourism is fuelwood. This resource is used for cooking, heating and light during the trek. The use of this fuel provides an important element in the tourist experience and generates income locally. Wood supplies are also necessary in the construction of separate tourist accommodation or additional rooms. The fuelwood demands from tourism add to the needs of the local population for this essential component of living.

Tourism demand for fuelwood is imposed upon areas where supplies are diminishing. The loss of fuelwood supplies in hill areas is directly connected to soil erosion, and threatens food production. Four major effects on the local economy have been identified as a result of the extra demands that tourism creates.

First, there has been a commercialization of fuelwood and food supplies so that a greater number of the local population have to purchase these items from their small cash incomes. Second, as a result of tourism and greater commercialisation of local supplies, demand has increased for both fuelwood and food, and so have prices. Third, where fuelwood is still collected for household use, distances have increased and a greater proportion of household time is spent on this essential task. Finally, as has been mentioned, the loss of wood supplies and increasing food production on hillside plots has resulted in a loss of soil fertility and soil itself.

Clearly, the extra demands of tourists for fuelwood have had a distributional effect on the local economy. Where commercialization takes place, supplies are redirected to those with greater purchasing power. In this context this is the tourists or more precisely the trekking tour operators who are able to command resources on the tourists' behalf.

Three responses have been considered. First, **price discrimination** could be introduced, increasing the price of fuelwood to tour operators and therefore tourists. This would not have a marked impact on tourism demand for fuelwood and would presumably generate larger incomes locally. However, it would be difficult to implement without affecting the local price of fuelwood as well. Traders are likely to benefit whilst the local population as a whole does not. Moreover, it would not reduce the physical demand for fuelwood and the resulting impact on soil and food production.

Second, an **additional tax** could be imposed on trekking operators and therefore tourists, which could be channelled to reforestation. In principle, this would generate larger incomes from tourism demand and ensure that fuelwood supplies were replaced. However, reforestation would not necessarily replace the natural forest being harvested for fuelwood in the same state. Access to forest areas would have to be restricted for several years, and the benefits might be too far in the future for present wood-users to appreciate.

Third, an **alternative fuel supply** could be provided by tour operators and tourists carrying bottled gas for lighting and cooking. This might resolve the physical problem of higher demand for fuelwood supplies to some extent. However, it would imply an increase in the foreign exchange of a low expenditure tourism—the canisters and gas would need to be imported—and would reduce local incomes from tourism. Moreover, there would be a change in the quality of the tourism experience. Trekking would become just a bit more like the organised mass tourism which trekkers seek to avoid.

It is not clear in this case what is the best solution. Neither is it clear who can take an initiative in this context. The distributional effects are important, even if they are imposed on changes that are taking place anyway. Separating tourism from those changes, by insisting on alternative supplies for tourists independent of the local markets, would require a government initiative in the form of a recommendation, regulation, or tax. Alternatively, the local environment could be valued so highly that tourism should be reduced until a larger volume can be sustained without detrimental effects. This latter option would also deprive some in the hill areas of a source of income, as well as removing a source of foreign exchange from the national economy, costs that might have to be borne to conserve resources for future generations in this case.

Jamaica in the 1990s

Tourism has become the main foreign exchange sector in Jamaica. It grew substantially in the 1980s on the basis of only a small amount of additional investment. The main forms of holiday tourism are hotel-based, and much of the hotel capacity is still concentrated in urban areas. There is a principal port of entry for tourists and virtually all arrive by air.

The growth of tourism has put a strain on the older urban areas that still provide a focus for tourism shopping and recreation outside hotels. Physically, there has been deterioration in roads, pavements, buildings and their surrounds. This is combined with problems of security and harassment. There is also an increasing problem in urban services such as water, cleansing and rubbish collection, partly owing to government expenditure cutbacks and lack of resources to local councils.

A privately funded organization called 'Jamaica Tourism Action Plan' has been set up. It acts as a source of pressure on central and local government to consider tourism-related issues in the provision of urban facilities, and in particular the several local areas who rely almost solely on tourism. It also represents a means of stimulating expenditure indirectly in support of tourism outside the government budget, and is therefore consistent with general budgetary policy.

The main focus of its activities is to rehabilitate tourism-frequented areas and to preserve tourism's acceptability through these improvements to local populations. Both are regarded as essential to maintain the quality of urban tourism for holiday-makers. Moreover, there is a risk that business incomes in shops and restaurants will simply decline unless improvements in the urban infrastructure are made.

An important distributional feature of its activities is the search for financial resources independent of government revenues. Improvements are intended to be financed by tourism enterprises in the improvement areas themselves. Little appeal is made in these circumstances to national levels of foreign exchange earnings, although implicitly this is seen to be bound up with tourism-financed expenditures carried out within the sector itself.

There is another element of the appeal to the self-interest of the tourism sector for maintaining the quality of the tourism experience. The alternative to urban improvements is regarded as a tourism increasingly centred just on secluded hotels, with little contact with, or income generation for, local traders. Hence this policy of urban improvement can also seem to be part of a dialogue within the tourism sector, between those basing their expansion on all-inclusive hotel developments, and those seeking to maintain the greater distributional effects of an older tourism which at the same time bears greater costs and risks.

Jamaica has no particular historical monuments with which it can sustain an urban tourism; it has to be done by small enterprises providing contemporary gratification. Moreover, tourism enterprises by themselves are not going to fund all the necessary expenditures implied by declining urban conditions. Nevertheless, it is argued that in looking after their own interests, tourism-related enterprises may provide an example of the urban regeneration that is more widely desirable.

Conclusion

International tourism often plays a key role in economic development strategies as a generator of foreign exchange and employment. In some countries—such as the Caribbean—tourism has become a major source of national revenue.

It is essential that the productivity of resources in tourism is maintained, which means either reinvestment or ensuring that policies in the first place are geared towards the long term. The success of tourism's sustainability depends upon the extent of the distributional impacts that it necessitates. For example, in extreme cases, the scaling down of tourism may be necessary to protect the physical environment. Since tourism is an industry which includes all key sectors of a national economy, its sustainability should be assessed within a macroeconomic context. Any trade-off between resources caused by developing tourism should be accounted for.

Tourism policies are most successful when directed at local participation and tailored towards local needs. Sustainable tourism may be a more achievable goal if the impact of tourism development at the micro-level is incorporated into macro-level planning.

Key areas which policies might include to be compatible with a sustainable development strategy are (1) long-term investment; (2) the participation of local people in decision-making, employment and therefore income distribution; and (3) preservation of the natural environment and the encouragement of ecotourism.

References

Bryden, J.M., 1973, *Tourism and Development: A Case Study of the Commonwealth Caribbean*, Cambridge University Press, Cambridge.

Chambers, Robert, 1987, 'Sustainable livelihoods, environment and development: putting poor rural people first', IDS Discussion Paper 240, December 1987.

Conway *et al.*, 1990, *Post-Green Revolution: Sustainable Development in Agriculture*, Macmillan, London.

Curry, S., 1988, 'Tourism and underdevelopment in Tanzania', PhD Thesis, Bradford University.

Farrel, B. and McLellan, R., 1987, 'Tourism and physical environment', *Annals of Tourism Research*, Special Issue, 14(1), pp. 1–9.

Farrell, B.H. and Runyan, D., 1991, 'Ecology and Tourism', *Annals of Tourism Research*, 18(1): pp. 26–40.

de Kadt, E. 1990, ' Making the alternative sustainable: lessons from development for tourism', Discussion Paper 272 IDS, University of Sussex.

Morvaridi, Behrooz, 1991, 'Sustainable development: an alternative to current development strategies?' paper presented to Development Studies Association Study Group Lancaster University, June.

Morvaridi, Behrooz, forthcoming, 'Sustainable development, rural poverty and structural adustment', in *Global Environmental Change*.

OECD, 1980, *The Impact of Tourism On the Environment: General Development*, Organization of Economics Co-operation and Development, Paris.

Pearce, D., Barbier, E. and Markandya, A., 1990, *Sustainable Development: Economics and Environment in the Third World*, Edward Elgar, London.

Roberts, J., 1983, 'The OECD's international study of tourism on the environment', in *Tourism and Environment: A Miscellany of Readings*, Occasional Paper, Development and Project Planning Centre, Bradford University.

Vigus, A., 1990, 'Tourism, development and environment', *Crown Agents Review*, l: pp. 28–31.

World Commission on Environment and Development (WCED), 1987, *Our Common Future*, Oxford University Press, Oxford.

11 Alternative tourism— a deceptive ploy

B. Wheeller

Over the last few years there has been a growing general awareness, and a belated acknowledgement by the tourist industry itself, of the impact problems that have invariably accompanied tourism growth. Tourism clearly brings benefits to the recipient region and of course to the tourists themselves. However, though sometimes the scapegoat for other negative forces, there is a catalogue of impact catastrophes that provide graphic evidence of tourism's destructive power.

Much of the blame for the current situation has (simplistically) been attributed to the demands of mass tourism. A school of thought has developed that appears to be based on the fundamental premise that changing those demands would somehow provide the solution to tourism impacts. *Apparent* hope lies (an appropriate word here) in the new forms of tourism being lauded by tourist practitioners, the media and many academics. Lane (1989), writing on the effects of mass tourism, believed that 'Perhaps the saddest feature of contemporary tourism is that there is an alternative, but we are ignoring it'. If the alternative was being ignored then, it certainly is not now. Currently, there is no shortage of verbose rhetoric in support of this new *alternative* as a requisite for tourism planning and development.

To suggest that there is only one alternative might seem to be misleading. Indeed, the bewildering variety of names allocated to the numerous strands of the new tourism movement is somewhat confusing—soft, green, eco, gentle, appropriate, responsible, sustainable, quality, harmonious, community, progressive—the list of names given to this new aware tourism seems endless. Nevertheless, though the nomenclature continually changes to reflect what appears to be little more than fine-tuning, the overall message coming through is roughly the same. What is needed, it is argued by many, is a more caring, aware form of tourism industry—small-scale developments, ecologically sound, local integration with indigenous ownership and control, seasonal and spatial spread of demand, etc.—and a more caring, aware tourist well versed in the ethics of 'travel'. The pace of any tourism development should be slow, controlled, sympathetically planned and managed and, of course, be sustainable.

Although numerous writers have obviously contributed significantly in raising tourism awareness and consciousness, arguably the two seminal pieces of work, both emanating in the mid-1980s, were Krippendorf's **Holidaymakers** (1987) and Murphy's **Community Approach** (1985). Even so, most of the ideological roots underlying this new aware tourism are, in fact, nothing new. It is however only relatively recently that they have, for a combination of reasons, been applied to tourism and gained acceptability and popularity in that context. Seaton (1992), in a brief, erudite exposition of what he calls 'Quality Tourism', highlights the fact that the concept of sustainability has long been associated with development economics although it has only over the last few years become in vogue in tourism. The emphasis has been on the environment with eco-tourism receiving a high profile. However, discussions on sustainability should not be restricted to ecological issues but should also, as Sofield (1991) believes, incorporate the environment as a whole, including culture. He develops this argument in his search for principles of sustainable ethnic tourism.

The surge of support for the movement is now in full flow. Warnings such as 'Making simplistic and idealised comparisons of hard and soft on mass and green tourism, such that one is obviously undesirable and the other close to perfection is not only inadequate, it is grossly misleading' (Butler 1990) are being ignored. New tourism is being ecstatically embraced with unbridled enthusiasm by virtually all sections of tourism — the thinking tourist/traveller; the tourism industry (both private and public); the media; and many academics. Apparently there is enough vociferous, vanguard support to endorse it fully as the green way forward. However, such wholehearted and unquestioning acceptance is desperately disturbing, though not at all surprising if one considers the power of vested interest. For the educated tourist/traveller, for instance, it is immediately appealing for it conveniently appeases any guilt while simultaneously providing the increased holiday options and experience desired.

A deluge of material endorsing *green* sustainable tourism is currently flooding the tourism consciousness. The industry, increasingly 'sensitive to criticism that it is in the business of destroying the very world it encourages us to see, is desperately trying to appear ecologically responsible' (Wickers, 1992). It is becoming difficult to find a brochure that does not allude to green tourism. However, Wickers explains,

Much of the noise is marketing babble—another front on which to fight the competition—and many companies are simply slapping the green label on any destination where nature is more rampant than concrete. What will happen to that nature as a result of their promotion of it is not a question they care to address.

The cynicism is well founded. To put into some perspective industry's support for the new tourism it is worth considering how selective they have been in deciding which components of new tourism to overtly adopt. International tour operators, for example, while ostentatiously (and ostensibly) going green do not seem too keen on relinquishing *control* to the *local community*.

In the United Kingdom, recent material from official tourist and related bodies vigorously wave the green flag—witness **Tourism in the National Parks. A Guide to Good Practice** (ETB, 1990), and the much vaunted **The Green Light. A guide to Sustainable Tourism** (ETB, 1991). Superficially both look good. However, do they actually deal with the issue of coping with increasing numbers of mass tourists, the real crux of the problem, or are they just glossy, sleek brochures—the public sector equivalent of private sector marketing hype? A similar question mark must also surely hang over the Government Task Force Publication, **Tourism and the Environment** (ETB, 1991). The Tourism Society (1991) the main professional body in the United Kingdom, has produced a short document on **Sustainable Tourism** setting out in a straightforward manner some of the considerations and examples of good practice, and suggesting principles to adopt. Tourism Concern (1991), a growing voice in the tourism debate, has also produced material suggesting the way forward. However, there remains the void between words—however genuine and well intentioned—and harsh reality.

There is also a spate of articles and books advocating the ethics of the new tourism and urging tourists to behave *correctly*, (see, for example, Stevens, 1990; Bramwell, 1991, Anscombe, 1991; Platt, 1991; and Wood and House, 1991). The latter, **The Good Tourist** described as 'a worldwide guide for the green traveller' is dedicated to all travellers of the next generation. Unfortunately for those believing that 'green behaviour' will solve the problem, it seems highly probable that the next generation will, globally, consist of a large number—the critical mass—of tourists not behaving *correctly*. Would-be travellers will be vastly outnumbered by mass tourists. It must be doubtful that Western tourists, experienced in the culture of going abroad, will radically change their holiday behaviour patterns unless it meets their immediate personal interest to do so.

It seems unrealistic to believe that all tourists from countries new to the international tourism scene will behave sensitively and sympathetically. For them it is a new experience and in the circumstances they will want as much from it as possible at as little cost (to themselves) as possible. Recent behaviour patterns of tourists from eastern Europe suggest this to be, understandably, the case. (Wheeller, 1992).

We have moved from travel to tourism to mass tourism. Pundits of the green movement advocate a kind of *back to travel* except the reality is that globally we are moving toward mega tourism. The gap between the solution and the problem is again alarmingly though conveniently forgotten.

Of particular concern to some critics of the new movement is this very gap, some would say chasm, between the appealing though theoretical notions of *good tourism* and the practical realities of its implementation. Cazes (1989) warns of the danger of 'insidious distortions between the ideological discourse on the one hand, and the effective practices in places of tourism on the other'. In the Third World, he laments, 'there are no examples of significant size that fully meets the requirements of the alternative model'. Pigram (1990) also argues cogently that though worthwhile policy statements may be espoused, they encounter formidable barriers when attempts are made to translate them into action. The problem is not deciding what should be done, but actually making it happen. His perceptive article on sustainable tourism concludes with the stark prospect that without the development of effective means of translating the ideal into action, sustainable tourism 'runs the risk of remaining irrelevant and inert as a feasible policy option for the real world of tourism development'.

The irony here should not be lost. Usually academics are criticized, often with justification, for theoretical *ivory tower* mentality. In this particular case, however, several academics are arguing that it is the limited practical application of alternative tourism, and the constraints that prevent wider actual adoption, which make the new tourist movement so questionable as a way forward for tourism planning and management.

I have argued previously (Wheeller, 1991) that the practical issues of implementation are being ignored by many advocates of the new movement. Glib, general assertions are frequently incorporated into policy statements without any attention being given to defining in a practical sense such phrases as, for example, *the local community*, *tourism education* or *good visitor management*. Who actually decides what is required/decided? If, for example, authenticity is the objective, then the popular assumption that indigenous ownership and control will automatically ensure its maintenance is, as Sofield (1991) illustrates, sadly misplaced. How are new forms of tourism to be co-ordinated and who is to be responsible and accountable for its success? Difficult questions remain unanswered.

That such criticism is being swamped is not surprising given the concerted support for new tourism—the easy comfortable *answer* that does not address the central issue. It must be stressed that the main problem with tourism is numbers, the sheer volume and their continued spatial spread—yet the solution identified by many seems to be small-scale, slow, restricted development. Hardly an answer, given the problem. True, recent example of supposed good tourism practice being cited have included Disney and Centre Parcs (ETB, 1991, Tourism Society, 1991). By citing these honeypots (itself to an extent at odds with the *spread the load, spread the jam* philosophy), advocates go some way to dealing with numbers. It is, however, going to take a considerable number of 'Centre Parcs' to syphon off mass demand on a global basis. And where, of course, does the *ghettoization* of tourism fit in with the notion of *being at one with the indigenous population*, so important to our new code of behaviour for the traveller. Surprise, surprise, it seems the ghettos are for the masses and the undiscovered (and as yet unspoilt) for the *sensitive* traveller.

However, are these really examples of what is meant by green, sustainable tourism? Are they examples of the mysterious, ubiquitous, *good visitor management*? Or are these synonymous? Improvements at Benidorm, Ibiza and Magaluf are also being cited as good examples of the new tourism. In reality, are they not all just good examples of attempts at providing a quality product, or up-grading an existing one, for the quality market? (Now, is this what is meant by alternative tourism?) The policy of *up-grading* fits perfectly with the tourism industry's continued obsession with *growth*. To counterbalance the hackneyed argument of the danger of killing the goose, the equally hackneyed Pavlovian response is that the product must be continually *enhanced*. Always an emphasis on quality for the discerning quality market. Unfortunately, while there might well be a quality market, all the market is not quality. As the tourist numbers, world-wide, grow are all these new tourists going to be up-market, quality tourists? The uncomfortable answer must certainly be no. If say, Magaluf is successful in changing its 18–30 image and goes up-market, ridding itself of the undesirable, holiday hooligan as it does so, will this solve the problem of tourism? Current thinking would have us believe so. However, although it might solve the problem for Magaluf, it just shifts the problem elsewhere. The lower end of the market will, presumably, go elsewhere for their pleasure—possibly somewhere even less able to cope than Magaluf. A case of passing the buck. A solution, or survival of the fittest?

Although numbers are of critical importance, it is not simply mass tourism that is the problem. So too is the psuedo-sophisticated, sensitive traveller: 'the vanguard of the package tour, where he or she goes others will, in every increasing numbers, eventually follow. They are forever seeking the new, the exotic, the unspoilt—the vulnerable' (Wheeller, 1991). Alternative tourism is somewhat vague in dealing with this matter of the desire for the new. Apparently it endorses it and the concomitant opening up and development of new destinations, provided this is under-taken sensitively, sensibly and is appreciated by those travelling. (Read the books before you go, behave with respect, etc. For eco-tourism, read ego-tourism.) If this sensitive development can be achieved, which I doubt, surely this will only encourage more to travel anyway. It seems most likely that destinations will continue to be developed and planning and regu-latory standards relaxed under pragmatic pressures, as demand increases. Either way, prospects are bleak. What seems certain, though, is that the traveller/tourist, seeking the new, will continue to fan outwards, one step beyond tourism's new frontier.

According to Butler (1990), 'Claiming one form of tourism is all things for all areas is not only pious and naive, it is unfair, unrealistic and unwise'. Alternative tourism is not the answer to the negative impacts of tourism. It must be treated with caution, indeed scepticism, scrutinized and critically analysed from a realistic, practical perspective. Its ineffectiveness is its popularity, enabling the tourist/traveller to enjoy the holiday experience they want with a clear conscience, impunity and no sacrifice: It provides the tourist lobby with the perfect foil to allay fears (superficially) while enabling the industry to continue its growth, spread and development, swathed in a green mantle. Cohen (1989), in an excellent review of alternative tourism argues that as 'contemporary tourism is an extremely varied and many-sided phenomenon its indiscriminate criticism and total repudiation stand in danger of being rejected as tendentious and inad-equate . . . as stale and unconvincing'. Although there is much truth in this, it must surely also be true that this very complexity and heterogeneity render tourism unmanageable. The main protagonists in tourism are now behaving much as before, although, thanks to alternative tourism, with a renewed vigour borne out of self-righteous virtue.

References

Anscombe, J., 1991, 'The gentle traveller' *New Woman*, June: pp. 51–3.

Bramwell, B., 1991, 'Shades of green tourism', *Leisure Management*, February: pp. 40–1.

Butler, R., 1990, 'Alternative tourism: pious hope or Trojan Horse?', *Journal of Travel Research*, Winter: pp. 40–5.

Cazes, G., 1989, 'Alternative tourism: reflections of an ambiguous concept', in Singh, Theuns and Co (eds), *Towards Appropriate Tourism*, Lang, Frankfurt, 117–26.

Cohen, E., 1989, 'Alternative tourism—a critique', in Singh, Theuns and Co (eds), *Towards Appropriate Tourism*, Lang, Frankfurt, 127–42.

English Tourist Board, 1990, *Tourism: The National Parks. A Guide to Good Practice*, ETB, London.

English Tourist Board, 1991, *The Green Light. A Guide to Sustainable Tourism*, ETB, London.

English Tourist Board, 1991, *Tourism and the Environment—Maintaining the Balance*, ETB, London.

Lane, B., 1989, 'Modern mass tourism: a critque', *The Independent*, 13 May.

Krippendorf, J., *The Holidaymakers*, Heinemann, London.

Murphy, P., 1985, *Tourism. A Community Approach*, Routledge, London.

Pigram, J., 1990, 'Sustainable tourism, policy considerations', *Journal of Tourism Studies*, 2, November: pp. 2–9.

Platt, S., 1991, 'The tender tax', *New Statesman and Society*, 9 August: pp. 19–20.

Seaton, A., 1992, 'Quality tourism sustained', *Tourisme Qualitatife Aiest Annual*, 33: pp. 209–37.

Sofield, T., 1991, 'Sustainable ethnic tourism in the South Pacific: some principles', *Journal of Tourism Studies*, 2(1), May: pp. 56–72.

Stevens, T., 1990, 'Greener than green', *Leisure Management*, September: pp. 64–6.

Tourism Society, 1991, '*Sustainable Tourism: Development in Balance with the Environment*, Tourism Society, London.

Tourism Concern, 1991, *Himalayan Code*, Tourism Concern, Roehampton Institute, London.

Wheeller, B., 1991, 'Tourism: troubled times', *Tourism Management*, June: pp. 91–6.

Wheeller, B., 1992, 'Is progressive tourism appropriate?', *Tourism Management*, 13(1): pp. 104–5.

Wickers, D., 1992, 'Whither green', *Sunday Times*, 5 January.

Wood, K. and House, S., 1991, *The Good Tourist*, Mandarin, London.

Quality in Hospitality

12 Quality management and the tourism and hospitality industry
D.C. Gilbert and I. Joshi

Introduction

Today quality has emerged as a key competitive component within the overall strategies of many service-based companies. There are three main factors which may account for the increasing importance being placed on *quality* by marketers in the tourism and hospitality industry:

— intensified national and international competition for the leisure consumer;
— increased consumerism and greater media attention on quality issues within the tourism industry;
— an increasing sophistication of consumer markets with non-price factors becoming more important.

This chapter sets out to identify the major conceptual foundations which underpin the promulgation of quality management in the 1990s.

Until relatively recently many practitioners and marketers have been slow to recognize and react to the fundamental shift in the market towards saturation, over-capacity and greater turbulence. However, the signs of a paradigm shift in consumer attitudes were evident to some researchers such as Peckron (1971), Sheridan and Gronroos in the early 1970s. They established that consumers were demanding higher levels of quality; becoming more conscious of value for money; and indicated that in the future price competition would become subordinate to *quality* competition. Hill (1985) went as far as saying that *good* quality has become a minimum requirement for market entry, and Haywood (1983) argued that the management of quality is one of three key areas which can lead to corporate success in the hospitality field.

In the tourism and hospitality industry the increasing realization of the adverse effects of price competition has led marketers to look at a range of *competitive weapons*. There are five main ways of competitive differentiation which can be identified from the literature, one of which is quality (Heskett, 1986; Hill, 1985; Voss *et al.*,1985).

1. *Range of services*. A company can provide a greater range of services than the competition.

2. *Price*. A company can charge lower prices than those charged for competing services.
3. *Availability*. A company can provide services that are more easily available to the customer than those of the competition.
4. *Uniqueness*. A company can provide a unique service that is not offered by any of its competitors.
5. *Quality*. A company can provide services that have a higher level of service quality than the competition.

The tour operator industry is an excellent example of a changing orientation towards competition. The two companies which dominated the UK overseas holiday market a couple of years ago—Thomson and Intasun Holidays—made major changes in their marketing policies. After nearly a decade of price wars between the two giants, both were in favour of a new emphasis on higher quality.

This new *quality awareness* was reflected in the changing of Intasun's long-running slogan—'Why pay more?'—in favour of a 'Better holiday, brilliant prices' line (Moyle, 1989). However, this policy change was never properly assessed owing to the collapse of Intasun in March 1991 when ILG, through cash flow problems, became the worst UK tourism business failure since Courtline in 1974.

Evidence of consumer dissatisfaction with quality

Many newspapers produce 'scathing attacks' on tour operators owing to the poor experiences of consumers when taking holidays abroad. In addition articles such as that of Gilbert and Soni (1991) have highlighted the problems of tour operator responsiveness to their consumers. A reliable source of evidence of trade problems comes from the Association of British Travel Agents (ABTA) (1985), who commissioned a research survey from the Harris Research Centre. The results of the consumer survey reflected those of an earlier World Tourism Organization survey. From a sample of over 500 holidays analysed, ABTA found that a high number of holidays give rise to some problem. The breakdown of complaints is shown in Table 12.1. Problems over package holiday arrangements are not isolated to the United Kingdom. Because the European tourism industry has failed to provide adequate control of the quality of its products, the EC has issued a directive which will lead to greater regulation of package travel arrangements (DTI, 1992).

On examining the nature of the complaints in Table 12.1, we believe the majority are easily controllable by management. In relation to quality assurance improvement, management policies which improve and control quality are an important issue within the tourism and hospitality industries. Evidence of attempts at control are sparse although a recent article by Callan (1992), provides an interesting case study of the way a hotel implemented a quality control scheme as an attempt to obtain the first British Standard 5750. Quality assurance in hotels has been examined by

Table 12.1 *Formal complaints made by holiday-makers*

Base: package holidays abroad (535 holidays)	535
Made formal complaint during holiday	13
Made formal complaint on return from holiday	6
Type of complaint	
Given wrong/sub-standard accommodation	5
Standard of food	2
Poor in-transit facilities, e.g., state of bus/train	1
Noise	1
Given wrong resort/hotel	1
Change in transport, e.g., different flight, train, cancellation	1
Luggage damaged/lost	1
Complaints about beds	1
Complaints about excursions	1
Standard of service	*
Theft	*
Having to pay extra for facilities/car hire	*
Lack of hygiene in accommodation	*
Overbooking	*
Other	7
Not stated	*

* = less than 0.5%

Walker and Salameh (1990) while Records and Glennie (1991) have explained how quality assurance can be improved through service management systems. However, Zeithaml, Berry and Parasuraman (1988), have pointed out that even when control is exercised, certain quality factors are beyond management control, such as the customer's personal needs, any past experience with the company and word of mouth recommendations.

Defining service quality

Quality appears to be a concept of which everyone claims to have an intuitive understanding while at the same time finding it difficult to define. The problem of providing a comprehensive definition is embedded in the fact that *quality* has traditionally been used as an adjective (e.g., as in a 'quality' product) to imply a high degree of excellence or as an associated distinguishing attribute. Gronroos (1984) deplores the use of the term *quality* as if it were a variable itself, rather than a function of a range of resources and activities. Parasuraman *et al.*, (1985) reiterate the problem faced by many academic writers and researchers that quality is an elusive and indistinct construct.

Therefore, there is a need for more thorough conceptualization in order to develop scholarly analysis and provide managerial prescriptions. We experienced some difficulty in trying to make order from the various ways *quality* has been defined in recent literature. The problem is that there appears to be no formal attempts to classify any of the concepts. We therefore propose that the approaches be distinguished on the basis of their emphasis into two categories:

1. *Product-attribute approach.*
2. *Consumer-oriented approach* (which can be further divided between: one focusing on needs and the other focusing on perceptions).

The product-attribute approach

Efforts in defining and measuring quality have come largely from the goods sector, which are clearly inappropriate for use in the service setting. Garvin (1983), for instance, measures quality by counting the incidence of **internal** failures (i.e., those observed before a product leaves a factory) and **external** failures (those incurred in the field after a unit has been installed). Scientists and engineers equate quality of a product with *technical quality*. They focus a product's quality rating on a set of *hard* or technical quality measures (e.g., conformance, weight, material).

Some researchers, in attempting to make a contribution to an understanding of service quality, have focused on the 'internal' operations view, such as Crosby (1984) who defines quality simply as 'conformance to requirements' based upon company specifications. This means the degree of conformance of all a service's features and characteristics to the service product requirement specification. Such an approach can be judged to be too product-oriented and technical to be of great use in the tourism and hospitality service setting. The increasing realization of the efficacy of adopting a marketing orientation in the tourism and hospitality industry has changed the quality emphasis to one of matching quality specifications to consumer needs. Unfortunately, management are often likely to evaluate the quality of the companies' products and services from an 'internal' product perspective. They forget that evaluation is often based upon the consumers' perceptions of the product's relative position to competing products.

The product-attribute approach is thus objectivistic. However, human behaviour, especially in the tourism and hospitality field, does not always follow rules of economic rationality, but rather is directed by idiosyncratic habits, psychological needs, perceptions and expectations. In addition, service quality in the tourism and hospitality industry is difficult to evaluate for it entails the holistic process of service delivery and a notion of consumer expectation of the required performance level.

The consumer-orientated approach

The following approaches show an emphasis on the consumer, but one focuses on the requirements of consumers while the other stresses their perceptions and expectations.

Consumer-requirement approach to quality. The following interpretations of quality move away from a focus on the product attributes and examine quality in relation to consumer needs and requirements.

Wyckoff (1984) defines service quality as 'the degree of excellence intended and the control of variability in achieving that excellence in meeting customer's requirements'. We believe this approach is positive owing to the fact that it

1. tries to incorporate the notion of control, thus making the definition all the more operational; and
2. implies that service quality should ultimately aim at meeting the needs of consumers.

The definition given by the British Standards Institute (1983) also embraces a consumer-orientation and revolves around the satisfaction of consumer needs: 'The totality of features or characteristics of a product or service that bear on its ability to satisfy a given need.'

Oakland (1986) defines quality as 'Fitness for purpose/function' and states that it concerns satisfying consumer needs.

We believe that these approaches to quality are beneficial, since they imply that customer needs should drive quality programmes. In relation to this approach recent publications such as Lewis and Nightingale (1991) reinforce the need for a customer-led level of service quality.

Consumer expectations orientation. Gronroos (1988) claims that consumers view service quality as a comparison between the service they expect with perceptions of the service they receive. Dore (1988) suggests that the key to providing good service is to understand that service is *not* the actions and behaviour themselves but the way in which guests perceive and interpret these actions. From his experience as a waiter, it was noticed that there were times when guests praised the quality of the service, which from the waiters' view was quite poor. The opposite also occurred. The guests did not seem to be evaluating the actions themselves but their perceptions of these actions. Zeithaml (1981) similarly contends that part of the literature on services tends to equate quality with perceived quality on the consumer's judgement about a service's overall excellence or superiority.

We believe that this approach is a positive one, for it acknowledges the importance of consumer behaviour in the evaluation of services. Such an approach implies that marketers need to expand their attention from understanding and manipulating the production process to understanding the consumer's perception and all the psychological, sociological and situational factors resulting from and impinging on a service interaction.

Conceptual foundations

An important underlying theme found in the literature is that service quality perceptions result from a comparison of consumer expectations with actual service performance. For example, Lewis and Booms (1983) contend: 'Service quality is a measure of how well the service level delivered matches customer expectations. Delivering quality service means conforming to customer expectations on a consistent basis.' On a similar note Smith and Houston (1982) claim that 'satisfaction with services is related to confirmation or disconfirmation of expectations'. However, the most prominent contributions to this area have been made by Gronroos (1982), and Parasuraman, Zeithaml and Berry (1985).

Gronroos (1982) developed a model to explain what he calls the 'missing service quality concept'. The model shown in Figure 12.1 rests largely on the construct of *image* which represents the gap between expected service and perceived service. Gronroos deplores the use of the term quality as if it were a variable itself rather than a 'function of a range of resources and activities'. He argues that this range includes what customers are looking for, what they are evaluating, how service quality is perceived and in what way service quality is influenced. Gronroos defines 'perceived quality' of the service as dependent on two variables: experienced service and perceived service; or collectively the outcome of the evaluation.

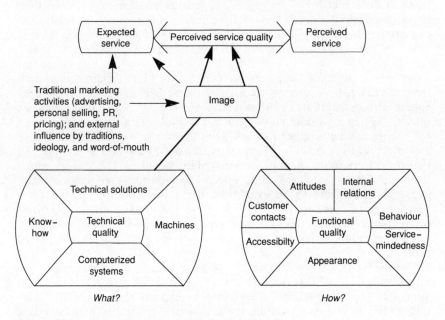

Figure 12.1   *Managing the perceived service quality*

Source: Gronroos, 1982.

Parasuraman, Zeithaml and Berry (1985) have also developed a model of service quality (see Figure 12.2), which hypothesizes that consumer evaluation of quality is a function of the difference (gap) between expected and perceived service. It highlights the main requirements for a service

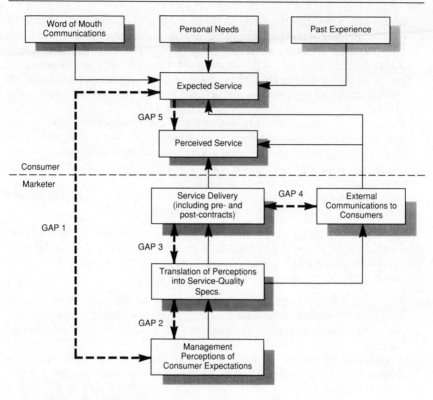

Figure 12.2 *Service quality model*

Source: Parasuraman, Zeithaml and Berry, 1985.

provider delivering the expected service quality. From the model we can identify five gaps that cause unsuccessful service delivery. In studying this model we believe that several of the gaps can be bridged through more effective use of market research techniques to provide the impetus for change.

1. *Gap between consumer expectation and management perception*. This may result from a lack of understanding of what consumers expect in a service. An extensive study by Nightingale (1983) confirms this disparity, by revealing that what providers perceive as important to consumers is often different from what consumers themselves expect.
2. *Gap between management perception and service quality specifications*. This gap results when there is a discrepancy between what management perceives to be consumer expectations and the actual service quality specifications established. Management might not set quality standards or very clear ones; or they may be clear although unrealistic. Alterna-

tively, although the standards might be clear and realistic, management may quite simply not be committed to enforcing them.

3. *Gap between service quality specifications and service delivery.* Even where guidelines exist for performing service well, service delivery may not be of the appropriate quality owing to poor employee performance. Indeed the employee plays a *pivotal* role in determining the quality of a service.
4. *Gap between service delivery and external communications.* Consumer expectations are affected by the promises made by the service provider's promotional message. Marketers must pay close attention to ensure consistency between the *quality* image portrayed in promotional activity and the *actual* quality offered.
5. *Gap between perceived service and delivered service.* This gap results when one or more of the previous gaps occur.

The focus on perceptions and expectations is similar to one of the approaches used to define service quality. On examining the model proposed by Parasuraman, Zeithaml and Berry, we believe that it has two main strengths to recommend it:

1. The model presents an entirely **dyadic** view to the marketing task of delivering service quality. The model alerts the marketer to consider the perceptions of both parties (marketers and consumers) in the exchange process.
2. Addressing the gaps in the model can serve as a logical basis for formulating strategies and tactics to ensure consistent experiences and expectations.

However, it is important to note that the researchers used the following four service categories for investigation: retail banking, credit card, securities brokerage and product repair and maintenance. One may question the applicability of these to the tourism and hospitality industry, which is uniquely characterized by high-risk, ego-sensitive and status-conscious purchasing. Following the work of Gronroos and Parasuraman, Zeithaml and Berry, various authors have attempted to develop a framework for carrying out empirical research into the differences of expected and derived satisfaction from service provision. In this mould we find authors such as Laws (1986), who has researched airline travel, and Lewis (1987), who carried out research into hotel service. In the tradition of the early work, reference is made to consumer gaps, yet it is interesting to find that other descriptions are utilized such as that of Blake *et al.* (1986) who refer to differences as disparity analysis.

Quality and process

A further underlying theme in the literature on which there appears to be a consensus is that quality evaluations are not made solely on the outcome of a service, they also include evaluations of the process of service delivery.

Nightingale (1985) examined perceptions of quality in the hospitality industry from both a management and consumer perspective.This contrasts sharply with the manufacturing industry where the consumer's evaluation of quality will centre on, for example the can of baked beans, not its production.

Prominent research in the area has been undertaken by Gronroos (1982), who distinguishes between two types of quality a customer receives related to service experience delivery:

1. *Technical quality*—which refers to what the customer is actually receiving from the service, and is capable of objective measurement as with any tangible good.
2. *Functional quality*—which refers to how the technical elements of the service are transferred. Thus a customer in a restaurant will not only evaluate the quality of food he consumes but also the way in which it was delivered (the style, manner and appearance of the waiter or the *ambience* of the place itself). Figure 12.1 shows that functional quality consists of elements such as attitudes, behaviour and general service-mindedness of personnel, all of which can be influenced by management.

In the research carried out by Bitner *et al.* (1985), respondents specify incidents in which good or poor service was delivered. By utilizing the Gronroos (1985) typology of technical versus functional service quality dimensions, the researchers discovered that 77 per cent of the service encounters mentioned as either satisfactory or unsatisfactory related to *functional* aspects of the service. In other words, the main concern for evaluation of service quality was on the *manner* in which the service was actually delivered. We believe that knowledge of this should be conducive to marketers directing greater efforts and resources to cultivating the right service personnel. Hopefully it will shift the focus of quality assurance and control from (for example) assuring the correct number of toiletry items per hotel room to a more *holistic* approach.

Research viewing service quality in a similar way, carried out by Lehtinen (1985), was based upon the fundamental premise that service quality is produced in the interaction between a customer and elements in the service organization. Three components of service quality are identified:

1. *Interactive quality*—the quality of the interaction between the service personnel and the customer.
2. *Physical quality*—the quality of tangible clues such as surroundings and facilitating goods.
3. *Institutional/corporate quality*—which involves the company's image or profile.

Similarly, the work of Sasser, Olsen and Wyckoff (1978) proposes three different dimensions of service performance:

— levels of materials;

— levels of facilities;
— levels of personnel.

The trichotomy implies that not only the *physical* outcomes are important but also the facilities and personnel who will influence how the service is delivered.

Marketing implications

We believe that it would be beneficial for tourism marketers to view services in terms of their technical and functional components. The marketer may want to try and assess the relative importance of each element for their particular service offering.

By way of example: in a *fast food outlet*, it may be found that consumers are more concerned about the technical quality (the output) than the functional quality (how the food is served). In the first class section of an airline, consumers may place equal importance on both elements, i.e., they will be concerned with both the service (the functional quality) *and* the meal they receive (technical quality such as whether the cutlery is metal or plastic and whether the drinks include champagne).

Knowledge of the relative importance consumers perceive for both elements can aid marketers to segment the market, and to develop service design and promotional activity accordingly.

The management of quality requires an emphasis on enhancing:

1. Preference and disposition toward the service, i.e., enhancing evaluative judgement;
2. the way in which the service is compared with others, i.e., improvement of the image and perceived benefits; and
3. the situational context in which the service is delivered, i.e., controlling the physical and social aspects of the service experience.

Quality control in service operations

On reviewing the literature, we found that although a range of quality control models have been proposed, there lacks a body of empirical research undertaken specifically with regard to the hospitality product. Many quality control models centre on the tangible aspects of the product (e.g., control of production, portion control, food cost control, labour standards, inventory control). However, a few exceptions were found, notably that of Jones (1983). The system proposed by Jones, seen in Figure 12.3, relies on defining management objectives in relation to market research findings.

Policy statements can then be made on the product design and development, from which precise documentation is produced relating to specific product-mix features. Jones then refines this documentation into two

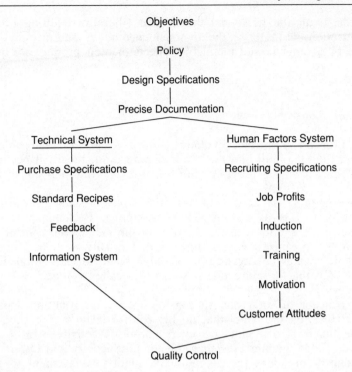

Objectives

Policy

Design Specifications

Precise Documentation

Technical System   Human Factors System

Purchase Specifications   Recruiting Specifications

Standard Recipes   Job Profits

Feedback   Induction

Information System   Training

Motivation

Customer Attitudes

Quality Control

Figure 12.3   *Quality control*

Source: Jones (1983).

areas: **technical** specifications and human factors (relating to recruitment, training, etc.). Control procedures are then applied, which determine the participation in the resultant attainment of quality.

Appraisal of the model

We believe that this quality control model shifts the emphasis from a mechanistic and technical base to incorporate the **human** dimensions within a management framework.

1. The model recognizes the centrality of consumer *attitudes* to drive the process of quality management. (Management objectives are made in accordance with market research findings.)
2. By including the *human factor* controls, it acknowledges that the restaurant product is seen by consumers not only in technical terms (portion control, etc.), but also in relation to *how* it is delivered. The model implies that the key to implementing and maintaining quality control standards lies with the successful communication of those stan-

dards to all the personnel taking part (thereby requiring training, motivation,etc.). Hence, the approach encourages marketers to ensure that both tangible and intangible aspects of their product are quality controlled.

Company culture and service quality

This approach concentrates on quality control as a general philosophy and mode of thinking built into the whole organization. Ideally it becomes a way of life, having a pervasive impact on everybody and all everyday activities.

Feigenbaum (1983) and Ishikawa (1985) have helped to widen the concept of quality as a management discipline. Feigenbaum expands the concept of quality control to cover all the managerial control functions of the organization and suggests that quality is in its essence a way of managing the organization through what he calls 'total quality control'. (In the literature this is sometimes called *company-wide quality control*.)

The concept of total quality control has come from the Japanese firms. It rests on the belief that quality control techniques can be used to raise the level of quality for every corporate activity, with a result of better yields, greater efficiency, higher productivity and lower costs. This concept broadens the definition of quality management to cover all aspects of corporate existence, and it is here where lies its strength. As Jones (1983) states, 'Consumers do not perceive the tangible and intangible elements of the totality, they perceive them as a unified whole.' Therefore a quality philosophy should embrace all aspects of company activity. Lockwood (1989) reinforces this by stating that to be effective, quality must be integrated into all activities of the organization and cannot be simply added at the end of the production cycle.

Katz and Kahn (1978) explain why climate and culture are so important in any industry. They suggest that human systems need some *glue*, some central theme or themes around which behaviour can coalesce. In the absence of any such themes, employees cannot know:

— when to direct their energies;
— at what to direct their energies; and
— how to direct their energies.

An appropriate culture provides this thematic coherence to the behaviour of employees, especially when the climate and culture are aimed at desired organizational behaviour.

While culture and company philosophy are always important management tools, they acquire enhanced importance for service organizations. Gronroos (1988) and Normann (1984) both contend that in a service context, a strong and well-established culture, which enhances an appreciation for good service and customer orientation, is extremely important. Service production cannot be standardized as completely as an assembly-line because of the human impact on the buyer-seller interface. Situations vary (according to individual, time, place, atmosphere) and therefore a distinct 'service-oriented' culture may be required in order to inform employees how to respond to new, unforeseen and even awkward situations. Bowen and Schneider (1985) support this and observe that 'service firms . . . need to manage and enhance their internal climate for service to positively impact the attitudes and behaviour of those who serve the customer'.

In organizational behaviour the issue of identification and commitment has a rich theory and database (Mowday *et al.*, 1980). It has been found that an increased sense of identity is correlated with improved job satisfaction, improved extra-role performance (going beyond the job description) and lower turnover. Schneider and Schmitt (1986) reveal that the quality experienced by the client increases if a positive, open and service-minded climate pervades the organization and is displayed to the client.

Having limited hierarchical power yet high responsibility levels for consumer satisfaction, the marketing manager has utilized internal marketing as a particular strategy to influence improvements in service quality. Internal marketing is especially relevant in service firms because in the majority more than 50 per cent of the personnel interact directly with the customer. We can therefore assume that given the level of interactive service encounters in tourism and hospitality industries, internal marketing assumes great importance. This is owing to the fact that it is the quality of employee performance which is a significant part of the 'product' the external customer buys.

In discussing internal marketing, it is important to realize that it is not to be seen as an isolated activity but indeed as an integral part of the wider objectives of a marketing-oriented philosophy. This complementarity between external and internal marketing was clearly identified by G.M. Hostage when interviewed as President of the Marriott Corporation (1975): 'In the service business, you cannot make happy customers with unhappy employees.'

Internal marketing

Berry (1980), Tarver (1987), Gronroos (1981), Teare and Gummesson (1989), have all provided contributions to the literature on the importance of internal marketing. The marketing function is weak in many service companies because the commercial personnel have for too long been subservient to the production function. Therefore, the latter tends to resist the will of the marketing department to influence the performance level of contact personnel. The question may thus arise: 'How can a marketing manager improve the service quality if he has little control over the people?'

Communication is especially important where units are geographically sparse. The development of internal communications at Thomson Holidays must ensure that over 2,000 employees working in small groups around the world do not feel isolated from the rest of the company's activities. Amongst the various channels of communication utilized is their in-house newspaper, which performs the particularly important function of acting as a two-way channel of information between the London Head Office and its staff overseas.

The Disney Corporation is often referred to as the classic internal marketer. It consistently achieves a high quality performance from its massive work-force. Everyone from part-time employee to the president has to attend an induction programme at Disney University and pass the *traditional* course.

Personnel recruitment

Appropriate recruitment and selection can provide organizations with the *raw materials* of a quality service firm. Whatever the overall focus, good recruitment can result in attracting the most appropriate candidates and discouraging others, and in the retention of people subsequently appointed.

Techniques now exist for developing work simulations that can be used to find persons with service-orientated skills and competencies (Schneider and Schmitt, 1986). Jones and DeCotis (1986) maintain that one of the ways to ensure a service-oriented staff is to select people who are guest-oriented in the first place. To this end they describe personnel-testing techniques such as video-assisted testing.

The importance of developing and educating the people who are recruited to supply services is so crucial that many service companies organize their own schools, as evidenced by Holiday Inn University, Marriott's 'learning centre' and the McDonald's Hamburger University. In the United Kingdom Forte International, have established a 'training' academy in a purpose-built site at a hotel near Heathrow Airport. In the tourism and hospitality industry, the product delivery from the service provider to the customer is both technical and interpersonal. This requires suitable training in both types of skills.

Voss *et al.* (1985) maintain the service provider cannot communicate technical skills to clients/customers independent of his/her service orientation or set of attitudes toward the client. Unfortunately many organizations tend to forget the ongoing nature of training and fail to persevere beyond initial induction. Mill (1990) contends that management too often see training as an expense rather than as an investment Voss *et al.* (1985) refer to training of new employees as an essential tool for enhancing employee motivation. It shows the company 'cares' and is committed to its employees, which in turn helps to sustain quality of service output.

Given the literature reveals a considerable body of knowledge on the enhancement of service quality, it seems surprising that many programmes have not proved successful. Leonard and Sasser (1982), Normann (1984) and Collier (1987) propose that one of the most common reasons for failure in quality management is a lack of top management's strategic support. Without personal example and the reinforcement of ideas from top management, quality standards are unlikely in the long run to be accepted and maintained.

A classic example of a quality assurance programme undertaken successfully by a service enterprise is that of British Airways (BA). An important reason for the success of BA's programme is the commitment of top management in bringing forth 'quality' as a key element of corporate strategy. Figure 12.4 represents the various stages through which the programme proceeded.

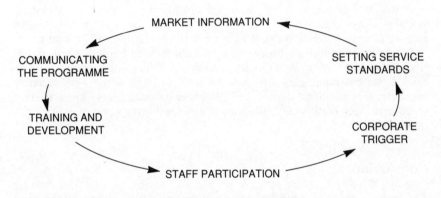

Figure 12.4   *The BA customer service quality programme*

Initial market research   Before the launch of the 'putting the customer first' programme, in 1983, BA embarked upon a major piece of qualitative market research amongst 700 fliers. The research objective was to identify the service expected at each point of customer contact from the very best airlines in the world (e.g. on the telephone, at the check-in desk, in the departure lounge and on board the aeroplane). It also aimed to find out how far airlines matched consumer expectations and how BA compared with these. In brief the main findings were that 20 per cent considered BA excellent, 60 per cent had no strong opinion and 20 per cent were dissatisfied. Therefore the main opportunity and target lay in the middle 60 per cent.

The research showed that customers expected the following from the very best airlines in the world:

1. recovering effectively when things go wrong;
2. showing care and concern;

3. being spontaneous—i.e. can the front-line staff use discretion on behalf of the customer and go beyond the rule book; and
4. solving customer problems.

These factors not only highlighted the key role of front-line customer contact staff, they indicated precisely which training objectives the customer would recognize as relevant. They demonstrated the need for staff to be encouraged to act with more independence and autonomy in all areas of service. An internal research project was also undertaken with customer contact staff to determine their views of customers. Part of this research revealed that few employees recognized the importance of the total team to service output. With the knowledge that consumers rarely *dissect* their service experiences, BA from 1983 onward have implemented programmes of 'putting people first' training schemes to ensure high levels of staff *consistency* in service delivery. In addition management have attended a 'managing people first' programme. One characteristic of the BA programme was to ensure service standards were delineated at each job interface with the customer.

It is interesting to note how service standards were implemented. Apart from a number of company-wide training schemes, management reinforced the customer care message to staff through some very creative means, e.g., calendars, diaries, videos, check-in computers. These service standards are continually reviewed and reinforcement schemes are ongoing.

Conclusion

The highly competitive market-place, increasingly active consumerism and a need to find alternative ways of differentiating products from those of competitors, have all led marketers to direct increasing attention on the management of quality. The body of literature on service industry quality management, which has been built up over the previous two decades, provides ample evidence of good practice. However, the tourism and hospitality industries need a greater cross-fertilization of the key concepts in order to be at the forefront of consumer quality expectations. The interrelationship between a quality management orientation and improved competitive advantage is a distinguishing feature which we believe will be a key emphasis for the industry in the future. On the research side it is believed greater attention will need to be placed on:

1. developing more sensitive instruments and measurements of consumers' service quality perceptions; and
2. establishing the usefulness of segmenting consumers on the basis of their service quality perceptions.

Overall, given the necessity to remain one notch above the service quality expectations of the consumer in order to squeeze greater intentional demand from the market-place, the management of quality will remain a focal point of interest to researchers and management alike.

References

Association of British Travel Agents, 1985, *Report on Holiday Complaints*, ABTA, London.

Berry, L.L., 1980. 'Services marketing is different', *Business*, 30(3), May–June: pp. 24–9.

Bitner, M., Nyquist, J. and Booms, B., 1985, 'The critical incident as a technique for analyzing the service encounter, in T. Bloch. *et al.*, *Service Marketing in a Changing Environment*, American Marketing Association, Chicago, 48–51.

Blake, B.F., Dexheimer, C. and Mercurin, N., 1986, 'Disparity analysis, a double-edged sword', *Marketing News*, 13 January: pp. 34–5.

Bowden, D.E. and Schneider, B., 1985, 'Boundary-spanning-role employees and the service encounter: some guidelines for management and research', in J.A. Czepiel and M.R. Solomon (eds), *The Service Encounter*, Lexington Books, Lexington.

British Standards Institute, 1983, *BSF, 4778 BSI Handbook*, p. 22.

Butterfield, R.W., 1987, 'A quality strategy for service organizations', *Quality Progress*, December: pp. 40–2.

Callan, R.J., 1992, 'Quality control at Avant Hotels—the debut of BS 5750', *The Service Industries Journal*, 12(1): pp. 17–33.

Chase, R.B., 1978, 'Where does the customer fit in a service operation?', *Harvard Business Review*, 56, November–December: pp. 137–2.

Collier, D.A., 1987, 'The customer service and quality challenge', *The Service Industries Journal*, 7(1): pp. 77–90.

Cowell, D.W., 1984, *The Marketing of Services*, Heinemann, London.

Crosby, P., 1984, *Quality Without Tears*, New American Library, New York.

Department of Trade and Industry, 1992, *Consultative Document re. Directive 90/314/ECC*, London.

Dore, C.D., 1988, 'The interpretation of service: an anthropological view', *Hospitality Education and Research Journal*, 12: pp. 81–91.

Feigenbaum, A.V., 1983, *Total Quality Control*, McGraw-Hill, New York.

Fitch, A. 1987, 'Tour operators in the UK', *Travel and Tourism Analyst*, March pp. 29–33.

Garvin, D.A., 1983, 'Quality on the line', *Harvard Business Review*, 61, September–October, pp. 65–73.

Gilbert, D.C. and Soni, S., 1991, 'UK tour operators and consumer responsiveness', *The Service Industries Journal*, 11(4): pp. 413–24.

Gronroos, C.A., 1978, 'A service-oriented approach to marketing of services', *European Journal of Marketing*, 12(8): pp. 588–601.

Gronroos, C., 1981, *Internal marketing—an integral part of marketing theory*, in J.H. Donnelly and W.R. George (eds), *Marketing of Services*, American Marketing Association, Chicago.

Gronroos, C., 1982, *Strategic management and marketing in the service sector*, Swedish School of Economics and Business Administration, Helsinki.

Gronroos, C., 1984, 'A service quality model and its marketing implications', *Journal of Marketing*, 18: pp. 36–44.

Gronroos, C., 1988, *Assessing Competitive Edge in the new Competition of the Service Economy: The Five Rules of Service*, Working Paper No. 9, First Interstate Centre for Services Marketing, Arizona State University.

Hales, C. and Oberoi, U. 1989, 'Assessing the quality of the conference hotel service product: towards an empirically-based model', *Journal of Contemporary Hospitality Management*, Launch Conference 1: pp. 90–113.

Haywood, K.M., 1983, 'Assessing the quality of hospitality services', *International Journal of Hospitality Management*, 2(4): pp. 165–77.

Heskett, J.L., 1986, *Managing in the Service Economy*, Harvard Business School Press, Boston.

Hill, T., 1985, *Manufacturing Strategy*, Macmillan, London.

Hostage, G.M., 1975, 'Quality control in a service business', *Harvard Business Review*, July–August: pp. 98–106.

Ishikawa, K. 1985, *What is Total Quality Control? The Japanese Way*, Prentice Hall, Englewood Cliffs.

ISO 8402, 1986, *Quality Vocabulary*, International Standards Organization, ISO Publications, London.

Jacoby, J., Olsen, J. and Price, 1973, 'Brand name and product composition characteristics as determinants of perceived quality', *Journal of Applied Psychology*, 50(6): pp. 570–9.

Jones, P., 1983, 'The restaurant—a place for quality control and product maintenance?', *International Journal of Hospitality Management*, 2(2): pp. 93–100.

Jones, P. and DeCotis, T., 1986, 'A better way to select service employees: video-assisted testing'. *The Cornell Hotel and Restaurant Administration Quarterly*, 27(2), August: pp. 68–73.

Jones, P., 1988, 'Quality, capacity and productivity in service industries', *International Journal of Hospitality Management*, 7(2): pp.104–12.

Katz, D. and Kahn, R.L., 1978, *The Social Psychology of Organization*, 2nd edn., Wiley, New York.

Lehtinen, V. and Lehtinen, J.R., 1985, *Service Quality: A Study of Quality Dimensions*, Helsinki Service Management Institute, Finland.

Lehtinen, V. and Jarmo, R., 1982, 'Service quality. a study of quality dimensions', unpublished working paper, Helsinki Service Management Institute, Finland.

Leonard, F.S. and Sasser, W.E., 1982, 'The incline of quality'. *Harvard Business Review*, 60(5), September–October: pp. 163–71.

Levitt, T., 1972, 'Production-line approach to service', *Harvard Business Review*, 50, September–October: pp. 41–52.

Levitt, T., 1976, 'The industrialization of service', *Harvard Business Review*, 54, September–October: pp. 63–74.

Lewis, R.C. and Booms, B.H., 1983, 'The marketing aspects of service quality in L. Berry and G. Shostack (eds) *Emerging Perspectives on Services Marketing*, American Marketing, Chicago, 99–107.

Lewis, R.C., 1987, 'The measurement of gaps in the quality of hotel services', *International Journal of Hospitality Management*, 6(2): pp. 83–88.

Lewis, R. and Nightingale, M., 1991, 'Targetting service to your customer', *The Cornell Hotel and Restaurant Administration Quarterly*, 32(2): pp. 18–27.

Lockwood, A., 1989, 'Quality management in hotels', in S.F. Witt and L. Moutinho (eds), *Tourism Marketing and Management Handbook*, Prentice Hall, New York.

Lovelock, C.L. and Young, R.F., 1979, 'Look to consumers to increase productivity'. *Harvard Business Review*. May–June, pp. 168–78.

McConnell, J.D., 1968, 'Effect of pricing on perception of product quality' *Journal of Applied Psychology*, 52, August pp. 300–3.

Mill, R.C., 1990, 'Human resources management within the hospitality industry', in C. Cooper (ed.), *Progress in Tourism, Recreation and Hospitality Manage-*

ment, Volume One, Belhaven Press, London 161–75.

Mowday, R.T., Porter, L.W. and Steers, R.M., 1980, 'Employee organization linkages', in *The Psychology of Commitment, Absenteeism and Turnover*, Academic Press, New York.

Moyle, F., 1989, 'Making the package a tourist attraction', *Marketing Week*, February: pp. 44–7.

Nightingale. M., 1983, 'Determination and control of quality standards in hospitality services', Unpublished MPhil thesis, University of Surrey.

Nightingale, M., 1985, 'The hospitality industry: Defining Quality for a quality assurance programme—a study of perceptions', *The Service Industries Journal*, 5(1): pp. 9–22.

Normann, R., 1984, *Service Management: Strategy and Leadership in Service Businesses*, Wiley, Chichester.

Oakland, J.S., 1986, 'Systematic quality management in banking', *The Service Industries Journal*, 6(2), July: pp. 193–204.

Parasuraman, A., Zeithaml, V.A. and Berry, L.L., 1983, 'Service firms need marketing skills', *Business Horizons*, November–December: pp. 28–31.

Parasuraman, A., Zeithaml, V.A. and Berry, L.L., 1985, 'A conceptual model of service quality and its implication for future research', *Journal of Marketing*, 49(4), Fall: pp. 41–50.

Peckron, H.S., 1971, 'Quality control program synthesis', *Marquette Business Review*, 14(4): pp. 192–203.

Pickworth, J.R., 1988, 'Service delivery systems in the food service industry', *International Journal of Hospitality Management*, 7(1): pp. 43–62.

Rathmell, J.M., 1974, *Marketing in the Service Sector*, Winthrop, Cambridge, Mass.

Records, M.A.and Glennie, M.F., 1991, 'Service management and quality assurance: a systems approach', *The Cornell Hotel and Restaurant Administration Quarterly*, 32(1): pp. 26–35.

Regan, W.J., 1963, 'The service revolution', *Journal of Marketing*, 27, July: pp. 57–62.

Sasser, W.E. and Arbeit, S.P., 1976, 'Selling jobs in the service sector', *Business Horizons*, 19, June: pp. 61–5.

Sasser, W.E., 1976, 'Match supply and demand in service industries', *Harvard Business Review*, November–December: pp. 133–40.

Sasser, W.E., Olsen, R.P. and Wyckoff, D.D., 1978, *Management of Service Operations*, Allyn and Bacon, Boston, Mass.

Schneider, B. and Schmitt, N., 1986, *Staffing for Organizations*, 2nd edn, Scott Foresman, Glenview.

Tarver, J.L., 1987, 'In search of a competitive edge in banking; a personnel approach', *International Journal of Bank Marketing*, 5(1): pp. 61–8.

Teare, R. and Gummesson, E.,1989, 'Internal marketing strategy for hospitality organizations', *Journal of Contemporary Hospitality Management*, Launch Conference 1: pp.126–36.

Voss, C., Armistead, C., Johnston, R. and Morris, B., 1985, *Operations Management in Service Industries and the Public Sector*, Wiley, Chichester.

Walker, J.R. and Salameh, T.T., 1990, 'The QA payoff', *The Cornell Hotel and Restaurant Administration Quarterly*, 30(4): pp.57–9.

Wyckoff, D.D., 1984, 'New tools for achieving service quality', *The Cornell Hotel and Restaurant Administration Quarterly*, November: pp. 78–91.

World Tourism Organization, 1981, *Tourism and the Consumer*, WTO Research Institute for Consumer Affairs, Madrid.

Zeithaml, V.A., 1981, 'How consumer evaluation processes differ between goods and services', in J. Donnelly and W. George (eds), *Marketing of Services*, American Marketing, Chicago, 186–90.
Zeithaml, V.A., Berry, L. and Parasuraman, A., 1988, 'Communication and control processes in the delivery of service quality', *Journal of Marketing*, 52(2), April: pp. 35–48.

13 Quality assurance and the mystery guest programme in Harvester Restaurants

S. Newton and C. van der Merwe

Establishing the mission

The constant motivation to be part of a winning team cannot be built by an executive team alone. It requires commitment from all its players. The way to drive that is through a *total quality culture*. Total quality is a way of life, not tactical action to solve short-term problems.

In Harvester, quality is taken to mean 'meeting the agreed needs of the guest, now and in the future'. The reference to the guest refers not only to the external guest but also to the internal guest, for example, the Regional Manager visiting one of the restaurants.

Total quality must involve everyone in the organization believing that everything they do must be right, first time, every time. This implies that total quality is a journey and not a destination. The root of Harvester's total quality philosophy is to be found in the mission statement, which is: 'Our business is hospitality. Our commitment is to help our people succeed. We all ensure our guests enjoy their visits. Their satisfaction guarantees our growth.' Taking the first statement of the company mission it is possible to identify how total quality becomes a way of life.

OUR	=	we all own Harvester.
BUSINESS	=	sales, controls and profit.
IS HOSPITALITY	=	treating our guests as if they were guests in our own home.

Translating mission into action

The way the mission is translated into action can be simplified by the diagram shown in Figure 13.1. At any one time it is possible to identify how we are going to make things happen. By simply looking down the chart we can see how from mission through to personal objectives. If there is doubt about why we are doing something, we can look up the chart to the mission and see why we are doing it. It is useful to follow the journey of total quality from its part in hospitality through to individual action.

The Harvester commitment and beliefs clearly state that 'our obsession

Figure 13.1   *The way we make things happen*

with total quality is reflected in everything we do' and 'everyone is accountable for total quality'. From there on to goals which are simply though powerfully stated as total quality. From this goal of total quality the company has been able to define clearly the following total quality objectives:

— to ensure quality systems are in place and constantly achieve their purpose;
— to measure the delivery of Harvester standards;
— to ensure Harvester standards always meet guest needs;
— to deliver Harvester standards first time, every time;
— to ensure our suppliers add value to our quality goal;
— to ensure that all Harvester standards and systems comply with the law;
— to integrate information technology effectively into the quality programme.

Once the objectives had been identified, the task to define the strategies became the role of operations and function management. Working in clearly defined teams, two days were given over to writing these strategies and presenting them to all the teams with a final presentation to the Directors.

For example, the objective 'to ensure quality systems are in place and constantly achieve their purpose' can be underpinned by the following strategies.

1. the quality of our quality systems must be measured by their effectiveness. They are; mystery guest, guest comments (complaints, compliments, feedback); quality assurance evaluation; meal critique; group hygiene and safety; financial audit fire reports. They will be reviewed half-yearly in consultation with experts at all levels in terms of their structure, user friendliness, effectiveness and reflection of a total quality culture.
2. To ensure that the philosophy, policy and procedure of all our quality systems are clearly documented in the appropriate manual.

Now knowing that everyone is accountable for total quality, the challenge is to convert strategies into action using the concept of personal objectives throughout Harvester. Commitment and ownership has to be created to ensure that action happens.

The quality assurance evaluation programme

Philosophy

Our mission is to ensure guest satisfaction, to help our people succeed and improve our business through hospitality. This can be done by

— improving the quality of our products, service and cleanliness standards;
— training and developing our people to maintain and improve quality in the jobs they do;
— gaining commitment to quality and motivating all our staff by actively sharing the quality assurance programme;
— teamwork throughout the business.

Policy

In order for Harvester to ensure that our standards of production, service and cleanliness are implemented in every unit, an evaluation form exists which not only defines and communicates those standards and expectations, but also reinforces them by

— monitoring unit and individual performance;
— identifying opportunities and their origins;
— identifying resources required;
— identifying core action plans;
— identifying training and development needs.

Quality assurance evaluation components

1. *Definition of standards.*   It is impossible to measure quality until a definite standard has been agreed and written in the appropriate manual. Everyone must know the standards to which they are working prior to any measurement.

2. *Evaluation.*   There are a number of components that make up a full quality assurance evaluation including hygiene, approved products, handling, bulk preparation, guest service and so on. The completion of the form is an objective, precise measurement of the standards at any one time and removes any subjective debate.

3. Problem solving. The quality assurance evaluation identifies opportunities for quality improvement caused by either people or equipment or procedures. This should lead to solutions being identified.

4. Action planning. Having measured the business, highlighting good and improvement points, the identification of the necessary corrective action is the most important part of the system. The action plan identifies the resources (people, time and money) required to solve the problems and identifies the people responsible and the target date for completion.

5. Follow up. This is to ensure that the opportunities identified have been resolved by corrective action or if further work is still required.

Structure

Every Harvester will carry out the minimum quality assurance evaluations per period. These are kitchen hygiene—once weekly; restaurant—monthly; kitchen production—monthly; and pub/cellar—monthly. All results are sent with a copy of the action plan to the Regional Manager to be discussed at the next business review meeting. All results are also entered on to a computer for periodic analysis and monitoring trends over the year.

The mystery guest programme

A mystery guest programme not only measures the key standards written in the appropriate manual, but also the true guest reaction to the meal experience. To be effective, a mystery guest programme should be awarded to an external company and managed by a single internal source.

Components of the programme

1. *Market research.* Before the criteria for the programme can be written, market research should be conducted to ensure that the guests' moments of truth are clearly understood. Moments of truth cover all the delivery points where customers and front-line staff continually make contact.
2. *Methodology.* Prior to initiating a mystery guest programme, a clear methodology must be written. This must include the moments of truth as well as the key standards that support the operation. This methodology must be clearly communicated throughout the organization prior to any visits taking place.
3. *Evaluation.* There are a number of components that make up a full mystery guest methodology. For Harvester, these are moments of truth, exterior, interior, restaurant personnel and pub personnel. The most

important area for our guests and therefore to the company are the moments of truth which are covered under the following headings: hospitality, telephone bookings, exterior, toilets, timing, options, meal quality, payment, and departure. These are the key areas which we feel will influence the guests' propensity to return.

4. *Problem solving*. The total delivery of the Harvester meal experience can be seen by following the moments of truth and the four other components that make up the total programme. Opportunities can then be highlighted which leads to solutions being identified.

5. *Action planning*. Like the quality assurance evaluation, that action plan is the most important part of the programme. However, the system is slightly different for this measurement has to be carried out by our external partners.

   — The report is read by the general manager and discussed with the duty manager.
   — The report is shared with all the management team. At this stage ideas are shared which will help formulate the action required.
   — The duty manager then discusses the report with the staff team who were on duty that session. At this point commitment to action is now required.
   — The report is then shared with all the staff teams.
   — Action is then written in the form of an action plan identifying the resources required, the areas of responsibility and the dates for completion.
   — The follow up ensures that the agreed action has taken place and any opportunities have been resolved.

Structure

Every Harvester receives a mystery guest report quarterly. The report is sent direct to the unit within four days of being carried out. A copy of the action plan must be sent to the Regional Manager for discussion at the next business review meeting. All results are also entered on the computer for trend and period analysis. All Harvester restaurants accumulate a quality bonus based on the mystery guest score which reaches 80 per cent or more.

The next step

So knowing that everyone is accountable for total quality, what has this process achieved for Harvester? It requires the participation of everyone. Every individual working for the company is an important member of the team. The opportunity to participate fully in the strategies for Harvester has clearly built an in-depth understanding and ownership of the company objectives and those strategies written to support them.

By using a team approach, individuals found themselves working in different teams, often with colleagues they normally had little contact with.

This proved to be an added bonus. Key lessons were learnt. Each goal team felt total ownership of the strategies they had written. Those not taking part in these particular strategies have to trust their colleagues and approach the presentation stage with a view to adding value.

The challenge ahead now is converting the strategies fully into action. The same commitment and ownership has to be created in the same way as it was in writing the strategies. The skill required is to ensure that objectives, relating to the strategies, are agreed at the right development stage for the individual whilst creating a climate that encourages spontaneous initiative taking. Working together for the future we shall

— identify and satisfy guest needs;
— measure our performance against predetermined standards and take necessary corrective action;
— create the awareness in every team member that our best efforts are essential to ensure guest satisfaction and our own success;
  –continue to develop the climate where there is dedication and commitment to Harvester's total quality culture.

14 Quality in the contract catering industry

G. Hawkes

Introduction

The food and drink industry requires total dedication to quality. Any deviation from the highest standard is immediately noticeable to the customer. Usually there is no middleman to filter complaints. Food can literally be thrown back into the face of the supplier. Without the most stringent quality controls, those operating in the catering industry will fail. Only the most dedicated to health, hygiene and cleanliness will survive in this industry.

Gardner Merchant is the world's leading contract caterer. That means we operate in more countries with more client contracts than any other catering company. At present we are expanding faster overseas than in the United Kingdom across Europe, the United States, in Australia and the Far East including Japan and Hong Kong. In all these markets our standards and commitment to quality and excellence, which have been developed and tested in the United Kingdom, are applied. Our company headquarters in Kenley, Surrey house the world's foremost contract catering and research centre, where universal standards are developed.

Essentially our business is to supply good, nourishing meals to people at work. We are not in the luxury restaurant business. Nor are we in the fast food business. We are in the unique business of supplying, to much the same customers their main meal of the day, every day. We are therefore, in some ways, a substitute for mother. We echo that tradition of attention to quality, nutrition and to producing a sense of satisfaction in those we feed.

Catering in the United Kingdom affects more than 30 per cent of the population. It is a growing trend. More and more employers and staff are recognizing the benefits of on-site hot meals and the relaxed networking environment the workplace restaurant offers.

Training—the key to quality

Gardner Merchant has some 45,000 employees. They are spread over sites from the North Sea where we feed off-shore oil workers to the Channel Tunnel where we cater for the English work-force. We have some 3,000 other operational sites in the United Kingdom offices, schools, hospitals, factories, central and local government. All staff are trained to a

high level. They also undergo continuing training both on the job and in
attending courses at the Kenley Training Centre.

Kenley Training

The Kenley Residential Training Centre offers two specialized areas of
training: Practical Craft Training and Management Skills Training. Both
are primarily concerned with quality and embody the aims expressed in our
mission statement: 'The core of Gardner Merchant is the quality of our
service. We shall continue to enhance and develop the skills of all our
staff.' Practical craft training concentrates on food quality and service. It is
an in-house two-week intensive course which develops maximum efficiency
while producing excellent quality food. Health and Safety Training courses
are run by region across the eight areas in the UK where Gardner
Merchant operates.

Attaining quality in contract catering

In one sense a common standard of quality is not possible across the
catering market. Although attention to health, safety and hygiene is always
of the same high standard, the so-called quality of ingredients used in the
preparation of meals, by definition, varies according to the client's taste,
requirements and budget.

However, the perception of quality, the atmosphere, the cleanliness,
efficiency, attitude and the general appearance of the food, the premises
and the staff, do provide a common denominator of quality in contract
catering. To that end the British Standards Institute has introduced a
certification for quality in the contract catering industry known as BS 5750.

The introduction of a quality standard BS 5750 to the catering industry

'I know it when I see it' is how most people describe the subjective value,
quality. Yet delivering quality has become so integral to business success in
the 1990s that the regulators have stepped in with the common standard:
BS 5750. Those who provide systems of sufficient quality can now be
recognized by this standard.

The introduction of BS 5750 to the catering industry is not unanimously
welcome. The Hotel Catering & Institutional Management Association
(HCIMA) is leading the drive to determine the relevance of BS 5750 to the
catering industry. Not only contract caterers, but also major airlines,
government departments, county councils and important institutions from
all over the country—who are providing good, fresh meals to multiple
mouths daily—have shown concern over the relevance of this particular
quality standard to the catering service.

The objections to BS 5750 stem from its origins. It was originally developed for the manufacturing industry. However the pressure for quality assurance, and the buzz-phrase of the past decade *total quality management* led others to press for an extension of this quality measure to all industries. The EC in pursuit of common standards for Europe has further increased pressure for the introduction of common quality standards.

Clearly a standard developed for manufacturing is not going to sit comfortably with an industry so fundamentally different as catering. The British Standards Institute who administers BS 5750 has adapted it for the catering industry. However, many continue to feel BS 5750 is not appropriate and they are calling for a standard tailor-made for the industry.

Gardner Merchant, as the UK market leader, sympathizes with some of the concerns voiced particularly from operators who claim the scheme is expensive and bureaucratic to operate. However, our own policies in the past have been to maintain standards at the same level as those required by BS 5750, and so our upheaval and costs in achieving that quality have been minimal.

Gardner Merchant and BS 5750

Internal review

Twelve months ago we conducted a review of the company as a whole with a view to the implementation of procedures necessary to satisfy quality standard BS 5750. We found we had some fifty codes and practices already in place which were used to satisfy our own stringent quality standards. However, achieving BS 5750 offered an ideal opportunity to streamline some procedures and prioritize the relevance of others. We also recognized that the formalized and documented procedure required by BS 5750 would provide a good internal auditing system—which would be of additional benefit to the company and avoid some *ad hoc* procedures.

External benefits

The award of BS 5750 requires the assessment of the quality system by an independent third party. The system is subsequently audited on a six monthly basis, also by an independent third party. These external checks provide an additional comfort factor for clients who in turn can satisfy their clients and suppliers of the quality standard achieved. While the requirement for this quality standard is by no means universal in the UK market at present, it demonstrates a trend driven by larger institutions and organizations which will become widespread in the future.

Gardner Merchant achieved its first BS 5750 quality rating—and the first in the contract catering industry early in 1992 at our site at Royal Insurance at Peterborough. The award recognized our ability to achieve quality management systems which met the requirements of BS 5750.

The first stage in achieving certification was the acceptance of our quality manual. This was followed by acceptance that all operating procedures followed those set in the manual and that the required quality specifications in the company's central purchasing systems were enforced under this contract. Those systems include details on how to ensure that the supplier meets requirements, the vetting of sources and suppliers, ensuring terms and conditions of supply are understood where necessary assisting in advising and training of personnel and exemplifying the standard required. In the client's premises—as in the case of Royal Insurance—quality assurance includes accounting for every step taken in the catering contract. These include identifying the quantities of goods ordered, receiving the goods and quality and condition on receipt, supervision of the quality of the goods until consumption and keeping records of the quality throughout the process. All such procedures are standard practice throughout our operations but we recognise that the process to meet BS 5750 is intrinsically worthwhile as a means of ensuring consistency to the client.

While restrictions remain on advertising the award of a BS 5750 certificate, we nevertheless believe its arrival heralds a general approach to the achievement of a universal quality standard, which we endorse, throughout all the markets beyond the United Kingdom in which we operate.

The HCIMA has set up a working party to inquire into the way BS 5750 is applied to the catering industry. Among the issues it will review are whether or not the industry needs to adopt one formal quality standard, or whether a series of standards specific to different sectors of the industry would be more appropriate.

Common standards of quality control in catering suppliers

Quality control starts with the purchase and receipt of raw materials. The selection of professional, quality suppliers is critical in the first instance. This includes both the adequate supply of the required standard of produce and a more subjective assessment of whether the supplier can continue to maintain the quality in future orders.

In order to make an accurate assessment of the supplier's potential, factors such as the well-being of the staff, including their demeanour and personal hygiene are noted. Other factors considered include evidence of staff smoking on the job, whether premises are kept pristine, whether storage facilities are kept at correct temperatures and what precautions are taken to prevent accidents, illness or other factors interfering with supply.

Particularly important in food processing operations is the employer's policy on dismissal of staff. Sabotage can all too often occur if disgruntled staff are asked to work out their period of notice.

Food processors also need to take particular care in the exclusion of naturally occurring and foreign materials in their product. It does not require much imagination to guess what sorts of human particles and articles have found their way into food-processing lines! The amount of care needed to prevent such things happening, such as use of metal detectors, and the wearing of protective clothing, is vital.

Equally important is the amount of care taken to prevent insects from entering the premises. We should expect all suppliers to use expert pest control contractors who work to our own specifications and conditions. We should also expect the same rigorous hand-washing disciplines and personal hygiene practices imposed on our own staff to apply to suppliers' staff.

We believe in establishing close and long-term relationships with suppliers, to both parties' mutual advantage. The aim is to give the supplier a measure of security for his business, although only on the basis of understanding our needs and adhering to our strict standards of quality control.

Hygiene and food safety in Gardner Merchant

Gardner Merchant's team of buyers backed by technical experts inspect the sources of supply and ensure that all goods strictly comply with our quality, health and hygiene standards. We apply the same stringent criteria within our own company, on all clients' premises and sites where we operate, as well, of course, as in our own offices and headquarters.

The technical areas of expertise, including health, hygiene, safety and food technology, are all grouped under one department: **Environmental Services**. The departmental aims are:

1. To ensure that all premises and equipment meet the requirements of our company and the law.
2. To ensure that all staff engaged in the food business are fit and competent in food handling.
3. To ensure that the catering practices used are safe and fall within the industry's operational codes of practice.

Food science and technology

This section of Environmental Services concentrates on the safety of the food we buy, prepare and serve. We pay special attention to:

1. *Microbiology:* checking the microbiological quality of food at a stages of preparation, setting safe standards for raw materials and finished products. Highlighting risk areas at all stages of production and imposing adequate controls to minimize contamination and prevent proliferation of harmful bacteria.
2. *Legal controls:* to ensure compliance with legal requirements on food name, composition and labelling.
3. *Chemistry:* To check on the nutritional quality of the recipes we use and the food we serve.

For each client and on each site the question is asked:

Does Your Food Business Meet the Requirements of the Law?

In order to answer the question we conduct a comprehensive audit which will identify:

— areas which need attention, now or in the future;
— areas in need of detailed, expert attention, such as water tanks, asbestos control, etc.;
— equipment in need of maintainence or replacement, which could be considered unsafe;
— effectiveness of heating or refrigeration equipment;
— staff competence and standard of food handling practice;
— safety policies, cleaning schedules, pest control arrangements, fire prevention, first aid and accident prevention.

In short, the audit aims to tell the operations manager whether the local Environmental Health Officer is likely to have any cause for complaint against the business. It also aims to tell how safe the operation is and whether there is any immediate risk to customers or staff. It will also tell whether food handling practices are safe or whether there could be any risk of food poisoning.

The audit is designed to highlight areas of the catering business most at risk and to recommend appropriate remedial action before problems occur. It is a preventive measure aimed at removing hazards, and minimizing and controlling risks.

Food Safety Act

The Food Safety Act, which came into force in early 1991, is the first major revision of food law in the United Kingdom since the 1930s. It introduces basic obligations that food must be safe, wholesome, of the quality demanded and properly described .

The Act also deals with enforcement of the law and imposes much more stringent penalties for non-compliance than in the past. For instance, premises can be closed down immediately and maximum fines are increased from £2,000 to £20,000. Businesses also need to respond to improvement notices within the time allowed. In particular the Act calls for the implementation and documentation of all quality systems in operation.

Written records will be needed to show temperature, quality and date marks of food received, and for frequent checks of storage of food on site.

Temperature control

One essential quality control issue, all too frequently in the news in recent years, relates to the correct temperature at which certain foods should be stored. It will no longer be good enough to regard the fridge as the cupboard in the corner of the kitchen and trust to luck that it is operating correctly. Caterers will need to check the temperature, probably once or twice a day, and keep a written log of the results, and take action when they find a problem.

The Food Act has given us the opportunity of carrying out a comprehensive review of our policies, codes of practice, systems of work, the equipment we used and how we maintain it.

We have looked carefully at our training systems and increased our efforts in this area. By building a new laboratory at Kenley, we are able to add more emphasis on safe systems of work and prevention of food illness. Our team of microbiologists and our chemist are able to set up experiments to demonstrate how bacteria can enter the food chain and grow. Our training emphasises how this growth can be safely controlled to prevent food poisoning. We are able to demonstrate temperature profiles, showing how long it takes to heat or cool foods, giving our Chefs and Managers attending craft courses a practical demonstration rather than a technical and theoretical talk, which can often be misinterpreted or misunderstood.

Our team of qualified Environmental Health Officers and Technical Assistants carry out annual audits of all our operations. These are designed to check the premises we manage and our food handling practices, making sure that we are operating well within the law. They will be on hand to advise on Health & Safety issues, cleaning procedures and Pest Control, as well as carrying out on-job training for our staff on all environmental issues. Clearly, the food industry faces many changes in food law, and there are more in the pipeline. There is a deliberate underlying policy on the part of government to place the responsibility where it belongs—on the management of food businesses who have in place active systems of management and control. Of course, to large companies like Gardner Merchant, who have always accepted these responsibilities, the new laws merely serve as reminders. But for many others, some of the regulations will be a novel concept.

Our business has grown out of a firm belief that our customers appreciate value for money and we can only achieve their satisfaction by continuing to give them the quality of food on their plate which they have come to expect from us.

15 Perceptions of hygiene and quality in food service operations

Y. Guerrier, M. Kipps, A. Lockwood and J. Sheppard

Introduction

A number of highly publicized *food scares* in the United Kingdom during the latter part of the 1980s brought renewed calls for improved hygiene practices within the hotel and catering industry. A series of official reports, from the public inquiry into food poisoning at Stanley Royd hospital in 1986 (Department of Health and Social Services, 1986) right through to the Richmond Committee Report in 1990 (Richmond, 1990), all underlined the need for substantial changes in food-handling if further safety problems were to be prevented. An earlier paper (Kipps *et al.*, 1990) identified a number of obstacles to the successful implementation of a Hazard Analysis Critical Control Point (HACCP) set of procedures. Some of these problems were of a technical nature concerned primarily with the systems of operation. These were discussed in the previous chapter. Others were less tangible and more concerned with the socio-cultural factors relevant to the hotel and catering industry. Because these had received little attention in the literature related to HACCP approaches, this chapter explores these aspects in more detail and reports on a small-scale exploratory investigation into some of these issues.

According to the World Health Organization, 'understanding the prevailing beliefs and practices' of the target audience is a crucial component of any successful educational initiative (WHO, 1988). Despite the importance which various official bodies have attached to hygiene education and training, very little is known about the relevant beliefs, opinions and attitudes of those employed in the hotel and catering industry. Nevertheless future education and training on hygiene must be guided by and tailored to the perceptions of this target group. Before further progress could be made in this area, research needed to be undertaken into the perceptions and beliefs of both those close to day-to-day operations and of more senior managers who have responsibility for those operations.

Therefore, it was decided to conduct a pilot study into caterers' attitudes and beliefs related to the two crucial notions of **hygiene** and **quality**. Traditionally quality has often been confused with excellence or even the absence of complaints. Inherent in this view is the problem of satisfactorily measuring quality in a reliable way and using it as a valid method of control.

Increasingly a much greater emphasis is being placed within the industry on those attributes which affect a customer's acceptance of a service or product. The customer's perception of quality is now being seen as a key to profitability.

The most widely accepted definitions of quality centre on the idea of satisfying the customers by meeting their requirements. According to Juran (1979), quality is 'fitness for purpose or use'. The British Standards (1987) definition of quality, which corresponds exactly to the International Standards Organization's approach, is 'the totality of features and characteristics of a product or service that bear on its ability to satisfy stated or implied needs'. The Hazard Analysis approach, originally developed as an effective means of assuring food safety, has an important application as a concept underlying the wider issues of assuring quality throughout a service or product delivery process.

Hence it can be seen easily that in a process producing a food product, or a service delivering such products to the consumer, HACCP, quality and hygiene become inextricably linked.

Our research had a number of objectives. The first objective was to explore how caterers perceived quality within their organizations. Despite the universally expressed commitment to achieving quality, it still remains a remarkably elusive concept (Nightingale, 1985).

Consequently, the research was concerned to elicit from practitioners their own perceptions of quality at different stages of the operational cycle. In addition the intention was to explore to what extent managers believed that quality was something that could or should be controlled, and what other considerations they thought relevant to its management. A further objective was to discover the significance that caterers attached to hygiene in their overall perceptions of quality. Finally, the study sought to investigate the decision-making itself, that is, how caterers decide on the priority they give to hygiene in the light of the many conflicting demands made upon them.

The study consisted of two identical one-day workshops using two groups of practitioners from a wide cross-section of the industry. Almost every sector of the industry was represented, including health authorities, local government, hotels, restaurant chains, contract catering companies, airlines and breweries.

Both groups took part in identical exercises although they were different in their composition. The first group (A) was made up of managers who were at least one remove from daily operational responsibilities. Their main concerns were with strategic policy and implementation, possibly for a group of outlets or for one large catering establishment. The group included regional catering advisers, group food and beverage managers, general managers and chief personnel and training officers. They were key decision-makers in the organizations in which they worked.

The second group (B) were invited from the same organizations as their

management colleagues in group A although with a different set of responsibilities. This group consisted of managers and supervisors with direct
'hands-on' experience and responsibilities, both for front of house and
back of house operations. They were in daily contact with production and
service staff and customers, and had an intimate knowledge of how their
operations functioned. Unlike their colleagues in the other group, they
were concerned not so much with formulating policy as with ensuring its
proper implementation.

The two different groups were selected in order to explore whether or
not perceptions of quality and responses to it varied within organizations.
It was not assumed that these subjects represented one homogenous group.
On the contrary, it was assumed that their different work experiences and
responsibilities would shape their beliefs and attitudes in rather different
ways. By comparing their responses to the tasks given during the workshops, the differences between their commitments to quality within their
organizations would be revealed.

Methodology

The method adopted was indirect. It was considered that respondents
would be likely to provide socially desirable answers. In response to a
direct question people are unlikely to say they are not concerned about
quality or hygiene, although when making an actual management decision
these considerations may play a minor part. A more subtle approach was
needed if we were to begin to understand how our respondents regarded
these concepts and how they affected decision-making.

These issues were explored through a series of exercises—both individual and group—with minimal intervention or prompting. Direct ques-
tioning was studiously avoided and only topics raised spontaneously were
discussed by the groups. The researchers' own attitudes towards the subjects under discussion were not communicated, no indication that particular responses were more 'correct' than others was given.

There are two problems characteristic of this style of research. The first
is that it is difficult to assess the influence the research has on the eventual
results. Despite attempts to avoid revealing the researchers' views to
participants, their active presence during the workshop undoubtedly communicates all kinds of subtle messages that may affect the outcomes. (As
will be seen, the researchers did to some extent set the agenda through an
initial discussion of the concept of quality.) Second, because of the nature
of qualitative data, results are often difficult to interpret.

The workshop sessions began with a review of different definitions of
quality. Three definitions were identified:

1. **quality in a comparative sense** where products or services are ranked
   relative to each other or according to some agreed standard;
2. **quality in a quantitative sense** as used in production processes for
   example, 'two defective parts per million' may be set as a quality level;

3. **quality in the sense of fitness for purpose** where the evaluation of a product or service relates to its ability to satisfy a given customer need.

Through open group discussion the participants identified quality in the last sense as the most appropriate to hospitality industries. Meeting the needs of customers was given a high priority by all. Thus, the ground had been prepared for the first exercise as described below.

The 'talking wall' exercise

Both groups were provided with a series of headings corresponding to the sequential stages in a service encounter based on the model developed by Johnson (1987). These were as follows:

— choice of outlet;
— on entering the outlet;
— initial contact with staff;
— waiting for service;
— the service itself;
— point of departure;
— after the event.

These elements are common to nearly all service encounters, and each stage was to be evaluated in its 'ability to satisfy a given customer need'. Each individual was asked to list the factors which they thought affected quality at each of these stages. For example, under 'choice of outlet' a wide range of factors could be thought relevant, such as location, off-street parking, recommendation or price.

At this stage in the exercise individuals had compiled long lists of variables under each of these seven headings. They were then asked in small working groups to take a heading each and sort through the various responses, grouping duplicate or similar responses together and summarizing them into a smaller, more manageable list. This process reduced a list of some twenty or thirty statements to perhaps six or seven key variables. These were then listed under each heading and individuals were asked to rank each factor according to its importance on a five-point scale, namely: very important; important; neutral; not important; not at all important.

This process elicited from participants the variables that they deemed important in the total quality mix. These variables were then scored to produce a list reflecting the relative importance attached to certain key stages in service. Without explicitly acknowledging the fact, the group had unwittingly used an approach similar to HACCP to identify critical variables that would have to be controlled if quality was to be maintained.

The critical incident exercise

This exercise was designed to explore several issues. The first was to use their experience to identify 'critical control points' in relation to critical service incidents that had occurred within their organizations. The second was to explore how participants decided between the competing claims of different priorities. In particular the research interest lay in the priority that participants attached to hygiene in practice compared with their stated intentions.

Working in pairs, individuals were asked to describe several 'critical incidents' that had occurred in their organizations. An incident was counted as 'critical' if it had the potential to generate complaints from either customers or others working within the organization, or garner compliments. For example, the non-delivery of crucial supplies before an important function, or last-minute staff absences would count as negative 'critical incidents'. However, not all critical incidents would be negative. Receiving a rave review from a prominent food critic, or a compliment from a conference organizer after a successful event would count as positive examples of critical incidents. Individuals were also asked to identify key factors that contributed to the occurrence of the incident.

The proforma used to describe the critical incidents in a standard format is shown in Figure 15.1.

CRITICAL INCIDENTS	
Setting	
People involved	
Description of the incident	
Critical points	
Positive/Negative	

Figure 15.1 *Critical incident report form*

Once examples had been compiled of both negative and positive incidents, small groups were asked to rank each incident against the two dimensions of probability of recurrence and the incident's significance. That is, the group had to assess how likely the incident was to recur in the future: very high; high; medium; low; and very low; and to assess its significance; a total disaster ('I might be looking for another job'); disaster; major problem ('things are really going wrong'); 'not much of a problem' or 'nobody notices but me'. With positive incidents each group was asked to perform a similar assessment ranging from absolute triumph ('I might be in line for promotion'); 'the compliments are coming thick and fast'; 'things are really going right'; 'it's nice when things are going right' to 'nobody notices but me'.

By the end of the group exercise a list had been compiled of critical incidents ranked by probability and significance (potential for compliments or complaints). This allowed us to locate each incident on a matrix that depicted the potential for compliments and complaints thus:

1. Low compliments, high complaints ('DISSATISFIERS')
2. Low compliments, low complaints ('NEUTRALS')
3. High compliments, low complaints ('SATISFIERS')
4. High compliments, high complaints ('CRITICALS')

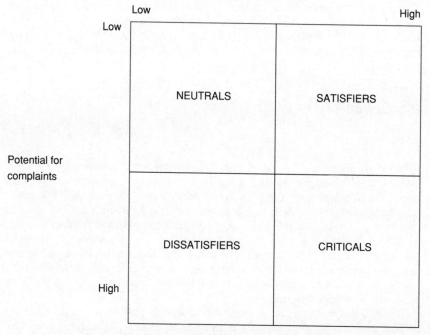

Figure 15.2 *Matrix of potential for compliments and complaints*

Each incident, whether negative or positive, was categorized on the matrix as a 'dissatisfier', a 'critical', a 'neutral' or a 'satisfier'. After the incidents had been located on the matrix, the group as a whole was asked to discuss which types of incidents they would pay most attention to within their operations.

Results

The talking wall

This exercise produced a wealth of data on the factors that participants deemed relevant to the maintenance of quality at each stage of service. These results are shown in Table 15.1.

Critical incidents

This exercise produced a wide variety of incidents. These were analysed as described in the methodology and then transferred to a proforma, an example of which is shown in Table 15.2. The number of 'negative' incidents recounted outnumbered 'positive' ones by over 2 to 1. The full results are shown in Table 15.3.

Although the imbalance between positive and negative incidents was not very apparent at the time, in retrospect this is an interesting finding in itself. It would be easy to conclude from it that the life of our average manager is, in reality, more characterized by failure and complaint than triumph!

Discussion

The talking wall

First, considerable agreement was found over what constituted quality. Both sets of managers shared a common perception of what constituted quality at different stages of production and service. Despite this consensus on what was deemed relevant, there was a marked divergence between the two groups on the significance they attached to each individual variable. Group A had a noticeably better-defined order of priorities. They were much more ready to rank different quality variables in order of significance than their colleagues in group B. Managers in group B were more liable to assign equal significance to several variables rather than ranking them in descending order of significance.

Second, despite the many recent 'food scares' published in the national media, it was apparent that food safety was not at the forefront of our participants' thinking about quality. Very few individuals in either group spontaneously mentioned the possibility of food-poisoning, although when

Table 15.1   *Results of the 'talking wall' exercise*

	GROUP A: Senior managers	GROUP B: Managers and supervisors
Choice of outlet	Quality and type of food Previous experience of outlet Personal recommendation Appropriateness to occasion Price	Price Quality and type of food Variety of facilities Location Advertising
On entry	Clean and tidy Appearance of good management and organization Welcoming Cloakroom facilities Ambience	Greeting Clean and tidy Ambience Decor Appearance of good management and organization
Initial contact	Feeling comfortable and at ease Polite and friendly greeting Clean and tidy staff Offered drink on being seated Staff knowledgeable about menu	Polite and friendly greeting Welcoming Clean and tidy staff Staff knowledgeable about menu Made to feel confident and comfortable
Waiting for service	Clean tableware Being made to feel at ease Speed of service Presentation of food Availability of menu items	Being made to feel at ease Speed of service Clean tableware Feeling comfortable Availability of menu items
The service itself	Clean tableware Meets expectations Customer-friendly Correct food temperature	Speed appropriate to outlet Clean and tidy staff Well-presented food Customer friendly
Point of departure	Bill arrives promptly Bill is clear and understandable Can vacate table at leisure Bill is correct Thanks and farewell from staff	Bill is correct Easy efficient payment Can vacate table at leisure Bill is clear and understandable Thanks and farewell from staff
After the event	Food does not cause illness Value for money Meets expectations All aspects of service met acceptable standards Worth recommending	Enjoyable meal Customer complaints followed up Wish to return Value for money Flexible speed

Table 15.2 *An example of the analysis of the critical incidents*

Rate by probability	Rate by significance	Negative incidents	Positive incidents	Rate by significance	Rate by probability
L	4	Undercooked eggs	Successful conference dinner at short notice	4	L
VH	3	Kitchen problem	Old-age pensioners' dinner	3	L
VL	2	Swimming-pool problem	Entertaining the Pope	5	VL
L	5	Soiled plaster in steak pie			

Table 15.3 *Summary of ratings of incidents*

	Negative incidents		Positive incidents		Totals			
PROBABILITY	A	B	A	B	A	B	−ve	+ve
VERY HIGH	3	5	1	1	4	6	8	2
HIGH	9	8	4	4	13	12	17	8
MEDIUM	1	1	4	0	5	1	2	4
LOW	4	2	2	0	6	2	6	2
VERY LOW	3	3	1	1	4	4	6	2
SIGNIFICANCE								
5	1	0	0	0	1	0	1	0
4	6	10	3	1	9	11	16	4
3	10	1	5	2	15	3	11	7
2	2	7	3	2	5	9	9	5
1	1	1	1	1	2	2	2	2
Total	20	19	12	6	32	25	39	18

several individuals in group A did mention the possible adverse effects of food-poisoning on the customers' perception of quality, this prompted the rest of the group to rank its significance highly. No one in group B discussed the possibility of food poisoning, and it did not appear in their subsequent ranking of significant variables.

There was, however, consensus concerning the importance of cleanliness in the customers' perception of quality. Cleanliness was rated highly by both groups. From informal discussion groups, it was clear that most individuals equated cleanliness with hygiene, and they tended to use the terms interchangeably. When hygiene was discussed it was viewed in aesthetic rather than safety terms—as a tangible characteristic that crucially influenced the consumer's perceptions of the operation. Cleanliness was seen as tangible proof that an operation was under control and well managed. From this it is possible to conclude that 'cleanliness' was not only an aesthetic feature but also a desirable moral characteristic.

Similarly food temperature was mentioned only on one occasion, and yet again, this was more influenced by aesthetic than safety considerations. Warm or tepid food was deemed as a lapse in quality because it affected the food's acceptability to the customer, not because it might endanger safety.

The critical incidents

The term 'critical' does for many people carry negative connotations, and this may have predisposed individuals to select negative rather than positive incidents. It is possible to argue that this predisposition probably does account for some of the imbalance. However, there is another, possibly more interesting hypothesis.

The term *quality* can have both negative and positive connotations. Attaining quality can be synonymous with avoiding faults or failure, that is, a 'zero defects' approach. On the other hand, it can also be seen as an equally positive orientation concerned with meeting and excelling certain agreed standards.

The imbalance between the negative and positive incidents cited by our managers perhaps indicates a preoccupation with one side of that quality equation at the expense of the other. It appears that managers in both groups were more preoccupied with avoiding 'getting things wrong' than with succeeding in 'getting things right'. This suggests that the fear of failure may be a significant factor in motivating managers.

Insufficient data was collected from this pilot study to explore this issue in any greater detail, although it may be a fruitful area for future research. Cultural attitudes towards success and failure may have an important role in explaining the different standards and commitment to quality in different countries or industries, or even within organizations.

The range of incidents described by our managers illustrated the complex demands now made on the average hospitality manager, both in the private and public sectors of the industry. Whilst critical incidents may not be daily occurrences, a plethora of petty irritations and occasional crises is obviously an accepted part of the day's work routine.

When all the incidents were analysed, it was discovered that the majority could be characterized as the results of failures in the organization's management system. This was either because critical factors had not been previously identified, or when properly identified had not been adequately controlled. Although some of our participants were able to identify the critical factors which had contributed towards incidents, very few mentioned the need for any systematic approach to control.

The picture emerging from these descriptions was of many managers spending a lot of time dealing with predictable, preventable and recurring problems. This did not, apparently, strike them as an inappropriate use of their time or skills. On the contrary, many believed that they were best employed in their role as 'trouble-shooters', responding to problems in an *ad hoc* way, plugging the gaps in the management system.

The incidents described in some detail by both management groups had another significant characteristic. Most of the incidents cited were 'critical' in an operational rather than customer-oriented sense. Despite their earlier commitment to a customer-oriented definition of quality, this was not evident in their choice of critical incidents. Their preoccupations were largely operational ones. This inability to take a consistently customer-centred view may help to explain why our managers were also preoccupied with avoiding failure. Whilst operators are concerned with not 'getting things wrong', customers, on the other hand, are only interested in their 'getting things right'.

When the incidents were analysed on the matrix shown in Figure 15.1, several interesting results emerged. It was found that the matrix was a reasonably reliable and useful guide to how managers perceived particular incidents. This increased the understanding of how managers decided on what priority to attach to incidents of different kinds. In subsequent discussions with both groups, however, it was discovered that there were many other intervening variables that affected their decision-making. Nevertheless, our matrix was a useful tool for thinking about the process by which managers decided to pay more attention to one incident rather than another.

'Criticals', for example, were more likely, other things being equal, to receive attention than 'neutrals'. 'Criticals' were incidents that had a high potential for generating either compliments or complaints. The incentives for attending to these types of incident are therefore correspondingly high. 'Neutrals', on the other hand, have a low potential for generating either compliments or complaints, and have, therefore, a lesser priority.

The situation concerning 'satisfiers' and 'dissatisfiers' was less clear-cut. 'Satisfiers' are incidents with a low potential for generating complaints but a high potential for garnering compliments. 'Dissatisfiers' have a low potential for compliments but a high potential for complaints. Most of the incidents described by the groups belonged to one of these two categories. As there was no obvious rank order of priority, this resulted in differences of opinion about which type of incident should legitimately command the most attention.

In group discussion the participants perceived hygiene as a 'dissatisfier'. Failures in this area were seen as having a high potential for complaints; conversely, however, 'getting it right' brought few rewards or compliments. This result is consistent with the earlier findings from the 'talking wall' exercise. The managers viewed hygiene as important only when it breaks down. Good hygiene is not, in other words, perceived as making any positive contribution towards quality, and is rarely adequately rewarded. Linking this point to the 'talking wall' finding that hygiene tends to be connected in the minds of caterers with cleanliness, we can hypothesise that many managers will, in any case, pay most attention to those aspects which are aesthetically visible to the customer.

The effects of this perception on subsequent priorities are difficult to gauge. For some managers, the high potential for complaints meant that they would automatically give hygiene a high priority. For others, different types of incident would be more likely to preoccupy their attention. Incidents with a high probability but low complaint potential, for example, would force them into action simply through sheer irritation. Another key factor cited by some managers was the ease with which a particular problem could be solved. Some acknowledged that they preferred to tackle problems where solutions were relatively easy to achieve, irrespective of their potential to generate complaints.

Conclusion

Several conclusions can be drawn from these findings.

First, the research indicates that hospitality managers do not view hygiene as a positive satisfier. Food hygiene is deemed significant only when something goes wrong. Food safety is not seen as making a positive contribution towards quality, and is unlikely to be viewed in the same terms as other quality variables.

Second, the views of these groups of managers represented a remarkable consensus of outlook on hygiene. However, this is a consensus that is increasingly at odds with the perceptions of customers. Caterers may either be ignorant of, or simply underestimate, the significance that the public now attaches to *safety*. For many consumers, safety is a positive quality attribute of food (AA, 1988; MAFF, 1988). By ignoring their customers' perceptions caterers are overlooking an increasingly important element in the marketing mix.

However, even if customers are concerned about food safety, how can they assess whether a caterer is meeting hygiene standards. A stomach upset after a meal may or may not be attributed to food-poisoning. Most customers probably do rely on superficial signs of cleanliness. Further qualitative research needs to be conducted into customers' perceptions of food hygiene. If customer pressure is to encourage caterers to take hygiene more seriously, then customers need a more reliable way of assessing the food safety standards of the restaurants and food outlets they frequent and caterers need new ways of publicizing their commitment to hygiene.

Third, although there is a strong consensus of outlook on food hygiene, caterers are not a monolithic group. It was found that different experiences and responsibilities could influence attitudes and approaches to problems. The research suggests that those closest to day-to-day operations have probably a less clear order of priorities than those with more strategic responsibilities.

Fourth, since a systematic approach to quality management relies on the ability to discern the difference between *critical* and merely *relevant* factors, the ability to control quality may not be distributed evenly throughout the organization's management.

Even taking into account the limitations of qualitative research and the small scale of this study, it is believed that this research provides, nevertheless, some useful insights and pointers to managers' perceptions of the important subjects of hygiene and quality. From an empirical standpoint, these findings are in agreement with the approaches proposed by other workers in the field (Oakland, 1989 ; Tenner and De Toro, 1992). Whilst hardly the last word on the subject, the findings are a starting-point for further, more structured research in a field that has so far been badly neglected.

References

Automobile Association, 1988, *Hotel classification system*, AA, Basingstoke.
British Standards Institute, 1987, *BS 4778: Quality Vocabulary—Part 1, international terms*, BSI, London.
Department of Health and Social Security, 1986, *The Report of the Committee of Inquiry into an Outbreak of Food poisoning at Stanley Royd Hospital*, HMSO, London.
Johnson, R., 1987, 'A framework for developing a quality strategy in a customer processing operation', *International Journal of Quality and Reliability Management*, 4(4): pp.35–44.
Juran, J.M., 1979, *Quality Control Handbook*, McGraw-Hill Book Company, New York.
Kipps, M., Sheppard, J. and Thomson, J., 1990, 'Hygiene and hazard analysis in food service', *Progress in Tourism, Recreation and Hospitality Management*, 2: pp. 192–226.
Ministry of Agriculture, Fisheries and Food, 1988, *Food Hygiene: Report on Consumer Survey*, HMSO, London.
Nightingale, M., 1985, 'The hospitality industry: defining quality for a quality assurance programme—a study of perception', *Service Industries Journal*, 5(1) pp. 9–22.
Oakland, J.S., 1989, *Total Quality Management*, Heinemann, Oxford.
Richmond, M., 1990, *Microbiological safety of food*, The Report of the Committee on the microbiological safety of food, HMSO, London.
Tenner, A.R. and De Toro, I.J., 1992, *Total Quality Management*, Addison-Wesley Publishing, Reading, Mass.
World Health Organization, 1988, *Health Education in Food Safety*, WHO, Geneva.

16 Taking quality on board! British Standard 5750

E. Pearce

Introduction

The British Standards Institution (BSI) has been the recognized standards-making body in the United Kingdom since 1901. There are now more than 12,000 British Standards covering virtually every type of industrial activity and a vast range of products. One standard in particular has won international acclaim as far as quality is concerned. This is the much-discussed BS 5750, the national standard for quality management systems.

The standard, which was first published in 1979, is based on a series of Ministry Defence supplier standards and other standards used in government procurement, particularly the AQAP (Allied Quality Assurance Publications) series. It is therefore not surprising that it was engineering and manufacturing companies who initially took the standard on board.

Registration to BS 5750 can be undertaken by BSI Quality Assurance (QA), the certification division of BSI. It means that a firm's management system has been independently assessed and checked by a team of experts, experienced both in quality assurance and the technical conditions that apply in that area.

By 1988, BSI QA had registered over 4,000 companies. This figure has now rapidly increased to 10,500 firms with BSI receiving over 3,000 applications for registration every year. The success achieved by the standard in this country resulted in its becoming the model for the equivalent international and European standards, ISO 9000 and EN 29 000 respectively. A company that has achieved registration to BS 5750 can therefore also claim compliance with ISO 9000 and EN 29 000.

Over the last two years, the service sector has developed a keen interest in registration to BS 5750/ISO 9000/EN 29 000 and a new part has been published to the standard, ISO 9002–4. This standard is a guidance document to the ISO 9000 series specifically for the service sector, covering such areas as service, delivery and customer satisfaction.

Currently in the service sector, BSI has registered hotels, caterers, general practitioners, solicitors, finance houses and contract-cleaning businesses. There are many other areas of the service sector introducing systems to BS 5750 and the next twelve months will see a significant rise in registrations in these sectors.

What is BS 5750 all about and how does it apply to the hotel and catering industries?

The standard is a very basic quality management system and requires a business to implement a framework of controls across their activities. BS 5750 defines quality as fitness for purpose: is the service provided or product designed and constructed to satisfy the customer's requirements? It does not define levels of quality as these will be dependent on the industry concerned, and the product or service being produced.

Let us examine quality assurance in the hotel and catering industry by addressing some of the arguments often voiced against BS 5750 and then looking closely at its requirements.

A firm can be registered and still produce rubbish

Yes, a registered firm can produce rubbish, although only if that is what the customer has requested. The clause, Contract Review, in the standard looks closely at the customer requirement and reviews it from two angles:

1. Is the customer requirement clear?
2. Does the supplier have the ability to meet that requirement?

Records of these reviews need to be maintained. In the hotel and catering sectors, contract review can happen at several different levels. The preparation of tenders being one level of review, with on-going reviews on a more regular basis with clients. For example, in a hotel a customer requesting a room for the night, or in contract catering, a customer requesting a buffet on a particular day.

It is bureaucratic and therefore extremely expensive to implement

BS 5750 does require a framework of documentation to be put in place. Many businesses will have a considerable amount of paperwork already in use. It is possible that these procedures go part of the way to meeting the requirements of the standard. These procedures can be used and where required, expanded upon or where duplication occurs, some procedures deleted. In fact, this can then lead to a reduction of existing paperwork.

One of the main benefits of having a documented system is that it provides a full audit trail. Only when this is in place can a business fully audit and check a system for its effectiveness. The maintenance of records will facilitate the ability to find root causes of problems and identify areas for improvement. These records could also help the business to demonstrate that it endeavoured to put things right first time.

The costs of implementing BS 5750 may be high in staff time and commitment, however these should be measured against the potential benefits of a formal quality management system.

You cannot put in controls for the intangibles of a service business

There are many intangibles in a service sector, and again the system can ultimately address these. This is done through several clauses of the standard: Process Control; Training; Internal Auditing; Corrective Action.

The Process Control clause states that criteria for workmanship should be defined. The business should therefore define what levels of training, qualifications and work instructions each member of staff in the system should have. Once this is in place, it is measured through the audit system and the identification of a training needs programme. Through contract review and corrective action, customer satisfaction is being measured and this will in turn highlight the need to amend criteria laid down for workmanship.

It has no implications on the quality of the product or service

BS 5750 is not product certification—it does not imply that a product or service is excellent. What it does say is that a business has an effective quality management system which ensures consistency to the customer and creates the framework for a continual improvement programme. The latter is catered for by the Non-conforming Product and Corrective Action clauses.

When a non-conformance arises—either through a customer complaint, a failed inspection or during an audit—measures need to be taken to prevent it from continuing. The systems should then be reviewed to identify the root cause: what was wrong with the system to allow this non-conformance to happen in the first place. Once identified, corrective action can be agreed to prevent this from happening again. A timescale should also be agreed for implementing the corrective action and when that time has passed, a check should be made to ensure it has been implemented. Here there is a system for monitoring the effectiveness of your operation, identifying and tracing problems and putting in measures to ensure they do not recur. How many of you have arrived at work only to be confronted with the same problem that has arisen several times before!

A documented system will stifle the flair of our people

There is not a need to document everything to the nth degree. Where a highly skilled individual has been employed for a particular task, there is no need to give them written instructions on everything they do. The documented system should specify the skills required for that particular job. In other words, there needs to be a balance between work instructions, training and expertise. It is very important that the system is flexible enough to allow the business to operate efficiently and not to smother originality.

BS 5750 does not consider the customer

BS 5750 is built around the customer. Contract Review is one of the most important clauses of the standard. If the requirement is not clearly understood and agreed in the first instance, the customer will never be satisfied. Everything done is geared up to meet the customer's needs, both stated and implied, therefore the quality management system will reflect this.

The successful implementation of BS 5750 in any business can bring many benefits, some of which have already been highlighted in this text. It can lead to reduced waste, lower overheads, better products and services and hence fewer customer complaints.

Job security and staff morale can also be improved. If staff are allowed input into the documentation of their own system, then they will start to feel more a part of the business and will therefore wish to give more commitment. Management responsibility is clearly defined at all levels through the business, so each member of staff knows exactly where he/she stand.

There are also marketing benefits in having the recognition of an independent third party. A registered company may carry the BSI Registered Firm logo on their stationery and promotional material. Finally, there is the increased customer confidence in dealing with a business who have been successfully assessed to BS 5750.

In response to demand from the industry, in February of this year BSI published guidelines on the application of BS 5750/ISO 9000 in the hotel and catering industry. The new guidelines were written in association with a number of catering organizations including the Department of Health, the Hotel, Catering and Institutional Management Association, the European Catering Association and the Leatherhead Food Research Association.

The Business Development Department of BSI Quality Assurance can provide guidance on the route to registration to BS 5750. If a company is in the early stages of looking at the standard, it may be worthwhile attending one of the monthly introductory seminars. Alternatively, the International Training Department carry out a number of courses, including Internal Auditor and Lead Assessor. They will also tailor training courses for individual businesses.

If a company has a system partially in place, then one of the Business Development Department team can visit, free of charge, to discuss the way ahead. However, it is important to remember that as an independent registration body, BSI cannot give consultancy on how to implement the system. BS 5750 does not set out to dictate to companies how they should run their business. It is simply a common-sense approach from which any company can benefit, whatever its size.

If you would like further information about BS 5750 or copies of the guidelines for the hotel and catering industry contact, Business Development, BSI Quality Assurance, PO Box 375, Milton Keynes, MK14 6LL. Tel: (0908) 220908.

Contemporary Themes

17 Development and innovation: the case of food and beverage in hotels

M. Riley and E. Davies

Introduction

The argument put forward in this chapter is that the commercial world of hotels and restaurants consists of two distinct forms of structure, the consequence of which is that each produces its own paradigm of development. These paradigms are maintained by the attitudes they engender and are expressed as *ways of thinking* about development. The purpose of this chapter is to show that the many problems associated with food and beverage in hotels, such as the lack of innovation and the struggle to interest house guests, result from these activities being trapped in the wrong paradigm. The case under examination is based on the UK hotel and restaurant industry. There is a whiff of a polemic in the air.

To be more specific, what is being asserted is that those concerned with hotel development share a set of assumptions and priorities which can roughly be described as room revenue-dominated, major destination and city centre-directed, project-centred, forecast-driven, *visitor*-fixated and group-obsessed. The management branch of this paradigm tends towards bureaucracy and cost-driven standardization. Those included in this paradigm are: Developers; Tourist Boards; Consultants; Corporate Hotel Managers and Educators who interact over time to produce a network. As these networks form individuals within them they exchange information as they interact. Over time they begin to share the same set of priorities and assumptions so that eventually formulas, ratios, reports and procedures grow up around 'projects' and become standard. Everybody accepts set ways of doing things. The closer the personal contact within the network the more mutual the assumptions. All this is perfectly legitimate.

By contrast, the world of restaurant development lives close to the market-place. Here, if a paradigm exists at all, it is about individual taste, fashion changes, influencing fashion and development through *try it and see*. For the small entrepreneur development entails much risk. For the large corporation development is a case of test marketing. In this world the big man and the little man share the same dangers of short product life cycles and consequently the same challenge to be innovative. Above all, the restaurant world must watch its customers closely and be able to react quickly. To see just how intimate the world of the cook the customer his fad and their trends are, see Wood (1991). Networks exist here although the currency of their exchanges tends to be customer tastes, staff skills and equipment.

The thrust of our argument is that hotel food and beverage is trapped in the wrong paradigm. It sits in the world of hotel development and as such it is always a secondary consideration. Although as an activity it should reside in the second more entrepreneurial paradigm, because it does not, its potential is not realized.

Some theoretical considerations

Whenever questions of innovation are raised in the context of organization it is inevitable that variables of size and structure with the corollary the degree of bureaucracy, will be invoked. Studies of hotels are no exception (Gamble, 1990; Riley and Jauncey, 1990; Shamir, 1978). Whilst not denying their relevance, these variables, have become, to borrow slang from the criminal world, something of a robber's dog, that is, someone who loyally gives a criminal an alibi. So often analysis stops at bureaucracy and it is not sufficient. The justification for this statement is simply that these structural factors are not truly explanatory variables; they are at best intervening variables. For example, Gamble (1990) uses large size and bureaucracy to explain resistance to technology, and has to struggle to find a structural explanation for the same resistance in small units. If an explanatory variable does not work in reverse then something else is at work. The real problem with structural arguments is they cannot explain intention and innovation is about intention. The arguments which follow are concerned with the formation of a knowledge *nexus* which becomes a working paradigm. By this is meant not just a cognitive map of *ways of seeing* but also a model of *ways of seeing and doing*. The only significance of structure here is whether or not it promotes or stifles the formation of a shared paradigm.

The fundamental idea at work here is that notions become entrenched within the individual through both a social and a cognitive process. The categorization schema that lies behind our perceptions is influenced by social processes. In every field social intercourse would be intolerable if there were not some consensus to what is similar. We learn to put the same things in the same perceptual categories. Consensus also helps us to evaluate so that there is general agreement on what is good and bad (Tajfel 1978). In this way our classification system of what goes with what and what is good is given to us by our social environments. By this means the structure of thinking of the atomized individual is influenced by the organization. For the organization to have such influence it must subtly persuade. The acceptance of a social group or an organization as a source of influence is both an intellectual and instinctive process. It is, however, a process related to the psychological terms of attachment. The appeal of the social group or organization is a claim for the legitimacy of all its ideas and assumptions on the basis of reason and analogy with nature (Douglas, 1987). Thus it is perfectly easy to assimilate the most common expression of the first paradigm, that is, 'rooms make more money'. It is rational and as it implies that rooms are *bigger* than something else it follows the laws of nature that it should be more important. Taken, as in the above example as one single assumption, it will not lead to bias against some other activity. It is when a group of ideas come together as a coherent set that the problem begins. For example, a preference for projects over continuous management and a favouring of groups over individual travellers fit nicely with the notion of room dominance. It is when a set of ideas congeal into a embracing example that matters outside the example receive less attention. In other words, working paradigms are useful in the same way that stereotypes are useful. They save a lot of rethinking (Morgan, 1991; Merton, 1968). What is being argued here is that shared systems of knowledge emerge through social processes. This argument is compatible with the isomorphic tendencies of organizations described by DiMaggio and Powell (1983).

There is clearly a process of normative isomorphism going on in the world of hotel development. Seen in this light, innovation may be a matter of breaking the existing paradigm (Kirton, 1976). However, it also follows that innovation may be a function of the *search for something new* being imbued into a system of knowledge. Alternatively, it may best thrive in situations where the influence of groups is minimal. What this analysis is suggesting is that questions of innovation should be addressed to social processes and the factors which maintain them.

The biased outlook on food and beverage

The basis of our argument is that the true value of food and beverage in hotels cannot be seen without taking a broader and longer perspective.For example, to see food and beverage in its 'project' context is to see it dwarfed by the importance of rooms. It follows quite naturally from this view that the transient aspects of the business come to the fore. In this scheme of things hotels emerge simply as a staging-post where tourists and businessmen come and go. A different view of things could see hotels having a longer-term and stronger relationship with their local community. However, they do not develop it because of a biased marketing outlook based on high volume tourists and businessmen. The lesson of recession is that cultivation of the local market is essential.

Working in conjunction with this outlook is the notion of the *group*. This primarily city centre and major destination phenomenon carries overtones of standardization and obscures the bulk of the industry which is more individualistic and more varied. There is a branch of this argument which at the unit level suggests that the future of food and beverage in hotels lies in standardization and strict cost centre control (Tiltscher, 1983). There is nothing wrong with this argument except that it produces boring restaurants and the kind of bureaucratic management that leads to 'The vegetarian dish of the month is . . .'

However, if it is assumed that the restaurant product must be compatible with the overall image of the hotel and yet must be the differentiating factor in the market segment, it follows that standardization must take on board those marketing criteria which enforce differentiation. Alas, the motive for standardization is as much cost-based as market-based. In other words, instead of seeing standardization as a base for differentiation it is seen as an end in itself for cost motives. In reality restaurant concepts have a short life cycle. This becomes important when the role of food and beverage is seen in its true context of marketing the whole hotel. It is the primary vehicle for leading and responding to market trends.

In a strange way the standardizers and the educationalist have something in common despite going in opposite directions. The traditional approach to food and beverage teaching is based on an established canon, and is very production orientated and very normative. With this approach they are as constrained as the standardizers in their inability to respond to the fluidity of market demands.

It is the volume-centred aspects of the industry that shout loudest and seek the attention of finance and development. Perfectly natural; however, the industry has a broader more varied, smaller scale, an entrepreneurial face which it is too easy to overlook—probably because this face is so fragmented. Food and beverage falls between two stools. On the one hand it is important simply because it is common to every aspect of the industry; on the other hand, however, it is marginalized out of the mainstream of thought on development. For whatever the reason, the net result is a story of lost opportunity. To put it simply there are some conspicuous problems:

— Innovation is totally absent from this area;
— Ideas are imported from the restaurant industry;
— There is no body of knowledge on marketing restaurants in hotels;
— Food and beverage plays little part in the marketing of the hotel;
— Often there is no access to food and beverage in hotels from the street;
— Standardization is seen as the only solution; and
— Food and beverage is not exploited as the link with the local market even after the good example of fitness centres.

The current position

Table 17.1 illustrates the composition of sales world-wide and indicates that, although not dominant in revenue generation terms, food and beverage makes a considerable contribution. Seen in this light the notion of *room dominance* has to be softened.

Figure 17.1 is a composite in which information from different sources expressed by different measures has been standardized by indexation. It compares the performance of food and beverage in hotels with hotel

Table 17.1   *Revenue distribution as a percentage of sales*

	Africa & Middle East %	Asia & Australasia %	North America %	Europe %	Latin America %	UK %
Rooms	46.0	54.1	63.9	49.2	53.8	47.4
Food	32.0	24.9	21.7	30.3	22.6	32.0
Beverage	9.6	8.8	6.1	13.9	11.4	14.3
Telephone	5.6	3.5	2.0	2.6	4.6	2.2
Minor departments	3.3	3.9	4.2	2.3	2.7	2.3
Rentals	3.5	4.0	2.0	1.4	4.6	1.7

Source: Horwath and Horwath International (1992), *Worldwide Hotel Industry 1991*, Horwath and Horwath, London.

occupancy and with the combined performance of eating out in pubs and fast food restaurants. The year 1987 forms the base year and is standardized to equal 100. As can be seen clearly hotels have not captured the rising market for eating out. This has been taken by pubs and fast food. Not only has hotel food and beverage not kept up with general demand, it has not grown at the same rate as the increase in hotel room occupancy. There is an overall picture here of opportunities missed.

The case for food and beverage

The case for food and beverage becomes clearer if hotels are viewed as a complete entity and their markets include the local population as well as transient customers. Then the full contribution of food and beverage can be realized. In support of this, five related arguments are presented below.

Image

The image of a hotel is defined by its service level and the quality of its food and beverage. In other words, within any market segment the differentiating factor is food and beverage. It is not necessary to have consumed these facilities for them to form part of the hotel's identity in the mind and memory of the customer.

Business in the locale

It is all too easy to overlook the importance of local business which can only be fostered through food and beverage. What is more, such contacts have direct relationship with room sales in that these customers represent

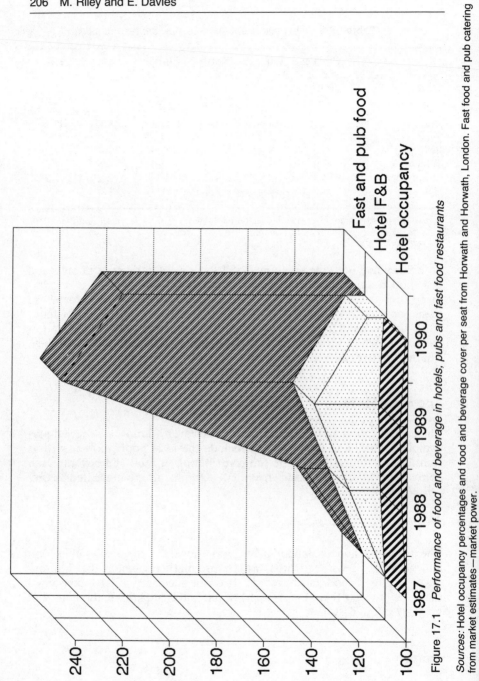

Figure 17.1   *Performance of food and beverage in hotels, pubs and fast food restaurants*

Sources: Hotel occupancy percentages and food and beverage cover per seat from Horwath and Horwath, London. Fast food and pub catering from market estimates—market power.

the purpose of the visits of others. In times of recession the loyalty of locals can be crucial to survival. There is always less volatility of demand in the local market. It does suffer from the massive political and social upheavals of the international market.

There is a connection between trends in eating out and room consumption

In qualitative terms eating out can be seen as a stage of consumption which leads towards travelling for leisure and a general opening out of life (Riley, 1984). In marketing for leisure it is often the case that the attraction is the style of life exemplified by good eating and drinking. In such cases the rooms are coincidental.

Profitability

In taking a broad view of the industry, Figure 17.1 shows that in some cases, the profitability of food and beverage matches that of rooms. Key areas here are banqueting, coffee shops and theme restaurants. There is nothing here which refutes the Tiltscher argument.

Contribution to cash flow

In times of recession, when the business and leisure markets are depressed, the hotel becomes more dependent on local business, and here food and beverage becomes the main attraction. In these circumstances where room revenues are low, the main contribution is as much to cash flow as to profits, exemplified by short-term credit and cash sales.

Conclusion

The arguments above may astound a practising hotelier because the merits of food and beverage are taken for granted and imbued by professional training. Indeed, this in itself may also contribute to the underestimation of the function. Whilst the same arguments circulate within hotel operations, they tend not to contain the bias so prominent in outsiders.

The joy of a polemic is that it can be highly biased and selective. This is true here. It is perfectly legitimate to dispute the facts as well the arguments. However, the purpose of our argument is to refute a fairly conspicuous view that down-grades a key component of the hotel package and unintentionally supports the movement towards safe mediocrity in this area.

References

DiMaggio, P.J. and Powell, W.W., 1983, The iron cage revisited: institutional isomorphism and collective rationality in organizational fields. *American Sociological Review*, 48, April: pp. 147–60.

Douglas, M., 1987, *How Institutions Think*, Routledge & Kegan Paul, London, 45–54.

Gamble, P.R., 1990, 'Innovation and innkeeping', inaugural lecture, University of Surrey.

Kirton, M., 1976, 'Adaptors and Innovators: a description and measure', *Journal of Applied Psychology*, 61: pp. 622–29.

Merton, R.K., 1968, *Social Theory and Social Structure*, The Free Press, New York, 104–12.

Morgan, G., 1991, 'Paradigms, metaphors and puzzle solving in organization theory', in J. Henry (ed.), *Creative Management*, Sage, London.

Riley, M.J., 1984, 'Hotels and group identity', *Tourism Management*, 5(2): pp. 102–9.

Riley, M.J. and Jauncey, S., 1991, 'Examining structure in decision making in hotels', *International Journal of Contemporary Hospitality Management*, 2(3): pp. 11–15.

Shamir, B., 1978, 'Between bureaucracy and hospitality—some organizational characteristics of hotels', *Journal of Management Studies*, 15 October: pp. 285–307.

Tajfel, H., 1978, *Differentiation of Social Groups*, Academic Press, London and New York.

Tiltscher, R., 1983, *An Investment Review of the UK Hotel Industry*. London, ch. 8.

Wood, R., 1991, 'The shock of the new: a sociology of nouvelle cuisine', *Journal of Consumer Studies and Home Economics*, 15: pp. 327–38.

18 Destination management systems: the challenge of the 1990s
S. Sussmann

Introduction

The 1980s saw the development and consolidation of powerful computerized reservation systems (CRSs), mostly initiated by airlines, and concerned primarily with air transport. Initially restricted to the reservation of seats on airlines, they have now extended their scope to incorporate accommodation, car rental and even attractions reservations. Their penetration as a global means of travel products distribution—beyond the air seat reservation—has been mainly aimed at the business or frequent traveller. There are now, however, clear indications that this market is becoming saturated and that the global CRSs are looking to the leisure market by building up connections with destination databases. At this point, the involvement of national and regional tourist organizations acquires particular relevance to ensure the marketing of the destinations is in their best interests and within their own agreed marketing plans (Travis, 1989). The availability of communications and networking technology, already anticipated by Bruce (1987; 1989), will make possible the efficient management of large destination databases, not limited to air travellers but also incorporating land transport, either by road or railway, and independent travellers. This is particularly relevant in Europe, as recently discussed by Lickorish (1991) and in some holiday locations in the United States.

This chapter will not enter into a detailed description of the current status of airline and global CRSs, which has recently been comprehensively reviewed (McGuffie, 1990a; Sloane, 1990; Truitt et al.,1991). Instead, it will analyse the arguments in favour of or against the creation or consolidation of destination databases, their connection with the distribution of travel products, and the conditions for their success, with examples of pilot or advanced projects from Europe and the United States.

The changing role of computerized reservation systems

The first computerized reservation system—**SABRE** from American Airlines—started in 1959 as a way of using the emerging tools of information technology to automate the mundane tasks of keeping track of seats sold. In 1976 it began to be used by travel agents world-wide and is currently installed in 20,000 travel agencies in fifty-four countries, with more than 128,000 terminals connected (Oliver, 1991). Its parent airline has become the archetypal case study for the competitive advantages to be gained from the use of information technology (McFarlan, 1984; Hopper, 1990; Ward, Griffiths and Whitmore, 1990), and a claim has often been quoted (Sloane, 1990) that in case of financial difficulties, the airline itself would be sold before **SABRE**.

The influence of deregulation in this expansion is well documented in Collier (1989) and the relative ranking of the remaining US large CRSs is extensively discussed in Truitt, Teye and Farris (1991). Impending deregulation in Europe, as well as the need to respond to the US challenge and the globalization of the markets, motivated the major European airlines into a united response, which was finally split into two rival global CRSs, **AMADEUS** and **GALILEO**. Their development is explained in Sloane (1990) and McGuffie (1990a) and their market coverage is illustrated in Truitt, Teye and Farris (1991). The latter authors also provide comprehensive coverage of the CRSs developments in other parts of the globe.

The CRSs are no longer used simply to reserve airline tickets. They now provide comprehensive services, in particular hotel reservations (McGuffie, 1990a; Sheldon, 1989) and car rentals. However, these extensions have so far affected only the business and frequent traveller markets.

With increased competition, some CRSs—**SABRE** in particular—decided to look into the opportunities available in the leisure market. In 1985 they introduced **Tourfinder**, a tour availability and reservation system, and the **SABRE Travel Guide**, an information system for tourist offices, with only modest success. An analysis of the characteristics of the leisure market led to the launch of **Leisure SABRE** established in 1990 and scheduled to introduce a global distribution product for late 1992/early 1993 (Oliver, 1991). This new product should consist of several software *modules*, interacting with existing **SABRE** products, and intended for **SABRE** travel agent subscribers. The product has been developed with input from Europe, United States, Canada and Australia and will consist of cruise, package tours and destination information modules, all wrapped around with a presentation manager to provide a user-friendly interface.

Another development along the same lines is the agreement between **Galileo** and **Autofile**, the main provider of software to the package tour industry, which allows travel agents who use Autofile's **ATOP** system to connect directly into **Galileo** (Sloane,1990).

Destination databases—the next generation

In November 1991, at a conference organized by the Italian Centre of Advanced Tourism Studies in Assisi, the European Commission representative, Mr Paul Watershoot, introduced his speech with the following scenario:

When I had to make my travel arrangements for Assisi last week, all I had to do was to switch on my computer and link up with our in house information databank. After browsing through some general information on travel to Italy and ordering some Italian Lira from my bank by electronic mail, I decided to switch, through a special connection, to the territorial databank on Umbria, where the system allowed me to call detailed and up-to-date information on accommodation on to my high definition colour screen. . . . Well, you may have guessed it was not quite like that. (Watershoot, 1991)

However futuristic this scenario sounds, the technology required to make it possible is tested, well proven and already in place in many areas of advanced countries. It basically requires fibre-optic cable and an integrated services digital network (ISDN) for the transmission of sound, voice, data and image (Knight and Silk, 1990; Shafer and Moeller, 1989). It is certainly available to the operators of the large CRSs, but is notoriously absent in the communications infrastructure of most medium and small tourist destinations, precisely those which national tourist organizations would be more interested in promoting.

A very important issue for the 1990s is the response of national tourist organizations and small and medium tourism enterprises to the expansion of computer networks and the creation of destination databases. Lickorish (1991) points out that 'tourism requires a partnership between the public and the private sector' and quotes research into impacts of technological changes of tourism flows and infrastructure as one of the important aims of the 'Community Action Plan to assist Tourism'.

A destination database is in its simplest form a collection of information, probably computerized and interactively accessible, about a destination. In its more sophisticated form it also includes accommodation and attractions, text and pictures, even interactive audio and video images using new multimedia techniques. However, the large investment required by the more sophisticated systems and the necessary networking infrastructure cannot be justified—if it is going to be undertaken solely by private corporations—unless the system can take reservations and bookings also.

The major areas of potential conflict between the interests of large CRSs in the leisure market and the national tourist organizations (Peroni, 1991) will undoubtedly be:

— selective versus generalized inclusion in the database;
— the information/transaction ratio; and
— the lack of agreed standards for the network and interface.

As concerns the medium and small tourism enterprises—both travel agencies and hotels—they will need to balance the potential gains in revenue against the increased investment in hardware, software and communications, as well as the additional booking commission. In hotels the costs have been calculated to increase room rates by 25 per cent (Go, 1991). There is also the problem of securing identity, achieved better through multimedia or graphical aids. Alternative methods of imaging—such as CD ROMs, which do not involve **transmission of images** and hence do not need optical fibre connections—are becoming more accessible and have been adopted in some pilot projects and even large hotel booking systems like **Utell International** and **Best Western**.

Most tourist boards or tourist organizations already have what amounts to either a basic or well-developed destination database in place (Lavery, 1989; Vogel, 1991). It is the management system developed to access, connect and extend them which will determine their success as a marketing tool. According to Haines (1991), they must be:

— complete: include all the available accommodation, effectively classified;
— accurate: both in terms of price and inventory; and
— provide instant confirmation and ease of payment.

Some examples of operational or planned destination management systems will be analysed in the following section.

Existing or planned destination databases: case studies

The following selection includes systems from Europe and the United States. They are either totally operational, in the initial planning stages, or pilot projects. They can be either information or information/booking systems, with different levels of connectivity to larger systems. They also include systems aimed at the road traveller, and as such totally independent from airline CRSs. The list is only illustrative and does not attempt to be complete.

Hi-Line

Hi-Line operates in the Highlands and Islands region of Scotland, a fairly remote area with very diverse tourist possibilities: seaside, climbing, sailing, skiing, shooting, fishing, golf. As a consequence of both remoteness and diversity, most of the demand is for touring and multi-centred holidays and most of the supply is from small independent business. Obviously, centralization is a very interesting proposition, and the Highlands and Islands Development Board funded an initial project in 1984. A detailed history can be found in Wayne (1991). The enterprise was reorganized in 1989, with only 30 per cent equity from the Highland and Islands Development Board, the rest coming from either corporate or private sources.

The mode of operation is both information and booking. A toll-free phone number is in all the brochures produced by the Highlands and Islands Development Board, and available either in tourist information offices or travel agents. Customers—either travel agents or individuals—can obtain either information or immediate confirmation of bookings, from their up-to-date room allocations database, which can be updated by either telephone or fax communication. This obviates the need for networking equipment at the small accommodation units.

For the future, on the demand side, they have already introduced a toll-free fax line to travel agents overseas and are engaged in negotiations with **Leisure SABRE** for direct connections to selected travel agents in the United States, who will have access to dedicated parts of the destination database, with search and reserve functions. On the supply side, they are looking into low-cost terminals for selected hotels.

Swissline

Swissline was founded in October 1991 (so it is strictly still in the planning stage) with funding from the Swiss National Tourist Office, Swiss Hoteliers Association, Swissair, Swiss Federal Railways, Swiss Tourism Association and the Swiss Post Office. The ultimate goal is the creation of a national tourism databank (Fisher, 1991) for Switzerland, accessible mainly through Swiss Tourist offices both internally and abroad. It will include both information and reservation functions.

Ulysses

This is a pilot project, funded by the EC IMPACT programme (Ploix, 1991). It comprises three parts:

— **Ulysses France**, sponsored by the International Federation of Automobile Clubs and including both information and reservations, attractions and in particular road information, based mainly on the existing Minitel telephone videotex system;
— **Ulysses Portugal**, sponsored by the Portuguese Automobile Club and initially only information;
— **Ulysses Ireland**, which extends the **GULLIVER** information database, already in place, with a reservation network.

An area that will see considerable developments in the future and deserves a separate analysis, is the application of *expert systems* to travel counselling (Bruce, 1989; Hruschka and Mazanec, 1990; Martin and Oxman, 1988). One such example is the **Minnesota Vacation Advisor** (Limback, 1991), a development of the travel information system described by Goeldner (1989).

Conclusions

The accelerated tendency of all areas of the developed world towards connectivity and the *global village* is clearly reflected in the marketing and distribution of tourism products. With air travel mostly dominated by a small number of large global reservation systems, the next stage will be the establishment, connection and management of destination databases, capable of both promoting and selling the tourism products of their own geographic areas. Both the public tourist organizations and the hospitality industry will need to be aware of the related potential advantages and pitfalls. The scope for enhancing and promoting the traveller's awareness of remote and underdeveloped areas is tremendous for as long as the control remains with those bodies concerned with the welfare of both the tourist and the destination.

References

Bruce, M., 1987, 'New technology and the future of tourism', *Tourism Management*, 8(2): pp.115–20.

Bruce, M., 1989, 'Technological change and competitive marketing strategies', in Witt and Moutinho (eds), *Tourism Marketing and Management Handbook*, Prentice Hall, Hemel Hempstead: pp. 455–8.

Collier, D., 1989, 'Expansion and development of CRS', *Tourism Management*, 10(2): pp. 86–8.

Go, F., 1991, 'The role of computerized reservation systems in the hospitality industry', presented at the conference Tourism and Hospitality Management: Established Disciplines, or 10 years wonders, 25–28 September, University of Surrey, UK.

Goeldner, C., 1989, 'Tourism information systems', in Witt and Moutinho (eds), *Tourism Marketing and Management Handbook*, Prentice Hall, Hemel Hempstead: pp. 503–6.

Hopper, M., 1990, 'Rattling SABRE—new ways to compete on information', *Harvard Business Review*: May/June: pp. 118–25.

Hruschka, H. and Mazanec, J., 1990, 'Computer-assisted travel counselling', *Annals of Tourism Research*, 17: pp. 208–27.

Knight, A.V. and Silk, D.J., 1990, *Managing Information*, McGraw-Hill, London, chs. 5 and 6.

Lavery, P., 1989, 'European destination marketing', in Witt and Moutinho (eds), *Tourism Marketing and Management Handbook*, Prentice Hall, Hemel Hempstead: pp. 141–6.

Lickorish, L.J., 1991, 'Developing a single European tourism policy', *Tourism Management*, 12(3): pp. 178–84.

Limback, L., 1991, 'Minnesota Office of Tourism Vacation Advisor Expert System', private communication.

McFarlan, I.F.W., 1984, 'Information technology changes the way you compete', *Harvard Business Review*, May/June: p. 98.

McGuffie, J., 1990a, 'CRS development and the hotel sector—Part I', *Travel and Tourism Analyst*, 1: pp. 29–41.

McGuffie, J., 1990b, 'CRS development and the hotel sector—Part II', *Travel and Tourism Analyst*, 2: pp. 18–36.

Martin, J. and Oxman, S., 1988, *Building Expert Systems*, Prentice Hall, New Jersey.

Shafer, E.L. and Moeller, G., 1989, 'Science and technology in tourism', in Witt and Moutinho (eds), *Tourism Marketing and Management Handbook*, Prentice Hall, Hemel Hempstead: pp. 381–6.

Sheldon, P., 1989, 'Travel industry information systems', in Witt and Moutinho (eds), *Tourism Marketing and Management Handbook*, Prentice Hall, Hemel Hempstead: pp. 589–92.

Sloane, J., 1990, 'Latest developments in Aviation CRSs', *Travel and Tourism Analyst*, 4: pp. 5–15.

Travis, A., 1989, 'Tourism destination area development (from theory into practice)', in Witt and Moutinho (eds), *Tourism Marketing and Management Handbook*, Prentice Hall, Hemel Hempstead: pp. 487–98.

Truitt, L.J., Teye, V.B. and Farris, M.T., 1991, 'The role of computer reservation systems. International implications for the travel industry', *Tourism Management*, 12(1): pp. 21–36.

Ward, Griffiths and Whitmore, 1990, *Strategic Planning for Information Systems*, John Wiley, Chichester, p. 20.

Papers presented at the International Conference on Public Networks and the National Tourist Organizations, organized by the Italian Centre for Advanced Tourism Studies, Assisi, Italy, 18–20 November 1991

Fisher, D., 'Swissline, new opportunities for Swiss tourism marketing'.

Haines, P., 'Qualities needed for destination management systems'.

Oliver, J., 'Leisure SABRE, a global means of distribution for tourism products'.

Peroni, G., 'Introductory speech: problems and prospects for the renewal of public tourism marketing in the computer network era'.

Ploix, D., 'Ulysses International', IMPACT Project No. 1004.

Vogel, H.M., 'Computer networking and new ways of tourism promotion and marketing for the public tourism system in Holland, Austria and Germany'.

Watershoot, P., 'The European Community: tourism and information technologies'.

Wayne, N., 'Hi-Line, a case study of a working computerised central reservation office in public sector tourism'.

19 1993 cross-Channel opportunities

A. Jefferson

Transport alternatives in 1993

The Channel Tunnel

At 11 a.m. on Saturday 1 December 1990 the historic service tunnel breakthrough took place. The Channel Tunnel—a dream of visionaries for more than two hundred years—was a reality. The land connection between Britain and mainland Europe was established and the Channel Tunnel was on target to open in June 1993, though since delayed until late 1993. Yet, in spite of the millions of words which have been written about this historic occasion, there is still ignorance about what the Tunnel is among future potential travellers. Many people believe that, like the Tyne Tunnel and the Mersey Tunnel, one will be able to drive through. In fact, the Channel Tunnel will be a railway system connecting terminals at Coquelles near Calais and Folkestone in Kent. It will carry three types of traffic:

1. cars and coaches on passenger shuttles operated by Eurotunnel;
2. heavy goods vehicles carrying freight in separate freight shuttles, again operated by Eurotunnel;
3. passenger trains and freight trains operated by the national railways on both sides of the Channel.

The shuttle trains will be double-decker for car carrying and single-deck for coach or heavy goods vehicles. Passengers will stay in their cars or coaches. There will be no provision for foot passengers, who will travel by high speed trains.

Thus leisure and business travellers will have a choice of travelling from a city centre, e.g., Paris–London, Brussels–London, as railway passengers or from a motorway in France to a motorway in Britain, using Eurotunnel's shuttles for the 35 minutes' journey through the Tunnel.

New high speed lines are being built between Calais, Lille and Paris and between Lille and Brussels. When the former is completed the journey times for through trains are forecast to be: London–Paris, three hours; and London–Brussels, a little over three hours. The latter should be reduced when the Lille–Brussels link is completed in 1995 to two hours forty minutes. French Railways (SNCF) is planning to build a TGV line around Paris connecting the new Lille–Paris line with Charles de Gaulle airport, Euro Disney, Lyons and Tours.

Alas, although British Rail is committed to a new high speed rail link, it is unlikely to be operational before the end of the century at the earliest. The reality is that passengers boarding in Paris will travel through the French countryside at 200 mph, travel through the Channel Tunnel at about 100 mph and finally in Britain at no more than 70 mph. The British government's decision in October 1991 to route the high speed rail link through Stratford begs a number of questions: timing and financing of the project are perhaps the most crucial. The Secretary of State claims that it could be developed and operational before the end of the century. In the House of Commons on 14 October 1991 he said:

We would like to see a private sector funded project and that is what we believe is most desirable. But if proposals come forward that fall short of that we will consider that in the circumstances at the time.

It seems that public money could be used to fund it, or at least part of it, if private sector finance is not forthcoming, notwithstanding the existing legislation. So, it appears that the engineering consultants Ove Arup's preferred route, which runs from Folkestone through north Kent before crossing the Thames at Dartford and thence to Stratford in East London to King's Cross, could well be operational before the end of the decade. A large freight terminal is planned for Stratford and there is the possibility of intermediate stations—at Medway Parkway for example. It is argued that this route will accelerate development in East London and Rainham Marshes.

The ferry operators

There has been considerable investment in new vessels and systems as the ferry companies gear up to face the new competition from the Channel Tunnel and to meet the needs of an increasingly sophisticated market. Today's cross-Channel ferries are more akin to cruise liners.

The ferry operators have segmented their markets and the product is increasingly designed to meet the wants and needs of leisure and business travellers alike. For example, P&O European Ferries, which has spent some £500 million on its fleet of twenty-three ships, has developed club class lounges where complimentary newspaper, tea and coffee are provided together with desks, telephones, fax and photocopying for the business traveller. This facility is available for a £5 premium on the fare. P&O European Ferries is also introducing a £5 million reservation and ticketing system in the autumn of 1991. This system, known as Dolphin, adds to the technological advances demonstrated in the Isocard machine-readable ticketing system which has considerably reduced check-in times. On the freight side a further £200 million has been invested in four superfreighters. Sealink Stena Line completed a £180 million investment programme during 1991, including buying new ships and up-grading existing ones. The Stena Invicta—a £40-million luxury superferry—now operates on the Dover–Calais route. P&O European Ferries operate the short sea crossings Dover–Boulogne, Dover–Calais and Dover–Ostend. Sealink Stena Line operate between Dover and Calais, Harwich and Hoek van Holland as well as Newhaven and Dieppe and Southampton and Cherbourg. Hoverspeed serves the Dover–Calais and Dover–Boulogne routes, and Sally Line ferries cover the Ramsgate–Dunkerque route.

The bulk of the traffic passes through Dover, which handled 15.5 million passengers in 1990. Day-trippers are an important source of revenue for the ferry operators, especially in the off-peak season, and at the moment the bulk of these trips are made by British residents. One of the attractions of such trips is the duty-free shopping. When this is abolished these trips will lose some of their appeal. However, EC Finance Ministers have agreed that 'duty-free' will not disappear with the start of the Single Market on 1 January 1993. It will be phased out over a period to be determined. Retention of the concession will give a competitive edge to the ferry operators—unless Eurotunnel decides to operate its own duty-free shops (not included in their current planning).

The airlines

On journeys of up to three hours SNCF claim that a TGV can capture 85 per cent of the market against 15 per cent travelling by air. Over three hours there is a reduced appeal. So Paris–London and Brussels–London business traffic could well switch to rail via the Channel Tunnel, which will provide a comfortable hassle-free journey from city centre to city centre in all weathers in about three hours. Eurotunnel's consultants forecast that more than 50 per cent of the existing air traffic on these routes will be diverted to the direct rail link. However, the Single European Act will be operating in 1993 and member states have agreed the following in principle:

— the introduction of a simple, more market-motivated system for setting fares;
— the ending of discrimination in favour of the national flag carriers through the introduction of uniform licensing criteria;
— the ending of bilateral capacity-sharing, which has artificially restricted the services which any individual carrier could offer.

Liberalization treaties have already been signed by the UK government with Germany (1984), Netherlands (1984), Luxembourg (1985), Belgium (1985) and Ireland (1988), and Britain fully supports the EC's liberalization programme. While the EC is creating the climate for more flexibility to enable airlines to set fares it is purely a matter of their commercial judgement. Where bilateral agreements have been reached to date, e.g., Ireland and The Netherlands, fares have come down.

One needs to make a distinction though between scheduled and charter traffic. The liberalization programme is geared to scheduled air services. Most holiday-makers from Britain to Europe use air travel by charter though the converse is not so true. There is another EC directive on packaged travel, which will impact on charter traffic, although this need not overly concern us here. There is a large amount of business traffic between Paris and London and Brussels and London which normally flies, and the Tunnel undoubtedly poses a threat to this traffic. On the other hand, services into London City Airport may develop strongly: Stansted with its rail link to Liverpool Street offers speedy processing, and a Heathrow–Paddington rail link is planned with a claimed journey time of sixteen minutes, though this too has been deferred.

The prices which will obtain in 1993 for the four transport modes—rail, shuttle, sea and air—are not known, although there seems little doubt that the airlines will have the ability to create attractive off-peak and excursion fares and could even use airports, such as Luton or Lydd, where landing fees and other airport charges are not nearly so high as Heathrow or Gatwick.

The prospects of a price war between the various transport modes are very real and there may well be casualties among the operators. The consumer though, at least in the short term, will benefit from the competition and the tourist traffic will increase. New traffic will be created through massive marketing campaigns. In my view the opening of the Tunnel and the response from sea and air carriers provides an opportunity to increase the market.

If P&O European Ferries and Sealink Stena Line merged operations, they could run ferries at least every hour with shared ticketing and revenues, there would be economies of scale and operation which could provide a better, cheaper service for the traveller. If they controlled their own terminals—the port of Dover is to be privatized—there would be further economies to be made, although P&O have announced that they are not interested in purchasing the port of Dover.

Ultimately, the ability to compete will depend on fares, frequency, quality of service and the provision of an adequate connecting transport infrastructure. Usually dominance in any two of these factors will guarantee success. The route, however, is a means to an end. The attraction and satisfaction at the destination remains the key element in the decision to make a journey. Results and success will depend on destination marketing in its widest sense.

Markets

Social, demographic, economic and political trends

Europe will undoubtedly continue to dominate the international travel picture in the foreseeable future. Western Europeans enjoy above-average standards of living compared with the world average. Although the EC population is not growing very much, it is ageing. By the end of the century one in four Europeans will be over 55, and since 1945 the average age of death has increased by ten years. Europeans are living longer and they are retiring earlier. In 1988 the average legal retirement age for men was 62.5 years and for women 58 years. Similarly the populations of Canada and the United States will grow slowly, and again retired people will account for a larger share of the total population than they do currently. Japan is the most rapidly ageing population in the world: even in 1985 one in ten people were over 64 and this is forecast to increase to one in seven by 2010.

Time, the desire to travel and income levels are the prerequisites of travel. Europeans have a much longer holiday entitlement than either Americans or Japanese—in many cases as much as six weeks.

Economic forecasts suggest that the EC will benefit from the competition of the Single Market, although growth will be constrained by its ageing population and its consequent drain on the public purse, and a rather inflexible labour market.

Rapid political changes in eastern Europe are creating a large new market with a pent-up desire for foreign travel, although in the short term the balance of traffic will be in favour of western tourists visiting eastern Europe. This new travel opportunity may, therefore, have a detrimental effect on traffic flows to Britain.

Consumer research

Qualitative research was carried out early in 1989 by the British Tourist Authority (BTA) and Eurotunnel to discover the views of continental leisure car-travellers about a trip to Britain and the Channel Tunnel. The Channel is currently seen as a physical and psychological barrier to continental car-travellers. The sea crossing is often perceived to be long, arduous and something that requires careful organization by tourists considering a short or spontaneous cross-border trip. Therefore, 'you do not go to Britain as to other European countries' for the journey is 'very long and you have to wait' and 'if you do not book you cannot cross'. However, amongst people who have visited Britain before and those planning a longer trip the sea crossing is considered to be a pleasurable aspect of a trip to Britain.

Many continental Europeans with experience of visiting Britain view it as an exotic short-haul destination—a concept which has reinforced by the need to cross the sea. This adds a quality of mystery and adventure which is not experienced by simply crossing a land frontier. This *exotic* appeal of Britain appears to be a unique feature amongst European destinations and one which we must protect after 1993. On the other hand, those who have not visited Britain may find the exotic appeal a negative factor and may therefore not wish to visit.

After the Tunnel opens there is some concern amongst continentals that Britain will lose its identity and will become similar to mainland Europe, for it will be 'so easy to go there, you will not have the impression of being there'. The research indicates that potential Tunnel travellers find the prospect of left-hand driving frightening. Some with experience of travelling in Britain find that with practice and local help it is easier than

Table 19.1   *Forecasts of visits to the UK by area of origin 1990–5*

	1990(P) 000s	1991 000s	1992 000s	1993 000s	1994 000s	1995 000s	Av. annual growth % 1990–5	Market share % 1990	% 1995
Americas	3,908	3,600	3,900	4,100	4,400	4,600	3	22	21
Europe	10,876	11,200	12,000	12,500	13,000	13,600	5	61	61
Pacific	2,000	2,000	2,200	2,400	2,600	2,900	8	11	13
Rest of world	1,166	1,200	1,100	1,200	1,200	1,200	1	6	5
TOTAL	17,950	18,000	19,200	20,200	21,200	22,300	4	100	100

Note: 1990 are provisional estimates based on monthly IPS figures. Visits are rounded to nearest hundred thousand. Percentages are based on unrounded figures.

Source: BTA/ETB

expected. Potential visitors need to be given much reassurance on this point.

While awareness of the construction of a fixed link is generally high amongst continental car-travellers, interest and knowledge diminish with distance from the coast. Consequently the French and Belgians are probably more aware of the opportunities afforded by the Tunnel than the Germans and the Dutch. The prospects are that when the Tunnel opens, 'Britain will be accessible at last', for it will provide a quick and efficient means of communication for businessmen and leisure travellers. This appeal means that the Tunnel is likely to attract traffic from both airlines and ferries.

Table 19.2   *Forecasts of expenditure in the UK by area of origin 1990–5*

	1990(P) 000s	1991 000s	1992 000s	1993 000s	1994 000s	1995 000s	Av. annual growth % 1990–5	Market share % 1990	% 1995
Americas	2,088	1,875	1,950	2,175	2,400	2,700	5	27	23
Europe	3,304	3,500	3,775	4,175	4,625	5,125	9	43	44
Pacific	1,271	1,375	1,550	1,775	2,075	2,400	14	16	21
Rest of world	1,062	1,100	1,150	1,225	1,300	1,375	5	14	12
TOTAL	7,725	7,850	8,425	9,350	10,400	11,600	8	100	100

Note: 1990 are provisional estimates based on monthly IPS figures. Estimated expenditure are at current prices, assuming an average annual inflation of about 5%. Expenditure figures are rounded to nearest £25m. Percentages are based on unrounded figures.

Source: BTA/ETB

Four travel modes competing for a share

By 1993 BTA estimates that over 20 million overseas residents will visit the United Kingdom—over 12 per cent more than in 1990. They will spend some £9,350 million.

France, Germany and the Benelux countries will provide the majority of Tunnel travellers, although Spain, Italy and Switzerland are also markets which offer potential. Neither must the long-haul markets like the United States, Australia, Japan and French Canada be overlooked—many visitors from these markets undertake European trips, taking in two or more countries (Tables 19.1 and 19.2).

Table 19.3   *Mode of travel between the UK and European countries, 1990*

No. of visits	Incoming versus outgoing					
	Total 000s	%	Air 000s	%	Sea 000s	%
UK–France						
Visits to UK by French residents	2,309	25	949	36	1,360	21
Visits to France by UK residents	6,865	75	1,699	64	5,166	79
UK–W Germany						
Visits to UK by W. German residents	1,878	51	1,000	49	878	54
Visits to W. Germany by UK residents	1,796	49	1,059	51	737	46
UK–Belgium/Luxembourg						
Visits to UK by Belgian/ Lux residents	572	37	236	43	336	34
Visits to Belgium/ Luxembourg by UK residents	958	63	317	57	641	66
UK–The Netherlands						
Visits to UK by residents of the Netherlands	993	45	530	45	463	45
Visits to the Netherlands by UK residents	1,216	55	639	55	577	55

Note: The definitions of incoming and outgoing travellers are somewhat different. An overseas visitor is counted regardless of whether the UK is the main country of visit, while a UK resident going to many countries is assigned to the main country visited.

Source: International Passenger Survey.

Table 19.4   *Mode of travel between the UK and European countries, 1990*

	All visits		Air		Sea	
	000s	%	000s	%	000s	%
UK–France						
Visits to UK by French residents	2,309	100	949	41	1,360	59
Visits to France by UK residents	6,865	100	1,699	25	5,166	75
UK–W. Germany						
Visits to UK by W. German residents	1,878	100	1,000	53	878	47
Visits to W. Germany by UK residents	1,796	100	1,059	59	737	41
UK–Belgium/Luxembourg						
Visits to UK by Belgian/Lux residents	572	100	236	41	336	59
Visits to Belgium/Luxembourg by UK residents	958	100	317	33	641	67
UK–The Netherlands						
Visits to UK by residents of The Netherlands	993	100	530	53	463	47
Visits to the Netherlands by UK residents	1,216	100	639	53	577	47

Notes: 1. Percentages total horizontally.
2. The definitions of incoming and outgoing travellers are somewhat different. An overseas visitor is counted regardless of whether the UK is the main country of visit, while a UK resident going to many countries is assigned to the main country visited.

Source: International Passenger Survey.

According to Tables 19.3 and 19.4, France is the biggest source market for visitors to Britain who come by sea—1.4 million in 1990 or 59 per cent of total visits. Germany accounted for 878,000 visits by sea in 1990, although it should be remembered that residents of Germany include the British forces there. Again sea traffic represents more than 50 per cent of visits. The Netherlands, Belgium and Luxembourg accounted for 799,000 visits by sea or 51 per cent of total traffic.

So ferry services are currently an important mode of travel to Britain from these source markets, carrying over 3 million passengers in 1990. They are even more important for outgoing passengers (7.1 million in 1990) who are resident in the United Kingdom.

Air travel is not so much in demand. Even so carryings are important, especially in Germany and The Netherlands, where air travel accounts for almost 50 per cent of total visits.

Foreign day-trippers are mainly from France (374,000 or 17 per cent of French visitors), The Netherlands (157,000 or 17 per cent) and Belgium/Luxembourg (161,000 or 26 per cent) (Table 19.5).

Eurotunnel has changed its forecasts over the past four years, generally reducing estimates for the first full year of operation, although increasing forecasts for 2003 as Table 19.6 shows.

Table 19.5 *Overseas visitors on an excursion to the UK by country of origin, 1989*

	Total %	(of which excursionists) %	Number of excursionists 000s
France	100	17	374
W. Germany	100	9	180
Netherlands	100	17	157
Belgium/Lux	100	26	161
Italy	100	2	11
Spain	100	1	6
Denmark	100	7	17
Total EC	**100**	**12**	**907**
Switzerland	100	5	21
Norway	100	8	22
Sweden	100	3	13
Total W. Europe (non-EC)	**100**	**4**	**60**
USA	100	1	30
Canada	100	1	5
N. America	**100**	**1**	**35**
Australia	100	1	5
Japan	100	1	3
Rest of world	**100**	**1**	**27**

Note: Excursionists: include business and leisure trips.

Source: International Passenger Survey.

Table 19.6 *Eurotunnel traffic forecasts*

	1993			2003		
Date of estimates	1987	1990	1991	1987	1990	1991
Shuttle pax m.	13.2	14.6	12.8	18.1	19.9	18.6
Rail pax m.	16.5	14.0	15.3	21.4	24.7	25.0

Note: 1993 figures are for the first full year of operation.

Markets offering potential for British tourism

Britain's tourism industry faces increased competition, particularly from France, in the domestic market. Euro Disney forecasts to have 11–18 million visitors by 1993 and 50 per cent of advance enquiries (outside France) have come from the United Kingdom. The Tunnel will syphon off travellers from London and South-East England, a prime market for Scotland, Wales and the North of England, especially the short-holiday market. The Tunnel, together with the fast and reliable rail network in the north, will win France a bigger share of the international tourism market. It will almost certainly take more travellers out of Britain than it will bring in. Already the ferry companies carry significantly more British to France, Germany and the Benelux countries than Britain receives from these markets. An increase of 10 per cent in British outgoing business would need a corresponding 25 per cent increase in incoming business. It follows then that Eurotunnel and the ferry companies will put the bulk of their promotional effort into the British market. To compensate for this loss of domestic market the British tourism industry will have to work very hard to secure new foreign business. The opening of the Channel Tunnel and the greatly improved ferry services offer opportunities for Britain to develop a number of market segments in both long and short-haul markets.

Already Americans and Canadians are crossing the Channel by ferry as part of a European tour. The improved services will encourage additional use of ferries as well as the Channel Tunnel, which will have a great novelty value for several years after its opening in 1993. The Brit–France rail pass, which is available in North America, is selling well. The French-Canadian market, independent youth and senior citizen travellers as well as those on European coach tours, all offer potential from this very important region for Britain.

Many Australians and New Zealanders are long-stay visitors. Increasingly Britain is not seen as *home*, so while easier Channel crossings could well encourage additional European touring by *non-British* Australians, it could conversely act to the detriment of length of stay by *British* Australians who will find it easier to travel more widely throughout Europe.

Round Europe Capital City tours will continue to be popular in Asian markets and the Tunnel will encourage coach travel, The Japanese market is fast developing, and while group touring will continue to be the favoured method for first-time international travellers, there is a distinct move to independent travel by repeat visitors to Europe and this should result in longer stays in Britain.

It will be the price-sensitive European markets though which will offer the greatest opportunities to expand the market for Britain as a destination. Identification of growth segments and closely targeted marketing campaigns to both trade and consumer will be the keys to success. The Tunnel will be unaffected by weather and will help increase autumn, winter and spring travel, and rail travel will appeal particularly to senior citizens. The novelty value of the Tunnel will also create new business travel opportunities. The additional links and easier access will have most impact on the French market, which is well placed to respond to short-term special offers which could develop *taster* trips by independent first-time travellers to Britain and lay the foundations for repeat business. Britain enjoys a high level (almost 80 per cent) of repeat visits. Independent rail travellers, senior citizen and *comités d'enterprise* coach travel, long-stay repeat motoring traffic, corporate conference and incentive groups as well as youth travel all offer good potential. The additional services will offer more short-break opportunities from Britain's Benelux markets and especially spur-of-the-moment travel. Britain will be perceived to be that much closer and more accessible for Spanish, Swiss and Italian visitors to Britain, and should particularly encourage motoring traffic in the summer from these burgeoning markets.

None of these opportunities can be taken for granted though. Markets, especially the near European ones, will look to competitive pricing between air, sea and Tunnel options and to off-peak discounting. The Channel Tunnel will provide an alternative, and novel, means of accessing Britain. Air and coach travel will benefit from deregulation and EC liberalization measures. The ferry companies are already responding to the new competition with vastly improved services. The psychological barrier of the Channel will disappear when the Tunnel opens. So far as Britain is concerned, there is a real opportunity for incoming business, which initially will benefit London and South-East England. On the other hand, this is a real threat to the domestic market. The extent to which this leakage can be replaced with foreign visits and the extent to which first-time visits can be retained in the longer term will be determined by the ability of tourist boards, local authorities and the tourist industry in Britain to exploit the unique opportunity which 1993 offers.

References

BTA, 1988, *The Channel Tunnel: An Opportunity and a Challenge for British Industry*, British Tourist Authority, London.
BTA, 1989, *The Channel Tunnel: Will Britain's Tourism Industry and Infrastructure be Ready for 1993?*, British Tourist Authority, London.
BTA, 1991, 1993, *Cross-Channel Marketing Strategy*, British Tourist Authority, London.
BTA, 1991b, *Guidelines for Tourism to Britain 1991–1995*, British Tourist Authority, London.
Hansard, 14 October 1991, HMSO.

20 Regional development and tourism within the European Community

E. Lowyck and S. Wanhill

Regional development in the European Community: an overall picture

Differences among the EC regions

In the 1960s the European Commission drew attention to the fundamental contrasts between the regions in the Community. However, it was not until the 1970s that a Common Regional Policy (CRP) for the member nations was implemented and financed. The objectives of the CRP were to 'create a greater convergence between the economies of the member states and to ensure a better spread of the economic activities throughout its territory' (Clout, 1987). In spite of the many efforts, at the end of the 1980s there still exist important regional disparities.

According to the 'Fourth Periodic Report on the Social-Economic Situation and Development of the Regions in the Community (1991)', there arise important disparities regarding income (gross domestic product per capita, see Table 20.1) and productivity (gross domestic product per employee) among the regions of the Community. At the end of the 1980s, the average income per capita of the ten least favoured regions—mostly Greek and Portuguese regions—was less than one-third of the average income per head of the ten most prosperous regions.

The Community's work-force rose by 9.5 million between 1984 and 1990. This represents an annual increase of about 1.25 per cent. Notwithstanding the increase in total employment, the regions still display considerable disparities in unemployment levels. In 1990 unemployment in the ten regions with the lowest unemployment approximated to an average of 2.25 per cent; in the ten regions with the highest unemployment, especially regions in Spain and Italy, the unemployment rate was 22 per cent (see Table 20.2). Also, other indicators such as levels of education and training, condition of research and innovation and competition circumstances, confirm the existence of fundamental regional imbalances within the European Community.

Regional policy of the European Community

One of the commitments of the member states, fixed in the Treaty of Rome, is the unification of the economies of all member states by decreas-

Table 20.1 *GDP per capita in the member states, 1980, 1985, 1990 (in purchasing power parties, EUR 12=100)*

Member state	1980	1985	1990
Begium	104.5	101.6	103.0
Denmark	109.0	117.0	107.2
Germany	113.8	114.4	113.4
Greece	58.2	56.8	53.0
Spain	73.4	71.8	76.3
France	111.9	110.7	108.6
Ireland	64.5	65.1	67.3
Italy	102.5	103.6	105.2
Luxembourg	115.6	124.0	128.7
Netherlands	111.0	107.2	103.1
Portugal	54.2	52.1	55.4
United Kingdom	101.1	103.7	103.7
EUR 3 (GR. IRL, P)	57.5	56.1	56.2
EUR 9 (Others)	103.2	103.4	103.4

Source: Commission of the European Communities, 1991.

Table 20.2 *Differences in regional unemployment percentages 1990*

Member state	Highest	Lowest	Mean
Belgium	13.1	3.8	7.6
Denmark	9.1	6.8	7.9
Germany	10.4	2.7	5.2
Greece	9.4	2.6	7.5
Spain	28.9	7.3	16.1
France	12.9	4.5	8.7
Ireland	—	—	16.4
Italy	22.6	2.4	10.2
Luxembourg	—	—	1.5
Netherlands	11.3	5.6	8.0
Portugal	12.6	2.8	5.1
United Kingdom	15.7	2.2	6.3

Source: Commission of the European Communities, 1991.

ing the regional imbalances and promoting the development of the least-favoured areas. This task is being accomplished by monitoring and controlling state aid and by financial aid to the less-developed regions. Community's control of state aid consists of supervision and ensuring that aid does not distort competition between the member states. In this chapter we concentrate on the Community's participation in financial aid for less-developed regions.

The European Regional Development Fund (ERDF) was created in 1975 with the aim of contributing to 'the correction of regional imbalances within the Community by participating in the development and structural adjustment of regions whose development is lagging behind and in the conversion of declining industrial regions' (Pearce, 1988). ERDF funds originally were granted on a quota basis and different reforms of the ERDF were attempted in 1979, 1985, and 1988 (Yuill and Allen, 1990).

The **first reform** undertaken established a non-quota section to finance specific Community regional development measures. Although the non-quota section represented only 5 per cent of the total ERDF budget, the European Commission obtained some independence from the member states in the assignment of the regional development grants.

The **second reform** of 1985 resulted in a replacement of the quota system with a system of upper and lower limits for each member state. The lower limit was the minimum amount guaranteed for each member state if it submitted an adequate volume of aid applications to the Commission. The assistance above the minimum amount depended on the extent to which projects submitted for ERDF grants were considered of value to the Community (Pearce, 1988). Also, more stress was placed on programmes rather than on project financing, and ERDF became the principal instrument available to the Community for supporting development of the regions under Community programmes, national programmes of Community interest, investment projects and ERDF-related studies. In 1985, when the second reform was implemented, the total budget of the ERDF amounted to ECU 2,290 million. For comparison, the start budget of ERDF in 1975 was ECU 258 million.

By the mid-1980s the objectives and implementation of the ERDF resources were increasingly overlapping with the European Social Fund (ESF), which has the task of increasing employment opportunities in the EC; with the European Agricultural Guidance and Guarantee Fund (EAGGF), which was set up to contribute to the development of rural areas and to adapt agricultural structures; and with other financial providers such as the European Investment Bank (EIB). Consequently, there was pressure for a more coherent approach towards social and regional development. Also, the enlargement of the EC with Spain and Portugal, which caused an increase in the number of least-favoured regions, and the growing complexity of procedures and mechanisms for providing assistance led to the need for a comprehensive reform of the Structural Funds. In 1988 the **new regulation** on the activities of the European Regional Development Fund was adopted in the reform of the Structural Funds (ESF, EAGGF, ERDF). The reform of the Structural Funds was based on three fundamental principles:

1. to transform structural policy into an instrument with real economic impact;
2. to use a multiannual approach for expenditure planning to assure member states of the stability and predictability of Community support; and

3. to implement a partnership with all the parties actively participating in structural policy, especially the regional authorities.
(Commission of the European Communities Annual Report on the implementation of the Reform of the Structural Funds, 1991)

The implementation of these principles required forward planning by the member states. They had to prepare **multiannual plans** reflecting their strategies and indicating the national resources available for the implementation and the Community assistance desired. In the next stage the Community determined priorities in the **Community Support Frameworks (CSFs)** in partnership with the member states and with the regional authorities designated by them. The CSFs are based on the needs formulated by the member states in their multiannual plans and they reflect the measures to be taken by the Community in co-operation with the member states. The CSFs also provide the framework for the applications for assistance.

According to Yuill and Allen (1990), the concrete impact of the reform is double: 'The reform has produced, first a co-ordination of the Funds according to six objectives to which the Funds are either jointly or separately assigned and, second, an increase in budgets'. To meet the first requirement, Community assistance is concentrated on regions experiencing difficulties (objectives 1, 2 and 5(b)) and on priority fields (objectives 3, 4 and 5(a)):

Objective 1:   Development and structural adjustment of regions whose development is lagging behind;
Objective 2:   Conversion of regions or parts of regions seriously affected by industrial decline;
Objective 3:   Combating long-term unemployment;
Objective 4:   Increasing youth employment;
Objective 5 (a): Adjustment of agricultural structures;
Objective 5 (b): Development of economic activities in rural areas, which creates jobs providing an alternative to employment in agriculture.

Objectives 1, 2 and 5(b) are regionally-targeted, while objectives 3, 4 and 5(a) are horizontal in character. This means that these objectives concern the entire Community. Since this article deals with regional development, full attention is paid to objectives 1, 2 and 5(b).

The main financial instruments which may be used for objective 1, 2 and 5(b) regions are the European Regional Development Fund the European Social Fund and the European Agricultural Guidance and Guarantee Fund, while financial instruments for objectives 3, 4 and 5(a) are mainly available from the European Social Fund, the European Investment Bank and the European Coal and Steel Community (ECSC).

The starting-point for the increase in budget was that the resources available to the Funds had to be doubled by comparison with 1987 (decision of the European Council February 1988). The Structural Fund assistance in the 1987 budget amounted to ECU 6,962 million (EAGGF,

ECU 1,017 million; ERDF, ECU 3,342 million; ESF, ECU 2,603 million) or ECU 7,233 million in 1988 prices. The budget in 1988 prices is the basis for the doubling. This gives a total of ECU 14,466 million for 1993 in 1988 prices. The Structural Fund financial resources available for the period 1989–93 in 1988 prices are shown below (Commission of the European Communities):

1989	ECU	8,980 million
1990		10,280 million
1991		11,580 million
1992		12,900 million
1993		14,466 million

The budget of the Structural Funds for the period 1989–93 comes to ECU 60,315 million (in 1989 prices). The following breakdown by objective was fixed by the Commission:

Objective 1	ECU	38,300 million
Objective 2		7,205 million
Objectives 3 and 4		7,450 million
Objective 5(a)		3,415 million
Objective 5(b)		2,795 million
Transitional measures		1,150 million
Total	ECU	60,315 million

A new situation has arisen from the events in Central and Eastern Europe in general, and in East Germany in particular. German unification has added another 16 million EC inhabitants. Generally, these new inhabitants are living in old industrial regions with very low productivity, or in agricultural regions with large and specialized, although low-productivity farms. The service sector in the former East Germany is underdeveloped in comparison with the West of Europe and infrastructure is mostly old and neglected. In order to cope with this situation in the former East German economy, the budgets of the Structural Funds have been increased by ECU 3,000 million.

The other Eastern and Central European countries are enduring similar problems of efficiency and productivity, general decay, lagging behind in development, and disturbed economic structures. Nevertheless, in the long run these countries will become important new sales markets and potential competitors for EC member states. These challenges should be supported by a long-term EC policy.

Community grants for tourism projects

Community actions in the field of tourism

All over the world tourism is seen as an industry with a positive economic impact on local economies. Europe currently enjoys 60 per cent of the international tourism business. The tourism sector in the EC employs 7.4 million full-time employees or 6.5 per cent of total employment in the member states (*Eurostat*). Total income from tourism in the EC represented 5.5 per cent of GDP in 1985 and tourism accounts for 8.1 per cent of final private consumption in the twelve member states. Notwithstanding the importance and impact of this new evolving industry, the European Community has been slow to formulate a Community tourism policy. It was not until 1986 that the Commission published a paper entitled 'Community action in the field of tourism'. In 1991 the European Commission adopted a 'Pluriannual Programme of Community Measures for Tourism'. This programme foresees two main axes strengthening the horizontal approach to tourism and supporting specific actions in the field of tourism in the EC:

1. Strengthening the horizontal approach to tourism includes:
   — improving knowledge in the field of tourism;
   — co-ordinating the Community and national policies;
   — improving the seasonal and geographical distribution of tourism; and
   — reinforcement of consultations of professionals and responsibles in the field of tourism.
2. In order to diversify tourism activities, the following medium-term measures are to be undertaken:
   — specific actions for the development of rural and cultural tourism;
   — specific actions for environmental protection; and
   — improvement of training programmes for the tourism industry.

The Community's regional policy for the tourism sector is directed towards two targets: First of all, the Community helps regions to develop their tourism potential by providing financial aid. Second, the European Community directs its regional policy towards regions likely to become too dependent on tourists or on the seasonal character of the presence of tourists. Resources available to cope with these problems will come from the Structural Funds (ERDF, ESF, EAGGF). Efforts for solving the first problem not only contribute directly to the development of tourism projects such as marinas, conference infrastructure or tourism animation, but also to investments of indirect importance. Indirect interventions in the domain of transport infrastructure, telecommunication or environment also contribute to the development of tourism. Similarly, the improvement of accessibility of certain regions whose development is lagging behind, creates the indispensable condition for the success of tourism initiatives in these regions. For regions becoming too dependent on tourism activities, funds are made available to solve problems in the environment, infrastructure, etc., on the one hand and to support efforts to diversify economic activities on the other.

Resources for structural interventions in the field of tourism in the Community are provided by the Structural Funds. For the regions of objective 1 (backward regions), 2 (regions affected by industrial decline) and 5(b) (rural areas) the reform of the Structural Funds permits plurian-nual actions for priority development goals (inclusive of tourism). In this way, tourism has been integrated into the global strategy of regional development.

Community assistance to tourism before the reform of the
Structural Funds

Since its start in 1975, the ERDF participated in an important number of projects, directly or indirectly linked to tourism. Grants have been awarded to a range of schemes: tourism infrastructure (marinas, develop-ment of coastal areas); infrastructure directly linked to the tourism sector (transport, energy and water supply); socio-cultural attractions (confer-ence and exhibition facilities, sport and recreation complexes, museums, libraries, theatres); services in the tourism field (tourism animation, infor-mation, promotion) and tourist accommodation.

Although most Community interventions in the field of tourism were met by the ERDF, the ESF and EAGGF have also contributed to initia-tives in favour of employment and of the development of complementary tourism activities on farms. In mountain regions and in other unfavourable agricultural areas EAGGF assistance assured the necessary conditions for the success of rural tourism.

Between 1975 and 1985 the ERDF awarded in total ECU 168 million of grants for projects directly and explicitly linked to tourism. This amount represented about 1.2 per cent of the entire ERDF budget over that period. Between 1986 and 1988 ERDF allocated ECU 732 million for tourism, representing 5 per cent of the overall ERDF budget over this period.

Next to ERDF assistance, Community efforts that are particularly important in the tourism field have been realized by the **Integrated Mediterranean Programmes**. By 1988 twenty-nine programmes had been approved for Greece, France and Italy. About 13 per cent of the total Integrated Mediterranean Programmes budget (ECU 3.2 billion) was re-served for financing the promotion of tourism activities and for the guid-ance of tourism policies in these countries.

Community assistance to tourism after the reform of the Structural Funds

When the CSFs were being drawn up, a section on tourism was included among the priorities for assistance. Actions in the tourism field, which are given priority in the allocation of the resources available from the Structural Funds, are the improvement of tourism supply, the geographical equilibrium of tourism supply, the reduction of the seasonal character of tourism, the revaluation of cultural heritage, the development of rural tourism, training for tourism careers and the protection of environment in tourism sites.

Structural Fund resources directly financing tourism activities in the regions of objective 1, covering the period 1989–93 come to ECU 1,613 million. This amount represents 5.5 per cent of the total Community assistance under the CSFs for this period, 86 per cent of which comes from the ERDF. The geographical distribution of this invention is shown in Table 20.3. For regions of objective 2, the Structural Funds support includes a budget of ECU 267 million for the period 1989–91 to favour tourism activity in a direct way. This means an allocation of 7.5 per cent of all Community assistance under the CSFs for the period in question. Countries taken into consideration for this appropriation are listed in Table 20.4. Regions of objective 5(b) receive ECU 176 million for the benefit of tourism initiatives in the period 1989–93, representing 6.8 per cent of total Community assistance under the CSFs. The geographical distribution of this assistance is given in Table 20.5.

Table 20.3   *Assistance in the field of tourism. Objective 1 regions (1989–93)*

Member state	MECU	% of total Community assistance under CSF
Greece	166.7	3.1
Spain	182.0	2.4
France	34.3	4.8
Ireland	188.6	6.6
Italy	780.0	12.5
Portugal	203.0	3.5
United Kingdom	58.2	10.5
Total objective 1	1,612.8	5.5

Source: Commission ot the European Communities, DG XVI.

All these measures concern only direct assistance. It is difficult to assess exactly the Community's total contribution for tourism, because other structural interventions also have an indirect influence on the development of tourism. Some assistance, particularly for transport, telecommunications and environment infrastructure indirectly benefits the tourism sector. It is, however, impossible to estimate the exact impact of these measures on the development of tourism.

Other Community initiatives for tourism are proposed by the Commission under the programmes **Envireg, Rechar and Interreg**. Envireg, the Commission initiative in the field of the environment, is of growing importance for tourism. One of the specific objectives of Envireg is to reduce pollution of coastal areas. Particular attention is paid to the Mediterranean regions, whose economy depends on tourism activity. One of the priorities, for example, is the important increase in the holiday

Table 20.4   *Assistance in the field of tourism. Objective 2 regions (1989–91)*

Member state	MECU	% of total Community assistance under CSF
Belgium	12.8	7.2
Denmark	0.5	1.6
Germany	1.32	0.4
Spain	—	—
France	44.1	7.3
Italy	24.6	9.0
Luxembourg	—	—
Netherlands	10.1	13.1
United Kingdom	173.9	12.8
Total objective 2	267.4	7.5

Source: Commission ot the European Communities, DG XVI.

Table 20.5   *Assistance in the field of tourism. Objective 5(b) regions (1989–93)*

Member state	MECU	% of total Community assistance under CSF
Belgium	4.4	13.5
Denmark	—	—
Germany	—	—
Spain	(*)	(*)
France	105.6	11.0
Italy	51.2	13.3
Luxembourg	0.4	16.0
Netherlands	9.0	20.5
United Kingdom	5.8	1.7
Total objective 5(b)	176.4	6.8

(*) not available

Source: Commission of the European Communities, DG XVI.

population during the summer in certain regions. Under Rechar—the Community initiative for the economic conversion of coal-mining areas—Community assistance may be granted for tourism promotion measures, and in particular for tourism promotion activities based on industrial heritage. Finally, under Interreg—the Community initiative for border areas—measures to encourage cross-frontier co-operation in tourism may receive Community assistance.

Operational arrangements

The purpose of this section is first, to report on the operational arrangements of the Community Structural Funds, and second, to deal with an overview of the successive steps a project promoter has to take.

The four different stages in the use of Community Structural Funds

The reform of the Structural Funds should help simplify and rationalize the Community's structural action. Uniformity of the procedures under which assistance is provided by the Structural Funds is a first step towards simplification. Rationalization has been assured by monitoring and assessing Community intervention.

The new simplified and rationalized procedure is in four stages (CEC, 1991):

1. Requirements are spelt out in multiannual plans by member states or by the competent national regional or other authorities designated by them. Multiannual plans cover five years for objectives 1 and 5(b) three years for objective 2.
2. Priorities are determined in the Community Support Frameworks (CSFs) by the Commission, working in close association with member states and with the competent national, regional, local or other authorities designated by them.
3. The operational stage is again based on partnership between the Commission and the member states concerned and/or by the competent authorities designated by the latter; it entails implementation of the CSFs through the use of the appropriate forms of assistance.
4. The CSFs and the assistance granted are monitored and assessed jointly by the Commission and the member states, and operations are then adjusted if necessary.

During 1989, the member states for the first time submitted multiannual plans under the five priority objectives. This approach was new for most of the member states and completely different from the submission of the regional development programmes under the old ERDF rules. There were two types of plan: regional plans concerning objectives 1, 2 and 5(b); and national plans covering objectives 3 and 4. As mentioned before, our attention here is to concentrate on the regional plans. Member states adopted different approaches to the preparation of the multiannual plans. Countries concerned with objective 1 decided to present a single plan with large regional sections. This is with the exception of France, which prepared five different plans per eligible region. All member states apart from Spain, opted for regional plans under objectives 2 and 5(b).

All the multiannual plans provided the Commission not only with an accurate, quantified and substantiated overview of the objectives and the financial needs of the member states, but also with an estimate of their financial commitments. This resulted in two striking considerations: first, the volume of funds requested was very large and exceeded the amount available; and second, the ERDF remained the Fund most in demand.

Based on the needs formulated in the multiannual plans, the Community drew up the Community Support Framework (CSFs), which represent the Community priorities for assistance and the funds to be assigned to each objective in each of the member states concerned. In accordance with the principles of the reform a CSF must include (CEC, 1991):

1. a statement of the priorities for action;
2. an outline of the forms of assistance and a regional breakdown at the appropriate geographical level;
3. an indicative costing plan specifying the financial allocations envisaged for the various forms of assistance and their duration;
4. information on the means available for any studies or technical assistance necessary for the preparation and implementation of the measures concerned; and
5. indication of the procedures for implementing the CSF.

The negotiations on the CSFs led to real exchanges between the Commission and the other partners at national and especially at regional level. Finally, each CSF was adopted by a formal decision of the Commission in agreement with each member state. The geographical level of the CSFs is normally the level proposed by the member states in the multiannual plans. Exception to this rule is possible if the Commission considers a more aggregated or a less aggregated geographical level to be more appropriate. The duration of the CSFs depends on the plans submitted and is between three and five years.

The third stage, the operational stage consists of the implementation of the CSFs with five different forms of assistance: operational programmes (OPs); global grants; individual applications for large-scale projects; part-financing of national aid schemes; and financing through direct loans. A brief commentary of the two most important forms of assistance is provided here.

The OPs are the predominant form of assistance. They are composed of multiannual measures covering two, three, four and five years. OPs may receive assistance from one or more Structural Funds. The global grants are to be managed by an intermediary designated by the member states in agreement with the Commission. Generally the intermediary is a specialized body or agency other than the national or regional authorities.

Finally, in the last stage the CSFs and the assistance are monitored and assessed, and the necessary adjustments are made. One of the aims of the reform of the Structural Funds was to ensure that financial control is as effective as possible. Efforts were made to improve monitoring methods especially in the light of the decentralization of the management of the Structural Funds to the member states or to intermediaries, which did necessitate an increase in financial control. The monitoring system is based on the gathering of three types of information: financial; physical, which is information on the material implementation of measures; and identification, linking each operation to a particular objective, form of assistance, type of action and CSF. Assessment includes the extent to which the objectives have been achieved. In fact, assessment makes an *ex-post* comparison with the corresponding forecasts in order to analyse any differences. The results of the assessment are used in the design of future Community policies.

Successive steps in promoting a regional development project

We conclude this section with an overview of the successive steps a project promoter has to take in order to receive assistance from the Structural Funds. Since the reform of the Structural Funds aimed at simplifying administrative procedures, a general scheme for project proposals is now applicable. In the first place a promoter of a project has to verify if the project meets a Community objective. Objective 1, economic development of regions lagging behind; objective 2, regions seriously affected by industrial decline, and objective 5(b), rural areas seriously depressed, cover all EC regions eligible for Structural Funds assistance. In the second place, the project promoter has to make sure that there exists a CSF to which his project may relate. If there exists no such CSF, the promoter has to notify the competent authorities of his project so that it can be taken into account in the next draft plan. If, on the other hand, the project fits into a CSF (if necessary the CSF can be modified), the promoter can move to the next question: How can the project progress to the application stage? Here five possibilities occur. The promoter can:

1. have his project included in an OP;
2. include his project in an application for a global grant;
3. submit an individual project if the total cost is greater than ECU 15 million for infrastructure projects or ECU 10 million for investment projects;
4. benefit from a national aid scheme part-financed by the Community; or
5. finance it with a direct loan.

At this point, the promoter has to contact the competent authorities designated by the member states concerned for further execution of the project.

Project appraisal

As stated earlier, ERDF monies are the main instrument of regional project support. Although there are many ways of presenting projects, tapping into ERDF grants requires that investment schemes are appraised from the standpoint of the regional economy as opposed to straightforward financial profitability. In this section we discuss the procedures used successfully by one of the authors for an urban tourism project in the industrial South Wales region. The project in question was the New

Theatre in Cardiff, which is the *home* of the Welsh National Opera (Cardiff City Council, 1988).

ERDF guidelines

It is clear that a project cannot stand alone: its wider relevance and impact within a CSF must be demonstrated, as well as ensuring that it meets one or more of the overall regional objectives laid down by the Community. As a rule, tourism projects in this category tend to be public sector-led and the principal aspects that should be addressed are:

1. The use of the project should be 50 per cent non-local.
2. The project should result in an increase in overnight stays.
3. The project should result in an increase in employment opportunities.
4. The economic position of the project within the local area should be examined.
5. The project should form part of a tourism strategy for the local area.
6. Tourist authority support will give weight to the application.

Project description

Cities offer important cultural venues for tourism purposes and are thus able to fit quite easily into the Community's tourism programmes, provided they are situated in a region designated for assistance. As the capital city of Wales, even if located in an area that had experienced industrial decline, Cardiff met all these conditions. The New Theatre was opened in 1906: it is listed for its architectural value and is one of a family of twelve theatres designed by Runtz and Ford, of which the best-known are the Adelphi and Garrick in London. The project was essentially one of refurbishing the theatre. Although the New Theatre is one of Cardiff's most significant venues for the performing arts, prior to ERDF and local authority support, it had suffered from cramped public areas and a steady deterioration in its structures both inside and out, to the point where standards of comfort and facilities were no longer acceptable in the market for a major theatre venue.

The business plan for the theatre was reviewed so as to position the project within the overall tourism strategy for Cardiff. The key to theatre planning is the box office, since this is the major revenue-earning activity. By appropriate pricing and setting a range of performances from amateur through to opera, pantomime and children's theatre, the modernized New Theatre expected to attract audiences not only from Cardiff City and South Wales, but also from beyond the region in a radius of one and a half hours' driving time. It would also draw tourists coming to the city, whether on holiday or on business.

Project impact

Given that the theatre was intended to be an ongoing project, its impact was evaluated at the target operating-capacity of 85 per cent. A breakdown of annual audience figures at this level of usage is shown in Table 20.6. The market analysis indicated that some 67 per cent of theatre attendances would come from outside the South Wales region, which would satisfy the ERDF guideline that at least 50 per cent should be non-local. The object of this rule is to ensure that tourist developments do not simply displace visitors from other parts of the region or other assisted areas. Table 20.7 indicates the revenues likely to be generated by the audience numbers shown in Table 20.6. For comparability the values are shown in ECUs at 1990 prices.

Table 20.6   *New Theatre visitor attendance at target capacity*

Market segment	Numbers
Staying Visitors	
Overseas	8,150
Domestic	65,700
Day Visitors	
Industrial South Wales region	91,250
Outside region	115,650
Total	280,750

Table 20.7   *New theatre revenue resources (1990 prices)*

	85% capacity	
Source	ECU (000s)	(%)
Activities		
Production		
Box Office	3,871	80.9
Sales	83	1.7
Theatre lettings	238	5.0
Fees and charges	87	1.8
Other[1]	33	0.7
Bars and Catering	359	7.5
Management and		2.4
Buildings[1]	112	
	4,783	100.0

Note: 1. Main item is grants and contributions.

Table 20.8   *Economic impact of trading operations*

Trading operating capacity	Direct, indirect and induced effects	
	Cardiff	Industrial South Wales
Household income (ECU thousands, 1990 prices)	1,729	1,976
Employment Full-time job equivalents	124	139
Employment headcount	168	188

The economic impact of the theatre in the local area falls into two parts: (1) the impact of the trading operations of the theatre; and (2) the impact of the additional off-site expenditure by audiences that may be reasonably attributed to the development.

The trading operations of the theatre affect local income and employment in three ways. First, there is the direct effect the theatre has in generating jobs and local income through its payroll; second, there is the indirect effect of purchases made by the theatre in the local area; and finally, there is the induced effect the respending of income (earned either directly or indirectly) by local people on goods and services in the local economy.

A summary of these effects is presented in Table 20.8: the values are calculated by applying appropriate tourism income multipliers to the expenditure components. This procedure gives household income (inclusive of employment benefits) which is then divided by average labour costs to give full-time job equivalents. The latter are then scaled up to allow for part-time work and thus give an employment headcount.

Clearly, the ripple effect of the multiplier is greater in the region than the local area. The values shown in Table 20.8 do include revenues generated from audiences coming from within the industrial South Wales region. Technically these revenues are displacement rather than additional and therefore outside the ERDF guidelines. However, the argument for including them rested on the view that without the modernization programme, there was little future for the theatre and in all probability the custom would go outside the region. Thus the continued operation of the theatre was safeguarding jobs and the project was creating further jobs.

At the operating capacity of 85 per cent, which was used to calculate the impact figures in Table 20.8, the theatre management indicated that they would be employing 86 persons (36 full-time and 50 part-time). Thus the additional employment created indirectly and through the induced effects of the theatre's trading operations is 82 jobs in the Cardiff area and a further 20 jobs in the South Wales area, to give a regional total of 102 jobs.

The expenditure, income and employment effects presented so far do not constitute the total economic impact of the theatre project. The refurbished theatre, as a prime cultural venue, contributes to raising tourism awareness and provides a reason for visiting Cardiff. Therefore, allowance must be made for how much of tourists' total expenditure (on accommodation, meals, shopping, transport, etc.) could be reasonably attributed to the New Theatre as one of Cardiff's important attractions.

This is not an easy calculation to make. A simple method would be to discover how many activities and attractions the tourists participate in during their stay and then allocate trip expenditure pro rata. An alternative approach, which was the one adopted in this instance, is to make use of survey information of visitors' intentions to see how individual attractions affect the decision to stay at a particular destination, a method also used by the UK Department of the Environment (1990).

From survey information, it was estimated that for staying visitors just over 10 per cent of their off-site expenditure could be allocated to the New Theatre, as can be seen in Table 20.9. Off-site expenditure generated by audiences from within South Wales are not included since they are likely to have incurred a similar level of expenditure elsewhere in the region, and so such expenditures are merely displacement within the regional economy. For theatre-goers coming from outside the region, the main purpose of their trip would be to visit the New Theatre, thus all of their additional expenditure was attributed to the project. The economic impact of the total allocated off-site expenditure shown in Table 20.9 can be found in Table 20.10.

Table 20.9   *Additional off-site expenditure by theatre-goers (ECU thousands, 1990 prices)*

Market segment	Total spend	Expenditure attributable to the New Theatre
Staying Visitors		
Overseas	2,170	260
Domestic	4,797	471
Day Visitors		
Industrial South Wales region	790	—[1]
Outside region	1,234	1,234
Total	8,991	1,965

Note: 1. Displacement expenditure within the region.

The summation of Tables 20.8 and 20.10 gives the overall impact of the theatre project on incomes and jobs, as shown in Table 20.11. Apart from the qualitative arguments for ensuring the future of an important cultural attraction within the city of Cardiff, the New Theatre project would generate annually ECU 2.6 million of household income in the region, of which ECU 2.2 million would be in Cardiff. Similarly a total of 241 jobs would be created in the region, with Cardiff taking 205 of them. Of the

Table 20.10   *Economic impact of additional expenditure*

	Direct, indirect and induced effects	
	Cardiff	Industrial South Wales
Household income (ECU thousands, 1990 prices)	451	641
Employment		
Full-time job equivalents	29	41
Employment headcount	37	53

Table 20.11   *Overall economic impact of the New Theatre*

Target operating capacity	Direct, indirect and induced effects	
	Cardiff	Industrial South Wales
Household income (ECU thousands, 1990 prices)	2,180	2,617
Employment		
Full-time job equivalents	153	180
Employment headcount	205	241

latter total, 86 would be direct jobs in the theatre. The overall cost of the theatre's refurbishment (including compensation payments) was estimated at ECU 8.3 million in 1990 prices. This gave a capital cost per regional full-time job equivalent of about ECU 46,000. The importance of this project to the city was acknowledged by the European Commission, and ERDF support was forthcoming for up to one-half of the assessed cost of restoring the theatre.

Conclusions

The European Community has not launched isolated initiatives favouring tourism. Tourism programmes have been included in different community actions. The most important interventions in the field of tourism in the Community are provided by the Structural Funds. The main financial instrument is the European Regional Development Fund. To be eligible for assistance, a tourism project must meet one or more of three Community objectives:

Objective 1:   Development of structurally backward regions;
Objective 2:   Restructuring regions in industrial decline;

Objective 5(b):   Development of rural areas.

In addition, a tourism project must be included within the strategic priorities of a Community Support Framework. The latter is jointly determined between the Commission and the member state. Finally, to be in receipt of grant aid, the evaluation of the project should be from the standpoint of the local and regional economies.

References

Annuaire Européen/European Year-Book, 1988, *Regional Policy*.
Main Developments, XXXVI, EC 40, Martinus Nijhof.
Cardiff City Council, 1988, *Cardiff Tourism Study*, City Hall, Cardiff.
Clout, H., 1987, *Regional Development in Western Europe*, David Fulton, London.
Commission of the European Communities, 1991, *Annual Report on the Implementation of the Reform of the Structural Funds*, Office for Official Publications of the European Communities, Luxembourg.
Commission of the European Communities, 1991, *The Regions in the 1990's: Fourth Periodic Report on the Social-Economic Situation and Development of the Regions in the Community*, Office for Official Publications of the European Communities, Luxembourg.
Commission of the European Communities, 1991, *Guide to the Reform of the Community's Structural Funds*, Office for Official Publications of the European Communities, Luxembourg.
Department of the Environment, 1990, *Tourism and the Inner City*, HMSO, London.
Pearce, D., 1988, 'Tourism and regional development in the European Community', *Tourism Management*, March: pp.13–22.
Yuill, D. and Allen, K., 1990, *European Regional Incentives*, Bowker-Saur, London.

21 The Atlantic-Caribbean cruise industry

C.W. Riley

Introduction

The Atlantic/Caribbean is by far the world's leading cruise destination. This archipelago of small nations, most of which are conveniently distanced, attract more than 6 out of every 10 sailings each year (Cruise Lines International Association, 1992). This definition of the region not only encompasses the islands within the Caribbean Sea, but also those further north such as the Bahamas and Bermuda as well as the Atlantic coast of Central and South America. In 1991 an estimated 3.5 million passengers descended upon its shores, up nearly 10 per cent from 1990. Based upon current orders for ships, that figure could increase by a similar amount each year until 1994 (Nissen-Lie Communications, 1991). This is a far cry from its early beginnings in the 1920s when there were just a few thousand cruise passengers visiting the region (Tassig, 1945). Such dramatic increases have raised new concerns about the economic value of such visitors, resulting in a tripartite debate between governments, cruise lines and hoteliers. The debate has increased in fervour with each new cruise berth, and it puts destinations, particularly the hotels, and cruise ships in opposing corners in an industry whose new buzz-word is *symbiosis*.

Foundations

Since the late 1930s, with the advent of commercial air travel, hotels have been a major part of the Atlantic/Caribbean landscape. In the 1960s and 1970s many of the islands obtained independence and placed greater emphasis on tourism since their agricultural base was declining. As a result, there was rapid hotel expansion. In 1980 hotel rooms totalled 76,200 but that figure had risen a dramatic 50 per cent to 116,600 by 1990 (Caribbean Tourism Organization, 1991a). Tourist arrivals for the same period were even more dramatic. They rose a hefty 72 per cent to 11.8 million. Several islands, such as the Dominican Republic, Jamaica and Aruba, considerably increased their capacity in obvious anticipation of continued growth. The tourists came, although they did not all stay in hotels.

About the same time as many Caribbean islands were gaining their independence, the transatlantic passenger trade was dying and more and more ships were being diverted to the Atlantic/Caribbean. The Mediterranean had, by this time, declined as a major cruise region as a result of World War II, (Lawton and Butler, 1987). Also, America grew quite prosperous after the war, was politically stable and was close to the region. All of these factors laid the foundation for the premier position in which the region's cruise industry finds itself today.

The economic impact on destinations

The 1980s were a period characterized by high spending and the acquiring of status symbols, including exotic vacations, and the Caribbean had established itself as one of the world's leading destinations, be it land or sea-based. That success was measured not just in the share numbers of arrivals, but also in expenditure. In 1990 the Caribbean Tourism Organization (CTO), the region's marketing and research arm, estimated that total expenditure was $8.9 billion, up 8.5 per cent compared with 1989. Nearly 94 per cent of that expenditure was made by the 11.84 million tourists (those persons staying longer than 24 hours) or approximately $700 each. Although CTO estimates that there were 7.45 million cruise passengers, this figure represents severe double counting, for ships often visit more than one destination. I was, however, able to establish that the actual number of cruise passengers is closer to 3.5 million (Nissen-Lie Communications, 1991). Cruise expenditure was $575 million, or about $165 per person. Unlike the land-based visitor, where the spending tends to remain with a single destination, cruise expenditure is divided among several islands, so its impact is further diminished.

The cost of a seven-day cruise, the standard in the Atlantic/Caribbean, was approximately $1,100 in 1990. Cruise lines serving the region, therefore, would have earned around $3.74 billion excluding on-board revenue. Thus the region benefited only fractionally, collecting about 15 per cent of the revenue earned by the cruise ships. While leakages in the hotel industry for some islands may leave as little as 35 per cent of revenues at the destination, this is more than double that for cruise ships (Archer, 1991). In fact, when leakages are taken into consideration for the cruise industry, the impact on destinations is minor. This is because the businesses at the destination also have to import goods to service cruise ship passengers, which have to be paid for in foreign currency.

Table 21.1   *Visitor expenditure by sector, 1990*

Sector	Number (m)	Expenditure ($m)	Expenditure per capita
Tourists	11.84	8,335	$703
Cruise passengers	3.5	575	$164

Source: Caribbean Tourism Organization, *Cruise Industry News*.

Table 21.2   *Cruise expenditure by selected island destinations, 1990*

Island	Passengers	Expenditure ($m)	Expenditure per capita
Bermuda	112,551	22.2	$197
U.S. Virgin Islands*	1,119,569	159.4	$142
Jamaica	385,205	27.3	$71
Cayman Island	361,712	22.2	$61
Bahamas	1,853,897	110.5	$60

Note: * Includes St Thomas, St Croix and St John
Source: National Tourism Organizations

Tables 21.1 and 21.2 show the spending of cruise passengers and tourists as well as cruise spending on selected island destinations. It can be seen that not only is expenditure by cruise passengers four times less than tourists, but there is also substantial variance among destinations. Bermuda comes out on top at $197 per passenger, although this is because the majority of its cruises visit no other island. The $142 recorded for the US Virgin Islands includes the three islands of St Thomas, St Croix and, to a lesser extent, St John. The per capita expenditure levels recorded for Jamaica, the Cayman Islands and the Bahamas reflect a truer picture of what each destination receives from a typical seven-day, multi-island, cruise passenger. Regional surveys have shown, however, that cruise passenger spending is similar to that of hotel visitors when accommodation costs are excluded, although this represents the major portion of spending by such visitors.

Differences between the cruise and the land vacation experience

Even though hotel visitors spend more per capita than cruise passengers, and therefore can be considered to be economically more important, one cannot escape the undeniable fact that cruise lines offer a highly desirable product. Standard cruises offer at least four meals per day, night club shows, health clubs, whirlpools, discos and 24-hour room service, all of which are included in the price of the cruise. Then there are casinos and shopping arcades. And for the children, games' rooms and organized programmes. Some offer golf ranges and tennis. While accommodations are basic, public areas tend to be luxurious. Staff are friendly and attentive. A recent study conducted by the Cruise Lines International Association (CLIA), the marketing and promotional body for the industry, found that out of fourteen attributes ranging from being pampered by staff to pleasurable dining experiences, cruises significantly outshone resorts in all areas except for comfortable accommodations (Cruise Lines International Association, 1992). In addition, because cruises often sail to several destinations, passengers can sample different cultures which enhances the overall cruise experience. That experience appears difficult for land resorts to duplicate. A study by one destination revealed that although a high 42 per cent of tourists had visited before, 66 per cent of all of its cruise passengers had been on a cruise before (Data Development Corporation, 1991).

Although the cruise experience may be different, is it so unique that it cannot be copied by land resorts? The answer may well be yes. Compared with land resorts, cruise ships operate with decided advantages. For starters, labour costs are much lower because cruise ships are normally registered under *flags of convenience* which allow them to recruit crew members from nations other than where the vessel is registered. Very often, therefore, crew members come from countries where wages are considerably lower than at the destination or the port of origin. Cruise lines are also able to, on most occasions, purchase their foodstuffs directly from the supplier, thereby avoiding high import duty costs. Indeed, all other costs associated with land resorts are all kept to a minimum. For instance, most destinations levy the absolute minimum, if any at all, passenger tax, for cruise lines would simply bypass a port if they felt that the tax was too high (Lee, 1991). Bermuda is the only exception where $60 is charged, by far the highest of any island. Hotel taxes throughout the region, on the other hand, are fairly standard, averaging about 7 per cent (Caribbean Tourism Organization, 1991b). Perhaps the most important advantage of all, however, is mobility. In the event of trouble at a cruise destination or region, cruise lines are able to pull out at short notice and divert their ships to other areas.

For their part, land resorts have attempted to duplicate the cruise experience. Club Med Inc. pioneered the all-inclusive resort concept back in the 1950s (Gibbons, 1980). Its members, who were young and independent-minded, were quickly attracted to a vacation that offered one price for all its activities and no supplements for single travellers. In recent years numerous such resorts have sprung up all over the Atlantic/ Caribbean, especially in Jamaica, and have been performing quite well compared with the traditional resorts, particularly in a depressed economy. However, they, too, are unable to relocate in times of social instability or other adversities.

A competitive market-place

With the popularity of cruises, hoteliers have become increasingly concerned about the prospect of lost business. In 1991 passenger capacity in the Caribbean was estimated to be 4.3 million. By 1994 that figure is expected to rise to 4.8 million, or by nearly 12 per cent. On the other hand, hotel rooms have remained at 116,000 since 1988 and new construction has so far only replaced lost beds. While cruise analysts expect actual passengers to keep pace with the new capacity, early results are that fulfilling this goal will come at a price. The cruise industry has always been associated with discounting, which was normally given for advanced bookings of six months or more. In 1990, when the effects of the recession were only beginning to be felt, discounts in the cruise industry were widespread and carried few restrictions. Offers of two people sailing for the price of one were common. In 1991, when the Gulf War broke out and the effects of the recession began to deepen, discounts became the norm. Although hotels and other sectors of the tourism industry likewise offered discounts, they were either of short duration or carried many restrictions. Even if economists may be uncertain when countries, particularly the key North American market, will recover from the recession, all agree that because of its cyclical nature, it will end. When that happens, however, the consumer is unlikely to be the same person encountered in the extravagant 1980s. The consumer in the 1990s will be cost-conscious and will have become used to the idea of not having to pay full price for anything. With the increased capacity of cruise ships, the likelihood is that heavy discounting will continue.

The concept that cruise lines are taking business away from land resorts implies that land resorts are owed a certain level of protection. The Bermuda government took steps in 1990 to limit cruise passengers during the peak season of May to October, although this was done more for the preservation of the quality of life of its residents and less for the protection of land resorts (Riley, 1991). Cruise lines argue that every visitor that is brought to a destination is a potential long-staying visitor. Although the CLIA are unable to offer any statistics to indicate to what extent this is true, a study by one destination found that just under 20 per cent of all cruise passengers who stated that they would return, would do so by plane (Data Development Corporation, 1992). The CLIA believes that both hotels and cruise lines operate in a competitive market and that destinations should put their best foot forward, as many are doing. Trinidad and Tobago, Dominica, Bahamas, and Guadeloupe have all recently renovated or built new cruise ports. In spite of the fact that cruise passengers spend considerably less than hotel visitors, the revenue obtained from cruise lines, when port charges are added, is still substantial for many islands. However, when cruise lines, such as Carnival, position themselves as the destination (Chicago Tribune, 1992), wounds which have not quite healed are reopened.

Conclusion

In the final analysis, while land resorts and cruise lines operate in a free and competitive market, governments are charged with the responsibility of managing the tourism industry for the benefit of its people. Discounting in the cruise industry has led to allegations by land merchants that a lower-grade visitor is being attracted who has little money to spend at the destination (CMP Publications, Inc., 1991). The question to be addressed then, is not whether cruise lines are taking business away from land resorts but whether destinations are extracting maximum benefit from the cruise industry. Resorts may have been derelict in their responsibility of taking advantage of a captive audience, 20 per cent or 700,000 of whom have indicated their intention to be a future land-based visitor. With cruise capacity expected to increase in the foreseeable future, this may be the appropriate time for a co-ordinated approach to deal with the challenges presented by the cruise industry.

The Caribbean Tourism Organization, and its 28 member states, have advocated such a coordinated approach for one main reason. Both the Atlantic/Caribbean and the cruise lines have considerable strengths—the former as a premier destination with luxurious resorts, the latter as a highly organized, influential sector (with a most desirable product) within the North American travel scene. Co-operation between the two bodies would likely yield mutual benefits. CTO's plan is as follows:

1. development of consistent and co-ordinated national cruise policies;
2. implementation of head taxes and port changes;
3. establishment and policing of environmental controls;
4. development of campaigns to promote 'sail and stay' vacations; and
5. encouragement of greater interaction between regional port directors and cruise officials. (Sobers, 1991)

For items 1 and 2, CTO used the example of a $3 minimum head tax throughout the region. With typical cruises going to a maximum of seven islands, only $21 will have to be added to the cost of a cruise ticket. Indeed, this is similar to a standard hotel tax. Steps to minimize the damage to the environment from tourism would benefit all concerned, as would the remaining points of the plan. The initial reaction to the plan by cruise lines was not positive although they are now collaborating with destinations to make it work. Even if the region itself may not have a history of internal co-operation, the collective importance of tourism may be the catalyst for bringing this about.

References

Archer, B., 1991, 'The Economic Impact of Tourism in Bermuda 1990', a report carried out annually on behalf of the Bermuda Department of Tourism, Hamilton, Bermuda (unpublished).
Caribbean Tourism Organization, 1991a, *Caribbean Tourism Statistical Report 1990*, Christ Church, Barbados.
Caribbean Tourism Organization, 1991b, *Statistical News*, October.
CMP Publications, Inc., 1991, *Tour and Travel News*, 18 March: p. 22.
Cruise Lines International Association, 1992, *The Cruise Industry—An Overview*, Marketing Edition, New York.
Data Development Corporation, 1991 and 1992, 'The Bermuda Cruise Study 1990 and 1991', carried out annually on behalf of the Bermuda Department of Tourism, New York (unpublished).
Data Development Corporation, 1991, 'The Bermuda Airport Study 1990', carried out annually on behalf of the Bermuda Department of Tourism, New York (unpublished).

Gibbons, R., 1980, 'Singles and Couples', speech to the Travel Research Association 11th Annual Conference.

Lawton, L.J. and Butler, R.W., 1987, 'Cruise ship industry—patterns in the Caribbean 1880–1986', *Tourism Management*, p. 329.

Lee, M., 1991, 'Tourism's triumph', *CanaBusiness*, August: p. 11.

Nissen-Lie Communications, Inc., 1991, *Cruise Industry News*.

Riley, C.W., 1991, 'Bermuda's cruise ship industry: headed for the rocks?', *Proceedings of the 1990 Congress on Coastal and Marine Tourism*, Volume 1, p. 159, National Coastal Resources Research and Development Institute, Newport, Oregon.

Sobers, A., 1991, 'Cruise Ship Issues', a presentation to the Council of Ministers, Caribbean Tourism Organizations, Barbados (unpublished).

Sofield, T.H.B., 1991, 'The Impact on Traditional, Socio-cultural Values in the South Pacific: Conflict, co-existence, and Symbiosis', *Proceedings of the 1990 Congress on Coastal and Marine Tourism*, Volume 1, p. 49, National Coastal Resources Research and Development Institute, Newport, Oregon.

Tassig, C., 1945, 'Caribbean Tourist Trade: A Regional Approach', paper prepared for the Anglo-American Caribbean Commission, Washington, DC, Guardian Printery, Port of Spain, Trinidad and Tobago.

22 The changing face of international tourism in Central and Eastern Europe

D.R. Hall

Introduction

The political and economic changes which have characterized Central and Eastern Europe since 1989 have exerted a number of influences on patterns of international tourism to, within and from the region. Just as the economic restructuring and social change have yet to establish a settled and coherent pattern, so too patterns of tourism development appear far from being stabilized. The picture is rendered further unclear by the fact that although some national tourism data for 1990 (and unconfirmed detail for 1991) are available, the most recent comparative international compilation (WTO, 1991) employs data up to only 1989. Familiar problems of data inconsistencies also hamper the study of the region's tourism patterns (Buckley and Witt, 1990; Hall, 1991b).

In summary (Table 22.1), Central and Eastern Europe experienced an increase in international tourist arrivals of 30–45 per cent overall during the second half of the 1980s, with particular growth over the 1988–9 watershed. Revealing a slight increase in its share of Europe arrivals during the period, 'Eastern Europe' returned the fastest average annual rate of increase in arrivals of the four WTO European regions, recording a figure of 9.7 per cent, compared with 5.5 per cent for Europe as a whole. However, when excluding Yugoslavia, the region's share of total world arrivals in the late 1980s was only half that for the regions of Western and Southern Europe within, an overall declining European share (from 65.07 per cent in 1985 to 62.88 per cent in 1989). Although large increases in receipts were recorded for the region for the second half of the 1980s, when excluding Yugoslavia the increase for 1988–9 appears relatively low. That increases in receipts had not kept pace with those elsewhere is reflected in the decreasing share of Europe receipts, which in themselves declined in importance from 50.12 in 1985 to 49.66 per cent of the world total in 1989. The average annual rate of increase for receipts within the region, at 7.5 per cent, was less than half that for Europe as a whole (15.6 per cent) (WTO *Yearbook*, 1991, 28, 30).

Tourism under state socialism

Although tourism was becoming increasingly popular in Central and Eastern Europe in the inter-war period, particularly in upland areas, the

Table 22.1 *Central and Eastern Europe: basic international tourism statistics for the region, 1985–9*

			1985	1988	1989	% increase 1988–9	% increase 1985–9
1.	International	} (a)	31.44	37.66	45.59	21.06	45.01
	tourist	} (b)	39.88	46.68	54.22	16.15	35.96
	arrivals	} (c)	35.54	40.67	46.47	14.26	30.75
	(millions)	}					
2.	% share of	} (a)	14.96	16.14	17.50	8.43	16.98
	Europe	} (b)	18.99	20.00	20.82	4.10	9.64
	arrivals	} (c)	16.92	17.43	17.84	2.35	5.44
3.	% share of	} (a)	9.74	9.86	11.01	11.66	13.04
	world	} (b)	12.36	12.22	13.09	7.12	5.91
	arrivals	} (c)	11.01	10.65	11.22	5.35	1.91
4.	International	} (a)	1,625	2,152	2,172	0.93	33.66
	tourist	} (b)	2,686	4,176	4,402	5.41	63.89
	receipts	} (c)	nd	3,960	4,152	4.85	–
	($US millions)						
5.	% share of	} (a)	2.79	2.10	2.08	–0.95	–25.45
	Europe	} (b)	4.61	4.08	4.22	3.43	–8.46
	receipts	} (c)	nd	3.86	3.98	3.11	–

Notes: (a) The region of 'Eastern Europe', as defined by the WTO, includes the former Soviet Union and excludes Yugoslavia, which is placed in 'Southern Europe'.
(b) This comprises the countries of (a) with the addition of Yugoslavia.
(c) This comprises the countries of (b) with the exclusion of the 'Soviet Union'.

Source: WTO *Yearbook*, 1991, Vol. 1, pp. 2, 24, 76, 137–8, 157–8.

post-war imposition of the Soviet model of political, economic and social development cut short previous development paths and introduced new roles and patterns for recreational activity.

Economic barriers, constraints on mobility, ideological hostility and the low priority given to service industries, coupled with general cold war perceptions rendered Europe behind the *Iron Curtain* a virtual *no-go* area for Western vacationers. Priority was given to domestic recreational activities, with organisation, transport and accommodation being subsidized by state enterprises and trades unions for the benefit of (usually urban/industrial) working families. Cross-border movement normally entailed exchanges of *friendship groups* between like-minded countries. Until the end of the 1980s, despite the human rights clauses of the 1975 Helsinki agreement, the region's nationals, other than Yugoslavs, were rarely permitted to travel westwards: currency inconvertibility, restricted access to hard currency, low living standards and stringent exit visa policies proscribed most forms of extra-bloc tourism.

Long-held fears of ideological contagion and social corruption delayed the harnessing of international tourism by the region's communist governments for diffusing employment opportunities and promoting positive national images abroad (Hall, 1984, 1990a, 1990b, 1990c, 1991b, 1992). Such structural characteristics of state socialism as centralized and inflexible bureaucracies and hostility towards 'capitalism' further inhibited international tourism development.

When, therefore, the West European package-holiday business was taking off in the 1960s, Central and Eastern Europe was ill-equipped to respond to expanding market demands, and was largely bypassed by Western tour operators. The one exception was Yugoslavia, which adopted a pragmatic attitude to labour and tourism mobility. As a consequence, a rapid growth in tourist arrivals from the West followed, unmatched elsewhere in the region. While absolute numbers of international tourists to Yugoslavia were not much greater than those to several other countries in the region (Table 22.2), the dominance of the Western market did secure a higher level of tourist income, which by the end of the 1980s was greater than the total for the rest of the region (and, moreover, was mostly in hard currency) (Table 22.3).

Table 22.2   *Central and Eastern Europe with selected Western destinations: international tourist arrivals 1970–89*

	International tourist arrivals (millions)				% change	
	1970	1980	1988	1989	1988–9	1980–9
Albania	nd	nd	nd	nd	nd	nd
Bulgaria[§]	1.3	2.1	2.6	2.8	6.0	30.6
Czechoslovakia	3.5	5.1	6.9	8.0	16.7	56.9
German Dem. Repub.[‡]	nd	1.5	2.2	3.1	39.0	106.7
Hungary*	4.0	9.4	10.6	14.2	34.8	51.1
Poland*	1.9	5.7	2.5	3.3	32.0	−42.1
Romania[†]	2.3	6.7	5.5	4.9	−11.9	−26.9
Yugoslavia[‡]	4.7	6.4	9.0	8.6	−4.1	34.4
Austria*	8.9	13.9	16.6	18.2	9.8	30.9
Fed. Repub. Germany*	8.5	11.1	13.1	14.7	11.7	32.4
Greece*	1.4	4.8	7.8	8.1	2.0	68.8
Spain[†]	24.1	23.4	35.1	35.4	1.0	51.3
Turkey*	0.4	0.9	3.7	3.9	5.5	333.3

Notes: nd, no data; * tourist arrivals at frontiers; † visitor arrivals at frontiers; ‡ notified arrivals at all registered accommodation; § 'visitor arrivals with tourist purpose'. Although the much higher 'visitor arrivals at frontiers' figures are presented in the WTO *Yearbook*, the more appropriate data used here are taken from *Tourism*, 1991, pp. 28–9 (see also Tables, 22.4 and 22.5).

Source: WTO *Yearbooks*; author's calculations.

Table 22.3 Central and Eastern Europe with selected Western destinations: international tourist receipts and average income per tourist, 1980–9

| | Receipts ($ US millions) | | | | | | % increase | | | |
| | 1980 | | 1988 | | 1989 | | 1988–9 | | 1980–9 | |
	(a)	(b)	(a)	(b)	(a)	(b)	(a)	(b)	(a)	(b)
Albania[†]	nd		nd		nd		nd		nd	
Bulgaria[†]	260	47.3	359	43.3	362	44.1	0.8	18.5	39.2	−6.6
Czechoslovakia*	338	66.3	436	31.1	450	56.0	3.2	80.1	33.1	−15.5
German Dem. Repub.[‡]	nd		nd		nd		nd		nd	
Hungary*	504	53.6	759	71.6	738	51.8	−2.8	−2.6	46.4	−3.4
Poland*	282	49.5	193	77.2	202	61.3	4.7	−20.6	−28.4	23.8
Romania[†]	324	57.9	176	32.0	170	35.0	−3.4	9.4	−47.5	−39.6
Yugoslavia[‡]	1,115	174.2	2,024	224.9	2,230	258.0	10.2	14.7	100.0	48.1
Austria*	6,442	464.1	8,520	513.3	9,317	511.9	9.4	−0.3	44.6	10.3
Fed. Repub. Germany*	6,566	590.5	8,449	645.0	8,658	590.9	2.5	−8.4	31.9	0.1
Greece*	1,734	361.3	2,396	307.2	1,976	244.5	−17.5	−20.4	14.0	−32.3
Spain[†]	6,968	297.8	16,686	475.4	16,174	457.5	−3.1	−3.8	132.1	53.6
Turkey*	327	375.9	2,355	636.5	2,557	655.6	8.6	3.0	682.0	69.3

Notes: nd, no data; * tourist arrivals at frontiers; [†] visitor arrivals at frontiers; [‡] notified arrivals at all registered accommodation; (a) receipts (US $ millions); (b) average income per tourist arrival (US dollars)

Source: WTO *Yearbooks*; author's calculations.

Yugoslavia aside, the economic impact of international tourism on Central and Eastern Europe remained small, certainly in comparison with Western Europe with average per capita tourist incomes notably lower (Table 22.3). In the 1980s, while Turkey experienced an almost 700 per cent growth in tourism receipts, for Poland and Romania they declined substantially during the decade, reflecting both countries' adverse image and domestic circumstances following martial law and Ceaușescu's austerity measures respectively. In Bulgaria, Hungary, Yugoslavia and Czechoslovakia, however, receipts increased at rates of between 33 and 100 per cent, comparable to some of the major Western tourist economies, although only in Yugoslavia did the average per capita income actually increase.

Patterns of the post-communist transition

While the countries of Central Europe—most notably Hungary and Czechoslovakia—are pursuing the difficult path from centralized to market economy through a peaceful and orderly period of transition, the picture for South-Eastern Europe is very different. For those countries which previously had *super-centralized economies*, such as Romania and Albania, upheaval has accompanied political change, prompting at least one observer (Popescu, 1992) to suggest that a four (rather than three) stage model of economic restructuring is appropriate in aiding an understanding of such countries' current dilemmas: *super-centralized economy—hiatus—transition—market economy*. The hiatus stage is characterized by a rejection of the past coupled with a residue of structures, institutions and resources seriously debilitated by past misuse. Already sensitive to change and upheaval, international tourism under such circumstances is likely to be greatly diminished in the short term, as in Romania (Tables 22.2 and 22.3). In Albania, international tourism activity came to a virtual halt during 1991.

For Yugoslavia, decentralization, reflecting the potentially fissiporous ethnic–historical framework of the country has been replaced, via a violent interim phase, with independent republics, with most notably a rump Serbia regressing into a centralized semi-state socialist anachronism. In the process, the Yugoslav tourism industry, previously unique in Eastern Europe with its predominance of Western tourists, has been all but dismantled. During the first seven months of 1991, tourism earnings dropped by 69 per cent with 62 per cent fewer foreign visitors and 68 per cent fewer overnight stays. Within domestic tourism, with a 40 per cent reduction in numbers on the Adriatic Riviera during the first six months of 1990, it was clear that Serbs were staying away from Croatian resorts. A $2-million tourism publicity campaign launched in Austria and Germany was soon overtaken by domestic events.

In Central Europe at least, there appears to have been a convergence of three major trends in post-war European tourism (Williams and Shaw, 1988):

1. an overall increase in long-term growth, reflecting absolute lower levels of tourism activity in Eastern Europe, and in part the response to a perceived *saturation* of tourism in Western Europe;
2. a shorter-term growth cycle related to creeping liberalization evident from the mid-1980s onwards; and
3. the major short-term *erratic* of the 1989 revolutions, generating substantial curiosity value and transforming the organizational, economic and social framework for tourism development through relaxing entry, exit and currency restrictions, modifying the *image* of the region and generating considerable Western media interest in it, and opening opportunities for more substantial Western participation in tourism development. (Hall, 1991b, 112)

Major regional changes to patterns of international tourism have so far come about largely without any commensurate improvement in transport facilities and with rather limited improvements in the region's accommodation stock. In transport, for example, heavy public subsidies are being removed from the public sector as a forerunner to privatization. Thus, in Poland, with the railways carrying only two-thirds of the 1.2 billion passengers transported in 1981, domestic fares were increased in September 1991 by 50 per cent, and, also reflecting a general downgrading of the role of the region's railway systems, 52 rakes of long-distance rolling stock were withdrawn. With the move to hard currency accounting in January 1991 for all international transactions, international rail, air and road transport fares within the region rose substantially. A deterioration of road conditions has resulted from both past under-investment and a current rapid increase in motor vehicle use, while additionally, conflict in Yugoslavia has necessitated avoiding routes both on land and in the air away from a major trunk corridor between Central Europe and the Balkans, placing a heavy burden on Hungary's underdeveloped road system. Despite some leasing of Western aircraft, long lead times for aircraft fleet replacement and airport rebuilding/expansion programmes are being experienced (Hall, 1993; Symons, 1993).

Central–East European contrasts: Hungary and Bulgaria

While Hungary and Bulgaria are comparable in area and population size, their cultural histories, geographical positions and orientations, and natural resources for tourism development are very different. Superficially, Bulgaria is far better placed than Hungary for tourism development (Carter, 1991; Compton, 1991). While the Balkan country has an extensive, sandy Black Sea coast, with several mountain ranges for both summer hiking and winter sports, land-locked Hungary has little notable relief. Yet, a more liberal image within the erstwhile Soviet bloc, a growing private accommodation sector during the 1980s, historical cultural ties with other Central European societies, ease of access from Austria and Germany, and the three major attractions of Budapest, Lake Balaton and the Danube Bend, have all contributed to draw large numbers of tourists to Hungary from both West and East. By contrast, the peripheral position of Bulgaria, its poor image for tourism services, inferior accessibility and eastward-looking traditions have tended to restrict penetration of Western tourist markets, a trend which has been perpetuated by the continuing political uncertainty within the country, while other East Europeans are now looking further afield. Thus, whereas Hungary recorded a 44 per cent increase in arrivals for 1990 and a 21 per cent growth in international tourist/nights, Bulgaria experienced decreases of 22 and 32 per cent respectively (Tables 22.4 and 22.5).

When comparing the major sources of tourist arrivals for 1990, and noting the almost tenfold difference in the scale of numbers between the two countries, Tables 22.4 and 22.5 highlight a number of interesting trends:

1. the decrease in German arrivals in both countries, reflecting the post-unification desire and ability of both eastern and western Germans to explore the other half of their own country;
2. the monumental increase in the number of Romanians crossing the border into Hungary, the result of both the freedom accorded to them after the execution of the Ceauşescus in December 1989 and the strong links which the ethnic Hungarians of Transylvania and Romanian Banat have with their *mother country*;
3. the general decline in both countries of arrivals from former Soviet bloc partners, as those countries' nationals used their newly found freedom to travel further afield;
4. the increase in numbers though actual reduction in tourist/nights of Soviet citizens in Bulgaria, reflecting the freedom of greater numbers of citizens from the now-dissolved USSR to undertake short visits abroad;
5. the large increase in the presence of Yugoslavs, most notably a more than fourfold increase in the number of tourist/nights in Bulgaria, indicating Serbs' forsaking Croatian resorts;
6. for Hungary, neighbouring Austria provides the most meaningful increases, after Romania, in both arrivals and tourist/nights, a sign of the ever-deepening ties between these two former imperial partners; and
7. somewhat perversely, the only major Western market to reveal growth in Bulgaria is the 11 per cent increase in tourist/nights from the United Kingdom, perhaps the result of marketing cheap Bulgarian winter sports holidays.

Future agendas

The requirement for systematic analysis and evaluation of tourism development, potential, constraints and future impacts within the region, presents a range of likely future agendas.

Table 22.4 *Bulgaria and Hungary: major sources of international tourist arrivals 1990*

Tourist arrivals, 1990 (millions)

		Bulgaria			Hungary		
Rank	Origin	Numbers	% share	% change 1989–90			
1.	Soviet Union	0.592	27.38	38.45			
2.	Poland	0.305	14.12	–44.45			
3.	Yugoslavia	0.278	12.86	26.36			
4.	Czechoslovakia	0.184	8.50	–43.49			
5.	Romania	0.162	7.51	4.57			
6.	Hungary	0.155	7.18	–47.61			
7.	Greece	0.137	6.33	–3.12			
8.	Germany	0.097	4.49	–69.89			
Total		2.161	100.00	–22.14			

Rank	Origin	Numbers	% share	% change 1989–90
1.	Romania	6.352	30.97	5,106.56
2.	Poland	2.742	13.37	–17.78
3.	Czechoslovakia	2.295	11.19	–3.12
4.	Germany	1.995	9.73	–27.00
5.	Yugoslavia	1.786	8.71	29.89
6.	Austria	1.661	8.10	56.99
7.	Soviet Union	1.464	7.14	–9.46
Total		20,510	100.00	44.07

Source: Tourism, 1991, 29; Próbáld & Hosszú, 1991, p. 2.

Table 22.5 *Bulgaria and Hungary: major sources of international tourist nights, 1990*

International tourist/nights, 1990 (millions)

	Bulgaria					Hungary		
Rank	Origin	Numbers	% share	% change 1989–90	Rank	Origin	Numbers	% share	% change 1989–90
1.	Soviet Union	3.739	29.30	−1.50	1.	Romania	32.087	31.83	4,457.81
2.	Czechoslovakia	1.856	14.55	−37.88	2.	Germany	13.597	13.49	−42.83
3.	Germany	1.459	11.44	−62.88	3.	Poland	11.977	11.88	−33.22
4.	United Kingdom	1.178	9.23	10.92	4.	Czechoslovakia	8.370	8.30	−30.75
5.	Poland	0.877	6.87	−74.24	5.	Austria	7.933	7.87	99.97
6.	Yugoslavia	0.764	5.99	409.33	6.	Yugoslavia	7.298	7.24	65.04
7.	Hungary	0.398	3.12	−28.03	7.	Soviet Union	5.737	5.69	−36.34
8.	Greece	0.311	2.44	−14.56					
9.	Sweden	0.281	2.20	−10.79					
10.	Romania	0.193	1.51	216.39					
Total		12.759	100.00	−31.87	Total		100.793	100.00	44.07

Source: Tourism, 1991, 36; Próbáld & Hosszú, 1991, 2.

Tourism as a vehicle for economic restructuring

The quality of the region's tourist services has often been low and very variable by accepted Western standards: accommodation, catering, utilities, transport and telecommunications have suffered from decades of neglect in which the economic and ideological cost of upgrading infrastructure to meet the needs of foreigners was considered too high. In accommodation, for example, the newly developing private sector will need to generate much more modest to medium-grade accommodation, and joint ventures for further investment in top quality accommodation will be necessary to develop and consolidate high-spending conference and business tourism.

There is clearly a considerable requirement for staff training at all levels of the tourism industry, not least in hotel management, catering, travel agenting, and in such areas as computing, telecommunications and foreign languages to cater for new growth markets such as Japan. This was recognized in late 1991 when American Express launched a $500,000 fund to develop tourism personnel skills in Czechoslovakia, Hungary and Poland (Hamilton, 1991).

For some time, however, there will continue to exist much uncertainty over the future organization of the tourism industry, as decentralization of state-controlled systems gives way to privatization. Legislative and regulatory frameworks appropriate for a restructured industry may be slow in coming about, particularly for potential foreign investors. How tourism administration will survive or re-emerge from the Balkan centres of conflict will be a matter of some speculation. Yugotours, Yugoslavia's largest tour operator, having abandoned its 1991 programme in the face of mounting conflict in the tourist republic of Croatia, forsook its home *country* to promote Mediterranean sailing holidays and packages to Malta, Greece and Turkey for 1992.

Overcoming mobility constraints

Since the events of 1989, exit visa requirements for Central and East Europeans have been abolished. Yet, fearing mass immigration, several Western governments have retained impediments. For example, although the United Kingdom has visa-free agreements with Czechoslovakia and Hungary, as well as with the erstwhile Yugoslavia, Poles and Romanians wishing to visit the United Kingdom still require visas costing one and two weeks' average income respectively, and are required to furnish letters of invitation from their host and confirmation from their employer that they are actually on leave during their visit.

Many of the region's border-crossing facilities need to be modernized to be able to cope with impacts of the EC Single Market and future accession, and to aid integration of local border economies. The task of reorganizing Hungary's border guard service, for example, was initiated in 1990. Twenty-two thousand soldiers are being replaced over five years with 5,000 professional border guards. A computerization of border checks at all 723 crossing-points is being completed in readiness for handling the coded EC passport.

Sustainable tourism

The extent to which the poor environmental image of the region has acted as a force of repulsion against tourism development remains to be assessed (see Carter and Turnock, 1992), sufficient reason for the careful monitoring of the environmental impact of tourism activities themselves. While official recognition is now being given to the need for *sustainable*, *green* and *eco* tourism, as, for example, in the Romanian national tourism programme (Romania Ministry of Trade and Tourism, 1990, p. 3), there is often little conceptual discussion and analysis of the appropriateness or otherwise of the adoption of what are often little more than fashionable buzz-words. This results in often contradictory and conflicting statements of policy. Further, a newly unleashed entrepreneurial sector may have neither the resources nor the inclination to take a longer view of tourism's environmental impacts.

Attempts to include local communities in tourism development are inhibited by the lack of experience of bottom-up development upon which citizens can draw. In Romania's Danube Delta, where a biosphere reserve has been established, researchers from the Danube Delta Institute have been surveying the local population on their attitudes towards accommodating tourists and on developing appropriate forms of transport and accommodation (DDTIRG, 1991). Yet crucial questions for such vulnerable natural and social environments as defining and recognizing *carrying-capacities* and *saturation levels* have barely begun to be addressed (Hall, 1991a).

Segmentation and niche marketing

The region's diversity of physical and cultural environments and attractions provides the potential for substantial market segmentatlon. Targeting niche markets—ideally high—spending groups with minimal adverse impacts and season-extending activities—highlights the future importance of conference/business tourism and exploitation of both West European and North American incentive travel. The region's substantial heritage potential and varied health resorts can be employed to supplement such activities. With a heightened awareness of nationality, ethnic tourism will also increase in importance (Ostrowski, 1991).

Conclusions

Out of the euphoria of the immediate post-communist freedom has come the realization that there are no easy or quick means of transforming the political, economic and social structures of Central and Eastern Europe after nearly half a century of communist *diktat*. Although tourism development may be viewed by impoverished governments as a likely short cut to employment and income generation, regional instability is likely to inhibit longer-term development. The apparently widening gulf between Central Europe and the Balkans is likely to be exacerbated in the short to medium term, with considerable implications for future patterns of European tourism.

Acknowledgements

The author wishes to extend his grateful thanks to David Harrison, Liz Hopkins, Claudia Popescu and Joanne Sizeland for their assistance.

References

Buckley, P.J. and Witt, S.F., 1990, 'Tourism In the centrally-planned economies of Europe', *Annals of Tourism Research*, 17(1): pp. 7–18.

Carter, F.W., 1991, 'Bulgaria', in D.R. Hall (ed.), *Tourism and Economic Development in Eastern Europe and the Soviet Union*, Belhaven, London, 220–35.

Carter, F.W. and Turnock, D. (eds), 1992, *Environmental Problems in Eastern Europe*, Routledge, London.

Compton, P.A., 1991, 'Hungary', in D.R Hall (ed.), *Tourism and Economic Development in Eastern Europe and the Soviet Union*, Belhaven, London, 173–89.

Danube Delta Institute Tourism Research Group (DDITRG), 1991, *Researches to Achieve a Tourism Based on the Support Capacity of Deltaic Ecosystems*, Danube Delta Institute, Tulcea.

Hall, D.R., 1984, 'Foreign tourism under socialism: the Albanian "Stalinist" model', *Annals of Tourism Research*, 11(4): pp. 539–55.

Hall, D.R., 1990a, 'Eastern Europe opens its doors', *Geographical Magazine*, 62(4): pp. 10–15.

Hall, D.R., 1990b, 'Stalinism and tourism: a study of Albania and North Korea', *Annals of Tourism Research*, 17(1): pp. 36–54.

Hall, D.R., 1990c, 'The changing face of tourism in Eastern Europe', *Town & Country Planning*, 59(12): pp. 348–51.

Hall, D.R., 1991a, 'New hope for the Danube Delta', *Town & Country Planning*, 60(9): pp. 251–2.

Hall, D.R. (ed.), 1991b, *Tourism and Economic Development in Eastern Europe and the Soviet Union*, Belhaven, London.

Hall, D.R., 1992, 'The challenges of international tourism in Eastern Europe', *Tourism Management*, 13(1): pp. 41–4.

Hall, D.R., 1993, 'The symbiotic relationship between transport and tourism', in D.R. Hall (ed.), *Transport and Economic Development in the new Central and Eastern Europe*, Belhaven, London.

Hamilton, G., 1991, 'Amex sets initiative for EE tourism development', *Business Eastern Europe*, 20(46): p. 412.

Kateraas, E., 1991, 'Boeing: keeping pace with competition in Eastern Europe', *Business Eastern Europe*, 20(41): pp. 352–3.

Kinnaird, V.H. and Hall, D.R. (eds), 1993, *Tourism Development: The gender Dimension*, Belhaven, London.

Ostrowski, S., 1991, 'Ethnic tourism—focus on Poland', *Tourism Management*, 12(2): pp. 125–31.

Popescu, G., 1992, 'Competition, labour and industrial change in transitory economy', paper presented at the Institute of British Geographers Annual Conference, University College Swansea.

Próbáld, A and Hosszú, K.P., 1991, *Tourism in Hungary 1990*, Hungarian Tourist Board/Paletta Publishing, Budapest.

Romania Ministry of Trade and Tourism, 1990, *The Programme of Modernization and Development of the Romanian Tourism in 1990–1992*, Ministry of Trade and Tourism, Bucharest.

Symons, L.J., 1993, 'Restructuring the region's air industry', in D.R. Hall (ed.), *Transport and Economic Development in the new Central and Eastern Europe*, Belhaven, London.

Tourism, annual, Central Statistical Office, Sofia.

Williams, A.M. and Shaw, G. (eds), 1988, *Tourism and economic development: Western European Experiences*, Belhaven, London.

World Tourism Organization (WTO), annual, *Yearbook of Tourism Statistics*, WTO, Madrid.

Tourism Statistics

Introduction

This section of **Progress** is primarily aimed at providing statistical information of international tourism world-wide. It covers key indicators such as arrivals and receipts, the split of international tourism by region, and the relative performance of the major generators and receivers. Information is presented in tabular form and is accompanied by a commentary.

Since this is the first edition of **Progress** with separate statistical section, in addition to providing up-to-date information (as far as deadlines allow), consideration has been given to historical trends over the past few decades and through the 1980s in particular. This not only enables current values to be seen in context, but also provides insight into the magnitude of likely changes over the next decade.

The two main sources used to construct the tables were publications of the World Tourism Organization (WTO) and the Organization of Economic Co-operation and Development (OECD). A full list of source material appears at the end of the section.

23 International tourism and statistics

J. Latham

Commentary

International tourism—trends since 1950

International tourism has, since World War II, grown at a remarkable rate and the period up to 1990 has seen its development on a massive scale (see Tables 23.1 and 23.2). Overall, the four decades 1950 to 1990 have produced an average annual growth rate of international tourist arrivals of just over 7 per cent. By 1990, every day well over one million people were taking an international trip. However, the average annual growth rate has slowed over the years as the market has matured.

Growth has not been evenly spread across countries or across regions. Table 23.3 shows the changing regional share of international tourist arrivals. Of particular note is the rapid gain in share of countries in the East Asia and Pacific region. This has been at the expense of the share of the Americas and, to a lesser extent, Europe.

The 1980s—a decade of continued but reduced growth

The 1980s saw a slowing of growth rates of international tourism to an average of just over 4 per cent per annum. The decade opened with economic recession, which had several negative impacts on travel (Goeldner and Frechtling, 1991). Falling disposable incomes and increased costs of travel depressed the markets. Length of stay fell, cheaper forms of accommodation were sought, and the consumer switched to cheaper or neighbouring destinations—or travelled domestically. Volumes did not recover until 1983.

The mid-1980s showed evidence of complete recovery, and 1984 and 1985 were record years with European destinations performing particularly well. However, international tourism movement in 1986 was considerably disrupted by the combined effects of the disaster at Chernobyl, the fall in the value of the US dollar, the Libyan bombing incident and an increase in terrorist activity. The result was a shift in world tourism flows away from Europe and North America. Tourists from North America in particular shunned European destinations, perceiving them as unsafe. The latter half of the decade saw a return to *normality* with substantial year-on-year

Table 23.1 *International tourism trends
—arrivals and receipts
world-wide 1950–90*

	Arrivals (thousands)	Receipts 1 ($US million)
1950	25,282	2,100
1960	69,296	6,867
1970	159,690	17,900
1980	284,841	102,372
1981	288,848	104,309
1982	286,780	98,634
1983	284,173	98,395
1984	312,434	109,832
1985	321,240	116,158
1986	330,746	140,019
1987	356,640	171,319
1988	381,824	197,692
1989	415,376	211,366
1990	443,477	254,767
1991	450,000 (E)	278,000 (E)

Notes: 1.   Excludes international fare receipts.
(E) Estimate.

Source: World Tourism Organization.

Table 23.2 *Rates of growth of international tourism*

	Average annual percentage increase	
	Arrivals	Receipts
1950 to 1960	10.6	12.6
1960 to 1970	8.7	10.0
1970 to 1980	6.0	19.1
1980 to 1990	4.5	9.5
1980 to 1985	2.5	2.6
1985 to 1990	6.7	17.0

Note: The average percentage increase is calculated as the
constant annual percentage increase which would result
in the overall change over the specified period.

growth in international arrivals and spending. The average annual growth in international tourist arrivals between 1985 and 1990 was 6.7 per cent, compared with 2.5 per cent for the first half of the decade, and more in line with the annual changes of the 1970s. Further disruption to tourism flows was soon to come in the form of the Gulf War and further recession.

The 1980s confirmed the continuing though slowing growth of international travel. They also highlighted its resolute nature against economic, political and other factors which act against it, and which can stabilize or even reduce demand for a time.

Current trends and analysis

According to estimates prepared by WTO, international tourist arrivals in 1990 numbered 443 million (Table 23.1), an increase of 6.8 per cent over the previous year. Receipts from international tourism world-wide (excluding expenditure on international transport) rose in 1990 to $US 255 billion, an increase of 20.5 per cent.

Since 1990 saw the build-up towards the Gulf War, these volume and value statistics for international tourism world-wide should not be seen as discouraging. Nevertheless, in the short term, the war in early 1991, its protracted build-up and the continuing situation have depressed international tourism. The war led initially to the virtual cessation of travel to the Gulf, Eastern Mediterranean and North Africa. In the medium term the impact upon many companies, particularly airlines, in the international tourism industry will be severe. Others may in fact benefit, particularly those destinations regarded as safe.

In April 1991, WTO brought together representatives of governments and the operational sector for a discussion and analysis of the immediate effects of the Gulf War. The WTO report (May 1991) describes regional market trends from August 1990 to the period following the formal cessation of hostilities. It also provides an initial analysis by the sectors airlines, accommodation and tour operators/travel agents.

The recession of 1990/1 experienced by the majority of industrialised countries has been made worse by the Gulf War. Many commentators believe that the recession will have a greater impact on tourism than the war (for example, see Goeldner and Frechtling, 1991). The provisional estimate for international tourist arrivals in 1991 is 450 million, an increase of about 1.5 per cent over 1990. However, the overall percentage change does conceal extreme variation in provisional estimates for the regions. Compared with 1990, international tourist arrivals to countries of East Asia and the Pacific, Americas and Europe were up by 6.4, 3.1 and 2.0 per cent respectively. On the other hand, arrivals to countries of South Asia, Africa and the Middle East decreased by 5.4, 14.7 and 26.3 per cent respectively.

Regional comment

The regional share of international tourist arrivals for 1990 is shown in Table 23.3. Tables 23.4 to 23.9 provide for each of the regions key statistics of international tourism. As appropriate, average annual growth rates for the decade 1980 to 1990 are given.

Africa (Table 23.4).   International tourist arrivals to African countries in 1990 numbered 15.2 million. This represented an annual increase of 9 per cent over the previous year, and was more than double the figure for 1980.

Inbound arrivals to African countries are predominantly from other African states, from Europe and from the United States. The major destinations in Africa continue to be those in the north of the continent. These are the ones which stand to lose most from the events in the Middle East and from depressed business conditions in the traditional tourism-generating countries.

The Americas (Table 23.5).   International tourist arrivals to the Americas in 1990 numbered 83.4 million. This represented an annual increase of 6 per cent over the previous year. Over the ten-year period 1980 to 1990, the average growth rate was just under 5 per cent.

The main generating markets for inbound tourism to the Americas are other countries in North America, Europe and Japan. However, over recent years there has been a marked growth in the numbers of arrivals from non-traditional markets. The main destinations remain the United States and Canada, with substantial movement between the two. Growth in arrivals over the past decade has, though, been greatest to Central and South America and the Caribbean.

East Asia and the Pacific (Table 23.6).   International tourist arrivals in East Asia and the Pacific (EAP) in 1990 numbered just over 50 million. This represented an annual increase of more than 15 per cent over the previous year. Over the ten-year period 1980 to 1990, the average growth rate was 9.8 per cent.

The EAP share of international tourism arrivals world-wide now stands at 11 per cent. This represents remarkable growth from a share of 1 per cent in 1960, 3 per cent in 1970 and 7 per cent 1980. EAP tourism destinations as a whole therefore attract an increasing share of an expanding market. There are a number of countries which have developed inbound tourism and have contributed to this growth, notably Hong Kong, Singapore, Japan, Korea, Indonesia and Australia. In spite of the rapid growth, international tourism of EAP countries represents only 5 per cent of exports, a low value in comparison with other regions.

The main generating markets of international tourism to EAP countries are Japan and the United States, followed by other countries of EAP and the major tourism generators of Western Europe.

Europe (Table 23.7).   International tourist arrivals to Europe in 1990 numbered 281.4 million. This represented an annual increase of 5.7 per cent over the previous year. Over the ten-year period 1980 to 1990, the average growth rate was a modest 3.7 per cent.

European countries as destinations now account for just under two-thirds of all international arrivals, a share which has decreased over the past thirty years. However, Europe's share of international tourism receipts has been remarkably stable over the same period. The European Economic Community alone hosts 40 per cent of arrivals, and accounts for 44 per cent of receipts world-wide.

Many West European countries are also major generators of international tourism. With the sole exception of the United States, the top ten generating countries for international tourism to European countries in 1990 are all to be found within Western Europe. West Europeans, particularly from Germany, the United Kingdom and France, also engage in long-haul travel and are regarded as important markets to attract all over the world.

The continued dominance of Europe can be explained in terms of the high disposable income of large segments of the population, the wealth of attractions, the large tourist industry and the necessary infrastructure (Shackleford, 1987). High priority is given to travel for pleasure purposes, and business travel has increased in recent years. Further, Europe consists of many small countries, and so international travel need not entail great distances. This contrasts with the size of the United States and Canada, which results in most of their populations taking holiday trips in their own country. The easing of border controls in Europe and the opening of the Channel Tunnel in the early 1990s may well consolidate its dominance in statistical terms.

The Middle East (Table 23.8).   International tourist arrivals to the Middle East in 1990 numbered 9.5 million, an annual increase of 2.3 per cent over the previous year. Over the ten-year period 1980 to 1990, the average growth rate was 3.2 per cent.

Given the ongoing unrest and tension in the region, the Middle Eastern countries find great difficulty in attracting the high-spending markets of North America and Western Europe. The performance of individual countries as destinations is wide-ranging. For example, international tourism to Egypt and Jordan increased by over 50 per cent in the last decade. On the other hand, international tourism to Syria and Iraq declined substantially over the same period. Following the Gulf War, business travel is expected to increase in connection with reconstruction work in Iraq and Kuwait. Barring further fighting and social unrest, tourism to countries not directly involved in the conflict may gradually return to normality (WTO, May 1991).

Southern Asia (Table 23.9).   International tourist arrivals to Southern Asia in 1990 numbered just over 3 million. This represented an annual increase of 3.8 per cent over the previous year. Over the period 1980 to 1990, the average growth rate was 3.4 per cent. This average is the result of much variation, with three of the ten years showing a decrease on the previous year's figure.

The performance of the region is linked closely to that of India, which receives well over half of its international tourist arrivals. The main generating markets for tourism to countries in Southern Asia are Western Europe (particularly the United Kingdom), United States, Japan and India itself. Absolute numbers though are relatively small, in no case reaching half a million. The WTO (May, 1991) reported that according to recent surveys, operators do not envisage the immediate future with excessive optimism.

Tourism destination countries (Table 23.10).

Table 23.10 lists the top twenty destinations for international tourism in 1990. For reasons described above, it is dominated by West European and North American countries. A fuller list, say the top forty, would demonstrate clearly the dramatic emergence of the East Asia and Pacific region. For example, the average annual growth rates of international arrivals over the past ten years to Japan was 14 per cent; Indonesia, 15 per cent; Korea, 12 per cent; Thailand, 11 per cent; Singapore, 9 per cent.

Given the different spending patterns at different destinations, a list based on international tourism receipts would provide different rankings. The world's top tourism earners in 1990 were, in order, the United States, France, Italy, Spain and the United Kingdom—an identical ordering to 1980. Interestingly, although Singapore, Thailand, Australia, Belgium, Korea and Denmark are all amongst the top twenty earners, they do not appear in the list of the top twenty based on arrivals.

Generators of international tourism (Table 23.11)

Table 23.11 lists the top twenty generating countries of international tourism, based on expenditure. With the exception of Japan, the only countries to be found in the top twelve generators are in Western Europe and North America. There is therefore much commonality in lists of major international generators and receivers, with only Japan providing strong competition. According to the OECD, Japan has pursued a policy of vigorous encouragement of foreign travel, partly as a means of reducing a positive balance of payments. As a result, Japan has moved into third position, behind only the United States and Germany, of top generators.

It is interesting to note that the top four generators—the United States, Germany, Japan and the United Kingdom—account for almost half of international tourism spending in the world. These countries, and others listed in Table 23.10, are regarded world-wide as important markets to attract.

Tourism in the 1990s

The long-term trend in international tourism is one of continued although slowing growth. Early predictions for the number of international tourist arrivals to reach the half-billion mark by the end of the century still seem reasonable. Economic performance within the main generating countries will continue to exert considerable influence on movements.

No doubt Europe will continue to be pre-eminent in the total volume of international arrivals. However, the trend of new destinations taking market share from the traditional destinations is clear and will continue in the 1990s. The major holiday and business travel-generating countries are those with developed economies. Countries with rapidly developing economies, such as those in Latin America and the Iberian peninsula, may well become important generating markets in the next decade.

The rapid and major changes of recent years as seen in Eastern Europe, the Middle East and the African continent will have considerable effects on tourism world-wide. Since international tourism is dependent on world events, the forecasting of movement is at best hazardous; the future may indeed bring further major upheavals.

References

Goeldner, C.R. and Fechtling, D., 1991, '1990: a year of transition', *Journal of Travel Research*, 29(4): pp. 47–50.

Latham, J., 1990, 'Statistical trends in tourism and hotel accommodation', in C.P. Cooper (ed.), *Progress in Tourism, Recreation and Hospitality Management*, Volume 2, Belhaven, London, pp. 117–28.

Latham, J., 1991, 'Statistical trends in tourism up to 1989', in C.P. Cooper (ed), *Progress in Tourism and Recreation and Hospitality Management*, Volume 3, Belhaven, London, pp. 130–9.

Organization for Economic Co-operation and Development, annual, *Tourism Policy and International Tourism in OECD Member Countries* OECD, Paris.

Shackleford, P., 1987, 'Global tourism trends', *Tourism Management*, 18(2): pp. 98–101.

World Tourism Organization, quarterly, *Travel and Tourism Barometer*, WTO Madrid.

World Tourism Organization, May 1991, *Impact of the Gulf Crisis on International Tourism (Special Report)*, WTO, Madrid.

World Tourism Organization, 1991, *Tourism Trends*, WTO, Madrid.

Table 23.3   *Regional share of international tourist arrivals, 1950–90*

	1950 %	1960 %	1970 %	1980 %	1990 %
Europe	66.6	72.7	70.8	68.8	63.4
Americas	29.6	24.1	23.0	18.9	18.8
East Asia/Pacific	0.8	1.0	3.0	7.0	11.4
Africa	2.1	1.1	1.5	2.5	3.4
Middle East	0.8	0.9	1.2	2.0	2.1
South Asia	0.2	0.3	0.6	0.8	0.7

Note: Columns do not necessarily add to 100 per cent, owing to rounding error.

Table 23.4   *International tourism in Africa, 1990*

International tourist arrivals 1990	—	15.2 million
International tourism receipts 1990	—	$US 4.8 billion
Receipts as a percentage of exports (1989)	—	8.9 %

Inbound tourism			Outbound tourism		
Origin	Arrivals to Africa (million)	Average growth rate 1980–90	Destination	Arrivals from Africa (million)	Average growth rate 1980–90
Africa	5.9	14.1	M. East	1.3	6.9
Europe	5.6	4.2	Europe	0.8	−9.3
M. East	0.6	9.9	Americas	0.2	21.1
Americas	0.6	3.0	S. Asia	*	14.0
EAP	0.2	6.1	EAP	*	5.7
S. Asia	*	8.0			

Major destinations in Africa			Major generating markets for Africa		
Country	Arrivals (thousands)	Average growth rate 1980–90	Country	Arrivals (thousands)	Average growth rate 1980–90
Tunisia	3,204	7.2	France	1,762	3.5
Morocco	2,978	7.6	Germany	1,151	4.7
Algeria	1,137	1.9	UK	855	3.7
S. Africa	1,029	3.9	Italy	496	5.9
Botswana	800	14.5	USA	473	3.0
Kenya	695	6.4	Spain	364	8.8

Notes: EAP, East Asia and Pacific; * less than 0.1 million.
Although the total tourist arrivals and tourism receipts at the top of the table are revised figures, the rest of the table is based on provisional estimates for 1990.

Source: World Tourism Organization.

Table 23.5 *International tourism in the Americas, 1990*

International tourist arrivals 1990	—	83.4 million
International tourism receipts 1990	—	$US 66.4 billion
Receipts as a percentage of exports (1989)	—	9.2%

Inbound tourism			Outbound tourism		
Origin	Arrivals to Americas (million)	Average growth rate 1980–90	Destination	Arrivals from Americas (million)	Average growth rate 1980–90
Americas	58.9	3.3	Europe	18.8	3.6
Europe	10.8	6.5	EAP	4.6	7.5
EAP	5.9	9.4	M. East	0.7	2.1
M. East	0.4	27.5	Africa	0.6	3.0
S. Asia	0.2	22.6	S. Asia	0.3	5.9
Africa	0.2	21.1			

Major destinations in the Americas			Major generating markets for the Americas		
Country	Arrivals (million)	Average growth rate 1980–90	Country	Arrivals (million)	Average growth rate 1980–90
USA	39.8	5.9	USA	29.4	2.2
Canada	15.3	1.7	Canada	18.1	4.1
Mexico	6.4	4.4	Mexico	6.9	7.4
Argentina	2.7	9.3	Japan	4.3	12.4
Puerto Rico	2.6	4.6	UK	3.8	7.2
Dom'n Rep	1.6	10.6	Germany	1.6	3.2

Notes: EAP, East Asia and Pacific.
Although the total tourist arrivals and tourism receipts at the top of the table are revised figures, the rest of the table is based on provisional estimates for 1990.

Source: World Tourism Organization.

Table 23.6 *International tourism in East Asia and the Pacific (EAP), 1990*

International tourist arrivals 1990   —   50.8 million
International tourism receipts 1990   — $US 36.7 billion
Receipts as a percentage of exports (1989)   —   4.8%

Inbound tourism			Outbound tourism		
Origin	Arrivals to EAP (million)	Average growth rate 1980–90	Destination	Arrivals from EAP (million)	Average growth rate 1980–90
EAP	22.3	8.3	Americas	5.8	9.4
Europe	6.3	9.5	Europe	5.7	6.9
Americas	4.6	7.5	S. Asia	0.4	5.9
S. Asia	1.0	7.4	M. East	0.2	9.5
M. East	0.1	–3.6	Africa	0.2	6.1
Africa	0.1	5.7			

Major destinations in EAP			Major generating markets for EAP		
Country	Arrivals (million)	Average growth rate 1980–90	Country	Arrivals (million)	Average growth rate 1980–90
China	10.5	6.3	Japan	7.3	8.5
Hong Kong	5.9	13.0	USA	3.3	5.7
Thailand	5.4	11.3	Korea	2.1	25.5
Singapore	5.3	8.7	Australia	2.1	6.7
Malaysia	4.2	7.3	UK	2.0	7.3
Japan	3.2	14.4	Germany	1.0	8.5

Notes: EAP, East Asia and Pacific.
Although the total tourist arrivals and tourism receipts at the top of the table are revised figures, the rest of the table is based on provisional estimates for 1990.

Source: World Tourism Organization.

Table 23.7 *International tourism in Europe, 1990*

International tourist arrivals 1990	—	281.4 million
International tourism receipts 1990	—	$US 138.5 billion
Receipts as a percentage of exports (1989)	—	6.7%

Inbound tourism			Outbound tourism		
Origin	Arrivals to Europe (million)	Average growth rate 1980–90	Destination	Arrivals from Europe (million)	Average growth rate 1980–90
Europe	240.2	5.4	Americas	11.0	6.5
Americas	19.2	3.7	EAP	6.2	9.5
EAP	5.8	6.6	M. East	5.8	11.4
M. East	4.5	3.4	Africa	5.6	4.2
Africa	0.7	–6.1	S. Asia	1.2	4.6
S. Asia	0.2	–1.7			

Major destinations in Europe			Major generating markets for Europe		
Country	Arrivals (million)	Average growth rate 1980–90	Country	Arrivals (million)	Average growth rate 1980–90
France	50.0	5.2	Germany	51.9	3.3
Spain	34.3	3.9	UK	27.1	5.8
Italy	26.7	1.9	Italy	19.9	10.4
Hungary	20.5	8.1	USA	15.7	4.6
Austria	19.0	3.2	Neths	15.1	2.8
UK	18.0	3.8	France	14.2	1.6

Notes: EAP, East Asia and Pacific.
Although the total tourist arrivals and tourism receipts at the top of the table are revised figures, the rest of the table is based on provisional estimates for 1990.

Source: World Tourism Organization.

Table 23.8   *International tourism in the Middle East, 1990*

International tourist arrivals 1990	— 9.5 million
International tourism receipts 1990	— $US 6.3 billion
Receipts as a percentage of exports (1989)	— 9.6%

Inbound tourism			Outbound tourism		
Origin	Arrivals to Middle East (million)	Average growth rate 1980–90	Destination	Arrivals from Middle East (million)	Average growth rate 1980–90
M. East	4.0	2.7	Europe	0.7	3.4
Europe	3.4	6.1	Africa	0.6	9.9
Americas	0.9	1.9	Americas	0.4	27.5
EAP	0.3	6.8	S. Asia	0.2	6.6
S. Asia	0.2	7.6	EAP	0.1	8.7
Africa	0.2	2.2			

Major destinations in Middle East			Major generating markets for Middle East		
Country	Arrivals (thousands)	Average growth rate 1980–90	Country	Arrivals (thousands)	Average growth rate 1980–90
Jordan	2,633	4.9	Egypt	1,272	7.5
Egypt	2,600	7.6	Jordan	568	0.8
Israel	1,063	–0.5	USA	506	0.6
Saudi Arabia	827	–1.9	Germany	403	3.5
Iraq	750	–4.8	UK	376	4.5
UAE	616	2.1	France	365	3.1

Notes: EAP, East Asia and Pacific; UAE, United Arab Emirates.
Although the total tourist arrivals and tourism receipts at the top of the table are revised figures, the rest of the table is based on provisional estimates for 1990.

Source: World Tourism Organization.

Table 23.9 *International tourism in Southern Asia, 1990*

International tourist arrivals 1990	—	3.2 million
International tourism receipts 1990	—	$US 2.0 billion
Receipts as a percentage of exports (1989)	—	5.1%

Inbound tourism			Outbound tourism		
Origin	Arrivals to Southern Asia (million)	Average growth rate 1980–90	Destination	Arrivals from Southern Asia (million)	Average growth rate 1980–90
Europe	1.2	4.6	EAP	0.9	8.0
S. Asia	1.0	16.4	M. East	0.6	22.3
EAP	0.4	5.9	Americas	0.3	22.6
Americas	0.3	5.9	Europe	0.2	−1.7
M. East	0.2	6.6	Africa	*	8.0
Africa	*	14.0			

Major destinations in Southern Asia			Major generating markets for Southern Asia		
Country	Arrivals (thousands)	Average growth rate 1980–90	Country	Arrivals (thousands)	Average growth rate 1980–90
India	1,775	4.0	UK	463	8.2
Pakistan	424	3.6	India	300	10.2
Sri Lanka	298	−0.8	USA	220	5.9
Nepal	210	2.6	Germany	166	−0.3
Maldives	195	16.6	France	155	2.2
Bangladesh	115	7.3	Japan	142	7.6

Notes: EAP, East Asia and Pacific; * less than 0.1 million.
Although the total tourist arrivals and tourism receipts at the top of the table are revised figures, the rest of the table is based on provisional estimates for 1990.

Source: World Tourism Organization.

Table 23.10   *The top twenty destinations for international tourism in 1990*
—based on numbers of international tourist arrivals

	Country	Tourist arrivals (millions)	Rank 1980	Average annual growth rate (%)
1	France	50.0	1	5.2
2	USA	39.8	3	5.9
3	Spain	34.3	2	3.9
4	Italy	26.7	4	1.9
5	Hungary	20.5	9	8.1
6	Austria	19.0	5	3.2
7	UK	18.0	7	3.8
8	Germany	17.0	8	4.4
9	Canada	15.3	6	1.7
10	Switzerland	13.0	10	3.9
11	China	10.5 (E)	13	6.3
12	Greece	8.9	18	6.3
13	Czechoslovakia	8.1 (E)	17	4.8
14	Portugal	8.0	21	11.5
15	Yugoslavia	7.9	12	2.1
16	USSR	7.2	15	2.6
17	Mexico	6.4	19	4.4
18	Hong Kong	5.9	27	13.0
19	Netherlands	5.8	20	7.6
20	Turkey	5.4	43	19.3

Notes: 1. (E) Preliminary estimate.
2. The top five destinations as measured by international tourism receipts in rank order are USA, France, Italy, Spain and UK.

Source: World Tourism Organization.

Table 23.11 *The top twenty generators of international tourism in 1990
—based on international tourism expenditures*

	Country	Tourism expenditure (billion $US)	Rank 1980	Average annual growth rate (%) 1980/90
1	USA	38.7	2	14.1
2	Germany	30.1	1	3.9
3	Japan	24.9	6	18.4
4	UK	19.8	3	11.1
5	Italy	13.8	13	21.9
6	France	13.5	4	8.4
7	Canada	8.4	9	10.4
8	Netherlands	7.4	5	4.7
9	Austria	6.3	10	8.2
10	Switzerland	6.0	11	9.9
11	Sweden	6.0	12	10.4
12	Belgium	5.7	8	5.6
13	Mexico 1	5.4	7	2.6
14	Spain	4.3	18	13.2
15	Australia	4.1	15	8.9
16	Denmark	3.7	16	9.1
17	Norway	3.4	17	10.0
18	Korea, Rep.	3.2	28	24.6
19	Finland	2.8	22	17.7
20	Singapore	1.4	29	15.9

Note: 1. For Mexico, the data are not strictly comparable owing to a change in methodology as from 1982.

Source: World Tourism Organization.